T0331434

Australia in International Politics

Australia in International Politics

AN INTRODUCTION TO AUSTRALIAN FOREIGN POLICY

3rd edition / STEWART FIRTH

Routledge
Taylor & Francis Group

LONDON AND NEW YORK

First published 2011 by Allen & Unwin

Published 2020 by Routledge
2 Park Square, Milton Park, Abingdon, Oxon OX14 4RN
605 Third Avenue, New York, NY 10017

Routledge is an imprint of the Taylor & Francis Group, an informa business

Copyright © Stewart Firth 2011

All rights reserved. No part of this book may be reprinted or reproduced or
utilised in any form or by any electronic, mechanical, or other means, now known
or hereafter invented, including photocopying and recording, or in any information
storage or retrieval system, without permission in writing from the publishers.

Notice:
Product or corporate names may be trademarks or registered trademarks, and are
used only for identification and explanation without intent to infringe.

Cataloguing-in-Publication details are available
from the National Library of Australia
www.trove.nla.gov.au

Text design by Emily O'Neill
Typeset in Minion Regular 12/14.5 pt by Midland Typesetters, Australia

ISBN-13: 9781742372631 (pbk)

Contents

Acknowledgements

The late John Iremonger of Allen & Unwin suggested I write the first edition of this book, and I did so only because John cajoled, encouraged and humoured me to the finish. John was a brilliant editor. The first edition also owed much to the scepticism and intellectual commitment of the late Michael Wills, who tutored and lectured Australian foreign policy with me at Macquarie University in the 1990s. I wrote the second edition in Fiji, where students and colleagues at the University of the South Pacific alerted me to the impact—not always positive—of Australian foreign policy on its small neighbours. And I taught the substance of this third edition to students in the Australian foreign policy course at the ANU College of Arts and Social Sciences in the first semester of 2010. They were interested and provocative, and I revised the book in the light of their reactions to it. I thank them.

I owe much to Elizabeth Weiss at Allen & Unwin for her patient encouragement with this edition, and to her colleague Clara Finlay, who wrought miracles in editing my words to publishable standard.

I owe most to my life partner Kate Hannan, a writer herself, who knows the demands books make and whose understanding is complete.

ACRONYMS

AANZFTA	ASEAN–Australia–New Zealand Free Trade Agreement
ABARE	Australian Bureau of Agricultural and Resource Economics
ABC	Australian Broadcasting Corporation
ACFID	Australian Council for International Development
ADF	Australian Defence Force
AFP	Australian Federal Police
AFTA	ASEAN Free Trade Area
AIF	Australian Imperial Force
AIG	American International Group
ALP	Australian Labor Party
ANZAC	Australia and New Zealand Army Corps
ANZUS	Australia, New Zealand, United States [Treaty]
APEC	Asia-Pacific Economic Cooperation [forum]
APP	Asia-Pacific Partnership on Clean Development and Climate
ARF	ASEAN Regional Forum
ASEAN	Association of Southeast Asian Nations
ASEM	Asia–Europe Meeting
ASIO	Australian Security Intelligence Organisation
ASIS	Australian Secret Intelligence Service
ASPI	Australian Strategic Policy Institute
AusAID	Australian Agency for International Development
AUSMIN	Australia–United States Ministerial Consultations
AWB	Australian Wheat Board Limited
BRA	Bougainville Revolutionary Army
CBRN	chemical, biological, radiological and nuclear [weapons]
CER	Closer Economic Relations Agreement [Australia–NZ]
CERD	Committee on the Elimination of Racial Discrimination
CERN	European Organisation for Nuclear Research
CFC	chlorofluorocarbon
CIA	Central Intelligence Agency
CTBT	Comprehensive Nuclear Test Ban Treaty
DAC	Development Assistance Committee of OECD
DFAT	Department of Foreign Affairs and Trade
DIGO	Defence Imagery and Geospatial Organisation
DIO	Defence Intelligence Organisation
DSD	Defence Signals Directorate
EC	European Community

ETM	elaborately transformed manufacture
EU	European Union
F-FDTL	Falintil-Forças de Defesa de Timor Leste
FIRB	Foreign Investment Review Board
FPDA	Five Power Defence Arrangements
FTA	free trade agreement
FUNCINPEC	National United Front for an Independent, Neutral, Peaceful, and Cooperative Cambodia
GATS	General Agreement on Trade in Services
GATT	General Agreement on Tariffs and Trade
GCC	Gulf Cooperation Council
GDP	gross domestic product
GICNT	Global Initiative to Combat Nuclear Terrorism
GNI	gross national income
GNP	gross national product
HDI	human development index
IAEA	International Atomic Energy Agency
ICISS	International Commission on Intervention and State Sovereignty
ICNND	International Commission on Nuclear Non-proliferation and Disarmament
ICRC	International Committee of the Red Cross
IDG	International Deployment Group
IMF	International Monetary Fund
INTERFET	International Force in East Timor
IPCC	Intergovernmental Panel on Climate Change
ISAF	International Security Assistance Force
ISF	International Stabilisation Force
JDSC	Joint Declaration of Security Cooperation (Japan–Australia)
JSCFAD&T	Joint Standing Committee on Foreign Affairs, Defence and Trade
KPNLF	Khmer People's National Liberation Front
MEF	Malaita Eagle Force
MPs	members of parliament
NAFTA	North American Free Trade Agreement
NASA	National Aeronautics and Space Administration
NATO	North Atlantic Treaty Organization
NGOs	non-government organisations
NPT	Nuclear Non-Proliferation Treaty
NICs	newly industrialising countries
NSC	National Security Committee of Cabinet

OECD	Organisation for Economic Co-operation and Development
ONA	Office of National Assessments
OPEC	Organization of Petroleum Exporting Countries
PACER Plus	Pacific Agreement on Closer Economic Relations
PBS	Pharmaceutical Benefits Scheme
PM&C	Department of Prime Minister and Cabinet
PNG	Papua New Guinea
PNTL	Policia Nacional de Timor-Leste
R2P	responsibility to protect
RAAF	Royal Australian Air Force
RAMSI	Regional Assistance Mission to Solomon Islands
RAN	Royal Australian Navy
SBS	Special Broadcasting Service
SIGINT	signals intelligence
SORT	Strategic Offensive Reductions Treaty (US–Russia)
SPNFZ	South Pacific Nuclear-Free Zone Treaty (Treaty of Rarotonga)
START I, START II	Strategic Arms Reduction Treaty
TRIPS	Agreement on Trade-related Aspects of Intellectual Property Rights
UK	United Kingdom of Great Britain and Northern Ireland
UN	United Nations
UNAMET	United Nations Mission in East Timor
UNAMIR	United Nations Assistance Mission for Rwanda
UNESCO	United Nations Educational, Scientific and Cultural Organization
UNHCR	United Nations High Commissioner for Refugees
UNITAF	Unified Task Force of Operation Restore Hope
UNMISET	United Nations Mission of Support in East Timor
UNMIT	United Nations Integrated Mission in Timor-Leste
UNOSOM	United Nations Operation in Somalia
UNOTIL	United Nations Office in East Timor
UNTAC	United Nations Transitional Authority in Cambodia
UNTAET	United Nations Transitional Administration in East Timor
USSR	Union of Soviet Socialist Republics
VCPOL	Vienna Convention for the Protection of the Ozone Layer
WHO	World Health Organization
WMD	weapons of mass destruction
WTO	World Trade Organization
WWF	World Wildlife Fund

Introduction

The study of foreign policy is located within a wider field called *international relations*. Making use of theory in the understanding of international relations is inevitable. In understanding the world, we adopt theoretical perspectives whether we know it or not, so it is better to be aware of what we are doing. Before proceeding, however, we need to clarify terminology.

Scholars in the field of international relations and foreign policy use the word *state* to mean 'independent country'. In this context state does not mean a constituent part of a federal system, such as Queensland in Australia, or California in the United States, but refers instead to Australia itself. The world of foreign relations is populated by 'states' of this kind, and Australia is one of 192 states that are members of the United Nations (UN), which is the international organisation of states. The distinguishing feature of these states is 'sovereignty', which means that their governments claim independent and exclusive authority over a clearly demarcated territorial area. The newest state in Australia's region is East Timor, which achieved independent statehood in 2002 after centuries of being controlled by other states: first Portugal and then Indonesia. The newest state in the UN is Montenegro, which joined in 2006. New Caledonia, which the French call an 'overseas country of France', is not a state because it is part of France itself, even though the local population has a degree of self-government. Not being a state, New Caledonia cannot be said to have a 'foreign policy'; nor can Hong Kong, which is a special autonomous region of a sovereign state called the People's Republic of China. Foreign policy is the business of states. The emergence of the European Union (EU) as a tightly integrated regional organisation of states complicates this story, because both the EU and its constituent member states can be said to possess foreign policies.

The study of foreign policy draws on a range of theoretical perspectives in international relations so broad that theorists disagree even on what the subject matter of this discipline is. One school of thought—traditionally known as *realism*—focuses on states, governments, and state power in the international arena. Realists stress the military dimension of state power and regard military issues as the core subject matter of international relations as a discipline. According to this approach, the fundamental logic of international relations is one of power. Since there is no world government to impose order, the international system is anarchic, and in the end states protect their interests through power politics. While structures of international cooperation, such as the United Nations, soften the hard edges of this global anarchy, states will never sacrifice their own national interests on vital issues for the greater international good. The edifice of international law, in realist thinking, is accepted by states only to the extent that it serves their interests, and exercises no real authority beyond that. States appeal instead to sovereignty—their legal and constitutional independence from all other states—and act in their own interests. Realists see themselves as continuing an ancient study with its roots in the work of Thucydides, Machiavelli, Hobbes and Clausewitz: the study of sovereign states, the state system, the balance of power and the origins of war and peace between states. A key realist thinker in modern times was E.H. Carr. His book *The Twenty Years' Crisis, 1919–1939: An introduction to the study of international relations* was published in 1939 as World War II loomed. At a time when everyone could see that the League of Nations had failed to bring international peace, Carr explained this failure as arising from the inevitable incapacity of the League of Nations to exercise influence over powerful states that believed in their own sovereignty, and would therefore never accept its authority. After World War II Carr inspired generations of scholars and students, and he was joined by Hans J. Morgenthau, whose *Politics Among Nations* (1948) became a key text for the highly influential realist tradition in international relations in the United States. At a time when two great superpowers confronted each other across the globe, each able to destroy each other and declaring their willingness to do so—the Cold War era—many theorists were attracted to the cold, sceptical logic of realism and to the idea that international peace is maintained only by the balance of power between states. Giving the name 'realism' to this approach conveys the misleading impression, however, that all other approaches are less realistic. In fact 'realism' is simply a technical term, and should not be understood as suggesting from the outset that it is better than the others.

A second school of thought in international relations draws inspiration from the *liberal* tradition. Liberals are more optimistic about human nature than realists, and believe that states, while constrained by the nature of the international system, can nevertheless exercise choices that produce a better world. For our purposes, the details of the different strains of liberal thought matter less than the fact that, to a greater or lesser extent, Australian governments tend to make foreign policy on the basis of liberal approaches, especially those that stress the importance of a growing web of international institutions. As James L. Richardson argues:

> Australian policy thinking for the most part endorses liberal institutionalism—both the general claim that the increasing recourse to international institutions makes for a more predictable, cooperative and thus peaceful environment, and also the specific thesis that it benefits a country like Australia that important sectors of international activity are regulated through generally accepted rules rather than through ad hoc bargaining among the strongest actors. Australian involvement in the World Trade Organization, arms control regimes, UN peacekeeping and regional economic cooperation can be seen in these terms.[1]

While most Australian governments have been liberal and internationalist in their foreign policies, many would say the Howard government was an exception and emphasised a realist orientation.

A third school of thought in international relations, the *cosmopolitan approach*, seeks to explain global inequalities and injustices of all kinds, economic and otherwise; that is, not just the rich exploiting the poor, but men dominating women, powerful cultures suppressing weaker ones, and economic systems that depend on never-ending growth while pillaging and despoiling the natural environment. For those who adopt this way of looking at things, governments and states are positive evils, standing in the way of popular movements of liberation and preventing the emergence of radically new ways of organising human social and political life. For them, the story of Australian foreign policy is that of a small Canberra elite, whose party labels and policy differences hardly matter, and who perpetuate global injustices while claiming to do otherwise. The Marxists among them see the central reality of international life as being the inequitable way the global economy is organised, both within countries and between them. They believe world politics is ultimately reducible to a single global socioeconomic system that divides the world into global classes. The critical and postmodern feminists among them believe 'knowledge about what should constitute the study of international relations is gendered to promote masculine characteristics'.[2] There are other schools of thought in international relations—*constructivism* and *critical theory*, for example—but they lie beyond the scope of this study.

This book is about Australian foreign policy, not about international relations in general or where power is located globally. Foreign policy is what governments do in the international arena. Foreign policy is about the positions governments adopt on international issues, the treaties they sign, the trading arrangements they enter into, the foreign aid they send, the international obligations they accept, the soldiers they despatch overseas, the military alliances they uphold, the treaties they ratify, the diplomatic representations they make, the foreign regimes they support or oppose, the international law they follow, the consular services they provide, and so on. To study foreign policy, then, is to examine part of public policy, not to attempt a comprehensive analysis of the way the international system works. Theoretical assumptions nevertheless underpin even this limited area of study, and those of this book broadly reflect those of the foreign policy-making community in Australia.

Like the liberal institutionalists who are important in Australia's foreign policy-making community, I assume that international law and international cooperation create a web of expectations and norms that influences state behaviour, and that Australia is well served by participating in diplomacy to enlarge the web on numerous issues, from global security, arms control and peace-keeping to climate change and global economic governance. I acknowledge the insight of the realists that state power, enshrined in the notion of sovereignty, is central to the international system. But I do not accord state power a monopoly place among influences on that system. The rise of terrorists as important non-state actors in international relations suggests a multiplicity of influences, and so does globalisation, the latest expression of that dynamic but destabilising economic system we call *capitalism*. I see economic forces, not least in the global financial crisis of 2008, as having a key influence on the space within which any state can conduct its foreign policy. Finally, like most Australians, I approve of Australian schemes to work with other states in assisting developing countries, giving disaster relief, advancing human rights, helping refugees, countering climate change and, perhaps, building states. Yet, at the same time, I assume that all such efforts are likely to fall short of expectations because of the nature of international politics.

The themes and subject matter of this book raise theoretical issues. The making of foreign policy directs our attention to the limitations of liberal democracy, and to the power exercised by government over arcane areas of policy. Globalisation raises issues about the global power of non-state actors such as multinational corporations, especially banks, and international non-government organisations. The global financial crisis of 2008 points to the precarious interrelatedness of a globalised economy run along neo-liberal lines, and to the shift in global power represented by the emerging importance of multilateral institutions that better reflect the rise of China, such as the G20. Defence reminds us of classical debates about sovereignty, alliances and the balance of power. The threat of terrorism makes us ask whether we live in a strategically transformed situation in which non-state actors imperil security more than states. Arms control and disarmament prompt the questions of whether humankind can survive indefinitely in a situation where some states have the capacity to destroy the world, whether nuclear weapons can ever serve ordinary political purposes, and whether, in a world of sovereign states, nuclear arms can be abolished. The UN and international security revive debates about collective security, its pitfalls and the usefulness of UN peacekeeping. Australia's experiments with intervention in its immediate region introduce us to debates about changing notions of sovereignty, humanitarian justifications for intervention, and the ethics and practicability of building states in other people's countries. Human rights and foreign aid raise issues about the moral claims of individuals in a world of states, the ability of one state to effect change in another, the rights of states to development, and the emergence of global norms of development. Climate change, a novel issue in international politics, requires us to imagine an unprecedented degree of global cooperation in the face of a threat to all humanity, and to ponder the limitations of sovereignty.

Theories of international relations also influence Australian foreign policy. Prime ministers, foreign ministers, cabinets, diplomats and government advisers reach decisions on the basis of assumptions that have their origins in political philosophy. While the entire policy-making community is deeply influenced by the liberal tradition, the two main sides of party politics bring different emphases to foreign policy.

The distinction is captured in different approaches to multilateral diplomacy, which is diplomacy conducted among a number of countries, in contradistinction to diplomacy conducted between two countries (bilateral). During the Howard years (1996–2007), 'multilateralism' became shorthand for everything the Howard government liked least about Labor's approach to foreign policy. Howard thought Labor placed too much faith in the UN as a source of international security and in UN agreements on human rights, arms control, the global environment and much else. The Howard government's first white paper on foreign and trade policy was produced in 1997. This statement of official policy insisted that:

> Australia must be realistic about what the multilateral system can achieve. The twentieth century has been both the incubator and the graveyard of a long list of initiatives for international cooperation. In most cases their failure reflected an inability to recognise that international organisations can only accomplish what their member states are prepared to enable them to accomplish. All too often international initiatives have failed to match aspirations with capability.[3]

The theme was one to which Alexander Downer returned throughout his eleven years as foreign minister in the Howard government. As Labor foreign affairs spokesperson in opposition, Kevin Rudd depicted Downer's position like this: 'Real men, according to Alex, do bilateral; not multilateral. Real men do bilateral security. Bilateral security is hard. Multilateral security is soft, be it disarmament, peacekeeping or the UN Security Council.'[4] The depiction was a caricature, but it captured the ambivalence of the Howard government towards the usefulness of the UN and the effectiveness of multilateral diplomacy. The tragedy of 9/11 confirmed the doubts Howard and Downer already held about multilateralism, and strengthened Australia's ties with a US administration that had little time for the UN and much faith in itself, acting alone or in 'coalitions of the willing', to solve global security problems. After Labor was elected in 2007, Australia returned to favouring the UN and multilateral diplomacy as solutions to global problems. Theoretical differences lie in the Coalition's scepticism about multilateralism and Labor's enthusiasm for it. John Howard and Alexander Downer, while in the broad liberal tradition, were influenced by the scepticism of the realist approach; Kevin Rudd, by contrast, wanted to make Australia a keen participant in negotiations over arms control, global security and climate change, and sought a seat for Australia on the UN Security Council, reflecting Labor's greater belief in the effectiveness of international cooperation. Party differences of this kind can be exaggerated, especially by the parties themselves, but they exist nevertheless and they arise from differing theoretical assumptions.

PART I

The evolution of Australian foreign policy

Foreign relations, 1901–83

- What was the impact of World War I on Australia's links with Britain?
- Was World War II a turning-point in the history of Australia's foreign relations?
- What were the origins of the ANZUS Treaty?
- Should the American alliance be central to Australian foreign and defence policy?
- What was the policy of 'forward defence'?
- Why did Australia send troops to fight in the Vietnam War?
- What were the achievements and failures of Australian foreign policy under the Whitlam government?
- What distinctive contribution did Malcolm Fraser make to Australia's foreign policy during his time as prime minister, 1975–1983?
- What is meant by the 'dependence issue' in the debate about Australian foreign policy?
- In what ways did Australia's relationship with Asia change during the twentieth century?

IMPERIAL CONNECTIONS: BRITAIN

An Act of the British Parliament, not a war of independence, created Australia the state in 1901. Australia was British, with a British constitution, a British head of state, a British flag and a British national anthem. Almost all Australians (though not the Aboriginal, German and Chinese, the most notable of the many minorities) were British by birth or descent.

Independent in many respects, Australia was still not a sovereign state. It lacked the legal capacity to make treaties with foreign states; it possessed no overseas diplomatic posts, except in London; the British government took charge of its foreign relations; and Britain had the main responsibility for its defence. Thinking of the British Isles as 'home' and of themselves as colonial British, Australia's political leaders found nothing odd in this state of affairs. On the contrary, they set great store by their intimate political and economic connection with the world's greatest power.

Australia had freedom to act, however, on immigration and foreign economic policy, and soon demonstrated a degree of independence in these areas. The first legislation passed by the inaugural Australian federal government was the *Immigration Restriction Act 1901* (the White Australia policy), which prohibited non-white migrants and effectively defined Australia as a white nation.

The new Commonwealth then abandoned free trade, at that time almost an article of faith in Britain, and embraced protection, imposing an external tariff on manufactured imports at the same time as removing interstate barriers to trade. Under the prime ministership of Alfred Deakin, this 'new protection' was a high-tariff policy which was meant to protect manufacturers from foreign competition and, in return, required them to pay reasonable wages to their employees. The Australian standard of living in 1908 was probably the highest in the world, higher than that of the United States or Britain and certainly far higher than that of Japan. Protection was intended to maintain this standard of living in an island of European affluence far from England and amid Asian poverty. Protectionism became the credo of every Australian government for the next 75 years.

The national interests of Britain and Australia were bound to diverge, though decades would pass before this became obvious. For one thing, Australia was on the other side of the world. From 1906 Australia possessed its own colony, a piece of Australian territory in the Pacific: the former British New Guinea, now renamed Papua. The defence of the Pacific was a more urgent national priority for Australia than it was for the Motherland, and many Australians came to distrust Britain's 1902 alliance with Japan that was renewed in 1911. As the British reduced their Pacific naval presence, the Australian Liberal prime minister, Alfred Deakin, pressed for an independent navy. Consequently, from 1913, Australia had its own small naval fleet, the Royal Australian Navy (RAN). Under the *Naval Defence Act 1910*, introduced by the Fisher Labor government, Australian boys and young men between the ages of twelve and 26 became liable to compulsory military training for home defence. These first Australian initiatives in defence all took place within a loyally imperial framework, but they were evidence of uniquely Australian priorities and of a specifically Australian patriotism.

Not only was Australia set apart from Britain by geography but it was also, even before World War I, a somewhat different kind of society. Australia was a more democratic, more egalitarian and less class-conscious society than the one from which it had sprung. A quarter of the population was Irish or of Irish descent; their ancestral homeland had been colonised by the British for centuries and they often thought of England and the British Empire as oppressors. With immense sacrifices, the Irish in Australia had constructed a separate school system where religious brothers and nuns preserved the Catholic faith in the rising generation and taught a patriotism which focused on Australia rather than England and the Empire. The Labor Party, which attracted most of the Catholic vote, also espoused a national rather than imperial patriotism, putting Australia first and the Empire second.

When war broke out in 1914, most Australians reacted to the news enthusiastically. Before the war Australian schoolchildren in the state and Protestant schools were constantly reminded that they belonged to the greatest and noblest Empire the world had ever seen. The most important part of the Australian flag, they were told, was the Union Jack in the corner, and the time would come when they would be called upon to fight for the Empire in foreign fields of battle. When that time came, as politicians were fond of saying, Australians would show their loyalty to the Empire to the last man and the last shilling. In August 1914, party leaders on both sides pledged Australia's support for the Motherland, and volunteers inundated the first Australian Imperial Force (AIF). While many wanted adventure, a chance to see the world, a job at five shillings a day or an escape from family problems, many were also filled with ideas of fighting for the glory of Empire.

The landing of Australian troops on the Turkish peninsula of Gallipoli in April 1915 was not Australia's first military action in World War I—an Australian force captured German New Guinea in 1914—but Gallipoli came to symbolise a new feeling of Australian national identity in what contemporaries called Australia's 'baptism in blood'. Before the Australian and New Zealand Army Corps—the ANZAC force—withdrew from Gallipoli in December 1915 almost 8000 Australians had been killed in a campaign which was to end in failure. As the war progressed and the demand for more troops grew, Australia divided sharply between those who thought young men should be conscripted for overseas military service and those who did not. Billy Hughes, the rabidly

pro-Empire prime minister, led the country into two bitterly contested referendums on conscription in 1916 and 1917, seeking a popular mandate to draft
young Australians for the murderous battles of the Western Front. With the
Catholic Church, much of the Labor Party, the radical left and many farmers
opposed to conscription, both referendums were lost. The 330,000 Australians
who went overseas with the AIF during World War I were all volunteers.

At Versailles, Billy Hughes proved to be a cantankerous and influential
voice for Australia. As he reminded the American president, Woodrow Wilson,
Australia had contributed 60,000 dead to the war against Germany and its allies
and deserved something in return. Most tangibly, that turned out to be German
New Guinea, or at least those parts of it south of the equator. Against Hughes's
protests, the former German islands north of the equator—most of the islands
of Micronesia—went to Japan, which had occupied them with Britain's approval
in 1914. Those Micronesian islands were to serve as Japan's springboards in
World War II at considerable cost to Australia and the United States. Though
Hughes would have liked to annex New Guinea outright, he had to accept the
next best thing: a 'C'-class mandate over New Guinea under the supervision of
the League of Nations; a form of territorial acquisition which allowed Australia
a virtually free hand yet did not completely abandon the idea of international
trusteeship. Australia, New Zealand and Britain shared the mandate over the
phosphate-rich island of Nauru and thereby ensured a steady supply of cheap
fertiliser to the farmers of the Antipodes.

The legacy of World War I for Australia's links with Britain was ambiguous.
In some ways postwar Australia was more British than ever, for the war had fatally
weakened that radical stream of opinion which wanted a separate and uniquely
egalitarian destiny for Australia, free of the constraints of the Old World. The war
conservatised the country. All state governors, and most generals, admirals, profes-
sors, Anglican bishops and Protestant school headmasters in the interwar period
were Englishmen. With one notable exception—in the person of Sir Isaac Isaacs,
appointed by the Scullin Labor government—all governors-general of Australia
were also Englishmen. Until the late 1930s Australian governments hardly interested themselves in foreign affairs—except on trade matters—and it was not until
the Labor Party was in office in 1942 that Australia bothered to ratify the *Statute of
Westminster 1931*. This complex piece of legislation, passed by the British Parliament, gave the self-governing dominions of the Empire the right to make their
own laws without British interference, to give their own advice to the Crown and
to make their own foreign policy. Apart from its representatives at the League of

Nations and a single counsellor appointed to the British Embassy in Washington in 1937, Australia had no diplomatic representative in a foreign country between the wars. Australia was content to let London represent it.

Australia's foreign economic policy between the wars was strongly pro-Empire. Under the *Ottawa Agreements Act 1932*, Australia entered a comprehensive system of imperial preferences which allowed Australian primary products into Britain duty-free; at the same time, Australia ensured that tariffs on British manufactured imports were always lower than tariffs on equivalent imports from elsewhere. The result was a pattern of trade that discriminated against Japan and the United States and tied Australia economically to the United Kingdom. The British people sat down to breakfasts of Australian eggs and Australian honey with toast made from Australian wheat, and what applied to breakfast was true of almost everything else. The United Kingdom was Australia's best market. At the same time, Australians ate their meals with knives, forks, spoons, plates, cups and saucers stamped 'Made in England'.

Yet popular sentiment for the Empire weakened after World War I. Gallipoli had become a symbol of uniquely Australian nationhood and Australians celebrated it more generally and more fervently than any English feat of war. ANZAC Day, which brought parades of veterans into the streets of Australian cities and towns every 25 April, far eclipsed Empire Day as a celebration of patriotism. At the depths of the Great Depression in the early 1930s, while tens of thousands of unemployed Australians were living in makeshift huts of galvanised iron and hessian bags, children at state schools were still being told of their good fortune in belonging to the greatest Empire the world had ever known. But many people blamed the British banks and bondholders for their poverty and despair. In addition, Japanese military expansion into China during the 1930s heightened Australians' fears that their country might soon face a direct threat from the north, and that the United Kingdom was not doing enough to protect them. Everything came to depend on what most Australians hoped was an impregnable bastion of British military power in the Far East: Singapore.

IMPERIAL CONNECTIONS: THE UNITED STATES

World War II was a turning-point for Australia's relationship with its first 'Great Protector', the United Kingdom. On 3 September 1939 Australian Prime Minister Robert Gordon (R.G.) Menzies told the Australian people in a radio broadcast that 'in consequence of a persistence by Germany in her invasion of Poland, Great

GREAT AND POWERFUL FRIENDS

Ever since Federation in 1901 Australian governments have regarded Australia as vulnerable, a country needing a great and powerful friend overseas to defend it against attack. That friend was first the UK and later the US. To keep the friend, Australia was ready to fight with it in wars overseas. Nowhere has this attitude been more obvious than when prime ministers have committed Australia to war or reaffirmed a commitment already made.

Robert Menzies on radio, 3 September 1939:

> It is my melancholy duty to inform you officially that, in consequence of a persistence by Germany in her invasion of Poland, Great Britain has declared war upon her, and that, as a result, Australia is also at war.
>
> R.G. Neale, ed., *Documents on Australian Foreign Policy 1937–49*, Volume II: 1939, AGPS, Canberra, 1976, pp. 221, 226.

Harold Holt in the presence of the American President Lyndon Baines Johnson (LBJ), June 1966:

> You have in us not merely an understanding friend but one staunch in the belief of the need for our presence with you in Vietnam.
>
> We are not there because of our friendship, we are there because, like you, we believe it is right to be there and, like you, we shall stay there as long as seems necessary to achieve the purposes of the South Vietnamese Government and the purposes that we join in formulating and progressing together.
>
> And so, sir, in the lonelier and perhaps even more disheartening moments which come to any national leader, I hope there will be a corner of your mind and heart which takes cheer from the fact that you have an admiring friend, a staunch friend that will be all the way with LBJ.
>
> *The Australian*, 1 July 1966.

Bob Hawke in parliament, 21 January 1991:

> On 2 August 1990, Iraq's armed forces assaulted, seized and subjugated Kuwait. Now, with the authority of the United Nations, and only after Iraq had made it clear that it would defy the United Nations by remaining in Kuwait, Australia has joined a great coalition of nations in a military commitment to defeat that invasion and to restore Kuwait's sovereignty and independence ... Mr Speaker, the allied nations, with Australia, shall prevail against Iraq's aggression. We shall restore the sovereignty of Kuwait, and in doing that we shall have done much more. We shall have established the conditions for peace and stability in the Middle East; we shall have protected the health of the international economy; and we shall have erected and strengthened the framework for a world order in which all nations can live in greater peace and harmony.
>
> House of Representatives, Hansard, 21 January 1991.

John Howard in parliament, 18 March 2003:

> Early this morning President Bush telephoned me and formally requested Australia's support and participation in a coalition of nations who are prepared to enforce the Security Council's resolutions by all necessary means. This request was subsequently considered and agreed to by cabinet. Around midday today, Australian Eastern Standard Time, President Bush delivered an ultimatum to the Iraqi leadership: Saddam Hussein and his sons must leave Iraq within 48 hours or face military conflict. Nobody wants a military conflict. The world has tried other means for years but, so far, to no avail. We cannot walk away from the threat that Iraq's continued possession of weapons of mass destruction constitutes to its region and to the wider world ... We have supported the Americans on this issue because we share their concerns and we share their worries about the future if Iraq is left unattended to. Alliances are two-way processes, and where we are in agreement, we should not leave it to the United States to do all of the heavy lifting just because they are the world's superpower. To do so would undermine one of the most important relationships we have and, in an increasingly globalised and borderless world, the relationship between Australia and the United States will become more rather than less important as the years go by.
>
> > Address to the House of Representatives, Canberra, 18 March 2003.

Kevin Rudd at Parliament House, Canberra, 29 April 2009:

> Today, I have announced an increase in our troop commitment [to Afghanistan] from 1100 to around 1550. We will also increase our police training presence as well as our governance and development assistance efforts.
>
> I have discussed this additional commitment with President Obama last week, following extensive deliberations by the National Security Committee of the Australian Cabinet.
>
> Cabinet yesterday, full Cabinet, endorsed this commitment.
>
> As I make these further commitments today, I am acutely conscious of the fact that I am placing more Australians in harm's way. And I fear that more Australians will lose their lives in the fight that lies ahead.
>
> I am also conscious of the price already paid by Australian service personnel in Afghanistan. I am conscious of the terrible toll on families and loved ones of the ten Australian personnel who have died and of the many who have been wounded. I am also conscious of the impact on our wider Australian community.
>
> But Australia will not bow to the threat of terrorism in Afghanistan. And we will continue to stand by our American ally in confronting this threat because failure to do so would only compound the terrorist threat to Australian, American and other nationals at home and abroad.
>
> > Press Conference, Parliament House,
> > <http://pmrudd.archive.dpmc.gov.au/node/5205>.

Britain has declared war upon her and that, as a result, Australia is also at war'. The phrase 'as a result' neatly captured Menzies's view that Australia and the United Kingdom should stand and fall together. Yet even Menzies, the most pro-British of prime ministers, realised that Australia must begin to develop its own diplomatic representation overseas and take its own initiatives in foreign policy. In 1940 Richard Gardiner (R.G.) Casey was sent to Washington as the minister in charge of the Australian Legation to the United States and Sir John Latham as the minister to Japan. The Australian government, for the first time, began to receive diplomatic information from a purely Australian point of view.

The crucial test of Australia's dependence on British military power came with the outbreak of the war in the Pacific in December 1941. Japan's attack on the American fleet in Hawai'i was followed six weeks later by its invasion of Rabaul, the capital of Australian New Guinea, and the rapid withdrawal of Australian forces south into Papua. The Australian government, now under the Labor prime minister John Curtin, faced the possibility—even the likelihood—that Japan would advance further south and invade Australia itself.

For the first time in Australia's history, as Alan Watt has said, 'an Australian Government was faced with the immediate problem of trying to ensure the survival of Australia'.[1] The problem was one that concentrated the mind, focused priorities and put the role of the United Kingdom in perspective. In those early months of 1942, as John Curtin argued sharply with the British prime minister Winston Churchill over the disposition of Australian military forces, Australians came to realise that depending on the United Kingdom was no longer the way to safeguard their national security. Curtin had already published a newspaper article in which he said that 'Australia looks to America, free of any pangs as to our traditional links with the United Kingdom. We know the problems that the United Kingdom faces ... But we know, too, that Australia can go and Britain can still hold on. We are, therefore, determined that Australia shall not go ...'[2]

Japanese forces captured British Singapore on 15 February 1942 and took 17,000 Australian servicemen as prisoners of war. The fall of Singapore shocked Australians more than any other event of their generation, and undermined the most cherished assumption of Australian defence planning—namely, that the British Empire in the Far East would always stand between Australia and Japan. Within a week the Japanese were bombing Darwin. It was vital, Curtin thought, for Australia to bring back its three AIF divisions then in the Middle East, more than 30,000 service personnel in all. But at this point Churchill asked for one of those AIF divisions, the Seventh, to be diverted to the defence of British Burma.

'We are all entirely in favour of all Australian troops returning home to defend their native soil', he cabled Curtin, 'and we shall help with their transportation in every way. But a vital war emergency cannot be ignored, and troops en route to other destinations must be ready to turn aside and take part in a battle.'[3] The British Admiralty sent the convoy carrying the Australian troops north towards Burma before Churchill heard from Curtin. Curtin was outraged and insisted the convoy turn around. Compelled to choose between Australia and the Empire, Curtin chose his homeland. He cabled Churchill demanding the immediate return of the Seventh Division: 'With A.I.F. troops we sought to save Malaya and Singapore, falling back on Netherlands East Indies. All these northern defences are gone or going. Now you contemplate using the A.I.F. to save Burma … We feel a primary obligation to save Australia not only for itself but to preserve it as a base for the development of the war against Japan.'[4]

Close as relations between Australia and the United Kingdom were to remain for many years afterwards, they would never be the same again. If Australia the nation was born at Gallipoli, Australia as a state with a distinctive foreign policy was born with the fall of Singapore.

At the same time, Australia turned from one Great Protector to another. The US military commander General Douglas MacArthur soon made Australia the headquarters for US forces in the South-West Pacific. The US Navy halted the southward advance of Japanese forces in the Battle of the Coral Sea in May 1942 and then inflicted heavy losses in the Battle of Midway in June. Within months of Britain's failure to protect them, Australians found themselves saved by the United States. The lesson was one which many people took to heart, and it sustained pro-American sentiment for decades afterwards. The Americans did not save Australia for Australia's sake. Indeed, President Roosevelt told R.G. Casey in 1941 that, while the United States would go to the defence of Canada if it were attacked, Australia and New Zealand were so far away that they should not count on American help. The circumstances of the Pacific War were the deciding factor. With the Americans driven by the Japanese from Guam and the Philippines, the British from Singapore, and the Dutch from the Netherlands East Indies, Australia was the only possible base for American forces to organise their military reply to Japan.

When World War II started, the British Empire acted as one on the international scene; when it finished, the colonies were restless and the dominions, such as Australia, were going their own way. The Labor Minister for External Affairs, Dr Herbert Vere Evatt, epitomised Australia's new independence on the world scene. He was an ambitious, self-assertive and humourless man who won

few personal friends overseas, but he pursued his vision of Australian independence tirelessly. He pushed for Australia and New Zealand to have a say in the
fate of Pacific Island territories after the war. He argued for an international
trusteeship system for colonial territories and was one of the shapers of the UN
Charter. He pressed, against the opposition of the British, for an independent
state of Israel and an independent Indonesia. He oversaw the transformation of External Affairs from a tiny corner of the bureaucracy to a significant
department, and ensured that by 1949 Australia had diplomatic posts across
the world from the United States, Canada, Brazil, the Netherlands, the Soviet
Union and France to China, India and New Zealand. While Labor was in office
in Canberra, the United Kingdom and Australia remained at odds on numerous
foreign policy issues. Where the British saw communist subversion in much of
the political strife in South-East Asia, for example, Evatt and the Secretary
of the Department of External Affairs, John Burton, were far more inclined to
see nationalists rightly trying to overthrow their colonial masters.

The idea that in 1942 Australia shifted from one Great Protector to another
contains elements of truth, but it simplifies a more complicated historical
process that occurred over a period longer than a single year. Australia did not
conclude a military alliance with the United States for almost another decade
and, in the meantime, such an alliance was far from being a foregone conclusion. Even when the American alliance was formally established, Australia's ties
to Britain in popular sentiment, trade, diplomacy and military commitment
remained close for many years.

The Chifley Labor government chose to remain firmly attached to the United
Kingdom economically. The Americans wanted an international economy
based on free trade, freedom of investment and the dollar as a reserve currency.
The British, on the other hand, wanted to keep control of what was known as
the *sterling area*: a bloc of British Commonwealth countries which traded in
sterling and accepted the financial dominance of London. Australia was caught
in the middle. Chifley and his advisers agreed that the American version of a
global economy would be to Australia's advantage in the long run because it
would stimulate international trade, but they feared embracing a scheme that
might compel Australia to use unemployment rather than import restrictions
as a way of dealing with excessive imports. With memories of the Great Depression fresh in his mind, Chifley wanted to keep in his hands the instruments of
regulation which he believed would enable Australia to avoid mass unemployment. Thinking the United States might plunge into another depression, Chifley

contended that the safe course for Australia was to remain in the sterling area with its trade protected by the imperial preference system with Britain.

In intelligence matters Australia cooperated with both the United Kingdom and the United States. The Australian espionage organisations were set up with British assistance and along British lines. Two of the most important were, and are still, the Australian Security Intelligence Organisation (ASIO), formed under the Labor government in 1949 to undertake internal surveillance, and the Australian Secret Intelligence Service (ASIS), which the Menzies government established in 1952 as an agency to spy on foreign countries. ASIS is Australia's version of America's Central Intelligence Agency (CIA). Under a secret agreement of 1947, the existence of which was not officially admitted until 1977, Australia cooperates with the United Kingdom, the United States, Canada and New Zealand in collecting and exchanging defence intelligence. The Howard and Rudd governments strengthened and expanded these intelligence agencies and others like them in the present era of international terrorism.

The ANZUS Treaty

The Chifley Labor government of 1945–49 certainly wanted a Pacific security pact that would involve the United States in the defence of Australia, but the Americans were not yet committed to establishing a ring of anti-communist alliances in East Asia and the Western Pacific. In any case, they distrusted Dr Evatt, who was openly critical of the United States and its anti-Soviet policies.

The circumstances which made possible the 1951 mutual defence treaty between Australia, New Zealand and the United States, known as the ANZUS Treaty, arose fundamentally from the Cold War: the intense antagonism that arose between the United States and the Soviet Union in the late 1940s, particularly because of the striking communist successes of 1949 and 1950 in China and Korea. Whereas Japan had been the enemy in 1945, by 1950 it was beginning to be seen by the United States as a crucial link in a web of pro-American military alliances directed against the Soviet Union and China. The Americans therefore believed that Japan should not be permanently weakened but instead permitted to re-arm, though this time for American benefit; that is, by the US negotiating a 'soft' peace treaty permitting Japan to re-arm, it might be able to make Japan a dependable ally of the United States, and it would be a useful thing to have Australia's support for such a treaty. Above all, a military alliance with Australia and New Zealand could become another link in the chain of anti-communist alliances.

The Americans were keen to conclude the ANZUS Treaty because the new alliance would contribute to containing what they feared most: Asian communism. On the Australian side, things had changed since the days of Dr Evatt. A Liberal–Country Party Coalition under Menzies had defeated the Labor government in 1949. Menzies was strongly anti-communist and his first Minister for External Affairs, Percy Spender, pursued a defence pact with the United States from the moment he came into office. The ANZUS Treaty partners did not include the United Kingdom.

The ANZUS Treaty, and the wider American alliance of which it was part, became the cornerstone of Australian defence policy and foreign policy during the Cold War, and remain central to Australia's security. The treaty established a military alliance between the United States, Australia and New Zealand. It did not establish a unified military command: article iv of the treaty affirms that 'each party recognises that an armed attack in the Pacific area on any of the Parties would be dangerous to its own peace and safety and declares that it would act to meet the common danger in accordance with its constitutional processes'. While the meaning of the phrase 'armed attack' is clear, Australians have never known exactly what is meant by the promise to 'act to meet the common danger' or even by the notion of the 'Pacific area'. Over the years, supporters of ANZUS have tended to see these words as a firm promise of American help in time of need, whereas critics have said they fail to guarantee anything. The treaty has been invoked on one occasion only in the last half-century, and in circumstances not envisaged by its founders, when the Australian prime minister John Howard said it applied to the terrorist attacks on the United States in 2001 and promised military help to the Americans in the war on terrorism.

The long-term significance of ANZUS lies outside these issues. The effect of the treaty was to formally initiate a process in which Australia's defence policy—and for many years its foreign policy in general—became integrated into the global military and diplomatic strategies of the United States. Whatever small measure of independence in foreign affairs Australia discovered during the 1940s was lost again by the staunchly pro-American Coalition governments which ruled Australia from 1949 to 1972. With ready access to American thinking on the course of international events, the Australian defence and intelligence community made that thinking its own, and Australian views eventually became scarcely distinguishable from those of the United States. In place of its first imperial connection, Australia now had a second; or, perhaps more correctly, Australia now had two Great Protectors and sought the security of both until the United Kingdom finally abandoned its global military role and withdrew its forces from South-East Asia and the Persian Gulf in the early 1970s.

The economic and military tide continued to run in the American direction and it is Australia's military commitments under Menzies and his Coalition successors that tell the story. For the United Kingdom, Australia sent aircraft to British Malaya in 1950, ground troops and more aircraft in 1955, and an infantry battalion to Borneo in 1965 at the time of Indonesia's confrontation with the newly independent state of Malaysia. For the United States, Australia sent a total of 15,000 service personnel to fight in the Korean War in the early 1950s and nearly 47,000 to the Vietnam War between 1965 and 1971. The last Australian army forces in Vietnam, a small training group, were withdrawn by the Whitlam Labor government elected in December 1972. In the meantime, the Coalition governments made Australian territory available for three important US military facilities, the functions of which were kept secret at the time: North West Cape, declared operational in 1967 with the principal purpose of communicating with American nuclear submarines; Pine Gap, an espionage base which went into service in 1969 under the control of the CIA for intercepting and collecting electronic intelligence; and Nurrungar, which from 1971 was a vital link in America's satellite system of early warning of Soviet nuclear attack. Nurrungar closed in 1999 but a US–Australia treaty signed in 2008 provides for military cooperation at North West Cape until 2033, and the joint defence facility at Pine Gap remains as a signals intelligence base linked to American and British facilities.

Ironically, Robert Menzies, who once said he was British to the boot heels, was the prime minister who began the process of breaking Australia's financial and economic ties with Britain. To the irritation of the British, Menzies raised a large dollar loan from the United States, imposed import restrictions that affected British companies exporting to Australia, renegotiated imperial preferences so as to reduce the United Kingdom's advantage and, in 1957, concluded a trade treaty with Japan. The Australia–Japan Commerce Agreement of 1957 generated a boom in Australian raw material exports to Japan and began the gradual process of Australia's economic enmeshment with East Asia. By that time America's global economic supremacy was uncontested, Japan was a rising power economically and the British connection was losing its economic relevance to Australia. From the mid 1950s to the mid 1970s about 28 per cent of the Australian workforce were employed in manufacturing, a proportion comparable with that of the United States and Canada, and much higher than it is today. Protection, mass immigration, foreign investment and rising prosperity in other Western countries transformed Australia into an industrial-ised country with a high standard of living.

FORWARD DEFENCE

Under the policy of 'forward defence', which dominated the defence thinking of the time, Australian forces engaged the enemy and did battle in other people's countries to the north. Had those forces been ordered simply to defend Austra-lia's territory or its northern approaches, Australia would not have fought wars at all and the lives of hundreds of Australians would not have been lost. This can be said with some certainty because in none of these conflicts did Australia count importantly in the outcome. Australia's forces were token in character, sent as auxiliaries alongside much larger forces and in order to produce a politi-cal effect in Washington and London rather than to turn the military tide, an approach echoed in later deployments of Australians to distant theatres of war by the Hawke, Howard, Rudd and Gillard governments. By giving military assis-tance, the Australian governments of the time sought the favour of the Great Protectors, especially that of the United States. At some future time of peril to Australia they reckoned the favour would stand a good chance of being returned. When President Truman asked for military help for South Korea in July 1950, for example, Australia's Minister for External Affairs, Spender, cabled Menzies with the argument for Australian commitment. He emphasised that

> from Australia's long-term point of view any additional aid we can give to the United States now, small though it may be, will repay us in the future one hundred fold ... Time in Korea is rapidly running out and if we refrain from giving any further aid we may lose an opportunity of cementing friendship with the United States which may not easily present itself again.[5]

Arguments of this kind became the stock-in-trade of official thinking about the defence and security of Australia. The mentality of ingratiation pervades it still.

The Vietnam War

The Vietnam War was the high point of Australia's dependence on the United States and identification with American foreign policy. For Australia, the war began with the despatch of military instructors in 1962. An infantry battalion of combat troops followed in 1965, then further battalions in 1966 and 1967, reaching a peak strength of 8300. The first Australian battalion in Vietnam was submerged in a larger American force, but from May 1966 to December 1971 the Australian Task Force in Phuoc Tuy province was an independent fighting unit. The Vietnam War, Australia's most significant overseas commitment since World War II, was also Australia's first war without Britain as an ally. It was accompanied by a considerable increase in the size of the Australian armed forces, achieved by selectively conscripting young men for overseas military service by means of a ballot based on birthdates.

Forty years later, Australia's involvement in Vietnam looks like folly born of two obsessions of the 1960s: a fear of threats from the north and a desire to please the Americans. Recommending from Washington in 1964 that Australia should respond to an American request for military assistance, the Australian diplomat Alan Renouf argued that the 'problem of Vietnam' was one 'where we could without a disproportionate expenditure pick up a lot of credit with the United States'.[6] While Australia wanted to gain credit in Washington, its decision to go to Vietnam should not be seen purely and simply as doing the bidding of the Great Protector. Rather, it was a case of a hawkish junior ally pushing the United States to commit itself more fully to a military solution. 'Far from being dragged into Vietnam by the Americans', the Minister for External Affairs, Paul Hasluck, said in 1966, 'the Australian government has been glad and reassured that the United States has been prepared to undertake such heavy commitments as it has undertaken in support of international security in a region where our own danger is immeasurably greater than any danger to America'. At the same time, the Americans were glad the Australians were by their side. They valued the Australian troops not so much for their military significance, which was slight, as for conferring moral legitimacy on the prosecution of the conflict. The US Secretary of State, Dean Rusk, said of the first Australian battalion that it 'would be worth many times its numbers both on the ground and in terms of the effect on public opinion in the world and in the United States'.[7]

When he announced the commitment of troops in parliament in April 1965, Menzies portrayed the decision as a response to a request for help from the government of South Vietnam. As we now know, the sequence of events was the other way round. Having first decided upon sending troops, Australia then had to set about prodding South Vietnam into asking for them. The Australian government was 'on tenterhooks that South Vietnam would not formally ask for the battalion now being pressed upon it, before the news was leaked'.[8]

Public opinion in Australia largely favoured the Vietnam commitment—at first. Menzies retired as prime minister early in 1966. His successor, Harold Holt, soon trebled Australia's commitment of forces to Vietnam and promised that Australia would go 'all the way with LBJ'. By contrast, the Labor Party under Arthur Calwell promised to end conscription and bring home the troops. At the invitation of Holt, LBJ himself—the US president, Lyndon Baines Johnson—visited Australia in 1966. Attracting vast crowds of sympathisers and anti-war demonstrators wherever he went, Johnson heaped praise on the prime minister and identified his Vietnam policies with loyalty to American friends in time of trouble. Labor was made to look unpatriotic. In the federal election a month later, Labor suffered its worst defeat since 1949; the Liberals emerged triumphant and the scene was set for a further increase in Australia's Vietnam commitment the following year.

But from 1968 onwards, the public perception of the Vietnam War began to change. On television, many Australians discovered the horror of war for the first time. They became aware that many Americans opposed their government on the issue. And, as hostilities dragged on for month after month, they began to realise that Australia was involved in a war which might never be won, a war which brought endless Australian casualties. By the latter half of 1969, public opinion polls were showing a majority in favour of withdrawing the troops. Vietnam and conscription split the country between those who thought Australia should help the Americans to stop the Communists at all costs and those who thought Australia had no place killing Vietnamese or forcing young men to go to fight. Demonstrators took to the streets, increasingly so as the war continued, until by the time of the Vietnam Moratorium marches of 1970 they included not just disenchanted youth but opponents of the war from all walks of life, the respectable and the unrespectable alike. For the Australian government, the Vietnam War became a political liability, something from which it wished to extricate itself. The Coalition governments withdrew almost all Australian troops by March 1972.

The strategic situation in North-East and South-East Asia changed dramatically during the years of the Vietnam War. Australia had seen Indonesia under President Sukarno as a threat, heavily influenced by communism. Between 1965 and 1966, hundreds of thousands of communist Indonesians were killed in the bloodletting which brought to power an anti-communist, pro-Western government. Australia hastened to support it and bent over backwards to be friends

THE VIETNAM WAR, 1962–72: AUSTRALIAN CASUALTIES

Service	Died	Wounded/ injured/ill	Total
Army	478	3025	3503
RAN	8	48	56
RAAF	14	56	70
TOTAL	500	3129	3629

Australian War Memorial,
<www.awm.gov.au/encyclopedia/vietnam/statistics.asp>.

with Indonesia. In what is known as the Guam Doctrine, the United States declared in 1969 that in future its allies in the Asia-Pacific region would have to bear the major responsibility for their own defence, and they could no longer rely on the Americans coming to their defence except in the case of nuclear threat. The economically weakened British had already announced that they would withdraw their forces from east of Suez; that is, from the Persian Gulf and South-East Asia. And in 1972, after a secret visit to Beijing by President Nixon's Special Assistant for National Security Affairs, Henry Kissinger, the United States normalised diplomatic relations with the country which it had long regarded as a communist outlaw and which Australia did not recognise: the People's Republic of China.

Within a few years the ground had shifted beneath the feet of the Australian government, undermining its assumptions about defence and security. In place of a monolithic communism endangering Australia from countries to the north, a threat which could be met only if Australia fought wars in South-East Asia, there was now seen to be a far more complex region in which some communist countries were America's friends and some were its enemies. The United Kingdom was gone as a military force. And America was indicating doubts about future military commitments of the kind that Australia, only a few years before, had considered vital to its security. The changes were too much for the Liberal–Country Party governments of the early 1970s and they were constantly left looking foolish. The Whitlam government, elected in 1972, hastened to adjust Australia's foreign policy to the new reality.

WHITLAM AND FRASER, 1972–83

In December 1972, the Australian people elected their first Labor government for almost a generation. Gough Whitlam was the new prime minister and, for the first eleven months, the new foreign minister as well. He was well versed in foreign affairs and determined to chart a new course for Australia internationally. Soon after his election, he explained that the direction of his thinking was 'towards a more independent Australian stance in international affairs and towards an Australia which will be less militarily oriented and not open to suggestions of racism; an Australia which will enjoy a growing standing as a distinctive, tolerant, co-operative and well-regarded nation not only in the Asian and Pacific region but in the world at large'.[9]

Whitlam acted as soon as he was prime minister. He withdrew the last Australian military advisers from South Vietnam, stopped all military aid to that country and abolished conscription. He established full diplomatic relations with East Germany and China. He ordered Australia's representatives at the United Nations to call more strongly for an end to colonial regimes in Rhodesia, Mozambique, Angola and elsewhere. He made Australia an outspoken opponent of apartheid in South Africa. He discarded the old policy of politely objecting to French nuclear tests in the South Pacific, still being conducted in the atmosphere, and brought a case against France in the International Court of Justice. He removed the last racial restrictions on immigration and made the White Australia policy a thing of the past. In time he was to increase Australia's foreign aid, oversee the transition by Papua New Guinea to independence, and demonstrate sympathy with a number of Third World causes.

The sudden emergence of an independent-minded ally in the South Pacific took the Americans by surprise, and the surprise turned to irritation when Whitlam and his ministers condemned American bombing of North Vietnam. One minister called it 'the most brutal, indiscriminate slaughter of women and children in living memory'; another thought the Americans were guilty of 'mass murder'.[10] Whitlam himself, in a personal letter to President Nixon, called for an end to the bombing. The Americans were not used to criticism from their friends the Australians, nor did they expect an Australian government to touch the sacred ark of Western intelligence. But in 1973 Attorney-General Senator Lionel Murphy sent federal police to raid the Melbourne offices of ASIO for files he suspected were being withheld from him. The ASIO raid, which was to pass into legend in the history of the Whitlam government, shocked the secret world of Western intelligence services. The CIA contemplated stopping the flow of information to its sister spy services in Australia. One CIA operative who was in Vietnam at the time said there 'was a complete alteration of our attitudes towards the Australians when the Whitlam government came to power'.[11]

Whitlam was not anti-American so much as pro-Australian. He defended the presence in Australia of US military facilities at Pine Gap, North West Cape and Nurrungar and resisted pressure from the left faction of the Labor Party to get rid of them. When New Zealand proposed a South Pacific nuclear-free zone in 1975, Whitlam joined with the Americans in opposing it. On East Timor, Whitlam, like the Americans, raised no objection to Indonesia's incorporation of the former Portuguese colony into Indonesian territory. He was an economic nationalist, but he had no plans to nationalise American holdings in Australia. In reality, he was no threat to American security or economic interests in Australia. Yet the US government, US corporations, the CIA and their allies in Australia were thoroughly alarmed by what they thought was happening in Canberra: a conservative, stable, pro-American ally seemed to have been replaced overnight by one that was radical, unstable and anti-American.

The Americans responded by appointing Marshall Green as ambassador. He was head of the Far Eastern and Pacific Affairs Division of the State Department, a professional sent to deal with a potentially troublesome government. The United States objected to the fact that Whitlam's personal staff were not required to undergo security clearances and succeeded in having the policy changed. The United States advised against releasing sensitive information to Dr Jim Cairns, a man they regarded as a potential security risk and who was also, at times, the acting prime minister of Australia. The CIA appears to have contributed to the fall of the Whitlam government in two ways: by supplying damaging information to ASIO so that ASIO could pass it on to the press; and by threatening an end to intelligence cooperation with Australia. The Americans were delighted when Whitlam was sacked as prime minister in 1975 and the Labor Party defeated in the subsequent election. But we cannot know how far, if at all, they and their friends in the Australian defence and intelligence community influenced the Governor-General Sir John Kerr in his decision to dismiss Whitlam.

The three years of the Whitlam government changed Australian foreign policy permanently in significant ways. After Whitlam, Australia would not return to restricting immigration on racial criteria, indeed it would open its doors as never before to migrants from the Asian region; it would not go back to regarding the near north principally as a place to send troops; it would continue to cultivate good relations with China and with the countries of South-East Asia; and it would proceed with the gradual dismantling of legal and ceremonial connections with the United Kingdom. Yet the tradition of dependence on the United States would return under the Liberal prime minister Malcolm Fraser and his Labor successor Bob Hawke.

Malcolm Fraser dominated the making of Australian foreign policy in his time almost as much as Whitlam dominated it in his. The two men differed in outlook. Where Whitlam was an optimist in international affairs and inclined to a tolerant view of Soviet intentions, Fraser was a pessimist who saw Soviet expansion as a serious threat to world peace. Where Whitlam sought greater independence from the United States, Fraser reasserted the central importance to Australia's security of the American alliance. And where Whitlam welcomed détente between the two superpowers, Fraser believed the Soviets were exploiting it to build themselves a military advantage over the West.

Fraser was an uncompromising opponent and critic of the Soviet Union, and he was prime minister during a period in which relations between the super-powers steadily deteriorated. By the time he left office in 1983, the United States and the Soviet Union were confronting each other as dangerously as at any time since the beginning of the Cold War. Fraser was quick to open Australian ports to US nuclear warships and to support the development of the atoll of Diego Garcia in the Indian Ocean as a US naval base. In a version of the old Australian desire to involve the Americans directly in the defence of Australia, he offered them Fremantle as the site for a US naval base, an offer which they declined. Instead, Darwin became a staging post for B-52 strategic bombers. Fraser's warnings of Soviet expansionism, initially dismissed by sceptics as conservative rhetoric, seemed to be borne out by the Soviet invasion of Afghanistan in 1979 and by the steady growth in Soviet deployments of missiles aimed at Western Europe. Yet, with Fraser as with Whitlam, a gap existed between rhetoric and action. Australia did not follow the lead of the United States in imposing an embargo on sales of grain to the Soviet Union; in fact, Australian grain exports to the Soviet Union almost tripled between 1979 and 1982, and Australian athletes competed in the 1980 Moscow Olympic Games.

For all his concern to repair the ANZUS alliance, Fraser was more than merely pro-American. He brought his own distinctive contribution to foreign policy, one that owed little to predecessors such as Menzies and Holt. Fraser associated Australia with the Third World on a number of issues, including the proposal for a common fund which would help to stabilise the prices received by Third World countries for primary commodities. He opposed racial discrimination in South Africa and played a role in bringing an end to white minority rule in Rhodesia, which became the independent state of Zimbabwe in 1980. Like Menzies, but for quite different reasons, Fraser was a Commonwealth man. Menzies liked the Commonwealth as the successor to the British Empire and for its British and white connections; Fraser valued it as an opportunity for rich and poor countries to come together, and as a forum for Third World issues, though whether the Commonwealth achieved much for its poorer members is open to doubt. The Fraser government stands in stark contrast to its Coalition predecessors on one issue: immigration. In accepting tens of thousands of political refugees from Vietnam, Cambodia and Laos for settlement in Australia, the Fraser government confirmed that White Australia was dead and that Australia as a nation was to have a partly Asian identity.

The fundamental reason for the massive defeats of the Whitlam government in 1975 and the Fraser government in 1983 was economic. During the long boom in Western economies from the late 1940s until the early 1970s, unemployment and inflation in Australia were low and real wages were rising. Australians enjoyed constantly growing levels of prosperity and security. Governments, it was thought, had removed the tendency of capitalist economies to enter periodic slumps or depressions by regulating the level of demand through taxation and the supply of credit. But in about 1973, Australia, like other Western industrialised countries, was pitchforked into a long economic recession. High unemployment became normal, inflation raged at record levels through most of the 1970s, and the period of general prosperity receded into history.

The causes of this prolonged recession were partly international and partly domestic. Events of the early 1970s, when the United States was forced to abandon convertibility of the US dollar into gold, permanently weakened the global financial and trading order established under American auspices in the 1940s. In effect, the United States began exporting inflation to the rest of the world. On top of these problems came the first 'oil shock' engineered by OPEC, the Organization of Petroleum Exporting Countries, which discovered in 1973 that by banding together as a cartel it could massively increase the price of oil sold to industrialised countries and cause a transfer of resources from the rich world to the oil producers. A second oil shock followed in 1979. Each shock produced a sharp economic downturn throughout the industrialised world, including Australia.

Yet international recession was not the only cause of Australia's economic problems. Australia's formula for economic success—to export raw materials while industrialising behind tariff walls—ran certain long-term risks that were becoming apparent by the 1970s. Australia's share of world trade was dropping. High rates of protection made most Australian manufactures too expensive to export and increased costs at home; dynamic economies, on the other hand, had lower tariffs and were building economic growth on exporting competitively priced manufactures, something Australia could never do. In order to revive its prosperity, Australia needed to reduce protection and diversify exports, restructuring the economy so as to allow the most competitive industries to flourish. That, at least, was the analysis of the problem that Australia's policy community came to accept. Experts said protectionism was becoming a halter around Australia's neck. Whitlam recognised the problem and cut all tariffs by 25 per cent in 1973, but he was blamed for unemployment and paid a heavy political price in 1975. Fraser took note and increased the effective protection enjoyed by Australia's least competitive industries—motor vehicles, textiles and footwear. Australia's foreign economic policy at the end of the Fraser government in 1983 was much as it had been since the 1950s.

As we shall see, the election of the Hawke Labor government in 1983, unlike that of Whitlam in 1972, brought no sudden change of direction in Australian foreign policy on matters of defence and political relations. On the contrary, Hawke the Labor man proved to be more concerned with what the Americans might think than Fraser the Liberal. But in foreign economic policy the Hawke government brought a revolution, dismantling the protectionism and regulation that had characterised Australia's approach since the early years of the century. From the perspective of the second decade of the twenty-first century, we can see that Whitlam's most significant foreign policy decision was to recognise the People's Republic of China, now Australia's foremost trading partner.

ASSESSMENTS

A few central themes recur in the history of Australia's foreign relations for most of the twentieth century: dependence, trade protection, and Australia's relationship with Asia.

The first theme is military and diplomatic dependence on more powerful states overseas. No Australian government, whether Labor or anti-Labor, has ever seriously considered emerging completely from under the comforting wing of a Great Protector from abroad. Many Australians, drawing on the conventional wisdom of politicians and the press, have assumed that depending on what Menzies called 'great and powerful friends' is an unavoidable condition for a small population in a big country. But throughout the century, except during World War II, a dissenting minority has refused to accept that Australia needs foreign help for its national security. The dissenters have interpreted dependence not as an advantage for Australia, but rather as the means by which Australia has been subjected to the interests of others. The campaigners against Australia's involvement in the Vietnam War or the 2003 war on Iraq were in the same dissenting tradition as opponents of conscription for overseas military service during World War I. In all three cases, Australia was seen to be sacrificing itself for the sake of a distant and dominant ally.

The dependence issue that is at the heart of most disputes about Australian foreign policy is really part of a more fundamental controversy among Australians over the identity and destiny of their country. For the mostly conservative politicians, diplomats and military officials who determined Australia's foreign and defence policy, Australia was defined by its 'imperial connection', first to the British Empire of dominions and colonies and later to a less formally organised but nonetheless real American empire of military alliances, economic investment and political influence. These decision-makers typically argued for foreign policy arrangements, calculated to please their class counterparts overseas in the United Kingdom and the United States, on a whole range of matters from foreign investment and anti-communism to the despatch of Australian soldiers to distant armed conflicts; and they assumed that Australia the nation would be best served by a foreign policy that promoted the political status quo at home. Their policies were the foreign face of domestic conservatism. The critics of such an approach regarded Australia's foreign commitments and obligations as shackles on the country's potential for creating a new and fairer society. For the critics, Australia's deliberate dependence on powerful allies opened the way for foreign political influence and, while preserving the class interests of wealthier Australians, it checked the potential for radical domestic reform.

The second theme is protection. For most of the century, the central issue in foreign economic policy was how much to protect Australian manufacturing industry from foreign competition. The answer to that question in the early years of Federation was unequivocally in favour of high protection, and when the newly formed Country Party complained in the 1920s that farmers bore the costs of such protection, a political settlement was reached whereby the rural sector received its own subsidies in the form of price supports, bounties and tax concessions. One way or another, Australian governments tried to do something for everybody: manufacturers had tariffs, farmers had subsidies, and the ordinary working man or woman was supposed to be protected by award wages and the arbitration system. That old political bargain came under strain during the Whitlam and Fraser governments and finally collapsed under the Hawke Labor government, which exposed Australia as never before to the influences of the international economy. Manufacturers began to lose their tariffs, farmers their subsidies, and workers their protections under a regulated wage system. By the 1990s the conventional wisdom in Canberra, shared by both sides of politics, was that Australia's economic salvation now lay in radical restructuring to make the country internationally competitive; and for that reason Australia would have to abandon tariffs and concentrate on its most efficient industries. The century-long debate about tariffs was resolved in favour of free trade.

The third theme in the history of Australian foreign policy, and one which is also about Australia's identity as a nation, is that of our relationship with Asia. The word 'Asia' is too convenient to abandon, but we should be aware of its pitfalls. As many scholars have pointed out, there is no such thing as Asia. The category of 'Asia', by some definitions, embraces every country from Iran in the west to the Philippines in the east, and includes the civilisations of India and China, the economic giant Japan and hundreds of different language and cultural groups—indeed, half the population of the globe! Thinking of this vast, populous and diverse area as one region and of its people as a homogeneous group of 'Asians', as if they drew upon a single cultural tradition and possessed a common identity, is an ethnocentric mistake made by many Australians even now. Ever since 1901 such ethnocentrism and much outright racial prejudice have exerted a powerful influence over Australia's interactions with the countries to its north. The first parliament after Federation devoted much of its time to White Australia legislation which was to prevent non-white foreigners from emigrating to Australia for the next 65 years. In doing so, the politicians were defining Australia as a country for white people, with ties to another white country on the other side of the world, an island of Europeans from which Asians in particular were to be excluded.

Australians' fear of Japan, dramatically realised in 1942 when the Japanese invaded New Guinea, bombed Darwin and captured thousands of Australian soldiers in Singapore, was slow to subside. After World War II it helped to sustain a popular fear of further military threats from the north, a sentiment used by the non-Labor governments of the 1950s and 1960s to justify sending Australian troops to Korea, Malaysia and Vietnam. To many Australians of the time, Asia was the place where our brave soldiers went to defend us against the Communists. Australia began to lose its reputation in the Asian region as a bastion of white racism only in the 1970s and 1980s, with the abolition of the White Australia policy and the influx of immigrants from countries such as Vietnam, China and the Philippines. In retrospect, Whitlam can be seen as the prime minister who broke the spell of fear which had inspired the policy of forward defence, and Fraser as the prime minister who did most to open Australia's doors to refugees from the region. Together, they began the gradual transformation of Australia from a nation which thought of itself as an isolated European outpost to one capable of assuming a partly Asian identity.

FURTHER READING

Overview

Beaumont, Joan, Christopher Waters and David Lowe, with Garry Woodard, *Ministers, Mandarins and Diplomats: Australian foreign policy making 1941–1969*, Melbourne University Press, Melbourne, 2003. (An authoritative history of the Department of External Affairs and its relations with the external affairs ministers of that period, Evatt, Spender, Casey, Barwick and Hasluck.)

Edwards, P.G., *Prime Ministers and Diplomats: The making of Australian foreign policy 1901– 1949*, Oxford University Press, Melbourne, 1983. (Scholarly evaluation of the early years.)

Goldsworthy, David, ed., *Facing North: A century of Australian engagement with Asia. Volume 1: 1901 to the 1970s*, Department of Foreign Affairs and Trade and Melbourne University Press, Melbourne, 2001. (A comprehensive official history tracing key aspects of the evolution of Australia's relations with its Asian, especially East Asian, neighbours from Federation to the Whitlam era.)

Millar, T.B., *Australia in Peace and War: External relations since 1788*, 2nd edn, ANU Press, Canberra, 1991. (First written a generation ago, and weak on economics, but can be useful.)

Woolcott, Richard, *The Hot Seat: Reflections on diplomacy from Stalin's death to the Bali bombings*, HarperCollins, Sydney, 2003. (An engagingly written autobiography by a leading diplomat who became head of the Department of Foreign Affairs and Trade; covers key issues in Australian foreign policy in the last half-century accessibly and perceptively.)

Relations with the UK and US

Bell, Coral, *Dependent Ally: A study in Australian foreign policy*, Oxford University Press, Melbourne, 3rd edn, 1995. (Emphasises strategic and security issues.)

Bridge, Carl, ed., *Munich to Vietnam: Australia's relations with Britain and the United States since the 1930s*, Melbourne University Press, Melbourne, 1991. (Economic as well as political relations.)

Day, David, *The Great Betrayal: Britain, Australia and the onset of the Pacific War 1939–42*, Angus & Robertson, Sydney, 1988. (Pacific War as the turning-point in Anglo-Australian relations.)

Goldsworthy, David, *Losing the Blanket: Australia and the end of Britain's Empire*, Melbourne University Press, Melbourne, 2002. (An historian surveys Australia's changing relationship with the UK in the 1950s and 1960s.)

Lowe, David, *Australia between Empires: The life of Percy Spender*, Pickering and Chatto, London, 2010. (Biography of the Australian foreign minister who negotiated the ANZUS Treaty, introduced the Colombo Plan and made Australians aware, for the first time, of the importance of East Asia in peacetime.)

Ward, Stuart, *Australia and the British Embrace: The demise of the Imperial Idea*, Melbourne University Press, Melbourne, 2001. (A scholarly history of the impact on Australia of the pivotal decision by the UK in the 1960s to seek membership of the European Economic Community, now the European Union.)

Waters, Christopher, *The Empire Fractures: Anglo-Australian conflict in the 1940s*, Australian Scholarly Publishing, Melbourne, 1995. (Australia asserts an independent foreign policy.)

Australia's involvement in South-East Asian wars

Edwards, Peter with Gregory Pemberton, *Crises and Commitments: The politics and diplomacy of Australia's involvement in Southeast Asian conflicts, 1948–1965*, Allen & Unwin with the Australian War Memorial, Sydney and Canberra, 1992. (Official history; detailed and comprehensive.)

Frost, Frank, *Australia's War in Vietnam*, Allen & Unwin, Sydney, 1987. (Chapter 1 summarises the reasons for Australia's participation.)

Pemberton, Gregory, *All the Way: Australia's road to Vietnam*, Allen & Unwin, Sydney, 1987. (The definitive scholarly account.)

Whitlam government

Albinski, H.S., *Australian External Policy under Labor: Content, process and the national debate*, University of Queensland Press, St Lucia, 1977. (Comprehensive.)

Camilleri, Joseph, 'Foreign policy', in *From Whitlam to Fraser: Reform and reaction in Australian politics*, Allan Patience and Brian W. Head, eds, Oxford University Press, Melbourne, 1979, Chapter 15. (Detailed and critical one-chapter summary.)

Hudson, W.J., ed., *Australia in World Affairs 1971–75*, Allen & Unwin, Sydney, 1980. (Authoritative scholarly survey.)

Lee, David and Christopher Waters, eds, *Evatt to Evans: The Labor tradition in Australian foreign policy*, Allen & Unwin, Sydney, 1997. (Foreign policy under the Curtin, Chifley, Whitlam, Hawke and Keating Labor governments.)

Fraser government, 1975–83

Boyce, P. and J. Angel, eds, *Independence and Alliance: Australia in world affairs 1976–80*, Allen & Unwin, Sydney, 1983. (Authoritative scholarly survey.)

——Diplomacy in the Marketplace—Australia in world affairs, 1981–90, Longman Cheshire, Melbourne, 1992. (Authoritative scholarly survey.)

Camilleri, Joseph, 'Foreign policy: Strategic and economic dimensions', in From Fraser to Hawke, Brian W. Head and Allan Patience, eds, Longman Cheshire, Melbourne, 1989, pp. 37–65. (Detailed and critical one-chapter summary.)

Renouf, Alan, Malcolm Fraser and Australian Foreign Policy, Australian Professional Publications, Mosman, 1986. (The only book-length study.)

An economics approach to writing the history of foreign policy

Lee, David, Search for Security: The political economy of Australia's postwar foreign and defence policy, Allen & Unwin, Sydney, 1995. (Foreign policy after World War II viewed from an economic perspective; original and perceptive.)

Documents

Australia's Military Commitment to Vietnam, Department of Foreign Affairs, Canberra, 1975. (Official documents showing how Australia became involved as American allies in the Vietnam War.)

Doran, Stuart and David Lee, eds, Australia and Recognition of the People's Republic of China, 1949–1972, Department of Foreign Affairs and Trade, Canberra, 2002. (Official documents showing why Australia did not grant recognition to the PRC until 1972.)

Holdich, Roger, Vivianne Johnson and Pamela Andre, eds, The ANZUS Treaty 1951, Department of Foreign Affairs and Trade, Canberra, 2001. (Official documents showing the diplomatic origins of Australia's security alliance with the US.)

Lowe, David and Daniel Oakman, eds, Australia and the Colombo Plan, 1949–1957, Department of Foreign Affairs and Trade, Canberra, 2004. (Official documents on the scheme that brought thousands of Asian students to Australia in the 1950s and inaugurated Australian bilateral aid to South and South-East Asia.)

Meaney, Neville, ed., Australia and the World: A documentary history from the 1870s to the 1970s, Longman Cheshire, Melbourne, 1985. (Well-chosen collection of official and unofficial documents.)

Way, Wendy with Damien Browne and Vivianne Johnson, eds, Australia and the Indonesian Incorporation of Portuguese Timor, 1974–1976, Melbourne University Press, Melbourne, 2000. (Official documents on Australia's policy on East Timor at the time of Indonesia's invasion.)

Foreign policy under Hawke and Keating, 1983–96

- What changes did the Hawke and Keating governments make to Australia's foreign economic policy, and what effect did they have on the Australian economy?
- What problems was the Labor government addressing in its two main trade initiatives?
- How did Australia respond to the ANZUS crisis of the mid 1980s?
- Why did Australia send troops to the Gulf War of 1991?
- What considerations determined the Indonesia policy of the Hawke and Keating governments?
- How did Australia's defence policy change in the 1980s?
- What was new about Labor's regional security policy?
- To what extent was Australian foreign policy under Hawke and Keating a characteristically Labor foreign policy?

Dramatic changes in Australia's external circumstances marked the years 1983 to 1996. Australia found itself alongside the world's fastest growing economies. In East Asia the economies of the 'Four Tigers'—South Korea, Taiwan, Hong Kong and Singapore—grew year by year and spread their prosperity across the region in a process that came to be recognised as a fundamental shift of global production towards that part of the world. Japan replaced the United States as the world's largest overseas investor. China, or at least parts of China, leapt from backwardness and isolation in the early 1980s to lead the world in economic growth by the mid 1990s.

Australia's strategic environment was also transformed after 1983. The Cold War was the defining fact of international relations when Labor came to office. By 1996 it was a thing of the past. Once divided into two camps, the world was now a more complicated scene of ethnic nationalist wars, civil conflict and regional tensions. The Soviet Union no longer existed. The threat of nuclear war between the Russians and the Americans, apparently so great in the early 1980s, had diminished to vanishing point as the two sides reduced their nuclear arsenals. In 1983 Communist Vietnam, a Soviet ally, confronted the five non-communist states of the Association of Southeast Asian Nations (ASEAN); by 1996 Communist Vietnam was a member of ASEAN and a major recipient of Australian aid and investment. Terrorism, the scourge of the new century, had emerged but was not yet a significant threat to international security.

Foreign policy, especially for a small country such as Australia, is the art not only of responding creatively to a changing external environment, but also of taking the initiative. Australia had a Labor government for thirteen years (1983–96), with Bob Hawke as prime minister until 1991 followed by over four years of Paul Keating. Labor's foreign ministers were first Bill Hayden and then, from 1988, Gareth Evans. Labor foreign policy was characterised not just by responses, but by initiatives on a wide range of issues from trade policy to arms control. After winning five federal elections in a row, Labor was swept from office in 1996 by a coalition of the Liberal and National parties under John Howard, who appointed the former Liberal leader Alexander Downer as his foreign affairs minister.

This chapter describes the mixture of response and initiative that was Australian foreign policy from 1983 to 1996, and asks whether we can speak of a distinctively 'Labor' approach to foreign policy.

FOREIGN ECONOMIC POLICY

When most Australians considered foreign policy during these years they conceived of international relations in traditional terms as the political and military contest of states. They thought of the American alliance, nuclear issues, wars, defence, regional security, political relations, the republic, and Australia's response to human rights abuses in foreign countries. The foreign policy issues that drew demonstrators on to the streets of Australian cities were all of this kind—the nuclear threat of the mid 1980s, Australian involvement in the Gulf War of 1991, Indonesian repression in East Timor and the French nuclear tests of 1995. These high politics issues are, however, only half the story of foreign policy 1983–96. The other half—some would say the core—was the economy, and Australia's economic relations with the rest of the world.

In 1983 Labor inherited an economy which, for long-term structural reasons, was losing international competitiveness. Whereas Europe, Japan and, to a lesser extent, the United States used efficient manufacturing to subsidise uncompetitive agricultural producers, Australia did the opposite. In Australia an efficient agricultural and mining sector subsidised an uncompetitive manufacturing sector through high tariffs. Australia had a First World standard of living based on a Third World pattern of exports, a solution that by many accounts left the nation dangerously exposed to fluctuations in world prices for its commodity exports.

As the long boom faded and the queues of unemployed lengthened, many economists embraced a new view about what Australia should do. Reports on industry and finance commissioned by Australian governments of the 1970s stressed the need for Australia to lower tariffs, deregulate the financial sector and restructure the national economy. The economists who wrote these reports did not share assumptions long held on both sides of politics in Australia: that the economy needed to be protected and regulated, for example, and that governments should use taxes and interest rates to moderate periodic booms and slumps, maintain full employment and preserve social harmony. They looked to a future where market forces would be liberated to do their magic work of stimulating efficiency and distributing goods, services and labour according to supply and demand. Government, they believed, had too large a place in the economy and needed to be restrained in favour of the market. If Australia was to remain prosperous, they said, it should begin exporting manufactures and services and reduce reliance on commodity exports. The government had no option but to unravel the web of protectionism and regulation that had been spun around the economy, for only in this way would international pressures for efficiency be felt and manufacturing industry become competitive.

When Bob Hawke was elected prime minister these neo-liberal ideas were not part of the Labor tradition. But the incoming Labor government confronted unemployment at its highest level since the Depression and was keen to try something different. The new treasurer, Paul Keating, still knew little about economics and Treasury officials found he could be persuaded to their viewpoint and then defend it convincingly to the public. On the basis of Treasury advice Keating soon made fundamental changes in Australia's foreign economic policy. The Australian dollar was floated in December 1983, in effect exposing the economy as never before to foreign competition and, in the long run, placing downward pressure on wages. The capital market was significantly deregulated, enabling foreign banks to invest in Australia and Australian companies to move capital offshore without difficulty. Capital began to flow in and out of Australia in unprecedented amounts and the Australian dollar became one of the most traded currencies in international foreign exchange markets. Like other countries following a similar policy path, Australia was exposing itself to the destabilising influences of deregulated international financial markets. From now on all Australian governments, when they pondered economic policy, would have to consider the likely reaction of the financial markets.

The effects of these developments were dramatically illustrated in 1986. Australia's net external debt grew fast in the 1980s and particularly rapidly in 1985 when world commodity prices fell (meaning that Australia received less for what it sold) and when the value of the dollar declined to a low of US60c (meaning that the existing debt in American dollars automatically increased). As monthly balance-of-payments figures worsened and foreign debt grew, the government became alarmed. More and more of the value of Australia's exports was being used to service the debt. In a radio interview Keating warned Australia was at risk of becoming a 'banana republic' crippled by chronic foreign indebtedness. Part of the solution, Keating claimed, was for government to cut spending, and in the 1986–87 Budget he made considerable cuts.

Another part of the solution was for Australia to sell more overseas. In a situation of growing foreign indebtedness, increasing exports was a vital national interest. Signalling that it now regarded trade diplomacy and foreign economic policy as lying at the core of Australia's national interests, Labor appointed an economist, Stuart Harris, as head of the Department of Foreign Affairs in 1984, merged Foreign Affairs with Trade in 1987 and moved the trade promotion organisation Austrade into the new Department of Foreign Affairs and Trade (DFAT) in 1991. Labor wanted diplomats mobilised and rejuvenated for tasks that went to the heart of national prosperity such as improving Australia's export performance, gaining access to new overseas markets and influencing the rules about international trading in Australia's favour.

Major hindrances stood in the way of Australia's exports, mainly in the form of subsidies paid by governments in Europe and the United States to agricultural producers. European governments paid their farmers handsomely to accumulate surpluses which were then dumped at low prices on world markets. The United States put export subsidies in the pockets of wheat farmers and then sold the cheap wheat into traditional Australian markets overseas, costing Australia hundreds of millions of dollars a year. America's Export Enhancement Program, signed into law in 1985, increased the American share of the world wheat trade at the direct expense of Australia. Labor thought it a disaster.

While Australia stood loyally by the United States the Americans were undermining Australian prosperity. The only bargaining chips Australia possessed were the nuclear-related US joint facilities at Pine Gap, North West Cape and Nurrungar. As tempers flared over wheat exports in 1986, Labor's foreign affairs minister Bill Hayden raised the possibility that Australia might have to reconsider its attitude to the joint facilities unless the United States stopped undercutting Australian exports. 'What contribution to Australia's security', he asked, 'could outweigh the subversion of Australia's economy? If Australia could not earn enough export income, it would be unable to purchase the military equipment for its own defence and that of Western interests in the region.'[1] As often happened, Hawke quickly corrected his foreign minister and refused to link trade with security issues in relations with the Americans. The issue lingered throughout the Labor period. All-party delegations went to Washington to put Australia's case; ministers talked tough about confronting the Americans; farm leaders even had a meeting with President George Bush senior on his visit to Australia in 1991. But the Americans, while praising Australia as a steadfast ally and key Pacific partner, never went beyond vague assurances. The truth was that, compared with the farm lobby in the United States, Australia had no leverage in Washington.

As a small and uninfluential player in international trade, Australia could never hope to achieve much bilaterally; that is, by doing deals over trading access with countries one by one, especially if those countries were large and powerful. Australia concluded the Closer Economic Relations Agreement (CER) with New Zealand but the best hope elsewhere was to work for a better set of rules about trade across the world and in the Asia-Pacific region. To use the technical jargon, Australia stood to gain most from rules-based trading regimes both globally and regionally.

Considerations of this kind led to Labor's two major trade initiatives, one global and the other regional. The global initiative was to form the Cairns Group of Fair Traders in Agriculture, so-called because its initial conference in 1986 was at the Queensland town of Cairns. The conference brought together fourteen countries (including Australia) which were efficient agricultural producers and which faced the same problem in exporting. The rules of the General Agreement on Tariffs and Trade (the GATT), which existed to ensure that international trade proceeded as freely as possible, did not include trade in agricultural goods. As Australia's Minister for Trade and Overseas Development, Neal Blewett, told the Cairns Group in 1991:

> Farmers in Australia—and in your own countries—are being placed in a financial vice by the economic vandalism of the world's strongest nations. It is indeed hard to reconcile that some Australian farmers face a future as welfare recipients while elsewhere in the world other 'farmers'—and I use the term loosely—live well on the public purse. Behind impenetrable barriers, inflated commodity prices stimulate the surpluses which are dumped on our export markets.[2]

The Cairns Group therefore campaigned to reform the GATT so that its rules covered agricultural commodities as well as manufactured goods. In 1994, after seven years of tortuous negotiations, the group was successful in extending GATT rules to agriculture. (Chapter 10 examines both the Cairns Group and the GATT in greater detail.)

Labor's regional trade initiative was the Asia-Pacific Economic Cooperation (APEC) forum, conceived by the Hawke government in 1989 to pave the way for liberalisation of trade and investment among the countries of the Pacific rim. APEC emerged at a time when similar trading arrangements were being reached in different parts of the region, such as the North American Free Trade Agreement (NAFTA) between Canada, Mexico and the United States and the ASEAN Free Trade Area (AFTA) among South-East Asian countries. The concept of APEC was to embrace all of these within a huge grouping that would unite half the world's economies.

Apart from giving leaders a chance to indulge in rhetoric about mutual benefit and cooperation, the APEC forum did not achieve much in its early years. But Australia claimed real progress at APEC's 1994 meeting in Bogor, Indonesia, where member states committed themselves to free trade and investment in a two-stage process over the succeeding 25 years. Developed countries undertook to meet the goals by 2010, and developing countries such as Indonesia and China were allowed an extra ten years. Keating made much of APEC and depicted the Bogor Declaration as a diplomatic triumph which would one day create tens of thousands of new jobs for Australians.

PAUL KEATING INSPIRES BILL CLINTON

As prime minister, Paul Keating played a key role in convincing the Americans to support APEC as a regional grouping of Asia-Pacific states, and President Bill Clinton convened the first meeting of APEC leaders in Seattle in 1993. The following year APEC leaders met in Bogor, Indonesia, and committed themselves to achieving free trade over the coming decades.

The US official most closely associated with East Asia was Stan Roth, who operated at the National Security Council in the White House and then as assistant secretary of state for Asian and Pacific Affairs. Roth said:

> What Paul Keating did was to offer a vision to President Clinton of what APEC could be. Not just a meeting—though no-one's diminishing the value of meeting once a year—but rather that it could be more substantive, namely, trying to forge an Asia-Pacific Community with the US in it. Clinton came to office more interested in economic issues than foreign policy and as a free trader. Keating seized his imagination by offering him a vision for APEC with the opportunity to do something different including big things like the Bogor vision of trade liberalisation. Paul Keating was thinking big picture. He didn't just say, we'll never get there because it's too hard. Instead he found an ally in Bill Clinton and got him motivated. It is not an exaggeration to say that Keating inspired Clinton. It's very clear to me having watched this from the White House that this was a special relationship.

> … In private Keating could be strongly critical of the United States in ways inconceivable to Howard. His dealings with Clinton were warm but tightly geared to Australia's objectives. He loved talking politics with Clinton and in one phone call spent a long time advising him how to sell free trade to the American people.

Paul Kelly, *The March of Patriots: The struggle for modern Australia*, Melbourne University Press, Melbourne, 2009, pp. 171–2.

While East Asia boomed, Australia possessed one natural advantage as a sophisticated economy situated alongside the fastest growing economies in the world. A Canberra economist and former ambassador to China, Ross Garnaut, expounded the potential of this situation in an influential report to the government in 1989, *Australia and the Northeast Asian Ascendancy*. The Garnaut Report said things which policymakers already knew but by giving coherence to those ideas Garnaut made them conventional wisdom. Pointing to the 'historic shift in the centre of gravity of economic production and power towards North-East Asia', Garnaut argued that Australians would have to transform their economy in order to share in the economic boom taking place to the north. Free trade, he said, should be embraced by 2000 and tariffs cut in the meantime; much greater efficiency should come to the electricity industry, the waterfront, coastal shipping, railways and aviation; foreign investment should be encouraged; more students should learn Asian languages; immigration should have a more economic focus; and the old Australian instinct to protect manufacturing industry should be abandoned. Like most officially commissioned reports, the Garnaut Report said what ministers wanted to hear, although the government would not commit Australia to all aspects of free trade. Labor aimed instead for an average tariff level of 5 per cent by 1996 with special exceptions for the motor vehicle, textile, clothing and footwear industries.

The virtue of Australia's economic integration with East Asia grew to be an official article of faith in Gareth Evans's years as foreign minister (1988–96). Austrade offices multiplied in East Asian cities. The East Asia Analytical Unit of the Department of Foreign Affairs and Trade examined the implications for Australia of the region's explosive economic growth. Ministers made frequent trips to the region, while Evans and Keating endlessly reiterated the theme that Australia's economic and strategic future lay in the Asia-Pacific.

THE AMERICAN CONNECTION

Ten years before Hawke was elected, a new Labor government under Gough Whitlam had come into office dissociating itself from US policy in Indochina and denouncing the American bombing of North Vietnam. When Whitlam was sacked in 1975, the Americans were glad to see him go and, according to some, played a part in his going. This time the new Labor prime minister was determined to reassure the Americans rather than unnerve them, not least because of American influence over Australia's image in the minds of international investors. So Hawke took the opposite line, expressing deep admiration for the United States and its president. Like Malcolm Fraser, the Liberal prime minister between 1975 and 1983, Hawke keenly supported the American alliance. Hawke said Australia and the United States would be 'together forever' and told President Ronald Reagan that there was no country the US would be able to rely on more as a constructive ally than Australia. 'Together forever' was a phrase that recalled 'all the way with LBJ', the resounding endorsement of America's Vietnam policy given by the Liberal prime minister Harold Holt in 1966. But Hawke did not mind. This time Labor—Hawke especially—was determined to keep the Americans happy.

The Hawke Labor government followed in the footsteps of its conservative predecessor on fundamental security issues, especially Australia's relations with the United States. Hawke reaffirmed the ANZUS alliance, sided with the United States during the 1985 ANZUS crisis caused by New Zealand, defended the presence in Australia of the nuclear-related joint facilities, and made Australia one of America's keenest allies in the Gulf War of 1991. At Hawke's first ANZUS Council meeting in mid 1983 Australia endorsed or congratulated the Americans on their approach to almost every major foreign policy issue, and when the Labor government conducted a review of the ANZUS Treaty it concluded that the American alliance was fundamental to Australia's national security and would be supported by Labor to the hilt.

Hawke defended the Americans' joint facilities at Pine Gap, North West Cape and Nurrungar. The 'American bases', as they were popularly known, were a sensitive issue for the government at a time of heightened superpower tension. As Hawke and Hayden conceded, the bases were potential nuclear targets in the event of war. For the sake of good relations with the United States, the government was putting Australia in the nuclear firing line and exposing Australians to the direct threat of nuclear annihilation. Peace activists in the Australian Labor Party (ALP) and the peace movement argued that hosting the bases ran counter to the responsibility of the Australian government for the security of its citizens, and should therefore be removed. In reply the government said the bases in fact contributed to peace. The Americans used them to ensure the Russians were not breaking arms control undertakings, it was argued, and the bases helped to maintain the 'stable nuclear deterrence' which in turn prevented the outbreak of nuclear war. The government's case showed that it completely accepted the 'nuclear balance of power' logic that so alarmed a sizeable minority of Australians.

Hawke rallied to the support of the Americans on the most important security issue faced by his government: the ANZUS crisis. New Zealanders went to the polls in 1984 and elected a Labour government committed to prohibiting nuclear-armed and nuclear-powered vessels from entering New Zealand ports. The policy represented a direct challenge to the Americans, whose policy was to neither confirm nor deny whether any particular US naval vessel was carrying nuclear weapons. For a few months the Americans hoped they would not have to put New Zealand's ship visits policy to the test. Some ambiguously phrased arrangement with the new government would soon be reached, they thought, and American ships would continue to be free to enter the ports of their ally.

The Americans had not counted on the strength of anti-nuclear sentiment, then at its height in New Zealand. Sixty-four per cent of voters in the 1984 New Zealand election chose parties that favoured a ban on nuclear ship visits. To many New Zealanders the route to security seemed to lie in being forgotten in a war rather than remaining exposed as a nuclear target whenever US Navy vessels were in port. When the Americans sought port entry for a guided missile destroyer, the USS *Buchanan*, early in 1985, the Labour government led by Prime Minister David Lange declined the request. In doing so, Lange precipitated a crisis in ANZUS, the military alliance that bound his country to Australia and the United States.

The Americans cut intelligence links with New Zealand, withdrew from joint naval exercises and eventually declared that America's defence commitments to New Zealand no longer applied. 'We part company as friends', said US Secretary of State George Schultz in 1986, 'but we part company'. New Zealand did not matter to the Americans strategically. On average only five US Navy ships visited New Zealand each year between 1976 and 1984. The reason for America's reaction lay in the precedent New Zealand created and the fear that others might follow. Anti-nuclear policies were sure to spread, said Reagan's Navy secretary, 'if foreign left-wing governments are able to assuage their left-wing, anti-nuclear radicals at the expense of the US Navy cost-free'.[3]

The response of the Hawke Labor government was to back the Americans—most of the way. ANZUS mattered far too much to the government for Australia to follow the lead of New Zealand, as some in the peace movement were demanding. In a letter to the New Zealand prime minister, Hawke stressed that Australia would welcome the visits of all US Navy vessels and would not ask about their nuclear status. He appears to have attempted secret negotiations with Lange to change or moderate New Zealand policy. Yet Australia was not willing to see New Zealand isolated, as some American officials wanted. Hayden stressed New Zealand's long record of support for Western interests, and Kim Beazley, as defence minister, arranged for Australian naval and military exercises to continue separately with New Zealand. Henceforth, though the old tripartite ANZUS alliance might have gone, Australia would continue to cooperate actively with both its alliance partners. The annual ANZUS talks were replaced by Australian–American ministerial (AUSMIN) talks, which have continued since.

Hawke's instincts were the same in handling the Persian Gulf crisis in 1990. The Gulf crisis arose when Iraq invaded Kuwait, a wealthy but small Middle East country whose oil supplies were regarded as vital to the economies of Western industrialised countries. Within days of the invasion in August 1990 Prime

Minister Bob Hawke announced that Australia was sending two guided missile frigates and a tanker to help the Americans enforce a blockade against Iraqi shipping in the Persian Gulf. The original commitment of Australian forces, it should be noted, was to the United States, though the government would later justify it as contributing to a joint action by the United Nations. For Hawke, it seems, the Americans came first and his Cabinet and party came second. He rushed to assist the Americans.

From a domestic political point of view, the Gulf War was almost the perfect armed conflict for Hawke. The allied counter-attack of early 1991 followed months of peaceful Western sanctions against Iraq. A resolution of the UN Security Council gave the attack the imprimatur of the international community and Hawke could depict it plausibly as a last resort after all other avenues had been tried. Led by the Americans, the allies swept to victory in under two months and without loss of Australian lives. The war did not threaten Australians and was played out on television screens like a gigantic video game. Though tens of thousands of Iraqis were being killed, many Australians appear to have treated the Gulf War as a form of entertainment. A Gulf peace movement opposed sending the frigates but was split between moderate and radical wings and failed to capture widespread public support; indeed the Australian people were more in favour of the United States, the ANZUS alliance and joint facilities at the end of the Gulf War than at the beginning. A greater contrast with the Vietnam War, which split Australia between supporters and opponents, is hard to imagine.

THE RELATIONSHIP WITH INDONESIA

The relationship with Indonesia represented another element of continuity in the foreign policy of the Coalition and Labor governments. Like every Australian prime minister since 1966, Hawke, Keating and Howard regarded the repressive but developmentalist New Order regime of President Suharto in Indonesia as a distinct security asset for Australia. For this reason, Labor went to great lengths to maintain good relations with Indonesia.

On this matter Labor came to office carrying political baggage which Hawke was determined to jettison as soon as possible. Groups of concerned Australians opposed Indonesia's occupation of the former Portuguese colony of East Timor from the time Indonesian troops invaded in 1975. As Indonesian atrocities continued in the late 1970s and scores of thousands of East Timorese died, support for East Timor's independence spread in ALP circles, especially in the left faction. The party embraced a policy that would have suspended Australian military aid to Indonesia until Indonesian forces withdrew from East Timor, only to see the policy reversed after Labor won government. By 1985 the government had reaffirmed de jure recognition of Indonesia's incorporation of East Timor. Like the Fraser government, the Hawke government formally accepted East Timor as legally part of Indonesia.

By 1991 the Hawke government, with Evans as foreign minister, could point to practical benefits for Australia from cooperating with Jakarta. The Timor Gap Zone of Cooperation Treaty, known as the Timor Gap Treaty, came into force that year, providing for the cooperative exploitation by Indonesia and Australia of 40,000 square kilometres of the Timor Sea. The treaty allowed both sides to gain from the oil and gas resources of the ocean lying between north-western Australia and East Timor. Hailed by Evans as a major achievement, the Timor Gap Treaty quickly came under fire from those who said it gave Australia a share in the spoils of Indonesia's conquest at the direct expense of the East Timorese.

When Indonesian soldiers shot dead scores of unarmed East Timorese protesters in November 1991, in what became known as the Dili Massacre, public outrage finally forced the government to condemn the resort to force and to express sympathy with the people of East Timor. But the government's reaction did not go beyond words. Australia's aid, trade, defence exports and defence cooperation were untouched and, in order to explain what went wrong in East Timor, the foreign minister Evans argued that the Dili Massacre 'was not an act of state but the product of aberrant behaviour by a subgroup within the country'.[4] Soon afterwards Indonesia was the first overseas destination of the new prime minister, Paul Keating, who was determined that East Timor should not dominate the official agenda.

Keating pursued good relations with Indonesia as a top priority in his years as prime minister (1991–96). He visited the country on a number of occasions and established a close rapport with President Suharto. At the end of 1995, with his eye on the coming election, Keating announced that Australia had signed a mutual security treaty with Indonesia providing for cooperation between the two countries in meeting 'adverse challenges'. The treaty was part of Keating's 'big picture' of a future Australia closely linked to its East Asian neighbours economically and strategically, but the treaty lasted only until 1999, when the Indonesians withdrew from it as a mark of their displeasure with Australia's military intervention in East Timor.

Prime Minister Paul Keating would not allow Australia's relations with Indonesia to be held hostage to the East Timor issue despite continuing objections from solidarity groups, churches and the small East Timorese community in Australia. In the government's view, too much was at stake strategically and commercially to risk upsetting the Indonesians in a situation where official protests from Canberra would achieve nothing practical for the people of East Timor. Critics claimed the government put profits before human rights and placed Australia on the side of an army of conquest against the conquered people. Australia's appeasement of Suharto, they said, only made things worse for the East Timorese.

A LABOR FOREIGN POLICY?

Not everyone in the ALP or the wider Australian community shared Hawke's unlimited enthusiasm for the Americans. In Hawke's time as prime minister, the ALP was a coalition of political groupings ranged along the political spectrum from left to centre-right. ALP members on the left and their parliamentary counterparts in the left faction, together with a broader peace movement outside the party, distrusted the Americans and their nuclear arsenal. They were alarmed by the American military build-up and the extravagant anti-Soviet rhetoric employed by Ronald Reagan in his first term as American president. They believed nuclear war was a genuine threat, and that the answer was to decouple Australia from its alliance and remove American nuclear-related installations from Australian soil. They also opposed the sale of Australian uranium on the grounds that it entailed Australia's complicity in the nuclear fuel cycle. The making of Australian foreign policy during the last years of the Cold War must be understood against this background of party and public opinion.

Even Hawke's first foreign minister failed to join him in embracing Washington. Hayden, not Hawke, criticised US policy towards Central American countries such as Nicaragua, where a popular revolution led by a group called the Sandinistas had overturned an American-backed dictatorship in 1979. He told the Americans that the 'Sandinista revolution stood for important principles which had received wide international support' and objected when Washington mined the Nicaraguan harbours and imposed an economic blockade on the country.[5] On a visit to Central America in 1984 Hayden called for a non-military solution to the problems of the region. With Hayden as foreign minister, Australia officially opposed American aid to the Contras, the counter-revolutionary army that sought to overthrow the Nicaraguan government. Irritated, the Americans told Hayden that Australia should stick to its own backyard and stop interfering.

On occasion Hawke pushed his friendship with the Americans too far for the Labor Party to stomach. Just when the New Zealanders were refusing entry to the USS *Buchanan*, word leaked out of a secret undertaking given by Hawke to the Americans. Hawke and a few key ministers, it emerged, had privately agreed that Australia would assist the Americans in a long-range test of their newest nuclear weapon, the 'missile experimental' or MX, which would be fired across the Pacific and land in the ocean near Tasmania. At a time of heightened public concern about American nuclear intentions, the Parliamentary Labor Party refused to join Hawke in supporting the MX test and threatened a revolt. Abandoned by his party, Hawke had no choice but to change his mind. Reagan and his administration were quick to distinguish between the two Antipodean prime ministers—Hawke, who they knew was their man despite this setback, and Lange, who they knew was not. To save Hawke embarrassment the Americans said that, of their own accord, they had decided to test the MX without Australian facilities. At the same time, they were sharply critical of Lange.

For most of its thirteen years in office, Labor acted vigorously on arms control and disarmament issues. To begin with, the government did so for political reasons. Confronted by a well-organised and popular peace movement, Labor presented itself as the 'true disarmament party' and endeavoured to impress the anti-nuclear constituency. At home the government created the post of Ambassador for Disarmament, established a peace and disarmament branch of the Department of Foreign Affairs, funded a peace research centre at the Australian National University and underwrote activities for the UN's International Year of Peace in 1986; abroad it negotiated the South Pacific Nuclear-Free Zone (SPNFZ) Treaty of 1985, known as the Treaty of Rarotonga, and embarked on a long campaign for a comprehensive nuclear test ban treaty at a time when the Americans repudiated the idea. The reasons for this flurry of activity were twofold. At the 1984 election the short-lived Nuclear Disarmament Party succeeded in electing a senator and drawing hundreds of thousands of Senate votes away from the ALP; in addition, the government feared that public sentiment against nuclear weapons, unless given some satisfaction, would eventually threaten the joint facilities and the American alliance. A strong symbolic response from the government was needed, senior ministers thought, to contain the effects of anti-nuclear feeling.

The arms control policy of Hayden's time as foreign minister (1983–88), is best seen as a symbolic gesture to divert criticism from ANZUS, which was what really mattered to the government. By the time Evans became foreign minister, arms control policy had gained an institutional momentum that ensured its survival. More importantly, he was attracted to the intellectual and political challenge of pursuing an intelligent arms control agenda. With Evans as foreign minister, Australia played an important role in international moves towards banning chemical weapons. Over a period of years Australia usefully facilitated negotiations to ban the use of chemical weapons, which are potentially instruments of mass destruction as deadly as nuclear weapons. It formed the Australia Group in 1985, a collection of countries concerned with controlling trade in the substances used in making chemical and biological weapons; lobbied for a chemical weapons ban in South-East Asian and South Pacific countries; smoothed the way for the cooperation of the worldwide chemical industry on the issue; and, by producing a draft text of the final treaty, intervened in 1992 to overcome diplomatic obstacles to final agreement on the Chemical Weapons Convention. When the convention went to the UN General Assembly it was sponsored by no fewer than 144 countries and passed by consensus. It prohibits an entire class of weapons of mass destruction (WMD).

When France announced in mid 1995 that it would once again test nuclear bombs in the South Pacific, Evans grasped a further opportunity to pursue his arms control agenda, this time in the nuclear field. Spurred on by public opinion, which was strongly anti-French, he argued that French testing posed a direct threat to nuclear arms control and disarmament. Australian diplomats pressed the case for a thoroughgoing, comprehensive nuclear test ban treaty, one that prohibited all tests however small. In normal times the argument for a zero-threshold treaty might well have been ignored. But with the world condemning France, the French government relented and agreed to support this version of the treaty. The decision was a success for Evans and a vindication of the policy Australia had promoted over many years.

As Labor left office in 1996, Australian arms control activism was continuing. The Canberra Commission on the Elimination of Nuclear Weapons brought together a group of international nuclear experts whose task would be to 'propose practical steps towards a nuclear weapons-free world'. Australia tabled a model text of the comprehensive nuclear test ban treaty at the Conference on Disarmament in Geneva. And the three nuclear powers—France, the United States and Britain—signed the protocols to the South Pacific Nuclear-Free Zone Treaty, thereby accepting its requirements and fulfilling a long-held Australian diplomatic objective. The Rudd government revived Australian interest in nuclear arms control but it was not a priority for the Howard government.

The government also brought a distinctively Labor approach to the Indochina issue. The Cambodian conflict, as Hayden said in 1983, was 'the greatest unresolved source of tension in South East Asia'.[6] Less obvious was the idea that Australia could help. But Hayden devoted much of his first two years as foreign minister to offering his services as an honest broker in negotiations between the parties in Cambodia. After three years under the murderous Pol Pot and his Khmer Rouge regime, Cambodia was invaded in 1978 by its neighbour Vietnam and placed under a Vietnamese puppet government. Khmer Rouge forces were not completely defeated, however, and they resumed hostilities against the government each dry season. To make matters worse, hundreds of thousands of refugees fled across the western border into Thailand where they languished in camps. Vietnam and its government in Cambodia were backed by the Soviet Union, and the Khmer Rouge received assistance from China, the United States and the ASEAN countries.

The Americans did not like Australia's attempt to broker peace in Cambodia. Secretary of State Shultz privately told Hayden his expectations in the matter were stupid, and Assistant Secretary of State for East Asian and Pacific Affairs Paul Wolfowitz expressed official doubts about the whole policy. Vietnam was a communist country in the Soviet camp, and that in itself was enough to propel the Americans to the opposite side. The Liberal and National Opposition agreed, accusing the Hawke government of being more willing to trust a Soviet client state than the United States, and of damaging Australia's reputation with South-East Asian countries. But Hayden persisted, hosting the Vietnamese foreign minister Nguyen Co Thach on a visit to Australia in 1984 and visiting Vietnam and Laos himself the following year. By then Australia's initiative had run into the sands, with fighting continuing.

Years later Hayden became convinced that Hawke had urged the initiative on Cambodia not for its own sake but as a way of distracting the Labor Party from East Timor. Whatever the truth of that, the initiative served useful purposes in the long run. It was a precedent for Australia's later contribution to settling the Cambodian problem and it gave Australia an early foot in the door when Vietnam changed tack in economic policy and began to welcome foreign investment after 1986.

The end of the Cold War provided another, far more promising chance to make peace in Cambodia. In 1989 Evans proposed establishing a transitional administration under the authority of the United Nations and sent the Deputy Secretary of the Department of Foreign Affairs and Trade, Michael Costello, on a mission to the region to solicit support. The mission was a success, and Australia's proposal was accepted. Under the plan, the UN assumed the role of a temporary administration in Cambodia while a UN military force repatriated refugees, cleared mines and supervised the democratic elections which took place in May 1993. The UN peacekeeping operation in Cambodia, the largest ever undertaken, brought peace of a kind to a stricken country but did not end the power of the Khmer Rouge or ensure that Cambodia would thereafter enjoy political stability.

Like his Labor predecessor H.V. Evatt, Evans made Australia a strong supporter of the United Nations. Under Labor, Australia was one of a small group of countries that paid their UN dues on time. Australia sent 500 troops to Cambodia and double that number to the UN's humanitarian intervention in Somalia, as well as sizeable contingents to UN operations in Namibia and Rwanda. The success of some UN operations and the failure of others prompted Evans to ponder the whole issue of the UN's security role after the end of the Cold War and document his thoughts. His 1993 book, *Cooperating for Peace: The global agenda for the 1990s*, known as the Blue Book, is a significant contribution to a debate begun by UN Secretary-General Boutros Boutros-Ghali the previous year; it suggested novel forms of international intervention for peace and argued that multilateral security regimes were the route to a less violent international scene.

Human rights, too, received closer attention from Labor than from earlier governments, especially during Evans's years as foreign minister. Evans claimed with some justification that Australia had become more active in making bilateral human rights representations than any other country. Labor's record was best on the human rights of individuals held for political reasons, many of whose chances of survival and release were enhanced by official representations made by Australian diplomats overseas. The larger human rights issues, involving whole peoples, merged into political questions where Australian national interests were at stake. They were therefore treated inconsistently and became a major focus of criticism from those who thought Labor's foreign policy lacked moral content. Critics pointed out, for example, that Australia imposed bans on investment, air links and government procurement in apartheid South Africa, yet did nothing to pressure the Indonesians over East Timor.

Australia's defence policy changed more under the Hawke and Keating governments than at any time since World War II. Some of this change was simply an adjustment to new external circumstances and would have come under any government, but in other ways it carried a characteristically Labor mark.

The concept of forward defence underlay Australian defence policy from the early 1950s, reached a high point during the Vietnam War and then lingered in attenuated form for another fifteen years. Under forward defence, the Australian Defence Force (ADF) was designed to fight wars against enemies in South-East Asia not on its own but in combination with the Americans or the British. International developments had made this approach to the defence of Australia increasingly anachronistic. In his Guam Doctrine of 1969 President Richard Nixon said America would no longer come to the aid of its South-East Asian allies in conventional conflicts, a policy interpreted in Canberra to mean that Australia could not rely on American assistance in a regional war. The British withdrew their forces from South-East Asia in the early 1970s.

Australia, it was clear, would have to be ready to defend itself. Yet not until the Hawke Labor government was there a comprehensive attempt to adjust defence policy to the new situation. It came in the form of a review of defence capabilities undertaken by a former intelligence officer, Paul Dibb, who in 1986 recommended a 'strategy of denial' focused on defending Australia from within Australian territory rather than concentrating on the forward projection of military power into South-East Asia. The strategy did not imply an active defence role beyond Australia itself except in a few limited areas such as training assistance. The Opposition challenged Dibb's view that Australia would not be significantly threatened for the next decade (though that turned out to be true) and said the whole concept, if adopted, would undermine the American alliance. As it happened, the Hawke government picked and chose from among Dibb's recommendations and did not fully implement his version of continental defence. Nevertheless, the essence of Dibb remained in Labor's new policy of 'defence self-reliance', which came into effect from 1987. One of the immediate consequences was that Australian fighter aircraft were no longer permanently stationed in Malaysia; another was the building of a new RAAF base at Tindal near Darwin in accordance with the plan of shifting military forces to the north.

Australia moved slowly towards greater military cooperation with its South-East Asian neighbours. In the 1993 strategic review the government said it wanted to move from more rigid traditional alliance structures of the Cold War towards new defence links with countries in Australia's region. Indonesian troops began to train with Australian troops in joint exercises such as Kangaroo 95.

Labor also enunciated a coherent regional security policy, which appeared in 1989. The impetus for this policy arose in part from political instability in the South Pacific and in part from the desire to clarify security relations with South-East Asia. Soldiers overthrew the constitutionally elected government of Fiji in 1987, rioters rampaged through the capital of Vanuatu in 1988, and in 1989 rebels on the Papua New Guinean island of Bougainville closed the Australian-owned copper mine and began a war to liberate Bougainville from rule by the national government. These developments alarmed the government and, in a regional security statement, foreign minister Evans sought to define the circumstances under which Australian military intervention might occur in the South Pacific. Military capability, he argued, was just one part of what ought to be a multidimensional approach encompassing diplomacy, trade and investment connections, development assistance and 'the exchange of people and ideas'. The theme of multidimensional security increasingly suited the times which, as the Cold War receded, were characterised by growing emphasis on the economic rather than the military foundations of national power and success.

The republic was a final area of Labor activism. Keating wanted to put a Labor stamp on his time as prime minister and to depict the Coalition as belonging to the past. He accused the Coalition of clinging to the British connection long after it had ceased to serve Australian interests and his description of Britain was scathing:

> [This is] the country which decided not to defend the Malayan peninsula, not to worry about Singapore and not to give us our troops back to keep ourselves free from Japanese domination. This was the country that you people wedded yourself to, and even as it walked out on you and joined the Common Market, you were still looking for your MBEs and your knighthoods, and all the rest of the regalia that comes with it.[7]

Only a republican Australia, he suggested, could be fully accepted as part of the region by its Asia-Pacific neighbours. Polls showed sentiment running in favour of the republic among a majority of Australians, especially the young, and in what was regarded as the best parliamentary speech of his career, Keating laid out the route to a minimalist version of the republic. By the time he left office Keating's venture in political symbolism had succeeded. He had created the republican agenda in contemporary Australian politics; however, Australians voted to keep the monarchy in the referendum on the republic conducted by the Howard government in 1999.

ASSESSMENTS

The initiatives of the Hawke and Keating governments on arms control and disarmament, French nuclear testing, the United Nations, human rights, regional security, cooperation with East Asia and republicanism all had roots in the mainstream Labor tradition, and in this sense constituted a Labor foreign policy. Precedents for many Labor positions can be traced to H.V. Evatt's time as Labor foreign minister in the 1940s, and for others to the Whitlam government of the 1970s. Bill Hayden was determined to assert Australia's independence and gained a reputation in Washington of being anti-American. He said Australia was independent as well as being aligned and acted accordingly. In Gareth Evans, Labor had a foreign minister who was young, energetic, academically trained and keen to leave his mark. The times were on his side. Australia was freer to pursue a new course as Cold War tensions faded. Evans seized the unique opportunities offered by the end of the Cold War to initiate a highly productive and original period in Australian foreign policy.

The distinctiveness in Labor's approach was that it sought to act in advance of events. Labor wanted to take the initiative in order to reposition Australia in the global economy. For thirteen years Labor was highly active in foreign economic policy, convinced that only fundamental changes to Australia's external economic relations would save the country from stagnation. Given Australia's traditions of protectionism and regulation, the change was momentous. Ministers and public servants grew adept at speaking the language of international economics, peppering their speeches with references to AFTA, NAFTA, ASEM, APEC, CER and WTO; that is, the ASEAN Free Trade Area, the North American Free Trade Agreement, the Asia-Europe Meeting, the Asia-Pacific Economic Cooperation forum, the Closer Economic Relations Agreement, and the World Trade Organization. An educated minority listened and approved. These were the institutions, after all, of a new order of regional and global economic integration. But the defeat of the Keating government in 1996 suggested that Labor left many Australians uncomprehending and uncertain in the wake of its enthusiasms, and that the benefits of rapid economic change and integration with East Asia were more evident to policymakers than to ordinary citizens. Yet the enduring legacy of foreign policy under Hawke and Keating was economic, for it was they who engineered Australia's transition from protectionism to free trade and embedded the Australian economy in East Asia.[8]

FURTHER READING

Overviews

Bell, Coral, ed., *Agenda for the Nineties: Australian choices in foreign and defence policy*, Longman Cheshire, Melbourne, 1991. (The view from the late 1980s.)

——*Dependent Ally: A study in Australian foreign policy*, Oxford University Press, Melbourne, 3rd edn, 1995. (Emphasises strategic and security issues.)

Boyce, P. and J. Angel, eds, *Diplomacy in the Marketplace: Australia in world affairs, 1981–90*, Longman Cheshire, Melbourne, 1992. (Indispensable.)

Cotton, James and John Ravenhill, *Seeking Asian Engagement: Australia in world affairs, 1991–95*, Oxford University Press, Melbourne, 1997. (Authoritative and scholarly.)

Keating, Paul, *Engagement: Australia faces the Asia-Pacific*, Pan Macmillan Australia, Sydney, 2000. (Australia's Labor prime minister, 1991–96, describes his part in foreign policy during those years, especially Australia's relations with East Asia. Readable and informative.)

Leaver, Richard and Dave Cox, eds, *Middling, Meddling, Muddling: Issues in Australian foreign policy*, Allen & Unwin, Sydney, 1997. (Essays on foreign policy at the end of the Labor period, some on theory, some on issues such as South Africa, arms control and the global environment.)

Lee, David and Christopher Waters, eds, *Evatt to Evans: The Labor tradition in Australian foreign policy*, Allen & Unwin, Sydney, 1997. (Includes the Hawke and Keating governments.)

Scott, Keith, *Gareth Evans*, Allen & Unwin, Sydney, 1999. (A readable biography with four useful chapters on Gareth Evans's time as Australia's minister for foreign affairs and trade, 1988–96.)

Foreign economic policy

Cooper, Andrew F., Richard A. Higgott and Kim Richard Nossal, *Relocating Middle Powers: Australia and Canada in a changing world order*, Melbourne University Press, Melbourne, 1993. (One of the best and most original accounts of foreign policy under Labor in the 1990s, with a focus on foreign economic initiatives.)

Higgott, Richard and Amitav Acharya, 'Problems in Australian foreign policy January–June 1986', *Australian Journal of Politics and History*, vol. 32, no. 3, 1986, pp. 359–77. (Covers a key turning-point in the history of foreign economic policy.)

Kelly, Paul, *The End of Certainty: Power, politics and business in Australia*, Allen & Unwin, Sydney, rev. edn, 1994. (Readable account of the politics of foreign economic policy under Labor.)

——*The March of Patriots: The struggle for modern Australia*, Melbourne University Press, Melbourne, 2009. (Covers, among other things, the foreign policy of the Keating government and Keating's policy of Asian engagement; readable and informative.)

Viviani, Nancy, 'Foreign economic policy', in *Hawke and Australian Public Policy: Consensus and restructuring*, Christine Jennett and Randal G. Stewart, eds, Macmillan, Melbourne, 1990, pp. 391–407. (Brilliant analysis of the interplay between foreign economic policy and bureaucratic restructuring under Labor.)

Defence and regional security

Cheeseman, Graeme, *The Search for Self-Reliance: Australian defence since Vietnam*, Longman Cheshire, Melbourne, 1993. (How defence policy changed, 1960s to 1990s.)

Fry, Greg, *Australia's Regional Security*, Allen & Unwin, Sydney, 1991. (Reactions to Labor's 1989 regional security statement, with a response by the minister.)

Goot, Murray and Rodney Tiffen, eds, *Australia's Gulf War*, Melbourne University Press, Melbourne, 1992. (Covers arguments for and against Australian participation, and the domestic reaction.)

Grey, Jeffrey, *A Military History of Australia*, Cambridge University Press, Melbourne, 1999. (Chapter 11, 'The post-Vietnam era, 1972–2000', traces defence policy from Whitlam to Howard.)

The view from the minister

Evans, Gareth and Bruce Grant, *Australia's Foreign Relations in the World of the 1990s*, Melbourne University Press, Melbourne, 2nd edn, 1995. (Comprehensive official account; the best account of foreign policy by any Australian foreign minister.)

Hayden, Bill, *Hayden: An autobiography*, Angus & Robertson, Sydney, 1996. (Includes recollections of his time as foreign minister, 1983–88.)

Foreign policy under Howard, 1996–2007

- Why did John Howard become one of George W. Bush's staunchest allies?
- Why did the Howard government send Australian troops to the war on Iraq and why did the Rudd government withdraw them?
- How did the Howard government restore good relations with Indonesia after the military intervention in East Timor in 1999?
- In what ways did Australian policy towards the Pacific Islands change under the Howard government?
- What approach did the Howard government adopt towards the UN and UN human rights processes?
- Why did the Howard government focus on bilateral trade diplomacy at the expense of multilateral trade diplomacy?
- How did the Howard government respond to the growing importance for Australia of China?
- Was the environmental foreign policy of the Howard government in Australia's national interest or not?

John Howard was prime minister of Australia for more than eleven years, from 1996 to 2007. Australian voters elected his Coalition of Liberal and National parties to government on four occasions, finally switching to a Labor government under Kevin Rudd at the elections of November 2007. Howard appointed the former Liberal leader, Alexander Downer, to the foreign affairs portfolio and he remained there throughout the Howard era, becoming Australia's longest serving foreign affairs minister.

From the start, Howard and Downer distanced themselves from the foreign policy legacy left by the Labor prime minister Paul Keating and his foreign affairs minister Gareth Evans. Labor liked the multilateral agenda—the political issues negotiated multilaterally in areas such as arms control and disarmament, UN peacekeeping, regional security, human rights and the environment, and the economic issues to which Labor responded with multilateral initiatives such as the Cairns Group and APEC. Gareth Evans in particular saw multilateral diplomacy as an opportunity for Australia, as a middle power, to 'punch above its weight' and make its mark internationally. The Coalition, by contrast, favoured bilateral relationships, which it called the *basic building block* of foreign policy, and it defined the national interest more narrowly than Labor. The Coalition government was unlikely to send 300 Australian personnel to a distant field of conflict for the sake of UN peacekeeping, for example, as Labor did when it despatched peacekeepers to Rwanda in Africa in 1994. The Coalition thought such operations had to be clearly related to immediate Australian national interests, as they were judged to be when Australia sent a much greater number of soldiers to East Timor in 1999 at the head of an international intervention force.

We can discern different political traditions and philosophical assumptions in these differences: Labor governments tend to be optimistic about schemes for international cooperation, whereas Coalition governments are more sceptical, seeing international relations as a domain in which power decides everything. Pragmatism, not ideology, drove the Howard government's reaction to many international events, and as the international scene changed, so did his policy. Howard had no grand vision of Australia's place in the world. His instincts were to side with the Americans on almost all issues, and to grasp opportunities to advance Australia's interests when they were offered. Alexander Downer, who was one of the prime minister's closest confidants, thought the same way.

THE RELATIONSHIP WITH THE UNITED STATES

Global terrorism burst to international prominence in what are known as the attacks of 9/11. Two hijacked passenger jets, American Airlines Flight 11 and United Airlines Flight 175, crashed into the north and south towers of the World Trade Center in New York on the morning of 11 September 2001. Within little more than an hour, both towers had collapsed into the streets below, creating devastation on a massive scale and killing 2752 people who had not been able to escape. A third plane, American Airlines Flight 77, ploughed into the Pentagon building in Washington, headquarters of the US Department of Defense, and a fourth—probably headed for the White House—crashed south-east of

Pittsburgh, Pennsylvania, after the passengers stormed the cockpit in a vain attempt to seize control of the aircraft from the hijackers. The crashes, credibly linked to Osama bin Laden's extremist Islamic terrorist organisation al-Qaeda, were the first foreign attacks on the continental United States since 1812. They demonstrated the vulnerability of the world's most powerful nation, and prompted a major change in American foreign and defence policy.

Terrorism reached Australia directly in the form of attacks in Indonesia. The first occurred on 12 October 2002, when a suicide bomber detonated a bomb in Paddy's Bar, a popular nightspot crowded with tourists at Kuta on the Indonesian island of Bali. Minutes later a much larger bomb exploded in the Sari Club not far away, triggering a fire that lasted eight hours. Ten Australians died in the World Trade Center in 2001. The Bali bombings killed a further 88 Australians in a total death toll of 202, and left others badly injured. Terrorists then exploded a large bomb outside the Australian Embassy in Jakarta on 9 September 2004.

At home, the Howard government responded by boosting the operations, increasing the funding and extending the legal powers of Australia's 'secret state', the intelligence and espionage agencies that collect information on those who are believed to threaten national security. Most Australians have heard of ASIO, the Australian Security Intelligence Organisation, but most know little about the other agencies—the Defence Signals Directorate (DSD), the Defence Intelligence Organisation (DIO), the Defence Imagery and Geospatial Organisation (DIGO), the Office of National Assessments (ONA) and the Australian Secret Intelligence Service—all of which assumed new importance. Australia is a member of the UKUSA Agreement, which provides for Australia to exchange communications intelligence with the United States, the United Kingdom, Canada and New Zealand. As Patrick Keefe says, UKUSA has spawned a global network of communications interception:

> The communications intelligence agencies of these five countries operate listening bases on remote islands, in secluded valleys, and in barren deserts the world over. They run a fleet of sophisticated eavesdropping satellites that hover miles above the earth's surface, intercepting signals. And the 'take'—the millions of conversations, faxes, telexes, and e-mails that are intercepted by this apparatus every day—is distributed by automated methods among the allies.[1]

Regionally, the Howard government responded with a strategy designed to boost the counter-terrorism capacity of Australia's neighbours. The government signed counter-terrorism agreements with Indonesia, Malaysia, Thailand, the Philippines, Cambodia, India, East Timor, Papua New Guinea and Fiji. The Australian Federal Police (AFP) gained more resources and personnel, forming the International Deployment Group (IDG) and becoming Australia's principal instrument of counter-terrorism in Indonesia, the Philippines and elsewhere. The AFP worked closely with Indonesian police after the Bali bombings, and their collaboration deepened after Australia and Indonesia joined in establishing the Jakarta Centre for Law Enforcement Cooperation in 2004. The possibility that terrorists might one day use weapons of mass destruction—the ultimate terrorism nightmare—prompted the Howard government to set up a chemical, biological, radiological and nuclear (CBRN) terrorism section within the Department of Foreign Affairs and Trade in 2006 and to join the US-sponsored Global Initiative to Combat Nuclear Terrorism (GICNT).

Globally, the key response of the Howard government to terrorism—and one that came to define the foreign policy of the second half of the Howard era—was to send troops to Afghanistan and Iraq, and to back the United States in all its endeavours to defeat the new enemy. John Howard was in Washington when terrorists attacked the United States, and on his return to Australia he invoked the ANZUS Treaty, the first time this had happened in the history of the ANZUS alliance. Notwithstanding the unexpected—that the United States rather than Australia had been attacked—the Australian government indicated its willingness to go to the defence of its ally. Melodramatic as this declaration was—given Australia's limited military capacities—it set the tone for the years that followed.

John Howard became one of George W. Bush's staunchest allies. He constructed Australian foreign policy around the fulcrum of the American alliance. He abandoned Australia's long-held and bipartisan commitment to the UN Security Council as the final arbiter in matters of global security. He supported the Bush administration's doctrine of pre-emptive military action, and he asserted an Australian version of it, to be applied to terrorist bases in South-East Asia. His government acquiesced in the detention by the United States of prisoners, including two Australians, without trial or charge at the Americans' naval base in Cuba, Guantanamo. His ministers reiterated the message that the American alliance was central to maintaining Australian and regional security. Arguing for the contemporary relevance of the alliance, Alexander Downer pointed to the critical role played by the Americans in the security and prosperity of the Asia-Pacific region:

In addition to strong economic links, the US strategic presence, and its leadership role in dealing with security challenges, provides [*sic*] an indispensable
underpinning to regional stability. In reinforcing US engagement, the ANZUS
alliance makes a strong contribution to that stability. The capabilities the United
States brings to bear in the campaign against terrorism are second to none ...
Bilaterally, Australia draws substantial benefit from our political contacts, our
intelligence exchanges, and our access to the advanced technology.[2]

In the immediate aftermath of 9/11, most Australians supported Howard's
initiatives in the 'war on terror'. Public opinion was behind the decision to send
150 SAS troops to Afghanistan in 2001 as part of a larger force of about 1500
who were deployed in Afghanistan, Kyrgyzstan and the Persian Gulf as part
of the United States' Operation Enduring Freedom. The Howard government
withdrew the troops from Afghanistan in 2002, at least officially. He sent them
back in 2005, and sent more in 2007.

Australia's decision to send troops to the Iraq War in 2003 was far more
controversial. A clear majority of Australians opposed Australia's participation
in the Iraq War before it started, then supported the government once troops
were on the ground. After that, support for the Howard government on the
issue ebbed away. President Bush declared victory in 2003, a year that proved
to be just the start of hostilities, and by mid 2004 opinion polls were recording
growing dissatisfaction with the presence of Australian soldiers in Iraq. As the
war dragged on and no decisive allied victory emerged, disenchantment grew,
and by April 2006 only 35 per cent of respondents to a Morgan poll said they
thought Australia should have 'a military presence in Iraq'. As Murray Goot
has shown, interpreting the polls is more complicated than this brief summary
suggests. People who were against the troops going to Iraq in the first place
might also believe that they should be kept there 'until the job is done'.[3] The
Howard government was helped, as well, by having most Australian troops in
a province out of harm's way. Few soldiers died, and the Australian public did
not have to confront numerous deaths on the battlefield. Overall, however, it
was an easy matter for the ALP to go the 2007 election promising to withdraw
the Australian forces from Iraq, because by then the majority of Australians
favoured withdrawal. The driving force of Australia's participation in the 'coalition of the willing' was Howard's conviction that Australia needed to back the
United States to the hilt in the wake of 9/11.

As new threats to security emerged, Howard fostered the nationalism of
the ANZAC tradition and revived the rhetoric of an earlier era. Speaking at a

Royal Australian Air Force (RAAF) base in 2004, he said he did not know a time since he had been in public life when there had been greater esteem for the individual men and women of the military forces. Defence was as much a matter of politics as a matter of policy for Howard. With an eye on the voters, the prime minister was tireless in farewelling troops, welcoming them home, wishing them well, and visiting them in foreign theatres. He believed Australians wanted to be reassured that their armed forces were protecting them. He made much of Australia's military commitments abroad to depict himself as a prime minister keen to defend Australia whatever the cost and to strengthen the defence forces. The ANZAC patriotism of John Howard, however, was hardly unique. Bob Hawke expressed similar sentiments when he sent Australian military forces to the Gulf War in 1991. Kevin Rudd was as keen as Howard to depict himself as a deeply patriotic national leader, concerned for the welfare of Australian troops abroad, proud of their exploits and appalled by the loss of a single soldier. In her first speech as prime minister, Julia Gillard described Australia as grateful for its soldiers and acknowledged 'the depth of the sacrifice that our serving men and women can be called on to make'.[4]

SEIZING OPPORTUNITIES

Howard's term as prime minister was long enough for him to confound critics on a number of issues and to seize opportunities created by a changing global scene in order to improve Australia's position internationally and regionally.

Australia's relations with Asia are an example. Critics accused Howard of squandering Labor's legacy of good relations. The Howard government claimed continuity with Labor in the priority given to the Asia-Pacific, especially to East Asia, close relationships with the United States, Japan, Indonesia and China, trade liberalisation, and strong support for the World Trade Organization and APEC. Yet Howard knew Keating had lost public support for his ambitious vision of Australia's place in the world, especially the idea that Australia should seek an Asian identity. The Howard government accepted engagement with Asia as a means to an end rather than an end in itself.

According to Howard and Downer, there would be no headlong rush towards integration with Asia, as Keating envisaged, but a practical and realistic engagement based on Australia's interests. One of those interests was to participate in East Asia's regional trade and diplomatic arrangements, and the Howard government actively sought Australia's admission to ASEAN Plus Three, a grouping that brought together ten South-East Asian countries with three others, China, Japan and South Korea. Australia would be happy to participate in ASEAN Plus Three if invited, Alexander Downer said in 2000, but nothing eventuated. More pointedly, Malaysia intervened in 2000 to prevent ASEAN from proceeding with negotiations for joining the ASEAN Free Trade Area with the Closer Economic Relations Agreement that had liberalised trade and investment between Australia and New Zealand. Until he stepped down as Malaysian prime minister in 2003, Mahathir Mohamad remained an obstacle to Australia's inclusion in regional institutions.

Howard wanted Australia to be invited to the first meeting of the East Asia Summit in 2005, sponsored by ASEAN, but ASEAN demanded that Australia first accede to the Treaty of Amity and Cooperation, a regional non-aggression pact already signed by China, India and Japan as well as the ASEAN member states. Howard at first refused to sign, saying it might be incompatible with Australia's obligations under the ANZUS Treaty with the United States. He subsequently agreed after the Bush administration gave its approval and an exchange of letters explained Australia's interpretation of the treaty. And when Howard attended the inaugural East Asia Summit in Kuala Lumpur, he claimed that Australia had better relations with Asia under his government than it had had under the Labor governments of Hawke and Keating.[5] Indonesia and Malaysia were newly cooperative, and ASEAN wanted Australia in rather than out of its diplomatic arrangements by 2005, not least to counterbalance China in the East Asia Summit. The leaders sitting around the table at Kuala Lumpur represented China, India, Japan, South Korea, Australia and New Zealand, and the ten ASEAN nations, Brunei, Cambodia, Indonesia, Laos, Malaysia, Myanmar, the Philippines, Singapore, Thailand and Vietnam. To use the language of diplomats, the meeting was ASEAN+3+3, and since 2005, as the East Asia Summit, it has taken place annually alongside the ASEAN summit. Changes in international circumstances smoothed the way for a foreign policy success.

Australia's relations with Indonesia are another example. Howard was generous in helping to bail out its South-East Asian neighbours at the time of the East Asian economic downturn, for example, and offered a sharp critique of the conditions which the International Monetary Fund (IMF) attached to its financial assistance to the region. Australia's relations with Indonesia remained stable, and Howard maintained Labor's East Timor policy, which was not to jeopardise the wider relationship for the sake of backing the independence aspirations of one Indonesian province, however justified its complaints about repression

ASSOCIATION OF SOUTH-EAST ASIAN NATIONS (ASEAN) AND THE EAST ASIA SUMMIT

South-East Asia encompasses eleven countries—Brunei, Burma, Cambodia, East Timor, Indonesia, Laos, Malaysia, the Philippines, Singapore, Thailand and Vietnam—in an area of fast growing economies with a total population of more than 600 million. All except East Timor are member states of ASEAN, which was formed in 1967 to foster regional economic and political cooperation, and has become a significant player in the global diplomatic scene.

The founding members of ASEAN were Indonesia, Malaysia, Singapore, the Philippines and Thailand. Brunei joined in 1984, Vietnam in 1995, Burma and Laos in 1997 and Cambodia in 1999.

ASEAN itself has never been a security organisation but its sister organisation established in 1994, the ASEAN Regional Forum (ARF), exists to foster regional security cooperation (see Chapter 6).

Australia does not belong to ASEAN and has not sought to join, but is a member of the increasingly important East Asia Summit of leaders, founded in 2005 and comprising the ten ASEAN states together with Australia, China, Japan, India, New Zealand and the Republic of Korea. With a further two states joining in 2011—the US and Russia—the East Asia Summit is growing in importance as a forum for high-level dialogue on strategic, environmental and trade issues in what has become the most dynamic region in the global economy. Australia is normally represented at the East Asia Summit by the prime minister.

might be. When the downturn triggered the fall of Suharto as president of Indonesia in 1998, however, the Howard government changed Australia's East Timor policy towards one that included the possibility of independence. Dragged along by events and pushed by Australian public opinion, the Howard government sent 5000 troops to East Timor in 1999 in order to guarantee the new country's independence. Outraged and humiliated, Indonesia abrogated the 1995 Australian–Indonesian security agreement. Critics said Howard had undermined good relations with Indonesia, a vital source of security for Australia. But the Howard government seized later opportunities to restore them. Australian and Indonesian police worked closely together against the common threat of terrorism after the first Bali bombings in 2002, when bomb blasts in two nightclubs killed 88 Australians, and they initiated cooperation that deepened after subsequent Bali bombings in 2004 and 2005. Australia helped Indonesia after the

2004 Boxing Day tsunami with medical and military assistance worth $1 billion, a gift deeply appreciated by Indonesia's President Susilo Bambang Yudhoyono. As individuals, Australians donated another $200 million. The tsunami, a natural disaster of cataclysmic proportions, killed hundreds of thousands of people and brought widespread destruction to Aceh, a politically sensitive province that in normal times would have been off-limits to troops from Australia. Under these circumstances the Indonesians welcomed Australian troops. By 2006 Alexander Downer had negotiated a new security agreement with Indonesia, the Lombok Treaty, covering defence, counter-terrorism, intelligence, natural disasters and maritime security. When Howard left office in 2007, Australia's relations with the new democratic Indonesia were as good as they had ever been with the old dictatorial Indonesia.

Australia's relations with the South Pacific are a third example. For the first seven years the Howard government gave low priority to the region and expected island states to resolve their own political problems, even when one of them, Solomon Islands, descended into serious disorder after a coup in 2000. But the Bali bombings altered Australian calculations about the security risks posed by

AUSTRALIA AND INDONESIA RETURN TO FORMAL SECURITY COOPERATION, 2006

Indonesia abrogated the 1995 Security Agreement with Australia because of Australia's role in leading the intervention force in East Timor in 1999. The Howard government strove to restore good relations with Indonesia. One result of these efforts was the Lombok Treaty, properly known as the Agreement between Australia and the Republic of Indonesia on the Framework for Security Cooperation. The Treaty was signed by Australian foreign minister Alexander Downer and his Indonesian counterpart Hassan Wirajuda on the Indonesian island of Lombok on 13 November 2006 and entered into force under the Rudd government on 7 February 2008. It provides for security cooperation in a wide range of areas, including intelligence, counter-terrorism and weapons of mass destruction as well as defence and law enforcement.

The Lombok Treaty
ARTICLE 3 AREAS AND FORMS OF COOPERATION
The scope of cooperation of this Agreement shall include:

Defence Cooperation

In recognition of the long-term mutual benefit of the closest professional cooperation between their Defence Forces,

1. Regular consultation on defence and security issues of common concern; and on their respective defence policies;
2. Promotion of development and capacity building of defence institutions and armed forces of both Parties including through military education and training, exercises, study visits and exchanges, application of scientific methods to support capacity building and management and other related mutually beneficial activities;
3. Facilitating cooperation in the field of mutually beneficial defence technologies and capabilities, including joint design, development, production, marketing and transfer of technology as well as developing mutually agreed joint projects.

Law Enforcement Cooperation

In recognition of the importance of effective cooperation to combat transnational crime that impacts upon the security of both Parties,

4. Regular consultation and dialogue aimed at strengthening the links between institutions and officials at all levels;
5. Cooperation to build capacity of law enforcement officials to prevent, respond to and investigate transnational crime;
6. Strengthening and intensifying police to police cooperation including through joint and coordinated operations;
7. Cooperation between relevant institutions and agencies, including prosecuting authorities, in preventing and combating transnational crimes, in particular crimes related to:
   a. People smuggling and trafficking in persons;
   b. Money laundering;
   c. Financing of terrorism;
   d. Corruption;
   e. Illegal fishing;
   f. Cyber-crimes;
   g. Illicit trafficking in narcotics drugs and psychotropic substances and its precursors;
   h. Illicit trafficking in arms, ammunition, explosives and other dangerous materials and the illegal production thereof; and
   i. Other types of crime if deemed necessary by both Parties.

Agreement between Australia and the Republic of Indonesia on the Framework for Security Cooperation, <www.austlii.edu.au/au/other/dfat/treaties/2008/3.html>.

unstable neighbours. Australia massively boosted aid to the region. More importantly, Australia embraced a new interventionism in its South Pacific policy, and sent troops and police to Solomon Islands in 2003 to restore order. The task of the regional mission led by Australia was nothing less than rebuilding the state in Solomon Islands over many years. Further instability in Solomon Islands, East Timor and Tonga in 2006 confirmed the policy: Australia sent troops in each case. In an approach which some called *cooperative intervention*, Australia would now intervene with security forces when island governments asked for security assistance. Under changed circumstances, an incoherent policy had become a new and enhanced form of direct engagement by Australia in its nearby region.

HUMAN RIGHTS

Together with Downer, Howard disparaged UN human rights processes and the UN in general. Howard demonised asylum seekers, playing to old Australian fears about Asian invasion rather than educating Australians about the complexity of the problem. Former diplomats and defence officials, academics, human rights activists and even a former Liberal prime minister were uneasy about these changes in Australia's traditional foreign policy stances. The veteran diplomat Richard Woolcott, who grew more critical of the Howard government over the years, said in 2006: 'Australia today is not the country I represented with pride for 40 years … Our standing is suffering because of a recrudescence of those atavistic currents of racism and intolerance that we have inherited from our past. With our participation in the Iraq War, the Howard government has also reinforced the image of an Australia moving back to the so-called Anglosphere.'[6]

The Howard government partially withdrew Australia from the UN human rights system, and placed barriers in the way of UN supervision of human rights in Australia. The government objected strongly to criticisms made by the Committee on the Elimination of Racial Discrimination (CERD) and by the UN Human Rights Committee. The government's view was that the entire UN human rights treaty system had become a tool for undemocratic countries with poor human rights records to criticise democratic ones with good human rights records, such as Australia. 'In the end we are not told what to do by anybody', John Howard told an ABC interviewer in 2000, arguing that Australia's human rights reputation compared with the rest of the world was 'quite magnificent'. The government thought the UN human rights treaty system required radical reform, and joined other states in mounting a campaign within the UN to make that happen. As a result, the old UN Human Rights Committee was replaced in 2006 by the UN Human Rights Council.

Why did Australia depart so sharply from previous practice? Middle powers such as Australia, after all, lack the diplomatic influence to shape the world as they would wish, and have most to gain from a global order founded on respect for international law. The answer probably lies in domestic politics. The Howard government subordinated foreign policy to calculations of political advantage within Australia, and did so to an unprecedented degree. In the process the government politicised human rights policy. In the Queensland state elections of 1998, Pauline Hanson's One Nation Party won almost a quarter of the vote with calls to end immigration, foreign aid and Aboriginal welfare. She spoke of international conspiracies against ordinary Australians, and she articulated an ignorant but powerful anti-internationalist and anti-globalisation ideology, in which the lost golden age lay in the 1950s and the utopia was a return to it. Howard countered the electoral threat from One Nation by occupying its ideological territory and identifying himself with Hanson's concerns about domination by international forces. As Robert Manne suggested, Prime Minister John Howard was a conservative populist.[7] His strategy was to win votes from traditional working-class Labor voters who wanted to hear that no one was going to push Australia around, and that the government was still there to protect them.

Under Howard, Australia's refugee policy came to possess four elements not found elsewhere: mandatory detention of people reaching Australian territory without a visa, a legacy of the previous government; the issuing of 'temporary protection visas' to those who succeed in obtaining asylum but arrived initially without a visa, a system condemned by the immigration minister when Pauline Hanson suggested it in 1998 and then adopted by the government a year later; 'upstream disruption' of the refugee flow from Indonesia, whereby Australia used the navy against small boats and entered into secret arrangements with the Indonesian authorities to ensure that boat people were hindered from travelling; and the removal of asylum seekers to third countries (Nauru and Papua New Guinea) where Australia maintained refugee detention centres. The government called this the Pacific Solution. All this was too much even for some Liberal members of parliament, and the government gradually eased the refugee policy, first by replacing the intransigent Philip Ruddock as immigration and ethnic affairs minister with the more liberal Amanda Vanstone in 2003, and later by easing the conditions under which refugees were held in detention. The government had released all children from detention by 2005.

The Howard government made some advances in Australia's international human rights position. Unlike the United States, Australia supported the establishment of the International Criminal Court in 2002 as a permanent tribunal to bring to justice the perpetrators of the most heinous crimes including genocide. The debate over the Howard government's human rights record nevertheless remained highly polarised. On one side were those who wanted Australia to assert its sovereignty and defy international bodies that sought to scrutinise the country's human rights performance. On the other were those who said Australia undermined international human rights law by refusing to accept that the UN had the right to criticise all governments within the system, including democratic ones.

Critics saw the Howard government's refugee policy, above all, as violating Australia's obligations under international law and abandoning national traditions of decency. The Rudd government abandoned the Pacific Solution, abolished temporary protection visas, and processed refugee claims more quickly than the Howard government had done, but it maintained the policy of placing asylum seekers in detention centres and tried to deter them by slowing the processing of claims when it sensed a loss of public support. In the end Rudd and Gillard, like Howard, acted as if asylum seekers—in theory protected by international law—were making unreasonable claims on Australia. Howard's legacy was to ensure that the refugee debate would be framed as one about border security, not about Australia's obligations under international humanitarian law.

GLOBALISATION AND TRADE

The Howard government welcomed globalisation. 'Let me put this clearly', Downer told the National Press Club in 1997, 'globalisation is an irreversible trend. It is happening. And it is good for all Australians, the region and the world.' Whatever their party, Australian ministers had little choice as the economic activities of humankind became increasingly globalised. More than ever before, the globe itself, not the nation-state, became the marketplace for goods and services, the site of producing them and the arena for the division of labour. Industrial competitiveness in one part of the world rapidly transmitted itself, in the form of recession and unemployment, to other parts less competitive, compelling governments to respond with policies that met the demands of international business. Capital flowed faster and faster across the borders of states in deregulated financial markets where investors profited from numerous new ways of selling debt, dealing in foreign exchange and speculating on changes in market values. The new power of the financial markets over every national economy was symbolised by the attention paid to the regular credit ratings given to Australia by merchant banks and ratings agencies. These institutions, by their ratings, could influence governments. As the East Asian downturn of 1997–98 showed, the financial markets now held the power to bring economies to their knees, to throw millions out of work overnight and to overturn governments. That downturn was confined to East Asia, however, and Western economists blamed it on policies pursued by East Asian governments. Few foresaw the comprehensive failure of the financial markets that occurred in 2008, nor the drastic economic effects it had on the economies of the United States, Japan and Europe, or the shift it represented in the distribution of global economic power.

Towards a bilateral free trade agenda

Labor's thirteen years in office (1983–96) coincided with a global push for free trade achieved through multilateral agreements in which a large number of countries removed trade barriers against each other. The Uruguay Round of the GATT began its negotiations when Hawke was prime minister and resulted in a major liberalisation of trade when it was concluded in 1994. Hawke initiated the Asia-Pacific Economic Cooperation forum as an instrument of free trade, and Keating laboured mightily to make it an effective regional grouping. The World Trade Organization emerged in 1995, when Paul Keating was prime minister, as the institution that would enforce the rules of free trade agreed among its member states. And the Cairns Group of agricultural exporting countries, founded by Australia in 1986, succeeded in having trade in agriculture added to the diplomatic agenda of the WTO. Labor was identified with Australia's historic shift from protectionism to free trade, and with multilateral diplomacy as the way to achieve it.

Australia's trade policy, on the other hand, changed during the Howard years. Howard was prime minister when the global push for free trade stalled, and when it seemed that Australia would be excluded from regional free trade arrangements in East Asia. The next series of WTO free trade negotiations after Uruguay was called the Doha Round, and its aim was to achieve a major liberalisation of trade in agriculture. The Doha Round opened in 2001 and by 2004 the 147 WTO countries had achieved a framework agreement, but negotiations made minimal progress after that and were still continuing in 2010 without result. The high tide of multilateral trade diplomacy had passed, and countries began to negotiate with each other over bilateral free trade agreements (FTAs). Strictly speaking, bilateral 'free trade' agreements cannot, by definition, achieve free trade, which is a removal of barriers to trade with *all* countries, or at least to a large number of countries in an organisation such as the WTO. Bilateral free trade agreements are not comprehensive but target particular areas of trade while leaving others out. That is why leading commentators on the issue call them *preferential trade agreements*.

Howard decided that Australia, too, would work towards bilateral free trade agreements. The first two, which came into effect in 2003, were with Singapore and Thailand. A third was reached with the United States in 2004. Under this agreement, the United States kept strong protection against imports of Australian beef, dairy products and sugar while at the same time gaining a much freer hand in investment, services and intellectual property. Australian agriculture, which was supposed to emerge the winner from the agreement, ended up with minor gains at most. The exercise showed that, as a small, open economy, Australia had limited leverage in negotiating bilaterally over trade with larger economies.

The negotiations also showed that modern free trade raises issues of domestic policy and has the potential to raise issues of sovereignty and independence. Australia wanted the United States to reduce protection on agriculture while the United States wanted Australia to reduce protection on services. The Americans sought change in the way Australia did things in a number of areas. The United States expected Australia to remove the monopoly of the Australian Wheat Board (AWB) Limited as the seller of Australian grain, and relax restrictions on foreign investment imposed by the Foreign Investment Review Board (FIRB). American drug companies sell more than US$6 billion worth of pharmaceuticals to Australia each year, and the Americans wanted Australia to modify or abandon the Pharmaceutical Benefits Scheme (PBS) under which the government acts as a single buyer, forcing down price and subsidising the cost of medicines to Australian consumers. The Americans objected to the local content rules that require Australian television companies to screen prescribed levels of Australian-made programs and advertisements, and wanted the door to be opened wider to American television material. When the free trade agreement was announced, the government claimed not to have conceded ground on pharmaceutical benefits or the film industry, but in fact had done so. On the issue of investment in Australia by American companies, the government abandoned most restrictions. Parliament needed to legislate before the free trade agreement could be approved, and the Labor Opposition insisted on two amendments to the government's legislation before it could pass the Senate. At that time, before the 2004 election, the government did not control the Senate. The amendments, which the Howard government accepted, were designed to protect Australian media content (though not Australian content in new forms of media) and to ensure that Australians could continue to buy medicines cheaply through the Pharmaceutical Benefits Scheme, by preventing drug companies from abusing patents.

While the Howard government embraced the bilateral trade agenda enthusiastically, it achieved little with it. Having liberalised already, Australia did not have much to offer as concessions to bilateral partners, and the big prize—a wholesale liberalisation of global trade in agriculture—was beyond the scope of bilateral diplomacy. As Ann Capling argues, the Howard government wanted bilateral free trade deals partly in order to maintain access to foreign markets that might be closed off by other such deals, such as the market for Australian cars and car parts in the member states of the Gulf Cooperation Council (GCC): Bahrain, Kuwait, Oman, Qatar, Saudi Arabia and the United Arab Emirates.[8]

A further motivation, especially in the case of the agreement with the United States, was strategic. Howard particularly wanted a free trade agreement with the Americans, who were, he said, 'the best exponents of capitalism and they are going to be the strongest economy in the world until the end of time, that's my view'.[9] For reasons of Australian security at a time of terrorism and war, he sought the closest possible trade relationship for Australia with the United States. Summing it up, Howard's trade minister Mark Vaile described the agreement as 'the commercial equivalent of the ANZUS Treaty'.[10]

However, one trade issue threatened to become a major scandal for the government. A UN inquiry into the UN Oil-for-Food Programme in Iraq revealed that between 1997 and 2003 AWB Limited, Australia's monopoly wheat exporter, had made side payments in the form of 'trucking fees' worth more than US$220 million to the Iraqi government of Saddam Hussein. They were bribes to the very regime that Australia wanted to overthrow, the same one that Howard claimed had weapons of mass destruction. The UN designed the Oil-for-Food Programme as a way of softening the impact of trade sanctions imposed after the Gulf War of 1991. Iraq was permitted to export oil but not to be paid in cash. Payment instead took the form of food and humanitarian assistance bought with funds from a special UN account. In practice, foreign companies funnelled money to the Iraqi regime in return for market access, enriching Saddam Hussein and his associates by US$1.8 billion, and AWB Limited was the largest contributor of such payments.[11] The Howard government set up a commission of inquiry, which cleared the government and DFAT of any involvement in the bribery scandal, but AWB Limited executives subsequently faced court action.

In theory, Rudd's Labor government was more committed than Howard's to the multilateral trade agenda, in particular to a successful conclusion of the Doha Round. One multilateral success for Labor is the ASEAN–Australia–New Zealand Free Trade Area (AANZFTA), covering twelve economies, a combined GDP of $3.1 trillion and a population of more than 600 million people. AANZFTA came into effect in 2010 and, over time, will open more and more South-East Asian markets to the free entry of Australian goods and services. The Howard government had sought AANZFTA as well, and in practice there was striking continuity in trade policy after Labor was elected in 2007. Under Howard, Australia reached FTAs with Singapore, Thailand and the United States and commenced negotiations for further FTAs with Malaysia, Japan, the Gulf Cooperation Council states and, most important of all, China. The Rudd government concluded a new FTA with Chile in 2009; continued existing bilateral negotiations; inaugurated others with Korea and the Pacific Islands; and began feasibility studies on FTAs with India and Indonesia.

Australian governments now seek trade and investment wherever it may be found, by both multilateral and bilateral means. Trade, which is an index of the extent to which a national economy is integrated into the global economy, boomed for Australia in the twenty years that followed the Hawke government's embrace of free trade in the 1980s. In constant dollars, the value of Australia's two-way trade (exports and imports) quadrupled from $118.1 billion in 1988–89 to $563.7 billion in 2008–09, and the share of Australia's GDP accounted for by trade grew from 32.5 to 47.1 per cent over the same period. Australia has become more of a trading nation than ever, and benefited both from the global economic boom that ended in 2008, and the commodity price boom that began in 2004. Tied economically to East Asia, Australia survived the global financial crisis of 2008–09 better than any other OECD (Organisation for Economic Co-operation and Development) economy.

CHINA, JAPAN AND INDIA

Australia's prosperity over the twenty years from 1989 to 2009 came to depend increasingly on China, which ranked eleventh among Australia's trading partners at the end of the 1980s, rose to second by 2005 and was first by 2009. As Australia entered the second decade of the twenty-first century, Japan and the United States, traditionally the two leading countries for Australian trade, were ranked second and third after China.

The Howard government was acutely aware that Australia's future would be closely intertwined with that of China, which year by year was buying more of Australia's coal, iron ore, wool, petroleum, aluminium, liquefied natural gas and other resources while Australian consumers increasingly bought all kinds of goods manufactured in China, from electrical appliances and electronic equipment to clothes and footwear. China alone dramatically improved Australia's terms of trade by forcing up the price of primary commodities by the sheer volume of its demand. In a 2003 report called *China's Industrial Rise: East Asia's challenge*, DFAT argued that Australia stood to gain from China's rise 'more than most economies', not least because of the high degree of complementarity between the two countries, with Australia a key supplier of raw materials and energy, and China the world's workshop of cheap manufactures. At the same time, China was becoming a major source of international students, tourists and migrants arriving in Australia, creating a firmer base for people-to-people relations between the two countries.

The Howard government responded to this situation by steering a careful course between the demands of Washington, which tended to view China as a growing threat to American global predominance, and those of Beijing, which sought to deepen its relations with the countries of South-East Asia and the 'broad neighbourhood' (*da zhoubian*). Howard and Downer did not indulge in the alarmist rhetoric about China heard so often in Washington during the Bush administration, and sought instead to build a web of political, diplomatic and military links with Beijing. Australia supported China's entry into the WTO in 2001, for example, and its bid to host the 2008 Olympics. Howard visited China more often than any previous prime minister, and high-level Chinese officials visited Australia. The most important was Chinese President Hu Jintao, who became the first non-elected foreign leader to address the Australian Parliament when he appeared before a joint sitting of both Houses the day after a similar address by President Bush in 2003. The symbolism of this invitation could not have been clearer. China had once been one among many of Australia's East Asian neighbours. Now it had a place of primary importance in Australian foreign policy calculations.

Visiting Beijing in 2004, Downer said that he agreed with Premier Wen Jiabao 'that Australia and China would build up a bilateral strategic relationship, that we would strengthen our economic relationship and we would work together closely on Asia-Pacific issues, be they economic or security issues'.[12] The statement appeared to put the ANZUS alliance in a new context, and although the government tried to counter this interpretation, the impression remained that Australia was repositioning itself in its relations with China and the United States. Under these circumstances, the annual human rights dialogue between Australia and China took on the character of a performance staged for the sake of Australian public opinion, and understood by both sides to be nothing more. Australia and China cooperated on counter-terrorism, and the Royal Australian Navy conducted a joint exercise with the Chinese navy. Even the defection in 2005 of a Chinese diplomat, Chen Yonglin, who claimed China spied on Australia, failed to disrupt the smooth course of a relationship built on substantial and growing economic interests.

Australia's move towards China had an impact on relations with Japan, a longstanding trading partner of great consequence and a strategic partner as well, but one that was sometimes inclined to take Australia and its resources for granted. The foundation of half a century of growing trade, during which Japan became Australia's key export market, was the 1957 commerce agreement negotiated by the Menzies government. The Fraser government confirmed the close relationship by concluding the Nippon–Australia Relations Agreement of friendship and cooperation of 1977, also known as the NARA Treaty. Japan saw China as a strategic competitor in East Asia. Australia looked at China from the perspective of export markets and economic opportunity. The Japanese were at first dismissive of the idea of a bilateral free trade agreement with Australia, but Australia played the 'China card', reminding the Japanese of its importance as a source of raw materials at a time when Chinese demand for them seemed limitless. The Japanese position on an FTA therefore softened, and Howard persuaded the Japanese government in 2005 to cooperate in a feasibility study on the concept. Full negotiations began in 2007. Whether an FTA will emerge from them depends on the extent to which any Japanese government is willing to allow foreign access to its highly protected and symbolically significant agricultural markets.[13]

Both 9/11 and the 'war on terror' also drove Japan and Australia closer together. The Australian military forces in the Iraqi province of Al-Muthanna in 2005 and 2006 had the task of providing security to Japanese forces engaged in reconstruction. Australia backed Japan's bid for a permanent seat on the UN Security Council, and in March 2007 the two countries signed the Japan–Australia Joint Declaration on Security Cooperation (JDSC), the first such defence agreement reached by Japan with any country other than the United States since World War II. The Howard government argued that the declaration was about cooperating on counter-terrorism, disaster relief and UN peacekeeping, but some observers saw the declaration as a balancing move by Australia to reassure the Japanese at a time of growing Chinese strategic influence in East Asia.

India was of far less consequence than China or Japan for Australian trade and investment, but the Howard government came to recognise the potential of a closer relationship with the world's second most populous country at a time when it was beginning to experience rapid economic growth. Australia froze relations with India when the Indian government conducted nuclear tests in 1998 and did not resume aid and defence links for another two years. By 2007, however, the Howard government had agreed to approve sales of uranium to India, a nuclear-armed state which is not a signatory to the Nuclear Non-Proliferation Treaty (NPT). He did so in defiance of longstanding Australian policy to limit the spread of nuclear weapons, to maintain the NPT non-proliferation safeguards system and to provide uranium only to states that had signed the NPT. One of the first acts of the incoming Rudd Labor government was to reverse this decision and restore Australia's traditional safeguards policy.

THE GLOBAL ENVIRONMENT

The Howard government is sometimes depicted as lacking environmental credentials of any kind. In fact, Australia under the Howard government remained a party or signatory to the major international environmental conventions of recent decades, dealing with a wide range of environmental threats, from depletion of the ozone layer to the persistence of organic pollutants and the accidental killing of albatrosses and petrels. The Howard government did not oppose multilateral mechanisms to protect the environment where it believed they served Australian national interests. At a time when fishing vessels were entering the Southern Ocean because stocks elsewhere were becoming exhausted, Australia fully supported the multilateral fisheries conservation regime. Australia has a huge maritime exclusive economic zone, more than twice the size of the Australian continent, and that zone is vigorously policed to prevent illegal fishing, especially of the valuable Patagonian toothfish. The Royal Australian Navy apprehended eight vessels fishing illegally in the region between 1997 and 2004. When HMAS *Warramunga* seized a Uruguayan fishing vessel with a catch of Patagonian toothfish worth $3 million in 2004, the authorities charged the entire crew with poaching.

The Coalition, whether in opposition or government, is as opposed to whaling as Labor or the Greens. Australia under Howard joined New Zealand in proposing another whale sanctuary in the South Pacific, stretching south of the equator across the region from Papua New Guinea to French Polynesia. The Howard government worked comfortably with the International Whaling Commission, which has the power to declare whale sanctuaries, and with the separate commission established under the Convention on the Conservation of Antarctic Marine Living Resources.

The problem for the Howard government was climate change. Australia under Howard remained a party to the UN Framework Convention on Climate Change, but refused to ratify the addition to that convention, the 1997 Kyoto Protocol, which for the first time committed states to curb emissions of greenhouse gases by accepting targets by 2012. In effect, nations undertook to be releasing agreed levels of greenhouse gases by that year so as to begin the process of averting possible global climatic catastrophe sometime later in the twenty-first century. The protocol allowed Australia to increase greenhouse gas emissions, but Howard still feared it would damage the economy. He told parliament in 2002 that 'because the arrangements currently exclude—and are likely under present settings to continue to exclude—both developing countries and the United States, for us to ratify the protocol would cost us jobs and damage our industry'.[14]

The Howard government, aware that its environmental policy was losing votes, took a number of initiatives before the 2007 election, joining the Asia-Pacific Partnership on Clean Development and Climate (APP or AP6)—a regional body focused on technological solutions to climate change—and giving aid to Indonesia in order to preserve forests in Borneo. Australia also joined China in a joint endeavour to develop clean coal. None of these initiatives, however, had the political impact—nationally and internationally—of the single and symbolic change promised by Kevin Rudd, leader of the Labor Party, in the election campaign, and that was for Australia finally to ratify the Kyoto Protocol. Yet Rudd's own environmental credentials were questioned in 2010 when, after failing to pass Labor's emissions trading scheme through parliament, he deferred consideration of the issue for another three years rather than continuing the fight for it. The public reaction to this decision played a part in his downfall as prime minister a few months later. In the end neither the Howard nor the Rudd government took decisive national action on climate change, and their failure pointed to the political difficulty of restraining the use of fossil fuels in Australia, a country where coal is the biggest export and the main source of electricity generation.

ASSESSMENTS

Deciding whether the Howard government succeeded or failed in its foreign policy is a matter of judgement, not fact. People and political parties disagree about what Australia should be doing in its relations with the rest of the world and their judgements depend on ideological assumptions. Australians on the left, for example, saw Australia's involvement in the Iraq War under Howard as a failure of policy and the withdrawal of troops by Rudd as a success, whereas those on the right saw things the other way around. The same applied to human rights, refugee policy and ratifying the Kyoto Protocol. Success or failure was in the eye of the beholder. People disagreed less about Australia's regional interventions in East Timor and the South Pacific, widely seen as foreign policy accomplishments, and on arcane areas of policy such as trade diplomacy. Any overall assessment of the Howard era in foreign policy, however, remains in the realm of opinion.

We can say with confidence that the foreign policy of the Howard government had plenty of critics. Howard brought a new tone to Australian foreign policy, and in the process refashioned Australia's image abroad. Howard eventually disowned the anti-Asian xenophobia of Pauline Hanson, who briefly led a political movement in the late 1990s, but not before he had revived Asian fears that the old, racist Australia had returned. Though he came to regret it, he endorsed a journalist's description of him as a 'deputy sheriff' to the United States in South-East Asia, reinforcing doubts held by regional leaders and the public about Australia's independence from Washington. He became one of the few world leaders to back George W. Bush unconditionally on the Iraq War, even though Bush ordered the invasion of Iraq without the approval of the UN Security Council, the key institution of global security. Howard remained committed to Australia's Iraq deployment to the end of his prime ministership. 'I know there are many people in Australia who do not agree with our commitment in Iraq', Howard said in 2007. 'And can I say to those people, I understand that, but I ask them to contemplate what will happen to the prestige of the West; what will happen to the prestige of the United States; what will happen to the fight against terrorism in our part of the world if al-Qaeda is seen to be triumphant in Iraq?'[15]

Some observers saw Howard's Iraq policy as a largely political gesture, designed for maximum effect in Washington while sending small numbers of soldiers to one of the safer Iraqi provinces. President Obama, then a candidate for the Democratic nomination, pointed out in 2007 that 'we have close to 140,000 troops in Iraq, and my understanding is Mr Howard has deployed 1400, so if he is … to fight the good fight in Iraq, I would suggest that he calls up another 20,000 Australians and sends them to Iraq. Otherwise it's just a bunch of empty rhetoric.'[16] Howard and Rudd agreed on the war in Afghanistan, and on the need for Australia to be there. Howard announced a series of build-ups in Australia's military commitment to Afghanistan in 2007 and the Rudd government confirmed them. Visiting Afghanistan, Rudd promised that Australia was there 'for the long haul', and, as soon as she became prime minister, Julia Gillard assured President Obama of Australia's continuing military commitment to that country. For the Labor government, Afghanistan was the good war that should have been fought to a successful conclusion in the first place, while Iraq was a disastrous diversion from the main task of defeating al-Qaeda and other terrorist groups.

The foreign policy environment shifted during the Howard era. Terrorism emerged as a global security threat, with attacks in Bali, Jakarta, London and Madrid, and, more intensely, in Iraq, Pakistan and Afghanistan. A province of Indonesia, East Timor, gained independence with Australian help in 2002, only to experience instability that prompted the return of Australian forces in 2006. Indonesia itself, home to 240 million people, turned from dictatorship to democracy after Suharto was forced from the presidency in 1998. Under the leadership of George W. Bush, the United States temporarily abandoned the UN and the multilateral system in favour of a unilateral application of power against its enemies in concert with willing allies. Australia changed its policy on the South Pacific following 9/11 and the Bali bombings, and led a regional intervention force into Solomon Islands, where it began a lengthy commitment to building the state, a novel undertaking in post-colonial times but in tune with a global shift towards intervention in fragile states. The place of China in Australian foreign policy calculations changed too. China's rapid economic growth and demand for Australian raw materials made Australians richer than ever before, and the Howard government began to talk of having a 'strategic economic relationship' with China. As the Howard era drew to a close, the strategic environment in East Asia was changing. China's economic and military power was growing fast, India was emerging from its long period of weakness, Japan was in relative decline, and for the first time since World War II it was possible to imagine a future—though one that is probably a long way off—in which US military supremacy in East Asia would be in question. How would Australia then manage its relationships with its 'strategic economic' partner, China, and its 'strategic military' partner, the United States—the two states that would compete for power in East Asia?

FURTHER READING

Overviews

Cotton, James and John Ravenhill, eds, *The National Interest in a Global Era: Australia in world affairs 1996–2000*, Oxford University Press, Melbourne, 2001. (Scholarly survey covering both bilateral relations and themes such as defence, the environment, human rights and globalisation.)

——*Trading on Alliance Security: Australia in world affairs 2001–2005*, Oxford University Press, Melbourne, 2007. (A comprehensive scholarly survey of key relationships and foreign policy issues, together with valuable chapters on public opinion and the management of intelligence.)

Gyngell, Allan and Michael Wesley, *Making Australian Foreign Policy*, 2nd edn, Cambridge University Press, Cambridge, 2007. (This indispensable analysis of the policy process includes case studies of the way Canberra responded to the Bali bombings, the crisis in Solomon Islands and the free trade agreement with the US.)

Kelly, Paul, *The March of Patriots: The struggle for modern Australia*, Melbourne University Press, Melbourne, 2009. (The foreign policy chapters cover the first five years of the Howard government to 2001 and focus on China, East Timor and the impact of 9/11.)

Ungerer, Carl, ed., *Australian Foreign Policy in the Age of Terror*, University of New South Wales Press, Sydney, 2008. (Includes chapters on less familiar foreign policy issues such as nuclear non-proliferation, unregulated migration and Australian policy towards South Asia after 9/11.)

The relationship with the US

Garran, Robert, *True Believer: John Howard, George Bush and the American alliance*, Allen & Unwin, Sydney, 2004. (A critic of the American alliance contends that Howard aligned Australia too closely with the US, to the detriment of Australia's relations with Asia and in a way that undermined multilateralism.)

Grant, Bruce, *Fatal Attraction: Reflections on the alliance with the United States*, Black Inc., Melbourne, 2004. (A veteran of Australian diplomacy argues that the military connection with the US has a fatal attraction for Australians, that Australia should not have joined in the Iraq War and that a more productive relationship with the US is possible.)

Sheridan, Greg, *The Partnership: The inside story of the US-Australian alliance under Bush and Howard*, UNSW Press, Sydney, 2006. (A strong supporter of the American alliance makes the case that, under Howard, Australia was a closer ally of the US than any other country except the UK, and that this intimacy served Australian national interests.)

Human rights

Brennan, Frank, *Tampering with Asylum: A universal humanitarian problem*, University of Queensland Press, St Lucia, 2003. (A considered and perceptive account of the asylum seeker issue in Australia, with proposals for returning to a humane policy.)

McMaster, Don, *Asylum Seekers: Australia's response to refugees*, Melbourne University Press, Melbourne, 2001. (An academic criticises government policy towards refugees, especially mandatory detention, and calls for a new approach.)

Manne, Robert, *The Howard Years*, Black Inc. Agenda, Melbourne, 2004. (A collection of critical essays, with an especially perceptive first chapter.)

Marr, David and Marian Wilkinson, *Dark Victory*, Allen & Unwin, Sydney, 2003. (How the Howard government used the *Tampa* affair and the refugee issue to win the 2001 election.)

Globalisation and trade

Kunkel, John, 'Australian trade policy in an age of globalisation', *Australian Journal of International Affairs*, vol. 56, no. 2, 2002, pp. 237–51. (Identifies challenges confronting trade policy, including the shift to bilateralism.)

Ravenhill, John, 'Australia and the global economy', in *The National Interest in a Global Era: Australia in world affairs 1996–2000*, James Cotton and John Ravenhill, eds, Oxford University Press, Melbourne, 2001, pp. 279–300. (Covers the East Asian economic crisis, bilateralism and multilateralism, APEC.)

——'Australia and the global economy', in *Trading on Alliance Security: Australia in world affairs 2001–2005*, James Cotton and John Ravenhill, eds, Oxford University Press, Melbourne, 2007, pp. 192–212. (Covers the growth of bilateralism, the Australia–US free trade agreement, APEC and the WTO.)

Australia in Asia

McDowell, Roy Campbell, *Howard's Long March: The strategic depiction of China in Howard government policy, 1996–2006*, ANU E Press, 2009. (The Howard government depicted

China as a friend and moved Australia closer to it economically and even strategically, while nevertheless harbouring concerns about China's rise to power.)

Wesley, Michael, *The Howard Paradox: Australian diplomacy in Asia 1996–2006*, ABC Books, Sydney, 2007. (The paradox is how Howard, who identified Australia so closely with the West and with the Bush administration in the US, should have achieved so much in improving Australia's relations with Asia, including Indonesia.)

4

The making of
foreign policy

- Why has the making of foreign policy become increasingly centralised in recent decades? Could it be more democratic?
- Who holds most power over the making of Australian foreign policy?
- What role in making foreign and defence policy is played by the National Security Committee of Cabinet?
- Why is parliament marginal to the making of foreign policy?
- What role is played by the three parliamentary committees which deal with foreign affairs?
- To what extent, and on what kinds of issues, does mass public opinion influence Australian foreign policy?
- What is the 'national interest'?
- Is Australia's growing 'secret state' a threat to civil liberties?
- Are the intelligence agencies sufficiently accountable to parliament? Are they sufficiently free from political direction?

This chapter examines the location of power in the making of Australia's foreign policy. We investigate the roles of senior ministers, the government, the bureaucracy, parliament, the intelligence services, the media and public opinion, and we ask whether foreign policy can be said to emerge from a democratic decision-making process.

MINISTERS, GOVERNMENT AND THE BUREAUCRACY

When Bob Hawke committed two RAN guided missile frigates and a tanker to support the Americans in the Persian Gulf in August 1990, he consulted five of his ministers and President George Bush of the United States. He acted before discussing the issue with the full Cabinet, the Parliamentary Labor Party or members of parliament, who all learned of Hawke's decision afterwards. Hawke was not the first Australian prime minister to make a major foreign policy decision without consulting Cabinet. The British asked the Liberal prime minister Robert Menzies in 1950 whether they could test their first atomic bomb on Australian territory, and Menzies agreed without discussing the matter with his Cabinet colleagues. Both Hawke and Menzies felt justified in proceeding with these decisions in secret, at least initially.

These examples, though extreme and unusual, point to the defining characteristic of foreign policy making in Australia: power is highly concentrated in the hands of the prime minister, foreign minister, trade minister, the Cabinet and the senior public servants and ministerial staff who advise them. Together, these people are the makers of foreign policy, and they are located in the executive under Australia's version of the Westminster system of parliamentary government. The executive's influence over foreign policy, moreover, is increasing.

Some prime ministers relish the challenge of foreign policy and monopolise it at the expense of foreign ministers. Gough Whitlam and Malcolm Fraser had strong views about the direction Australia should take internationally and put a personal stamp on foreign policy, leaving foreign ministers such as Don Willesee and Tony Street (though not Andrew Peacock) to be forgotten by history. Bob Hawke and Paul Keating were less dominant prime ministers in foreign policy and Bill Hayden and Gareth Evans are remembered for their contributions as foreign ministers. John Howard concentrated power over foreign affairs in his own hands, though few think he overshadowed his foreign minister Alexander Downer. Rudd, a former diplomat, took a higher profile in dealing with the world than his foreign affairs minister, Stephen Smith, and counted his diplomatic initiatives among his major achievements as prime minister. Rudd then replaced Smith as foreign affairs minister after the 2010 elections. The prime minister needs to maintain a close working relationship with his foreign minister if policy is to be consistent and credible. When Hayden was foreign minister, from 1983 to 1988, the Americans were able to question Australian policy because they knew Hayden and Hawke disliked each other and often disagreed. Policy kept a steadier course when Evans was foreign minister, from 1988 to 1996, because he had good relations with his prime ministers, and the same has been true of policy in the years since 1996.

The Cabinet consists of government ministers. Under the Howard, Rudd and Gillard governments the heart of foreign policy making has been a committee of

Cabinet called the National Security Committee (NSC), which Howard established in 1996. The NSC gathers in one room the political, bureaucratic, military and intelligence elite of Australia, and usually meets every month. In the Rudd and Gillard governments the committee consisted of the prime minister as chair, the deputy prime minister, the treasurer, the Cabinet secretary, the Attorney-General, the Minister for Defence and the Minister for Foreign Affairs. Under Howard it also included the Minister for Immigration. At the bureaucratic level, the senior public servants who are the heads of relevant government departments—the 'secretaries'—participate in the NSC meetings and bring their expertise to the committee's deliberations. They come not only from Foreign Affairs and Trade, Defence, Treasury and Attorney-General's, but also significantly from the Department of Prime Minister and Cabinet (PM&C), which answers directly to the prime minister and which is concerned, as is the prime minister, with the domestic political effects of foreign policy decisions. The commander of the Defence Force and Director-General of the Office of National Assessments, an intelligence analysis organisation answering directly to the prime minister, also come to NSC meetings. Rudd created two new positions, those of national security adviser and deputy national security adviser. The national security adviser comes to NSC meetings and is responsible to the secretary of PM&C. The Ambassador for Counter-Terrorism, whose task is to coordinate national counter-terrorism efforts and negotiate counter-terrorism agreements with other countries, also makes policy recommendations to the NSC.

The brief of the NSC is to focus on 'major international security issues of strategic importance to Australia, national responses to developing situations (either domestic or international) and classified matters relating to aspects of operations and activities of the Australian Intelligence Community'.[1] When a crisis arises, the NSC convenes and makes decisions: the 2002 Bali bombings took place on a Saturday night, government and the Defence Force swung into action early the next morning, and the NSC was in session by the Monday afternoon to decide what action Australia would take in relation to the Indonesian government; and when Israel misused Australian passports for its agents involved in assassinating the Hamas military commander Mahmoud al-Mabhouh in Dubai in 2010, government agencies gave the NSC a comprehensive briefing on the issue. The government responded by expelling an Israeli diplomat.

The bureaucrats—the public servants—are the ones who advise ministers and who draw on professional expertise in formulating that advice. Bureaucrats wield influence over foreign policy for three reasons. First, they control information, a vital resource which in the case of foreign affairs tends to be formidably complicated and arcane. Second, armed with this information, bureaucrats may set the policy agenda themselves unless their minister is gifted, knowledgeable and forceful: a combination of qualities found in Gareth Evans but not in most foreign ministers. And third, even if ministers determine the agenda, senior bureaucrats are uniquely placed to exert influence because they have privileged access to governments and they know how things have worked in the past. Unlike Howard, Rudd made few changes to the appointed personnel of Australia's foreign policy, intelligence and defence community when he took office, leaving the heads of Defence, DFAT, the Australian Security Intelligence Organisation and the Office of National Assessments in place, and confirming the appointments of Australia's key ambassadors overseas. Rudd was a centralist, even more so than Howard, and happily inherited the administrative arrangements that put the prime minister and his own department at the centre of foreign policy making. More and more bureaucrats were appointed to work on foreign affairs in PM&C under Howard and Rudd, and that department's National Security and International Policy Group grew fast in each of its four divisions: the International Division; the Homeland and Border Security Division; the Defence, Intelligence and Research Coordination Division; and the International Strategy Unit created by Rudd.

For two reasons the foreign policy-making process is more politicised than it used to be. In the first place, as Gyngell and Wesley argue, the federal public service has been subject to the managerial revolution. Instead of serving as neutral public servants from one government to the next, today's senior public servants are on short-term contracts that require performance, and performance is related to the expectations of their political masters in government. In the second place, ministerial advisers have emerged over the last 30 years as increasingly influential players in the policy-making process. Under the law they are not public servants, though many advisers come and go from the public service during their careers. Their appointments are directly political, and they are expected to demonstrate loyalty rather than objectivity. The most influential ministerial advisers on foreign issues under the Howard government were the prime minister's senior advisers on international affairs, located in PM&C. Their influence over the direction of Australian foreign policy ranked with that of ministers themselves and the departmental secretaries heading DFAT and PM&C. Some say that helps to explain why foreign policy under the Howard government was unusually influenced by calculations of its political effects within Australia.

The Department of Foreign Affairs and Trade (DFAT) is the contemporary version of a federal government department that originated in 1935. The Department of External Affairs, as it was called, first flowered when Australia broke from the diplomatic dominance of London during the 1940s to establish a unique Australian identity in international affairs. The Hawke government incorporated the old Department of Trade—once one of the most powerful parts of the Canberra bureaucracy—into the Department of Foreign Affairs in 1987, in a change indicating the new centrality of economics in Australian foreign policy. The Australian Agency for International Development (AusAID) functions as a separate foreign aid bureau within DFAT. DFAT is housed in a building opened in 1996 and named by the Howard Coalition government after a long-serving foreign affairs minister in the Menzies Coalition government of the 1950s, R.G. (Lord) Casey. As a department that deals with both foreign affairs and trade, DFAT usually answers to two ministers, one responsible for each. Rudd's Minister for Trade was Simon Crean, and he also appointed two parliamentary secretaries or junior ministers, one for international development assistance and one for Pacific Island affairs. When Julia Gillard became prime minister in 2010, she briefly made Stephen Smith minister for both foreign affairs and trade. After the 2010 election Gillard split the portfolio again, with Rudd as foreign minister and Craig Emerson as minister for trade.

DFAT is the home base of a network of diplomatic missions that represent Australia around the globe. Successive governments have reduced Australia's overseas representation to save money, and considerably fewer diplomats work abroad now than in the 1970s or 1980s. The Howard and Rudd governments hastened this process by cutting the number of diplomatic missions by a third from 128 in 1997 to 89 in 2009. Australians serving in embassies, high commissions, consulates and multilateral missions abroad are expensive to maintain, and a small minority of DFAT staff, around one in seven, work there. The remaining Australian employees of the department work in Canberra or in the states and territories. More than two in every five people working for DFAT are foreigners recruited and working in an Australian mission in a foreign country. The geographical distribution of these missions accords with Australia's view of its commercial and strategic interests. A third is located in North and South-East Asia and the South Pacific, a quarter in Europe, an eighth in the Americas and the rest elsewhere around the globe. A legacy of Empire remains in the fact that embassies in Commonwealth countries are called 'high commissions'. Where overseas missions are few, ambassadors are usually accredited to a number of neighbouring countries as well as the one in which they live. A sizeable number of missions are managed for trade promotion purposes by Austrade. Some missions are not to other governments but to multilateral institutions such as the UN, the Organisation for Economic Co-operation and Development (OECD) and the World Trade Organization (WTO), and there is the Australian Embassy to the Holy See in Rome, where Australia is represented by a former National Party minister, Tim Fischer.

Some say we no longer need diplomats in an age of instant electronic communication, but that is to forget what they do. Diplomats protect the interests of Australian citizens in other parts of the world by ensuring, for example, that tourists are warned of possible dangers and that Australians accused of crimes in a foreign country receive proper trials. Diplomats assist Australian citizens overseas if they are hospitalised or need medical evacuation, if they are arrested or imprisoned, and even if they run out of money. Australian embassies regularly make loans to Australians who find themselves penniless in a foreign country. The 2002 Bali bombings showed how important such consular services could be in an emergency. Within 36 hours DFAT had organised the evacuation of 66 injured Australians, and answered tens of thousands of phone calls from concerned relatives. Less well known was DFAT's role the same year in arranging the rescue of three Australian mountain climbers in Tibet. War between Israel and Lebanon in 2006 prompted the mass evacuation of Australian citizens from Lebanon. Within days of the crisis emerging, 12,000 Australian citizens had registered with a crisis centre established by the Australian government. Australian governments now emphasise this consular side of Australia's diplomatic activities on the assumption that people understand it readily and will reward a government that offers citizens protection and assistance.

Diplomats act as Australia's eyes and ears abroad. Political and economic developments in most countries are best understood by those who live there and whose training and linguistic skills enable them to interpret intelligently what they observe. They are likely to have an accurate idea of how foreign governments will react to decisions made in Canberra, and they develop personal contacts that enable them to negotiate effectively on Australia's behalf. Far from rendering diplomats redundant, modern communications can make them participants in the making of policy. Helping tourists and reporting from overseas are only the most obvious tasks performed by the diplomatic service, which undertakes a whole range of complicated functions vital to Australia's security, prosperity and international reputation. Diplomats represent Australia, for example, in the specialised agencies of the UN. They argue Australia's case in the World Health Organization (WHO) and the International Atomic Energy Agency (IAEA). They negotiate bilateral agreements with regional states on countering the threat of terrorism. They master the daunting complexities of international trade agreements overseen by the WTO, and of international financial arrangements supervised by the World Bank, the International Monetary Fund (IMF) and the Asian Development Bank. They negotiate trade access, confer on free trade agreements and take up cases using the WTO's dispute settlement system. They negotiate treaties, often over a period of years.

Yet the prime ministerial centralisation of power has combined with the terrorist threat to leave the traditional home of Australian diplomacy on the sidelines of policy making. Recent Australian governments have neglected DFAT in favour of PM&C, the Department of Defence and the intelligence agencies. DFAT's funding has fallen in comparative terms while that of Defence and intelligence has massively increased. By 2009 Australia had fewer overseas missions than most OECD countries, despite its growing enmeshment in the global economy and multiplying foreign interests. A 2009 Lowy Institute report concluded that Australia's overseas network of diplomatic missions was 'overstretched and hollowed out'. Australia did not have enough missions or diplomats overseas 'to build vital contacts with other governments and other important international actors, to interpret events in emerging centres of power, to advocate our interests or to help distressed Australian travellers'. The report recommended that Australia open twenty new diplomatic missions by 2019, with a number of them in the regional areas of India, China and Indonesia, and reinvest heavily in language skills while expanding 'language-designated positions'.[2]

As we have seen, DFAT is only one among a number of government departments that influence foreign policy. Others with particular influence include not only PM&C and Defence, but also Treasury and the Department of Immigration and Citizenship. In recent years the business of almost every Commonwealth department has acquired international dimensions. Under these circumstances, coordinating the different streams of policy advice has become a vital task, one that is performed above all by PM&C, the NSC, and an arm of the Canberra bureaucracy called the Strategic Policy Coordination Group, which brings together DFAT, Defence and PM&C.

To ask who among the prime minister, the foreign affairs and trade ministers, Cabinet, the NSC, senior public servants and ministerial advisers exercises

THE EXPERTS CALL FOR AUSTRALIA TO ENHANCE ITS OVERSEAS DIPLOMATIC REPRESENTATION

Australia's network of overseas diplomatic missions—the government's most important point of immediate contact with the world, and the best way it has of influencing it—is overstretched and hollowed out. It has not kept pace with our interests or with a changing world. This diplomatic deficit is even starker because Australia does not belong to any natural regional grouping or economic bloc to multiply our influence. Our geopolitical circumstances are also significantly more challenging than those faced by most other developed nations.

Australia has fewer diplomatic missions than all but a few OECD countries, leaving us badly underrepresented, particularly in emerging centres of power of significance to our interests. DFAT staff numbers have been steadily falling—particularly front-line positions overseas—with further cuts planned. Years of underfunding have diminished its policy capacity and rendered many overseas missions critically overstretched. Specialist skills—particularly foreign languages—are badly lacking. Over the same period, the consular workload has more than doubled, further displacing our diplomats' capacity to contribute to wider national objectives.

As a result we don't have enough diplomatic missions or trained diplomats overseas to build vital contacts with governments and other important international actors, to interpret events in emerging centres of power, to advocate our interests or to help distressed Australian travellers. Public diplomacy is lacklustre, poorly integrated and untargeted, and Australia's aid program faces significant challenges . . .

Our ability to understand our international environment, to anticipate developments affecting Australia's security and prosperity and to generate appropriate responses to them is degrading. Without urgent action to rebuild the intellectual infrastructure needed to support international policy we will fall further behind.

Blue Ribbon Panel Report, *Australia's Diplomatic Deficit: Reinvesting in our instruments of international policy*, Lowy Institute, Sydney, 2009, p. vii.

the greatest influence over foreign policy is to ask the wrong question. Power over foreign policy, it is safer to say, is held by a foreign policy elite consisting of all these people with the prime minister and foreign minister at the top. By and large, they have a common outlook on Australia's place in the world. The key point is that they all, in one way or another, belong to the executive.

PARLIAMENT

Parliament has little say in foreign policy. Parliament cannot veto the appointment of ambassadors, prevent treaties from being ratified or even stop the government from declaring war. All parliament can do is gather information and subject the government's performance in foreign policy to public scrutiny through Question Time and parliamentary committees. Tight party discipline ensures that the Cabinet rather than parliament has power over decisions. Members of the governing parties vote automatically with the government on all important occasions, so Cabinet can count in advance on the support of a parliamentary majority and act accordingly.

Cabinet and ministerial control is even greater over foreign policy than over other areas of government activity. For one thing, foreign policy requires comparatively little legislation or budgetary support. The government needs parliamentary approval for the annual appropriations that pay for DFAT and for some of the security services. The aid budget, too, depends on annual appropriations approved by parliament and therefore subject to scrutiny and debate. But foreign affairs is a minor area of government expenditure compared with, say, social security or education. What does a government do, after all, when it implements a 'foreign policy'? Most of the time it responds to events overseas by issuing statements, takes positions on international issues, negotiates treaties, represents Australia abroad and explains policy at home. None of these things needs the approval of parliament.

Second, foreign policy is usually, though not always, less contentious than other areas of policy. The major parties usually disagree over the way the government implements policy, how well the foreign minister performs and how much emphasis the minister puts on one issue rather than another, not on what the general direction of foreign policy should be. Australia has bipartisanship on the key issues of foreign policy.

'Bipartisanship' can mean consensus, and can convey the idea that MPs or opinion leaders or party members think the same way about Australia's foreign policy regardless of party affiliation and preference. Bipartisanship can also imply continuity. It can mean that Australian foreign policy is continuous from one government to the next because incoming governments adopt the foreign policy of predecessors, at least on fundamentals. Many observers say defence and security are fundamental elements of foreign policy. They say Australian foreign policy is bipartisan in the sense that the major parties agree on a common approach to defence and security. That approach is along these lines: Australia's military security depends upon our alliance with the United States, and ANZUS should be defended to the Australian people; good relations with Indonesia are a strategic asset for us and we must therefore maintain them; enmeshing commercially and diplomatically with East Asia—in good times and bad—is vital to our future wellbeing. Yet people differ in defining 'fundamental'. Some see big differences between the parties on foreign policy, and the opposition of the Labor Party to Australia's involvement in the 2003 Iraq War showed that bipartisanship cannot be taken for granted.

The political parties provide tendencies in foreign policy rather than having a determining impact. The parties have foreign policy committees which reflect rank-and-file opinion to a greater or lesser extent, and they adopt policy at party conferences. But no government feels bound by party policy. Party leaders, once elected to government, change direction 'for the sake of the broader national interest' or 'in the light of secret information which cannot be divulged'. Bob Hawke and Bill Hayden jettisoned Labor policy on East Timor when they reached government in 1983, for example, and then used their authority to persuade the party to agree. The Rudd government's climate change policy fell far short of the expectations of many who voted for it.

Whether bipartisan or not, the approach of the major parties to foreign policy in parliament tends to enhance the power of the executive. The major political parties agree on its general direction, and so the Opposition has less incentive to use foreign policy to embarrass the government. Foreign policy debates in parliament are unusual, and except in 1966, no federal election has been fought primarily on a foreign policy issue in the last 50 years unless one counts the 'Tampa election' of 2001. In late August 2001, the Australian Maritime Safety Authority identified a vessel sailing towards Australia as being in distress, and requested the captain of a Norwegian container ship, the Tampa, to rescue the passengers. He reached the boat, took its complement of 438 people on board, and then headed for the nearest port, which happened to be the Australian territory of Christmas Island. But, before the Tampa could land, SAS commandos came aboard with instructions to prevent it from doing so. For eight days the Tampa stood offshore, its fate swiftly becoming an international incident, while the Howard government concocted a way out that would leave the prime minister looking like a tough defender of Australia's borders. Under the 'Pacific Solution', the navy took the refugees to hastily established detention centres in Nauru and Papua New Guinea, where their claims for asylum were to be processed. Some people believe the *Tampa* affair won the election for Howard by arousing popular fears that Australia would be swamped by asylum seekers.

Most of the time, parliamentary debate over foreign policy, when it occurs, is conducted within conventional limits. Maverick opinions on foreign policy surface only occasionally. The short-lived Nuclear Disarmament Party of the 1980s called for Australia to withdraw from the American alliance, close the nuclear-related joint facilities and ban nuclear vessels from Australian ports. The independent MP Pauline Hanson, elected in 1996, wanted Australia to stop giving aid to foreign countries. But these are exceptions.

Parliament's most active role in foreign affairs is in three committees, two long established and one that dates from 1996. The most important is the Joint Standing Committee on Foreign Affairs, Defence and Trade (JSCFAD&T), dating from 1952. The committee is 'joint' because it draws members from both upper and lower Houses and 'standing' because it lasts throughout the life of each parliament. It has a membership of 32, consisting of twelve government and eight Opposition MPs from the House of Representatives together with twelve senators—five from the government, five from the Opposition and two from the minority parties or independents. The joint standing committee holds inquiries, takes evidence from interested parties at public hearings, inspects defence installations, observes defence exercises, and meets visiting parliamentary delegations and notable individuals. Ministers may refer matters to the committee for examination, or references may come from either House of parliament. Delegations of parliamentarians serving the JSCFAD&T Committee may make overseas visits, such as the one in 2009 to Australian defence personnel serving in East Timor, and report to parliament when they return.

The joint standing committee produces some of parliament's most informative reports. Their subject matter demonstrates the breadth of the JSCFAD&T Committee's interests and its growing stature as a parliamentary institution. Those who give evidence to joint standing committee inquiries are those with a stake of some kind in the outcome of foreign policy decisions: business people wanting to influence foreign economic policy, compatriots of foreigners suffering from human rights abuses, defence personnel with opinions about defence policy, academics with specialist knowledge of foreign affairs, and so on. Together, they constitute an important part of what has been called the *attentive public* in foreign policy matters, a much smaller public than the one to which the government must respond in domestic policy.

The Senate Standing Committee on Foreign Affairs, Defence and Trade, formed in 1971, is smaller than the joint standing committee—membership varies between six and eight senators and from parliament to parliament—but it generates a steady stream of reports on foreign affairs. The committee is divided in two. One committee deals with legislation, and the other with references; that is, matters referred to it for inquiry. In 2010, for example, this committee presented a report on security challenges facing Papua New Guinea and the island states of the South Pacific.

These two committees usually request a government response to their reports. Governments are quicker than they used to be, generally replying well within a year, but they rarely respond within the time specified by parliament, and responses tend to reiterate official policy rather than take recommendations seriously except on minor details.

The Howard government established a third foreign affairs parliamentary committee in 1996, the Joint Standing Committee on Treaties, with sixteen members in all: nine government, six Opposition and one other. The Coalition parties set up this committee because they did not like what happened to treaties under Hawke and Keating. The power to make a treaty in Australia belongs solely to the executive under section 61 of the constitution. When the Australian government signs a treaty, it commits Australia to support the principles of that treaty. But many treaties require the further step of 'ratification' or its equivalent 'accession', which comes after laws have been amended in accordance with treaty obligations. Once the Australian government has ratified or acceded to a treaty, Australia is bound under international law to observe it.

Successive governments since the 1970s, especially those of Hawke and Keating, increasingly ignored parliament both in signing and in ratifying treaties. An older tradition faded, in which governments waited to ratify treaties until they were 'tabled' in parliament; that is, until treaties had 'lain on the tables' of both Houses so that MPs could examine them. Labor tabled treaties in job lots twice a year but acted on them without waiting for parliament. When the Keating government tabled 36 treaties in one day in 1994, seven had already come into force and sixteen others had been ratified or acceded to. While this approach was perfectly constitutional, the Coalition claimed it centralised power and undermined parliament.

The Coalition was particularly concerned about the link between treaties and the external affairs power in section 51(xxix) of the constitution. Labor used the external affairs power in 1983 to prevent Tasmania from damming the Gordon

River, saying it was required to take this action by obligations under a treaty. In this case Labor relied on an international treaty to support a domestic law, a procedure repeated throughout the Labor years to modernise Australian legislation on issues such as race and sex discrimination. Many Coalition supporters came to see treaties (especially those dealing with human rights) as the means by which Labor acted without consulting parliament or the states. Had Labor been using treaty obligations for different purposes, ones of which the Coalition approved, treaties would probably not have become a political issue.

The Joint Standing Committee on Treaties is the means by which treaties now receive parliamentary scrutiny. Among the matters being considered by the committee in 2010 were the UN Convention on the Use of Electronic Communications in International Contracts and amendments to the Convention on International Trade in Endangered Species of Wild Fauna and Flora. The government tables treaties for at least fifteen sitting days, accompanying each text with a national interest analysis explaining how Australia will benefit, and outlining the treaty's obligations and costs together with its expected economic, environmental, social and cultural effects. During this time the Treaties Committee organises public hearings and gathers material for reports. In circumstances where the government must 'safeguard Australia's national interests, be they commercial, strategic or foreign policy interests', the government bypasses parliament and binds Australia under international law without first tabling treaties. The escape clause on treaties and governments' treatment of reports from parliamentary committees should not surprise us. They merely confirm that government dominates the stage of foreign policy making and that parliament is a bit player.

Parliament might inquire and report, but the executive decides. Parliament involves the public in its foreign policy inquiries, governments answer foreign policy questions in Question Time, and the hearings of the Senate Estimates committee on the operations of DFAT make governments marginally more accountable. Yet Gyngell and Wesley conclude that it is 'hard to find any significant role played in the formulation of Australian foreign policy by Federal Parliament'. They find little to suggest the Joint Standing Committee on Foreign Affairs, Defence and Trade exercises 'any compelling influence' on foreign policy. The DFAT officers they surveyed in 2001 agreed, ranking the impact on policy of the joint standing committee well below that of the prime minister and foreign and trade ministers, their advisers, departmental secretaries in Canberra, and ambassadors overseas. The equivalent committee in the

PARLIAMENTARY COMMITTEES AND FOREIGN POLICY

. . . several factors militate against parliament as a whole holding the government to account for foreign policy decisions. These include a small number of sitting days, the fact that the conduct of foreign policy rarely requires the consent of parliament, and the emergence of an inner sanctum within the Prime Minister's department which has largely displaced the Department of Foreign Affairs in making sensitive foreign policy decisions. Committees, with their powers to call for witnesses and documents in their role as the watchdog of the government, are regarded by many as the last bulwark against irresponsible and unaccountable executive behaviour.

. . . this optimism is often misplaced, especially in relation to committees that oversee foreign and national security policy. For a start, the usual barriers that confound most parliamentary committees come into play, including: obfuscatory techniques employed by public servants; serving and former ministers who refuse to appear before an inquiry; and committees that are unwilling to exercise the full range of their coercive powers, for fear of being accused of heavy-handedness or suffering retribution when the political tables are turned.

More intractable barriers, however, appear in inquiries into foreign and national security policy. Bipartisanship is the first. Foreign and security policy are seen as too important to be left to the minor players in the political scene. Senior figures in the two main parties share the privileges and responsibilities of managing what some regard as parliament's most sensitive committees. Consensus, rather than dissent and rigorous questioning, is the normal modus operandi. As a result, difficult questions about the rights and wrongs of certain foreign policy decisions are not always asked, or are not asked of people in a position to know.

The second barrier is self-censorship. 'Once brought into the tent, people recognise their responsibilities', is how one person interviewed for this study explained the phenomenon. National security, it is argued here, has a powerful pull that leads its self-styled keepers, including those on committees, away from principles of open and accountable government and into a murkier world which can encourage obfuscation, complicity and, sometimes, deliberate misrepresentation of the facts.

Kate Burton, Scrutiny or secrecy? Committee oversight of foreign and national security policy in the Australian Parliament, Commonwealth of Australia, 2005, p. xi, <www.aph.gov.au/library/pubs/monographs/burton/scrutinyorsecrecy.pdf>.

Senate is even less influential, and the greatest impact of the Joint Standing Committee on Treaties is not to make the government more accountable but to burden DFAT officers with the task of researching and writing an endless succession of national interest analyses.[3]

THE MEDIA AND PUBLIC OPINION

Most foreign policy issues are too complicated to lend themselves to popular media treatment. Apart from terrorism, the issues that matter most in contemporary foreign policy—multilateral and bilateral trade negotiations, regional monetary arrangements, foreign economic analysis and global economic governance—do not make good television or even good radio for a mass audience. That is why most serious reporting of foreign news and foreign policy in the electronic media comes from the ABC and the Special Broadcasting Service (SBS), and in both print and electronic forms from the *Australian*, the *Sydney Morning Herald*, the *Age*, the *Canberra Times* and the *Australian Financial Review*, the major Australian newspapers directed at a well-informed readership. These are the newspapers that provide most of the material for DFAT's regular collection of Australian print stories on foreign affairs, aid and trade issues. DFAT keeps relevant ministers aware of how the media are covering foreign affairs and the government's performance, and provides an official interpretation of events to journalists through its media office and media releases.

Like other ministers, foreign ministers have a symbiotic relationship with the press. They need journalists to publicise the government's successes and journalists need them to supply stories. Ministers or DFAT officials often give senior journalists and newspaper editors background briefings 'off the record', where they defend policy more frankly than in public in the hope that they will get sympathetic media coverage.

The media have the capacity not only to embarrass the government but even to influence Australia's relations with other countries. The *Sydney Morning Herald* published an exposé of high-level corruption in Indonesia in 1986, prompting a sudden cooling in relations between Australia and Indonesia. The media affected relations with Malaysia in 1993 by seizing on a remark made by Paul Keating describing the Malaysians as 'recalcitrants' over South-East Asian regional integration. The publicity gave the Malaysian prime minister the chance to pose as wronged by Australia. Relations between China and Australia cooled in 2009 after wide media coverage of the arrest of Stern Hu, an Australian citizen working for Rio Tinto, and the visit to the Melbourne Film Festival of Rebiya Kadeer, an activist for the rights of the Muslim Uighur minority in the Chinese province of Xinjiang.

For reasons of this kind, no foreign minister or prime minister has an entirely easy relationship with the media. All foreign ministers think the media treat sensitive matters of national interest in a cavalier way. Bill Hayden argued that the media 'cannot divorce itself from the responsibility of avoiding unnecessary damage to our national interests with other countries'.[4] Gareth Evans said the press swung between accusing governments of upsetting good relations, and accusing them of 'not being aggressively objectionable enough on matters like self-determination for East Timor or human rights in China'. He thought the media risked becoming irresponsible in the search for the dramatic and controversial. As foreign minister, Evans thought that 'if the media sees advantage for itself in running a manifestly national security–sensitive story, its collective instinct is to publish come what may'.[5] The Labor prime minister Bob Hawke was unimpressed with the ABC's reporting of the 1991 Gulf War. He accused the ABC of indulging in a 'parade of prejudice' by employing experts whose views were 'loaded, biased and disgraceful'.[6] Some ministers in the Howard government saw the ABC as a bastion of left-wing opinions.

Governments worry about the media because the media influence public opinion. But what is 'public opinion'?

We may approach this question by distinguishing between 'mass public opinion' of the kind which the media influence and even manipulate, and 'organised public opinion' of the kind expressed by informed pressure groups on particular issues. Mass public opinion about much of Australia's foreign policy hardly exists. The issues are complicated, governments control the agenda, they keep information secret and the media see no reason to publicise matters that have little news value. Yet one set of foreign policy issues is different. Peace, war and foreign threats mobilise mass public opinion and attract media attention on a scale large enough to influence governments. So governments are especially sensitive to the way the media report issues of this kind.

The Vietnam War and conscription—extensively covered by the media— helped the Coalition to win by a landslide in 1966 when public opinion backed the government, and contributed to their defeat in 1972 when public support had faded. The equivalent issue in the 1980s was the threat of nuclear war and Australia's role in the American nuclear alliance. Again the media gave extensive coverage, especially to protest events staged by peace activists to attract media attention, such as sending flotillas of dinghies and surfboards to dramatise the nuclear threat by surrounding visiting nuclear warships. French nuclear tests were the major foreign affairs media story of 1995, combining patriotic appeal, drama and powerful images with a simple dichotomy of the bad French exploding bombs and the good Australians resisting them. Australian media coverage of French nuclear tests was uniformly antagonistic to France, responding to public outrage and creating it at the same time. In this case, media and public opinion compelled the government to toughen its original position on the issue and condemn France in the strongest terms.

Sometimes media coverage, public opinion and government policy confirm each other. Such was the case on the question of East Timor in 1999. Most Australians were shocked by the revenge taken on the East Timorese when they voted for independence from Indonesia. Night after night, Australian television screens showed chaos on the streets of Dili, terrified East Timorese seeking refuge in the UN compound from the machine-gun fire of the militias, and the RAAF Hercules C130 aircraft flying rescue missions to evacuate people to the safety of Darwin. Many of the evacuees were East Timorese. A few weeks later, Australian troops landed in Dili as the first wave of a UN-mandated intervention force, INTERFET (International Force in East Timor), was sent to stop the killings and restore order. As Greenlees and Garran say, 'they went with more faith in the justice of their cause, and support at home, than any departing army since World War II'.[7] In this case, media coverage of foreign conflict strengthened public opinion in favour of Australian military intervention and backed the government unreservedly. Broad popular support for government also followed the terrorist attacks on New York and Washington of 11 September 2001, conveyed live on television in some of the most arresting images of our times. Most Australians were fully behind the prime minister when he invoked the ANZUS Treaty and committed Australia to join with the United States in the war against terrorism, and when he announced that the Australian Defence Force would send more than 1500 troops overseas as part of the American-led attacks on the Taliban and al-Qaeda in Afghanistan. The Afghanistan War of 2001–02 was a popular war, and continued to be so after Australia sent troops back there in 2005.

The war on Iraq in 2003 was different. The Labor Party opposed Australian participation, many Australians protested against it, and some media coverage— particularly on the ABC and SBS—reflected the nation's divisions. Like Bob Hawke twelve years before, John Howard and his communications minister

Senator Richard Alston were sharply critical of the way the ABC reported a war involving Australian troops. Senator Alston produced a dossier of ABC reports, finding numerous examples of what he regarded as beat-ups, exaggeration, lack of evidence, ridicule, bias and abuse on the part of journalists. An ABC internal inquiry into the allegations dismissed most of them, and so the government in turn dismissed its findings. The whole affair showed that governments hold a stake in favourable war coverage and that global television can powerfully influence Australians' opinions. Popular support for Australia's participation in the Iraq War faded as the war progressed, leaving the Labor Party well positioned in the 2007 election to promise Australia's withdrawal.

Mass public opinion may be dramatically influential on a few foreign policy issues but it is transient. It disappears with the issues and when media coverage fades. Organised public opinion is less transient, more knowledgeable and more influential over the long term.

Gyngell and Wesley distinguish between four kinds of organised public opinion on foreign policy, or what they term *foreign policy issue publics*.[8] The first, which they term *economic-utilitarian publics*, focuses on the impact of foreign policy on particular industries or the economy as a whole. Some are producer organisations with a stake in access to overseas markets, tariff policy and international trading arrangements. Such organisations possess the political leverage that goes with being creators of investment and employment. Soon after coming to office the Howard government confronted lobbying from the automotive industry and from the textile, clothing and footwear industry, both of which sought protection from foreign competition. Companies and trade unions joined in a common campaign to save jobs, a formidable combination in regional cities such as Geelong, and Howard agreed to check the pace of tariff reduction.

A second kind of organised public opinion arises from *ethnic-religious issue publics* with an interest in events taking place in an overseas country, either because it is their country of origin or because they wish to demonstrate solidarity with people suffering somewhere else in the world. They may seek to use Australia to advance their political objectives overseas, protect compatriots there, enable relatives to come as migrants, and provide assistance for refugees once they reach Australia.

A third kind of organised public opinion is humanitarian in character, and represents *normative-cosmopolitan issue publics* concerned about a global or regional political issue such as human rights, the environment, disarmament or aid for developing countries. Amnesty International Australia, Greenpeace Australia Pacific and Oxfam Community Aid Abroad are examples. Gareth Evans described the non-government aid organisations such as Oxfam Community Aid Abroad as 'the most formidable external lobbyists—certainly the noisiest, especially around Budget time'. The aid lobby had little influence on the Keating or Howard governments. For many years the lobby called on successive governments to increase Australia's aid to the rest of the world, yet aid fell as a proportion of gross national income (GNI), and started rising only in the last years of the Howard government and after the election of the Rudd government in 2007. The aid lobby has resisted the commercialisation of aid, yet Australian governments have continued to create an aid industry of consultants and companies that bid for aid contracts. The threat of terrorism and state failure in the South Pacific region has had a much greater effect than the aid lobby on Australia's policy, which is now to increase aid to developing countries.

Finally, there are many organisations with a *national issue focus* that has foreign policy implications. The concern of the Australian Conservation Foundation for the natural environment in Australia cannot be separated, for example, from global warming and the government's weakened position on climate change following the failure in 2009 of the United Nations Climate Change Conference, also called the Copenhagen Summit.

Generally speaking, even the best informed groups representing organised public opinion exert only minor influence on foreign policy unless they possess political leverage such as a threat to jobs or votes.

THE NATIONAL INTEREST

Labor and the Coalition both appeal to 'the national interest' in explaining and defending foreign policy to the Australian people.

Gareth Evans saw Australia's 'overriding geo-political or strategic interest' as being 'the defence of Australian sovereignty and political independence'. In saying this, he echoed the sentiments of almost every sovereign government that has ever existed. States put their own survival first in foreign policy priorities, and close links are always to be found in state bureaucracies between departments of foreign affairs and departments of defence. In economic affairs, Evans said, Australia's interest was 'in trying to secure a free and liberal international trading regime' so that the country could add to its income from exports. And he found a third set of national interests in being 'a good international citizen' on issues such as the global environment, peacekeeping, arms control and international health problems.[9]

Howard dropped Labor's phrase 'good international citizenship' from the moment he became prime minister. Howard was no less concerned than Labor about the national interest but defined it more narrowly. His government called its 1997 foreign affairs white paper *In the National Interest*, defined as 'the security of the Australian nation and the jobs and standard of living of the Australian people'. Six years later, seeking a title for the next foreign affairs white paper, the government chose *Advancing the National Interest* and defined it as 'the security and prosperity of Australia and Australians'.[10] Meantime the foreign policy bureaucracy peppered its reports with references to 'the national interest'. The standard DFAT description of what it does, repeated in annual reports under the Howard and Rudd governments, is that it protects and advances 'Australia's national interests through contributions to international security, national economic and trade performance and global cooperation'.[11]

States have natural interests that derive from their geographical position, size, population, military strength, economic situation and so on. Each state's interests will endure, the argument goes, and governments of quite different political persuasions will end up reaching much the same conclusions about them. At one level this kind of categorising is commonsense. The larger a state is, the more numerous are likely to be its connections with other states on matters of trade, investment, migration and defence, and the more far-flung its range and influence. And the position of states on the globe, in particular the position of borders, certainly exercises a continuing effect on the way political leaders conduct foreign policies. Consider, for example, the natural defencelessness of a country like Poland, sandwiched for centuries between more powerful states on the flat plain of Northern Europe; the natural protection from invasion enjoyed by New Zealand, a chain of islands far from other states; the necessary deference which Canada and Mexico must show to their powerful neighbour the United States; or the likelihood of border problems wherever populations are driven to flee from political persecution or famine.

Geography matters. But much else also determines foreign policy, especially in a world increasingly bound together by an integrated global economy. Any oversimplified schema of what lies behind national interests—like the one based on geography—is bound to mislead. The risk in all such oversimplifications is to impute to international events an inevitability which they do not possess, and to assume that foreign policy is the product of a careful weighing of the national interest. Foreign policies are far less planned and far more haphazard than neat theories allow. Governments, after all, consist of human beings. Ministers are often unaware of what other ministers are doing, government departments sometimes compete, and 'policy' is frequently a matter of responding to the flow of events.

What states do externally, moreover, is often deeply influenced by internal politics and by the attempts of governments to make themselves popular. A foreign war, for example, can divert attention from the failures of a government on the home front, bolster its standing and—in liberal democracies—add to its chances of re-election. Some observers believe such considerations encouraged both the Argentine and British governments to go to war over the Falkland Islands in 1982. Domestic pressure groups such as the pro-Israel and Cuban-American lobbies in the United States modify the way in which governments define national interest.

'National interest', 'national security', 'vital interest', 'strategic interest': phrases such as these abound in the debate among policymakers and advisers over the direction of Australian foreign policy, and they are rarely defined because their meaning is supposedly obvious. Not everyone in Australia would agree with the present government's way of defining Australia's national interests, however. And this disagreement, like disagreements among Americans or Japanese or Indonesians over their national interests, points to the fact that 'interests' are political in meaning. They do not exist in an indisputable way; instead, people in authority appeal to them as a way of garnering support for particular foreign and defence policies. When people argue for a course of action as being in the national interest, they really mean that others should adopt their view of what the national interest is. Some argue, for example, that governments pursue class interests in foreign policy by seeking to preserve an economic order that enriches part of the population while keeping the rest poor; others see precisely the same policy as one that serves the nation as a whole.

SECRECY AND FOREIGN POLICY

The making of foreign policy is far from being a democratic process if by *democratic* we mean 'determined by the people'. And while the same may be said of all kinds of policy, the description applies particularly to foreign policy.

In the foreign policy context, *intelligence* means 'information', a vital resource in formulating foreign and defence policy. Information is what the public lacks and the government has. Some of it comes from secret or semi-secret intelligence-gathering organisations based in Canberra. Since 11 September 2001 all these organisations have mattered more to the Australian government, some are now better funded, and one has had its legal powers considerably extended.

Three are located within the Department of Defence and specialise in collecting or interpreting military information. The biggest is the Defence Signals Directorate (DSD), whose primary task since it was founded in 1947 has been to work with sister agencies in the United States, Britain, Canada and New Zealand to collect signals intelligence (SIGINT) by intercepting electronic communications of all kinds made by telephone, radio and the Internet, for example. DSD also advises and assists federal and state governments on maintaining the security of their information, most of which is now stored electronically. DSD used to collect satellite imagery of the earth as well, but that task has been performed since 2000 by the Defence Imagery and Geospatial Organisation (DIGO), which directly supports the Department of Defence with precision navigation and targeting as well as providing information to government for important events and venues with security implications. The responsibility for analysing and interpreting military intelligence falls to the Defence Intelligence Organisation (DIO), which has specialists working on developments in different parts of the world such as the Middle East, on security threats such as terrorism, and on weapons systems, missiles, defence systems and weapons of mass destruction (WMD).

Three more intelligence organisations operate outside the Department of Defence. The Australian Security Intelligence Organisation (ASIO) has a domestic focus and answers to the Attorney-General. ASIO's task is to protect Australia from politically motivated violence, espionage, attacks on Australia's defence system and acts of foreign interference. Since the Bali bombings ASIO has taken a special interest in Jemaah Islamiyah, the extremist Islamic group in Indonesia, and conducted investigations into Australians who have trained with al-Qaeda and other terrorist organisations. The Howard and Rudd governments increased ASIO's funding, a new central office building for it appeared in Canberra, and ASIO staff tripled in numbers to about 1800 between 2003 and 2011. Rudd added a counter-terrorism control centre to ASIO.

In the wake of the terrorist attacks in the United States and Indonesia, the Australian Parliament passed a new ASIO Act: the *Australian Security Intelligence Organisation Legislation Amendment (Terrorism) Act 2003*. The Act widened ASIO's powers, and permitted the detention of suspects as young as sixteen for

48 hours without charge and for longer if further warrants were obtained. The Act also allowed the police to prevent detainees from making contact with their families and lawyers. Critics see it as an unnecessary assault on civil liberties and a weakening of traditional legal protections for the accused.

The Office of National Assessments (ONA), established by the Fraser government, provides broad-ranging political assessments of foreign developments directly to the prime minister and maintains close liaison with PM&C. ONA officers, who often specialise in a particular area or country, become accustomed to producing reports that are succinct enough to be read by the prime minister. ONA has a much smaller staff than ASIO, but has also been given its own building. According to budget statements, ONA appears to cost about $50 million a year.

The Australian Secret Intelligence Service (ASIS) is responsible to the foreign affairs minister and works from DFAT headquarters in Canberra. The function of ASIS is to obtain intelligence about the capabilities, intentions or activities of people or organisations outside Australia in cases where the government believes they are relevant to national security, to liaise with equivalent organisations overseas such as the American CIA or Britain's MI6, and to conduct counter-intelligence operations. ASIS cost $263 million in the financial year 2009–10, and its funding has increased considerably in recent years.[12]

In order to coordinate the activities of these rapidly expanding intelligence organisations, the Rudd government established the National Intelligence Coordination Committee in 2008, and announced plans to establish a national security college at the Australian National University. The *secret state*, as these organisations have been called, is not quite as secret or unaccountable as it used to be. Intelligence agencies now maintain websites with unclassified information for the public, including, in some cases, how much they cost the Australian taxpayer. And the *Intelligence Services Act 2001* gave DSD and ASIS a clear legislative basis as well as providing for the establishment of a parliamentary committee to exercise oversight of key intelligence organisations. This is called the Parliamentary Joint Committee on ASIO, ASIS and DSD. It has seven members, four from the government and three from the Opposition.

Yet the traditions of the secret state remain strong. This is a parliamentary committee that works under restrictions. It lacks a 'broad right to call witnesses', and key ministers—the Minister for Foreign Affairs, the Minister for Defence and the Attorney-General—must check its reports to ensure that it does not reveal sensitive matters of national security. Intelligence became a matter of public controversy in Australia after the 2003 Iraq War, when the government sent Australian troops to Iraq partly on the basis of intelligence pointing to the dangers of weapons of mass destruction in the hands of the regime of Saddam Hussein. The Senate, which was not under government control, referred the issue to the Parliamentary Joint Committee on ASIO, ASIS and DSD, asking it to establish the nature, accuracy and independence of the intelligence available to the government, and the way the government used that intelligence to justify its decision. The committee concluded that a divergence of emphasis and judgement over the weapons issue emerged between intelligence assessment agencies in the six months before the war on Iraq and that the DIO was more 'sceptical and circumspect' than ONA in reaching firm conclusions about WMD.[13]

The affair raised two key issues. One was the dependence of Australian intelligence organisations on their foreign counterparts, and the problem that arises when different parts of foreign intelligence bureaucracies, such as the American Department of Defense and the American Central Intelligence Agency, disagree in their assessments or are engaged in institutional competition. Another was political influence, and the extent to which intelligence agencies might be tempted to offer the information that their political masters want rather than report things as they are. One ONA employee, Andrew Wilkie, resigned on the grounds that 'the war had little to do with weapons of mass destruction and almost nothing to do with al-Qaeda'. He was alarmed by the sudden change of tone in the reports going from ONA to the prime minister in 2002, from carefully qualified assessments to 'a more gung-ho position on Iraq', and he attributed it to the government's 'extraordinary request in mid September for an unclassified report for use in the preparation of the Prime Minister's and Foreign Minister's speeches'. Wilkie believed the request 'sent a clear signal to ONA to deliver something much stronger' even though its experts knew this to be potentially misleading.[14] Clearly, if intelligence agencies are to be of any use, they must be free to report their findings without fear of government criticism or direction.

The secret side of making Australia's foreign and defence policy is a reminder of continuities in the way sovereign states behave. Under the British monarchy from which Australia's system of government ultimately derives, the Crown claimed a prerogative (or exclusive privilege) to deal with other states on behalf of the nation and to enter into treaties with them. This tradition, which gives governments extraordinary freedom of action in foreign and defence policy, survives in modern Australia. As Hawke told parliament at the start of the 1991 Gulf War, the 'decision to commit Australian forces to combat is of course one that constitutionally is the prerogative of the Executive'.[15] The state in the twenty-first century retains its old association with the exercise of political power in its crudest form—physical violence—and with the universal practice of spying.

Foreign policy possesses a mystique which arises from this historic association of the state with defending national territory, waging war, spying on enemies and raising armed forces. People tend to treat with respect and even awe the area of government activity dedicated to preserving and protecting the state itself. Governments depend on the mystique when they say foreign policy decisions serve 'the national interest', when they censor parliamentary reports, and when they act without reference to the customary institutions of accountability such as Cabinet and parliament. As much as anything else, this mystique explains why the making of Australian foreign policy remains secretive, centralised and insulated from democratic pressures.

FURTHER READING

The policy-making process

Blue Ribbon Panel Report, *Australia's Diplomatic Deficit: Reinvesting in our instruments of international policy*, Lowy Institute, Sydney, 2009.

Connery, David, *Crisis Policymaking: Australia and the East Timor crisis of 1999*, ANU E Press, Canberra, 2010. (How Australia made policy on East Timor in 1999, pointing to the dominance of the executive, the importance of the National Security Committee of Cabinet, and the impact of the crisis on national security policy making.)

Gyngell, Allan and Michael Wesley, *Making Australian Foreign Policy*, 2nd edn, Cambridge University Press, Cambridge, 2007. (The most comprehensive and informed study of the making of Australian foreign policy, based in part on survey evidence.)

The 'national interest'

Marsh, Ian, ed., *Australia's Choices: Options for a prosperous and fair society*, UNSW Press, Sydney, 2003. (Chapters 8–10 are perceptive essays by Michael Wesley on different ways of conceiving Australia's 'national interest'.)

Media

Tiffen, Rodney, *Diplomatic Deceits: Government, media and East Timor*, UNSW Press, Sydney, 2001. (An evaluation of Australian reporting on East Timor 1975–99, arguing that it took cues too often from official policy.)

—— 'Marching to whose drum?—Media battles in the Gulf War', *Australian Journal of International Affairs*, vol. 46, no. 1, 1992, pp. 44–60. (How the military managed international media coverage of the Gulf War.)

Parliamentary foreign policy committees

Burton, Kate, *Scrutiny or Secrecy? Committee oversight of foreign and national security policy in the Australian Parliament*, Parliamentary Library, Canberra, 2005. (A perceptive analysis of the role of the executive in making foreign policy, barriers to parliamentary scrutiny, the notion of national interest and the mystique of national security.)

Capling, Ann and Kim Richard Nossal, 'Parliament and the democratization of foreign policy: The case of Australia's Joint Standing Committee on Treaties', *Canadian Journal of Political Science*, vol. 36, no. 4, 2003, pp. 835–55. (A rare analysis of the role of the JSCOT.)

Verrier, June, 'Parliament and foreign policy', in *Trading on Alliance Security: Australia in world affairs 2001–2005*, James Cotton and John Ravenhill, eds, Oxford University Press, Melbourne, 2007, pp. 305–28. (Examines, inter alia, the roles of the Joint Standing Committee on Foreign Affairs, Defence and Trade and the Joint Standing Committee on Treaties, the parliamentary debate on the Iraq War and the 'adversarial relationship between the Executive and the Legislature'.)

Secret state

Cotton, James, 'After the flood: Foreign policy and the management of intelligence', in *Trading on Alliance Security: Australia in world affairs 2001–2005*, James Cotton and John Ravenhill, eds, Oxford University Press, Melbourne, 2007, pp. 329–51. (Argues that the Howard government managed intelligence poorly, especially over Iraq, and in ways that did not serve Australia's interests.)

Gyngell, Allan and Michael Wesley, *Making Australian Foreign Policy*, Chapter 7: 'The Australian intelligence community'. (A valuable one-chapter guide to Australia's intelligence agencies.)

Parliament of the Commonwealth of Australia, *Intelligence on Iraq's Weapons of Mass Destruction*, Parliamentary Joint Committee on ASIO, ASIS and DSD, Canberra, 2003. (Censored but revealing on the operations of the intelligence agencies.)

Richelson, Jeffrey T. and Desmond Ball, *The Ties That Bind: Intelligence cooperation between the UKUSA countries—the United Kingdom, the United States of America, Canada, Australia and New Zealand*, Allen & Unwin, Sydney, 2nd edn, 1990. (Exhaustive.)

Wilkie, Andrew, *Axis of Deceit: The story of the intelligence officer who risked all to tell the truth about WMD and Iraq*, Black Inc. Agenda, Melbourne, 2004. (The man who resigned from ONA over the decision to invade Iraq tells why he considered the war 'neither justified nor lawful'.)

Websites

Joint Standing Committee on Treaties: <www.aph.gov.au/house/committee/jsct/index.htm>
Parliamentary Joint Committee on Foreign Affairs, Defence and Trade:
    <www.aph.gov.au/house/committee/jfadt>
Senate Standing Committee on Foreign Affairs, Defence and Trade:
    <www.aph.gov.au/Senate/committee/fadt_ctte/index.htm>

PART II

Security

The United Nations and international security

- What was the impact of the end of the Cold War on the role of the UN in international security?
- Did the Allied invasion of Iraq weaken the authority of the UN Security Council in international security?
- What are the limitations of collective security as an instrument for maintaining global peace?
- How has UN peacekeeping changed since the end of the Cold War?
- Why did Australia send peacekeepers to Cambodia, Somalia, Rwanda and East Timor?
- In what ways is the international community, or parts of it, redefining the meaning of sovereignty in the international system of states?
- Should UN peacekeepers be given the authority to enforce peace or should they be returned to their traditional and more restricted role?
- Is the 'responsibility to protect' a useful global norm in international relations or one that is likely to be misused?

Large states can exercise influence by themselves. Smaller states depend on international organisations for their voice to be heard. Like most middle powers Australia has long had a positive attitude towards participating in the UN and contributing to its diverse activities. These include social and economic development, education, the care of refugees, humanitarian relief, health, labour standards, human rights and arms control. Except on the fringes of politics, Australians do not share the strong anti-UN sentiment of many Americans.

Yet the two major political groupings have differed in enthusiasm for the UN in its international security role. Like the American president George W. Bush,

John Howard did not think the UN should always be central to international peace and security. That is why Australia sent Australian troops to the 2003 war on Iraq without the approval of the UN Security Council and in the face of opposition from traditional Western friends such as France and Germany. The Howard government proved little inclined to encourage a vigorous UN role for Australia, except where UN objectives coincided with Australia's, as in East Timor. East Timor, however, is a very large exception, and Australia's military and civilian commitments to a succession of UN operations there since 1999 have been on a scale that dwarfs anything previously undertaken by Australia in this field. In the words of the former foreign minister Alexander Downer, 'East Timor was a UN, and Australian, success story'.[1]

Labor has traditionally favoured the UN more than the Coalition has. The Labor foreign minister of the 1940s, H.V. Evatt, played a significant part in drafting the UN Charter and was president of the UN General Assembly from 1948 to 1949. Labor governments have welcomed the internationalism of the UN more than Coalition ones, and Australia under Hawke and Keating became, more than ever, an active UN participant. Hawke appointed his best foreign affairs officers to the Australian mission to the UN in New York and defended UNESCO, the United Nations Educational, Scientific and Cultural Organization, when other Western countries were condemning it for being politicised and poorly managed. Keating headed the government that sent unprecedented numbers of Australians overseas as UN peacekeepers. As foreign minister, Gareth Evans was a strong defender of the UN from the start, he was intimately involved in expanding UN peacekeeping after the Cold War and he campaigned for reforms aimed at making the UN effective in international peace and security. During his time as foreign minister Australia participated in a number of UN peacekeeping operations, including the largest one ever, which was in Cambodia.

Prime Minister Kevin Rudd followed in the Labor tradition by seeking closer involvement for Australia in the UN after the Howard years. In particular, he committed Australia to seek a non-permanent seat on the UN Security Council in 2013–14. After talks with the UN Secretary-General Ban Ki-moon in 2008, Rudd told journalists: 'We need to enhance the United Nations' activities in terms of multilateral security, multilateral economic engagement, and also in the area of social policy and human rights as well. And on top of that, climate change and the environment. To be fully effective in that, we have to be fully engaged with the United Nations, and that is what we intend to do.'[2] Rudd's first overseas trip as foreign minister was to the UN in New York.

THE RISE AND FALL OF THE 'NEW WORLD ORDER'

The defining fact of international life after the end of World War II was the Cold War. For more than 40 years the world lived in a condition of long-term confrontation between two great states, two ideologies and two political systems, with each side organised in military alliances and close to general military mobilisation. Then came the events of the second half of the 1980s. In the space of a few years reforms introduced by the Soviet leader Mikhail Gorbachev led to the removal of communist governments in Eastern Europe and the collapse of communism in the Soviet Union. The Cold War was in retreat from 1987, when Gorbachev and Reagan agreed to remove intermediate-range nuclear weapons from Europe under the Intermediate Nuclear Forces Treaty. By 1989 Gorbachev was no longer willing to intervene to keep communist governments in power in Eastern Europe. They quickly crumbled in Poland, Hungary, East Germany and Czechoslovakia. By 1990 the Cold War was over and the United States was left the world's only superpower.

The central authority of the Soviet Union collapsed in 1991 and its constituent parts broke away to form new states, fifteen in all including Russia. The first to achieve international recognition were the Baltic Republics of Lithuania, Latvia and Estonia, which regained the political independence lost half a century before when Soviet troops occupied them in 1940. In the wake of a failed coup in Moscow, the rest of the Soviet Union unravelled in a succession of declarations of independence by new countries: Armenia, Azerbaijan, Georgia, Moldova; the Central Asian republics of Kazakhstan, Kyrgyzstan, Tadjikistan, Turkmenistan and Uzbekistan; and, after the Ukrainians voted for independence in December 1991, the three Slav republics of the Ukraine, Belarus and Russia. At the end of 1991 the Red Flag no longer flew over the Kremlin, the Soviet Union ceased to exist and Russia took its place on the Security Council of the UN.

The end of antagonism between the superpowers focused attention on the future of global peace and security. The Cold War was itself an international security system in which the superpowers had the final say about what happened in international politics. Now that the Cold War was over a new system was needed to replace it. Some observers claimed that a new system, international business civilisation, was already working. The world, they said, was entering an era when a peaceful struggle for market shares in a liberal economic order had finally superseded geopolitics and the resort to war by the major powers. They argued that the new interdependence between states was different in character from all previous interdependence; in the global village, economies are linked by transnational corporations and financial institutions to such a degree that governments must cooperate with each other and with large multinational business corporations in order to maintain their domestic legitimacy. In their view there is nothing to gain in this interdependent economic order by the forceful acquisition of territory and everything to gain from playing by the rules. International business civilisation, it was argued, is inherently peaceful. The American scholar Francis Fukuyama believed that people almost everywhere now accepted the virtues of the market economy and democracy and wanted to follow the American example.

A further source of optimism for some was that the end of the Cold War meant the end of proxy wars fought by the superpowers. For decades the United States and the Soviet Union, unwilling to risk direct military confrontation, had backed opposing sides in Third World conflicts in order to inflict indirect damage on each other. In Cambodia and Afghanistan, for example, the superpowers lent military support to opposing sides in civil wars. At the end of the 1980s new opportunities for peace appeared in both countries as the superpowers withdrew military assistance, and some observers predicted that the new international security situation would bring peace elsewhere as well. Without the Cold War, they argued, external powers would lack the incentive to perpetuate internal and regional conflicts, and the world would be more peaceful.

The end of the Cold War also offered the UN the chance to play a much greater role in global peace and security. Some said the moment had arrived in twentieth-century history when the international community could at last create a global security system of the kind proposed by the American president, Woodrow Wilson, after World War I. This was a system in which all the leading states would be committed to peace and would join together in a common cause against international outlaws. After the extraordinary disaster of World War I, Wilson was foremost in believing that the way to world order was by establishing a system of international rules of conduct which would make war a thing of the past. In effect, war would be outlawed, just as violence between individuals within states was outlawed. To enforce the rules, the League of Nations was established, and the principle of collective security provided that states which broke the rules were to be punished by the rest. The idea was that, if a state engaged in an act of armed aggression, all the other states would join in acting against it, the aggression would be checked and peace would be restored. But collective security came to grief in the 1930s, as Japan invaded China, Italy conquered Ethiopia, and Hitler's Germany expanded its borders by force and embarked upon a path of world domination, all without effective resistance from the League of Nations.

World War II destroyed illusions about outlawing war but a concept of collective security remains in the UN Charter, which says the UN's primary purpose is 'to take effective collective measures for the prevention and removal of threats to the peace, and for the suppression of acts of aggression …' The mechanism for collective security under the UN may be found in the peace enforcement provisions of Chapter VII of the charter, which allows the Security Council to 'take such action by air, sea, or land forces as may be necessary' for the restoration of international peace and security. For as long as the Cold War lasted, however, this section of the charter remained theoretical. Genuine collective action of a military kind by the UN against states was out of the question because it required the most powerful countries to agree about the form that security should take, and no such agreement could be reached while the United States and the Union of Soviet Socialist Republics (USSR) were at loggerheads. The Americans favoured the extension of their idea of security worldwide while the Russians favoured theirs.

Under the UN Charter the United Nations consists of the General Assembly to which all member states belong (currently 192) and the Security Council which has five permanent members and ten non-permanent members elected by the General Assembly for terms of two years. Australia has been a non-permanent member four times since World War II, most recently between 1985 and 1986. The five permanent members of the Security Council are the major states that emerged victorious from World War II: the United States, France, Britain, China, and the Soviet Union which, since 1991, has been replaced by Russia. The Security Council is meant to deal with the settlement of disputes and with international acts of aggression. The important point for collective security is that each permanent member state has veto power over any Security Council decision and can unilaterally prevent the UN from acting. On some occasions during the Cold War—the Korean War is one—ways were found to circumvent the veto so as to give a major military action the imprimatur of UN legitimacy, but these were the exception. In general, the superpowers, the Soviet Union especially, exercised veto power to prevent large-scale militarised peace enforcement under the UN.

Collective security and Iraq

The test for collective security came when Iraq invaded the oil-rich state of Kuwait in 1990. For the first time since World War II the Soviet Union and the United States stood together on a major international security issue. They voted together in the Security Council for economic sanctions against Iraq and later for military action authorised by the UN. In the Gulf War of 1991, allied military forces led by the Americans inflicted a crushing defeat on the Iraqis and drove them out of Kuwait in less than two months. Australia enthusiastically supported action against Iraq, sending two guided missile frigates and a tanker to the Persian Gulf to help the Americans even before the UN had become involved, and later it sent a medical team to serve on US Navy vessels. Afterwards, Iraq was compelled to open its borders to UN inspection teams, and Australian naval forces continued to contribute to patrolling the Gulf. The Security Council subsequently authorised the deployment of a peacekeeping mission to monitor the ceasefire between Iraq and Kuwait.

Bob Hawke and Gareth Evans depicted the Gulf War as a watershed between past and future. From now on, they said, there was a good chance that global security would be based on respect for international law, collective security and an effective UN, and Australia should participate in the Gulf War in order to hasten the arrival of what the American president George Bush senior called the 'New World Order', one in which the UN would function as originally intended. The Security Council authorised member states to 'use all necessary means' to 'restore international peace and security' in Kuwait, and 37 countries joined the United States in the military campaign against Iraq.[3] While Operation Desert Storm was in essence an American military campaign directed from Washington and for American reasons, the principle of obtaining UN authority for the war had been maintained, and international law had been upheld.

The same applied to the first war fought by the United States and its allies after the attacks of 11 September 2001, the war against the Taliban regime in Afghanistan. The Security Council supported those in Afghanistan who sought to overthrow the Taliban, and condemned it for providing sanctuary for Osama bin Laden and his al-Qaeda terrorists. So when Australia sent 1550 troops, including special forces, to assist the United States in the war against terrorism, it did so with the general support of Security Council resolutions. Resolution 1368 of 12 September 2001 called on states to bring the perpetrators of the terrorist attacks on the United States to justice and recognised 'the inherent right of individual or collective self-defence in accordance with the Charter'. The Taliban crumbled quickly in the face of overwhelming American air power and intense fighting by their Afghan enemies in the Northern Alliance. Kabul, the capital, fell in November and the last large city, Kandahar, was surrendered by Taliban forces a month later. The UN helped to maintain security after the defeat of the Taliban through the UN-authorised International Security Assistance Force (ISAF), and in providing humanitarian assistance to a country that had been racked by armed conflict for many years.

What would happen to UN collective security, though, if the world's only superpower were itself to become the aggressor? According to many experts in international law, that was the situation when the United States led a 'coalition of the willing' in the 2003 invasion of Iraq without Security Council approval. They said a pre-emptive strike against a regime that had not attacked first was illegal and therefore constituted aggression. In 2002 President George W. Bush announced a new doctrine of pre-emptive military intervention, according to which the Americans would take military action against states believed to pose threats even before they acted against the United States:

> The United States has long maintained the option of preemptive actions to counter a sufficient threat to our national security. The greater the threat, the greater is the risk of inaction and the more compelling the case for taking anticipatory action to defend ourselves, even if uncertainty remains as to the time and place of the enemy's attack. To forestall or prevent such hostile acts by our adversaries, the United States will, if necessary, act preemptively.[4]

Iraq was the country that attracted the United States' first experiment with pre-emptive military intervention. The country was under the dictatorship of Saddam Hussein, the same man who had led his nation when the American-led coalition drove Iraqi troops out of Kuwait twelve years before. The American president is reported to have said that this was 'the guy who tried to kill my dad'.[5] In 1991 the Americans had considered going all the way to the capital Baghdad to depose Saddam Hussein, but decided against it, leaving him in charge while the international community imposed sanctions on Iraq. The Americans created a kind of protectorate for the minority Kurdish population in northern Iraq, freeing them from rule by Saddam Hussein, while the UN required him to surrender and destroy Iraq's stockpiles of weapons of mass destruction (WMD). UN inspection teams visited Iraq on numerous occasions during the 1990s in order to enforce these requirements, but without being finally satisfied that all the weapons had been accounted for. War threatened in 1998, when the United States wanted to force Iraq to open its weapons sites to inspection, but was averted when the UN Secretary-General Kofi Annan negotiated a peaceful resolution of the dispute. On that occasion Australia sent

110 Special Air Services troops, together with 100 intelligence and technical officers, to the Persian Gulf to join the Americans in an expected assault on Iraq. They were not needed, but they were a tangible sign of Australia's loyalty to its great and powerful friend across the Pacific.

We cannot yet know precisely when the United States decided to invade Iraq. Some say President George W. Bush intended to invade Iraq from the day the terrorists struck New York and Washington in 2001, others that he determined upon it sometime in 2002, while Bush depicted himself as driven unwillingly to war in 2003 only after exhausting all avenues for peace. Whatever the timing may have been, Saddam Hussein had no clear connection with the terrorists of 9/11—indeed, fanatically fundamentalist Muslims such as Osama bin Laden saw him as an apostate—but Bush knew he could use the threat of international terrorism as cover in justifying the forceful overthrow of the Iraqi regime. To do that convincingly, he needed to emphasise the threat posed to world security by Iraq's possession of WMD and by its repeated refusals to cooperate with UN weapons inspectors. Chemical, biological and nuclear weapons held by a regime like that of Saddam Hussein, he argued, might well find their way into the hands of international terrorists, with incalculable risks to targeted populations. From September 2002 onwards, President Bush and his British and Australian allies, Tony Blair and John Howard, stressed Saddam Hussein's possession of WMD as a key reason he posed a threat and why he ought therefore to be removed.

The role to be played by the UN in the Iraq dispute mattered a great deal. The UN is imperfect but also indispensable, and since World War II has been responsible for developing mechanisms of international cooperation that have moderated the natural tendency for a law of the jungle to operate in global affairs. If the Security Council were to approve armed action against Iraq under the UN Charter, as it had done in 1991, the precedent of international cooperation on issues of global security would be upheld. The same would be true if the Security Council failed to give approval and the United States accepted its ruling. But if UN approval was not forthcoming, and the world's one superpower proceeded to invade anyway, then international law and the international security system would be weakened.

In the end, this third possibility is what happened. At the insistence of the British prime minister Tony Blair, the United States went to the Security Council in November 2002 and succeeded in persuading it to pass resolution 1441, which gave Iraq 'a final opportunity to comply with its disarmament obligations' and warned that, otherwise, it would face 'serious consequences'.

While the US military build-up in the Persian Gulf continued, the inspectors of the UN Monitoring, Verification and Inspection Commission, with a staff of 260 drawn from 60 countries, undertook hundreds of inspections of likely sites where WMD might be stored, only to find nothing beyond a few old missiles and cluster bombs.

The Bush administration poured scorn on these UN efforts, claiming to have firm evidence of Iraq's WMD through its own intelligence agencies. Then in March 2003 the United States introduced a second resolution into the Security Council seeking authorisation for war, even though the inspection teams were reporting progress and seeking time to complete their work. With the hotter weather in Iraq approaching, the United States was keen to launch the invasion. This time the historic alliances across the Atlantic failed to hold, with Germany and France promising to vote against the resolution, and with the French veto ensuring it would be defeated. So the Americans withdrew their resolution and went to war anyway, denouncing the UN as ineffective because it did not follow their wishes.

Australians split on the Iraq issue. Demonstrations in the capital cities against Australia going to war were larger than any since the Vietnam War. The Labor Opposition in parliament, which had supported sending troops to Iraq in 1991 and 1998, voted against Australia's involvement in the war. Australia 'pre-deployed' troops in the Persian Gulf from January 2003, the prime minister claiming he had not made a final decision about Australia's military involvement. Critics thought his argument disingenuous, and were not surprised when he committed Australia to the war in March. 'The government's principal objective', he told parliament, 'is the disarmament of Iraq', and in an address to the nation he stressed that 'we are determined to join other countries to deprive Iraq of its weapons of mass destruction, its chemical and biological weapons, which even in minute quantities are capable of causing death and destruction on a mammoth scale'. The Saddam Hussein regime, far weaker militarily than its opponents, soon collapsed and the war was over within weeks, the Americans assuming control for a transitional period while they endeavoured to replace dictatorship with democracy. Keeping the peace in a turbulent Iraq was to prove far more deadly for American soldiers than fighting the war.

The record of the last half-century suggests that, when Australia goes to war alongside the United States, the principal motivation is to reassure the Americans that Australians are the most reliable of allies. 'It wasn't a time in our history to have a great and historic breach with the United States', Downer later said of Australia's decision to participate. 'If we were to walk away from the American alliance, it would leave us as a country very vulnerable and very open.'[6] The disarmament of Iraq is therefore unlikely to have been the government's principal objective in joining in the war, and has since proved a slender reed on which to support the decision, any more than the defeat of the Taliban is likely to have been the main reason for the presence of Australian troops in Afghanistan under the Rudd and Gillard governments. Once they had charge of Iraq, the Americans despatched their own teams of experts to comb the country for WMD, only to discover after months of searching that their intelligence agencies were wrong and the UN was right. No WMD could be found. Contrary to American claims, the UN inspection process had in fact achieved Iraq's disarmament.

AUSTRALIA AND UN PEACEKEEPING

The war on Iraq showed that UN collective security which, after all, is another name for UN war making, has inherent limitations as a basis of international security. Yet collective security is only one approach to the problem. The end of the Cold War gave the UN an enhanced role in using another, more modest instrument of international peace and security. This is peacekeeping in the form of military observer missions and peacekeeping forces, a UN invention that has operated since the 1940s under the authority of the UN Charter. Once the superpowers began to cooperate in the Security Council, the way was open for the UN to send peacekeeping missions all over the world. Within a few years the number and size of UN peacekeeping operations rose dramatically. In the 40 years from 1948 to 1988 the Security Council authorised a total of thirteen peacekeeping operations, including observer missions; in the next twenty years to 2008 it authorised a further 48, some on a scale never seen before. UN operations since the end of the Cold War have taken peacekeepers not only to traditional destinations in the Middle East and South Asia, but also to South-Eastern Europe, Africa, Central Asia, Central America and South-East Asia. More than 100,000 military personnel, police and observers were serving in UN peacekeeping operations in 2010, an unprecedented number.

The tasks, or mandates, given to peacekeepers have multiplied. Peacekeeping during the Cold War, except in a few cases, was confined to tasks that presupposed warring parties had at least reached a truce even if they had not signed a formal ceasefire agreement. Lightly armed, and with instructions to shoot only in self-defence, peacekeepers during these years commonly manned observation posts, patrolled buffer zones, maintained checkpoints at borders, supported local monitoring teams and took other peaceful measures to ensure that the military status quo was preserved. Their success in keeping the peace, in some cases for decades, rested on maintaining absolute impartiality between contending parties.

Most UN missions now have wider mandates, and most peacekeepers do much more than patrol ceasefire lines and report violations. Peacekeepers have become responsible for demobilising armies, training military forces, repatriating and resettling refugees, organising national elections, removing landmines, defending safe areas declared by the UN, securing the delivery of humanitarian aid and, in some cases, assuming the administrative tasks of an entire national government for a limited period. Confronted by countries that are disintegrating because of civil conflict, the international community has given the UN the task of doing nothing less than rehabilitating states. UN peacekeeping is being transformed and redefined, so that the general term *peacekeeping* is now used to encompass a variety of different UN functions. Previously restricted to being Chapter VI operations under the UN Charter, many recent UN peacekeeping missions have been under Chapter VII mandates which allow for peace enforcement and robust rules of engagement.

The international community expected countries like Australia to contribute to the increasing number of UN peacekeeping missions authorised after the Cold War. Unlike Canada, Australia had rarely been a generous supplier of UN troops even though the UN traditionally looked to middle and small powers for peacekeeping contingents. Just as the new era of peacekeeping arrived, however, and with Evans as foreign minister, Australia abandoned its traditional reluctance and sent significant numbers of troops—more than 300 in each case—to complex peace operations in Namibia, Cambodia, Somalia and Rwanda. Australia also sent smaller contingents to Afghanistan, the Western Sahara and Mozambique in the early 1990s. By far the largest commitment of UN peacekeepers by Australia, numbering more than 5000 troops at its peak, came under the Coalition government in a series of missions to East Timor. Under Kevin Rudd and Julia Gillard Australia made small contributions to UN peacekeeping missions while reserving most of its troops and police serving overseas for operations under Australian command, though even those operations were usually in support of UN missions. Australia had more than 3000 troops overseas in 2010 but fewer than 300 directly deployed in UN peacekeeping missions in Cyprus, Sudan, Afghanistan, East Timor and Iraq.

Until East Timor, the high point of Australia's diplomatic and military involvement in UN peacekeeping was in Cambodia. As foreign ministers, Hayden and Evans gave Cambodia a greater priority in foreign policy than might have been expected for a poor South-East Asian country with a population of fewer than 8 million, minimal trade with Australia and—apart from a recent intake of refugees—few links of any kind with Australia. One reason was that official Australian perceptions of South-East Asia shifted during the 1980s. Canberra policymakers recognised that a peaceful, prosperous Cambodia could contribute to a general regional stability that was in Australia's long-term interest, especially in view of the potential importance of South-East Asia to Australian standards of living. Another reason was that Cambodia's strategic circumstances changed with the end of the Cold War, making peace possible rather than merely desirable. The civil war that ravaged Cambodia during the 1980s was nurtured from outside by powers supporting one or other of the country's four armies. Cambodia was under a Vietnamese military occupation endorsed and backed by the Soviet Union. When Gorbachev changed course, so did Vietnam, withdrawing its forces in 1989 and leaving the way open for a peace settlement.

Evans seized the opportunity to involve Australia by devising a blueprint for major UN intervention in Cambodia, *Cambodia: An Australian peace proposal* (1990), a series of working papers which suggested in detail how the parties could be brought to an agreement, how the UN could organise a transition to legitimate government and what it all would cost. The Red Book, as these papers were known, was then refined in diplomatic negotiation to become the basis on which the peacekeeping operation proceeded. Just as Australia offered technical expertise to the Cairns Group and over the chemical weapons issue, helping accelerate the conclusion of the Chemical Weapons Treaty in 1992, so it did the same to expedite diplomatic progress over Cambodia.

The origins of the Cambodian conflict lie in a decade of disaster during the 1970s. Under Norodom Sihanouk, Cambodia succeeded throughout most of the 1960s in quarantining itself from the war which was raging in the country next door, Vietnam. But Sihanouk was overthrown in 1970 by a CIA-sponsored coup and replaced by a client of the Americans, Lon Nol, whose government was soon engaged in a civil war with communist insurgents, above all with a previously obscure group of revolutionaries called the Khmer Rouge. In a vain attempt to help Lon Nol, the Americans targeted rural Cambodia in massive bombing campaigns which continued even after the bombing of Vietnam stopped. Bombing had the opposite effect to that intended. Far from strengthening the Lon Nol regime, which grew ever weaker, the American bombing boosted the popularity of the Khmer Rouge, whose military forces came to control more and more of the countryside and finally occupied the Cambodian capital, Phnom Penh, in April 1975.

The Khmer Rouge was good at rebellion but its leaders were loathsome rulers. Just as the horror of civil war ended, the horror of the new Khmer Rouge government began. Led by Pol Pot, the Khmer Rouge comprised communist fundamentalists whose bizarre vision of revolution entailed forcing all 3 million residents of the capital to leave and work in the countryside. Pol Pot was fascinated by power and by war. The Khmer Rouge abolished the use of money, forbade all forms of private property, closed most schools, separated children from parents, attempted to eradicate Buddhism, persecuted ethnic minorities and divided the population into two groups—*base people*, who were under Khmer Rouge control at the time of the takeover, and *new people*, who were not and who were therefore immediately suspected of disloyalty. The Khmer Rouge summarily executed tens of thousands of the country's most talented people, including many doctors and nurses, on the grounds that their educational level showed they belonged to the exploiting classes. Directly and indirectly, the Khmer Rouge caused the deaths of between 1.5 million and 2 million people in three and a half years.

Vietnam decided in 1978 to intervene in Cambodia and put an end to the chaos on the other side of the border. Backed by a mutual security pact with the Soviet Union, Vietnam invaded Cambodia on Christmas Day 1978 and overran all but the mountainous Thai border region in three weeks' fighting, installing an army of occupation that was to remain until 1989. Vietnam established its own puppet government, one which ensured Vietnam's own border security and which brought a far more moderate kind of communist rule to Cambodia. The international community condemned the invasion as a breach of the UN Charter, as indeed it was. Yet among the choice of evils which then faced the Cambodian people, Vietnamese military occupation was preferable to continued rule by the Khmer Rouge. The point was not lost on Australia, which at first recognised the Khmer Rouge as part of the legitimate government of Cambodia and then withdrew that recognition in favour of the view that no faction was legitimate.

Many of the problems which UN intervention addressed in the 1990s arose in the first years of Vietnamese occupation. Vietnam conquered most, but not all, of Cambodia. As a result, fighting continued, abating each wet season and resuming again when the rains stopped. The fighting was mostly between the Cambodian government and Vietnamese forces on one side, and the Khmer Rouge on the other, but the Khmer Rouge was not the only Cambodian faction with its own armed forces. There were two others as well, the royalist National United Front for an Independent, Neutral, Peaceful, and Cooperative Cambodia (FUNCINPEC) and the Khmer People's National Liberation Front (KPNLF) which were dug in like the Khmer Rouge along the Thai border where they could receive assistance from foreign patrons and attempt to harass and undermine the Cambodian government. The Thai border was also where South-East Asia's largest refugee problem surfaced as about 600,000 Cambodians sought security in refugee camps outside their country. Those who stayed behind had to live with the danger of landmines laid just beneath the surface of the soil where they could be detonated by a footfall. Troops on all sides laid millions of landmines which, over the years, have given Cambodia one of the world's highest proportions of physically disabled people.

In the Agreements on a Comprehensive Political Settlement of the Cambodia Conflict, signed in Paris in 1991, the four Cambodian factions joined nineteen interested countries in laying the basis for UN intervention. The Paris agreements gave the UN a formidable list of tasks, one that went far beyond the traditional mandate for peacekeeping forces. As its name suggested, the United Nations Transitional Authority in Cambodia (UNTAC) was to become the effective government of the country during the transition from war to peace, and from authoritarian to democratic government. UNTAC's task was to disarm and demobilise about 400,000 troops, regulars and irregulars, from all factions including the Khmer Rouge; to repatriate and resettle 370,000 refugees from the Thai border camps; to verify the complete withdrawal of Vietnamese forces; to clear landmines; and to organise a democratic election for a new government. The 16,000 troops deployed by UNTAC came from 32 countries, a further 3600 police were sent from abroad, and administrative personnel numbered over a thousand. Altogether, UNTAC cost US$1.9 billion.

Australia contributed to the diplomacy that led to UNTAC and to UNTAC itself. UNTAC's force commander was an Australian, Lieutenant General John Sanderson. Australia sent senior Defence Force staff for UNTAC headquarters, a small group of Australian Federal Police, staff from the Australian Electoral Commission to help organise the election and, for UNTAC's military component, about 460 troops who were joined by 40 New Zealanders in the Force

Communications Unit. Small detachments of this unit spread across Cambodia to set up a communications net based on radio, telex, fax, telephone, modem and a helicopter courier service. One detachment used purifying equipment to produce Cambodia's purest drinking water from the muddy and contaminated Mekong River. Australia provided the largest national contingent of electoral officers. UNTAC benefited Australian companies. Morris Catering Australia won the contract to feed all 16,000 UNTAC troops and in the final phase of the program the military handed over communications to the Australian company Telstra, whose international telephone exchange and pay phones have since become a large commercial investment in the country.

UNTAC was a notable accomplishment. It succeeded in repatriating refugees from camps where they had been languishing for more than a decade. Against all expectations, the elections under UNTAC proceeded as planned, giving ordinary Cambodians their first experience of choosing a government. UNTAC's human rights program encouraged Cambodian activists to form human rights groups as catalysts of opposition to corrupt and authoritarian government. And at a broader level, the UN peace process released Vietnam and Cambodia from diplomatic isolation and prompted a flow of aid from Western countries.

Australia also sent soldiers for the UN to Somalia on the Horn of Africa. Anarchy engulfed the desert country after the overthrow of its president in 1991. As fourteen different factions fought for control, government collapsed, its place taken by marauding groups of militia, bandits and what were called *technicals*. The technicals were teenage gang members who survived by initiating protection rackets, manning checkpoints, providing escorts and driving four-wheel-drive vehicles armed with machine guns. As order disintegrated, Somalia suffered widespread starvation: about 300,000 people died during 1992. Non-government aid agencies sent food but, lacking military force, they could not get it to those who were starving. The technicals and militias took it instead.

Public opinion was decisive in the UN's intervention in Somalia. As television took news of the Somalian crisis to Western publics, they demanded that the governments do something to help. People held high expectations for the UN intervention in Somalia. They expected armies in the post–Cold War world to be able to save starving people. In fact, the intervention was a mixed success at best, and demonstrated the considerable limitations of the UN in such circumstances.

The UN intervention proceeded in three stages, each representing a different way in which the UN is now becoming involved in security and humanitarian crises. In effect, the UN experimented with new forms of intervention as the Somali political situation changed and as American public opinion pushed the Clinton administration first one way and then the other. The first stage, UNOSOM (United Nations Operation in Somalia), was traditional Chapter VI peacekeeping, designed to maintain and monitor a ceasefire. The ceasefire quickly failed and so the Security Council authorised a peace enforcement oper-ation under Chapter VII.

Unlike earlier peace enforcement authorisations, however, the Security Council's resolution 794 of 1992 was not in response to an act of international aggression or to end a civil war. It was purely for the purpose of ensuring the delivery of humanitarian aid. This part of the intervention, while authorised by the UN, was under the command of the United States, which led a coalition of countries, including Australia, in what was called UNITAF, or the Unified Task Force of Operation Restore Hope. When UNITAF came to an end in May 1993, the Security Council again broke new ground by creating the first UN peace enforcement operation under direct UN control, UNOSOM II.

Most of the Australians involved were part of the early, successful period of UN intervention and were in and out of Somalia quickly. The 937-strong Austra-lian battalion group was not in Mogadishu, where some Somalis resented the UN presence, but in south-western Somalia in a district called Baidoa. After the main Australian contingent departed, the situation in Somalia (as it happens) deterio-rated. UN peacekeepers were caught up in the murderous factional politics of the country they had come to help. While UNITAF had at least restored some order and fed starving villagers, UNOSOM II degenerated into hostilities between the UN and the powerful Somalian faction leader General Aidid, whose militia succeeded in killing and humiliating UN troops. Aidid's forces ambushed Paki-stani UN peacekeepers, killing 24. The UN responded by waging a minor war in which American and Malaysian peacekeepers as well as Somalis lost their lives. Then American television news showed Somalis dragging the body of an American peacekeeper through the streets. Reacting to public outrage, President Clinton withdrew American troops in 1994. All UN peacekeepers of any nationality were gone by 1995, leaving looters to steal what they could from the ruins of the UN compound in the capital Mogadishu, and leaving the idea of UN peacekeeping blemished in the eyes of Western publics, especially in the United States. Somalia still had no effective government in 2010. A tiny proportion of Somalian children went to school, roads had become sandy tracks, and traders sold weapons and passports to anyone who could pay for them.

The small central African country of Rwanda presented the international community with an even more desperate situation than Somalia. Conflict between the two ethnic groups of Rwanda was not new, nor was the slaughter of one side by the other, but the mass killings of Tutsis by Hutus in 1994 was on an unprecedented scale and amounted to an act of genocide. Half a million people were killed and 2 million displaced from their homes in the space of a few months. Rwanda was a charnel house. The UN withdrew many of its 1500 peacekeepers during the worst of the massacres and was unable to construct a new force large enough to put an end to the chaos. By this time the United States and European countries were wary of new military involvements in peacekeeping. Apart from Canada, Australia was the only Western country to send substantial contingents to UNAMIR, the United Nations Assistance Mission for Rwanda. The two Australian medical support force contingents, each with more than 300 personnel who were in Rwanda in 1994 and 1995, were part of a force of over 5000 mainly drawn from African countries such as Ethiopia, Ghana, Zambia and Tunisia. Their task was to run a hospital for UNAMIR forces and, when they could, to treat refugees and assist with distributing food, water and medical supplies.

In comparison, since 1999, Australia's commitment to East Timor, in terms of personnel and resources, to the complex peace operations of the UN, has been on an unprecedented scale. The UN operations have been in six missions approved by the Security Council. The United Nations Mission in East Timor (UNAMET) organised the popular consultation at which the people of East Timor, after 24 years under the Indonesians, were able to vote on their future. The International Force in East Timor (INTERFET) followed, with a Chapter VII mandate permitting the use of 'all necessary measures' to restore security following the outbreak of widespread violence and destruction, a task quickly accomplished by thousands of troops from different countries under the command of an Australian, Major General Peter Cosgrove. Then came the UN Transitional Administration in East Timor (UNTAET), with the mammoth task of assuming responsibility for government in the territory and preparing it for independence. UNTAET was supported by a peacekeeping force drawn from 30 countries, and began by supplying emergency relief before moving to the politically difficult job of establishing a working government and civil service in a country devastated by disorder. The UN was attempting to create an independent and viable state where none had existed before, even more than it had attempted in Cambodia. Once East Timor declared itself independent on 20 May 2002, the Security Council established the UN Mission of Support in

East Timor (UNMISET) to provide law enforcement and security and to assist in developing the country's police force for the following two years. The United Nations Office in East Timor (UNOTIL) followed in 2005 but proved too small to respond to the disorders that broke out in 2006, and was replaced by the far larger UN Integrated Mission in Timor-Leste (UNMIT), a peacekeeping mission that has been there ever since.

The circumstances that gave rise to INTERFET point to the political complexities of organising a major UN military intervention at short notice. The 1999 ballot conducted in East Timor by the Australian Electoral Commission produced a nightmare result for the pro-Indonesian East Timorese militias which, with Indonesian military backing, had worked so hard to intimidate voters. Not only did almost everyone vote (98 per cent) but, of those, a mere 21.5 per cent opted to stay with Indonesia. The rest, an overwhelming majority of 78.5 per cent, wanted independence. Stunned and outraged, the militias set all to the torch in a rape of East Timor that was conveyed graphically to the world by the television organisations that had sent journalists to cover the vote. The British ambassador to the UN, Sir Jeremy Greenstock, travelling with a Security Council mission to East Timor in the midst of the chaos, found shops and businesses in the capital ransacked, and more than half the houses destroyed. He described Dili as 'hell on earth'.[7] World leaders from President Clinton to UN Secretary-General Kofi Annan and the Pope condemned Indonesia's patent failure to maintain security. As the international community determined upon intervention, Australia worked closely with the UN on how an intervention force might be organised. For the sake of speed, the force would need to be a 'coalition of the willing' with UN authority sent to restore order in advance of a normal UN peacekeeping operation which would take much longer to arrange. It would also need regional participation from South-East Asian countries, the agreement of Indonesia, and the backing of the United States. As it happened, national leaders and ministers from APEC countries were meeting in New Zealand at the same time. They included President Clinton, his Secretary of State Madeleine Albright, and senior representatives of four of the five permanent member states of the Security Council. Clinton, Howard and other leaders delivered a stark message to the Indonesian representative at the meeting: unless Indonesia agreed to accept an international intervention force, the IMF would consider blocking its access to funds, the lifeline of the government in Jakarta since the collapse of the economy in 1997. Indonesia therefore agreed, and the INTERFET operation proceeded.

One of the biggest challenges faced by the UN in East Timor was the repatriation of refugees. More than 500,000 people, or 70 per cent of the population, were estimated to have become refugees in the terror that followed the independence referendum. Some were internally displaced, and INTERFET soon provided the security that enabled them to go home and rebuild shattered villages. A greater difficulty was posed by the 250,000 people who crossed the border into Indonesian West Timor, some fearing retribution for having voted for integration, and the many others who were deliberately driven out of East Timor by pro-Indonesian militias who kept them in refugee camps. The key UN agency in this case was the UN High Commissioner for Refugees (UNHCR), whose staff was able to go to the camps in West Timor, reassure people they would not be killed if they returned, and arrange for them to go back across the border. The UNHCR workers were at great personal risk because the militias regarded them as the enemy. On one occasion militia fighters attacked the UN office in Atambua, West Timor, killing three UNHCR personnel with machetes in an attempt to bring the repatriation program to an end. Since the Indonesian government was unable or unwilling to provide security, the UN then withdrew from West Timor for a year. Nevertheless, more than 188,000 refugees had returned to East Timor by the end of 2001.

THE EVOLUTION OF A NEW NORM: THE RESPONSIBILITY TO PROTECT

Norms influencing the international system are standards of international practice that states come to accept as a consequence of changing circumstances. Such is the case with the responsibility to protect, now widely accepted as a permissible infringement of sovereignty if states fail to protect their populations from the grossest violations of human rights. The change in the way the international community defines sovereignty has come only since the 1990s; before then, sovereignty was seen as guaranteeing, without qualification, the right of a state to exercise authority within its territorial borders.

The UN experienced a renaissance after the end of the Cold War, and nowhere more than in peacekeeping. In effect the UN—no longer confining itself mainly to conflicts between sovereign states—acts on a new principle, the right of humanitarian intervention in the internal affairs of sovereign states. The UN, it was argued in the 1990s, should intervene to end civil wars like the war in Bosnia, stop countries like Somalia from falling into anarchy and mass starvation, prevent one community from massacring another as in Rwanda, and stop militias from wrecking a whole country as in East Timor. Public opinion, spurred on by television reports, pushed national leaders and the UN to do something, anything, to relieve human suffering in a succession of crises.

The fragmentation of states is now an important threat to international peace and security. While the end of the Cold War brought peace in some places, it encouraged armed conflict in others by removing the fear that a local or regional war would escalate into a global confrontation between the superpowers. The upsurge of ethnic nationalism in Eastern Europe and the former Soviet Union is an example. Ethnic nationalism in much of the Third World has been a constant presence since former colonies gained independence as new states in the 1950s and 1960s. Its origins in Africa, South Asia and South-East Asia lie in the mismatch between national groupings and state borders. Many new states formed after World War II embrace the territories of diverse peoples whose common history dates only from the time when Europeans came and established colonial borders. The 1990s saw a rise in ethnic nationalism and the outbreak of especially violent ethnic conflict in the Third World, as in the wholesale massacre of Tutsis by the Hutu people of Rwanda.

In part because armed conflict between ethnic groups is increasing worldwide, many more wars now occur within states than between them. The characteristic modern war is a civil war fought between government forces and rebels. Wars of this kind pose special problems for the UN, which was designed to deal with threats to peace and security of a quite different kind. The framers of the UN Charter had World War II in mind when they devised the Security Council and gave it powers to intervene in disputes. They thought of strong, unified states like Germany or Japan as threats to security, not weak, disintegrating ones such as Yugoslavia, Somalia or Rwanda. They imagined cross-border aggression, as when Hitler invaded Poland in 1939, and wars with clear lines separating the opposing forces, not complicated internecine wars where frontlines constantly shift, if they exist at all. In short, they constructed the UN to deal with wars between states, not wars within them.

The internecine conflicts that emerged in the 1990s were quite unlike wars between states. In Bosnia and Somalia the UN was drawn into peacekeeping situations where there was no peace to keep because the warring parties had not agreed on a ceasefire. The UN's solution was to give peacekeepers authority to use armed force in order to realise UN objectives such as the safe delivery of humanitarian aid. Peacekeepers became peace enforcers under the provisions of Chapter VII of the UN Charter. The new peace enforcement was not on the massive scale characteristic of a collective security action such as the Gulf War, but it was peace enforcement just the same. UN peacekeepers lost their customary neutrality and became participants in warfare. A number lost their lives in military actions directed against UN forces. Critics of the shift towards peace enforcement such as Ramesh Thakur said turning UN peacekeepers into a fighting force 'erodes international consensus on their function, encourages withdrawals by contributing contingents, converts them into a factional participant in the internal struggle, and turns them into targets of attack from rival internal factions'.[8]

The new situation prompted a wide-ranging debate about the proper role of the UN in international and intrastate security. In 1992 the Security Council asked UN Secretary-General Boutros Boutros-Ghali to propose ways of improving 'the capacity of the United Nations for preventive diplomacy, for peacemaking and for peacekeeping'. Boutros-Ghali replied with *An Agenda for Peace* (1992), in which he proposed a notion of peace that was positive (peace as justice) rather than negative (absence of war), and called for a more energetic and interventionist role for the UN in crisis situations. He said the UN should do a number of things it had not done before, among them preventively deploying troops where hostilities were likely and using peace enforcement troops to maintain ceasefires.

By 1995 Boutros-Ghali, dismayed by what had happened in Bosnia and Somalia, was counselling against peace enforcement in the typical conflicts into which the UN was now being drawn. These were civil wars, 'usually fought not only by regular armies but also by militias and armed civilians with little discipline and with ill-defined chains of command'. Now he thought there was nothing more dangerous for a peacekeeping operation than 'to require it to use force when its existing composition, armament, logistic support and deployment deny it the capacity to'.[9] Peacekeeping and peace enforcement were different and should be strictly separated. Peacekeepers should not also be peace enforcers, and the UN should return to traditional peacekeeping in which troops are impartial and do not use force except in self-defence.

The problem with limiting UN peacekeeping in this way is that it fails to allow for the complexities of conflict that actually emerge. The UN success in East Timor, for example, arose not from limiting peacekeepers but from giving them the robust mandate needed to intimidate militias who would otherwise have continued to lay waste to the country. East Timor also pointed to the difference between multinational forces such as INTERFET, 'coalitions of the willing' with UN authority, and blue-helmeted peacekeeping forces under direct UN control such as the force that supported UNTAET. When General Cosgrove commanded INTERFET, he answered to Canberra, and his operational head-quarters was well prepared to conduct military operations. His successor in command of the UNTAET force was appointed late, and had to create an oper-ational headquarters with minimal planning and resources, commanding his soldiers in accordance with UN regulations and financial requirements. The key advantage of multinational forces is that, unlike regular peacekeepers, they can intervene quickly. In East Timor's case, the intervention occurred fast enough to stop the militias carrying out even worse calamities, such as seizing the western districts of the country for Indonesia. Even under the UN Standby Arrangement System, which is meant to hasten interventions, national forces are committed to serve as peacekeepers in complex missions only within 90 days. For this reason, the UN is likely to continue to authorise multinational intervention forces to restore security while UN peacekeeping forces are organised.

Not everyone thinks humanitarian intervention is a useful practice to introduce into international affairs. Who, after all, is to determine whether an intervention is humanitarian or not? States will always say they are acting from the highest motives, and that their military forces are killing in a moral cause. However, the appeal to the principle of humanitarian intervention might be just a cover for imperialism. Others think the principle should be invoked, but only sparingly and carefully.

The UN Secretary-General, Kofi Annan, appealed for the international community to reach agreement on this issue, and the Canadian government responded by setting up the International Commission on Intervention and State Sovereignty (ICISS), co-chaired by former Australian foreign minister Gareth Evans. Annan asked: 'If humanitarian intervention is, indeed, an unac-ceptable assault on sovereignty, how should we respond to a Rwanda, to a Srebrenica—to gross and systematic violations of human rights that affect every precept of our common humanity?' Or as his successor Ban Ki-moon put it, 'Could sovereignty, the essential building block of the nation-state era and of the United Nations itself ... be misused as a shield behind which mass violence could be inflicted on populations with impunity?' In response to questions of this kind, the ICISS's report, *The Responsibility to Protect*, proposed a series of principles by which humanitarian intervention could be justified, arguing that there must be just cause involving large-scale loss of life or large-scale 'ethnic cleansing', and that the intervention must have the primary purpose of halting or averting human suffering. The intervention must be a last resort after all other avenues for resolving the crisis have been exhausted; it must be on a scale and with a duration and intensity proportionate to achieving human protection; and there must be reasonable prospects of success. ICISS pointed to the UN Security Council as the obvious body 'to authorise military intervention for human protection purposes'.[10]

The UN endorsed the principle of the responsibility to protect at its 2005 World Summit. The UN declared that just as every state 'has the responsibility to protect its populations from genocide, war crimes, ethnic cleansing and crimes against humanity', so too does the international community, acting through the United Nations, also have 'the responsibility to use appropriate diplomatic, humanitarian and other peaceful means, in accordance with Chapters VI and VIII of the Charter, to help to protect populations from genocide, war crimes, ethnic cleansing and crimes against humanity'.[11] The UN restricted the application of the responsibility to protect to four crimes and violations—genocide, war crimes, ethnic cleansing and crimes against humanity—and made the UN Security Council solely responsible for authorising force in implementing it. By then it was clear that states could use the new global norm on intervention for their own purposes. The Bush administration wanted to use the newly qualified definition of sovereignty to justify its foreign policy. Bush and Tony Blair, the British prime minister, argued that the US-led invasion of Iraq in 2003 was justified by the responsibility to protect the Iraqi people from the crimes of their leader Saddam Hussein. In 2009 Ban Ki-moon attempted to refine the principle, and restrain the misuse of the new norm, in a major UN report on how the international community should implement the responsibility to protect.

Australia's recent interventions in East Timor and Solomon Islands have been influenced by the changing international attitude to such intrusions into foreign states, but they are not cases of invoking the principle of the responsibility to protect as the UN defines it. Some see them instead as cases of cooperative intervention in which Australia proceeded at the request of the sovereign authorities in each case: the Indonesian government for East Timor in 1999, the East Timor government in 2006, and the Solomon Islands government in 2003 and 2006. Given the ability of more powerful states to engineer invitations to intervene from weaker ones, however, cooperative intervention is also potentially problematic.

THE UNITED NATIONS ADOPTS THE DOCTRINE OF THE RESPONSIBILITY TO PROTECT

Following the World Summit in 2005, the UN General Assembly adopted the '2005 World Summit Outcome', which included a global commitment to the new doctrine called the 'responsibility to protect'. The resolution included the following paragraphs:

138. Each individual State has the responsibility to protect its populations from genocide, war crimes, ethnic cleansing and crimes against humanity. This responsibility entails the prevention of such crimes, including their incitement, through appropriate and necessary means. We accept that responsibility and will act in accordance with it. The international community should, as appropriate, encourage and help States to exercise this responsibility and support the United Nations in establishing an early warning capability.

139. The international community, through the United Nations, also has the responsibility to use appropriate diplomatic, humanitarian and other peaceful means, in accordance with Chapters VI and VIII of the Charter, to help to protect populations from genocide, war crimes, ethnic cleansing and crimes against humanity. In this context, we are prepared to take collective action, in a timely and decisive manner, through the Security Council, in accordance with the Charter, including Chapter VII, on a case-by-case basis and in cooperation with relevant regional organizations as appropriate, should peaceful means be inadequate and national authorities are manifestly failing to protect their populations from genocide, war crimes, ethnic cleansing and crimes against humanity. We stress the need for the General Assembly to continue consideration of the responsibility to protect populations from genocide, war crimes, ethnic cleansing and crimes against humanity and its implications, bearing in mind the principles of the Charter and international law. We also intend to commit ourselves, as necessary and appropriate, to helping States build capacity to protect their populations from genocide, war crimes, ethnic cleansing and crimes against humanity and to assisting those which are under stress before crises and conflicts break out.

140. We fully support the mission of the Special Adviser of the Secretary-General on the Prevention of Genocide.

UN General Assembly, Resolution 60/1, *2005 World Summit Outcome*.

ASSESSMENTS

When the Howard government won office in 1996, it did not share Labor's eagerness for Australia to play a notable role in global organisations such as the

UN, especially a security role. The government argued that Australia had 'no strategic interests at stake' in situations such as those that arose in Somalia and Rwanda.[12] With just 52 peacekeepers in the field in September 1997, Australia came forty-third among countries contributing troops to UN operations. Yet two years later successions of RAAF Hercules C130 aircraft were landing at Comoro airport in East Timor with the Australian troops who were to begin Operation Stabilise under the authority of the Security Council. INTERFET was so successful that by the end of 1999 Howard had come to see East Timor as a triumph of Australian diplomacy and military prowess. 'I don't think this country has stood taller and stronger in the chanceries of the world than it does at the present time', he proclaimed.[13] The East Timor success shifted the emphasis in the Howard government's approach to the UN role in international security, and so did the terrorist attacks on the United States. The official tone became cautiously more positive. In a world where failing states could become incubators of terrorism, the UN could, after all, play a valuable role in reconstructing them.

Under Howard, Australia backed the UN on some issues of international security and not others, pulled one way by ideology and the other by the logic of events. The government that came to office determined to reduce Australia's participation in UN peacekeeping became the largest force contributor to one of the largest UN peacekeeping operations in the world, not just for a few months, but over a period of years. In the wake of the East Timor experience, the government predicted that 'coalitions of the willing', with UN endorsement, would be centrally important to maintaining global security in the future. When the next 'coalition of the willing' emerged, however, it was organised by an American president determined to proceed without UN authority. Forced to choose between the UN and the United States, Australia chose the United States. That could hardly have surprised anyone familiar with the Howard government's position, which was that, in cases where the UN was not able to respond to a security crisis, Australia would join coalitions in accordance with its national security and global interests. The war on Iraq placed Australia where the Howard government wanted it to be: with the United States under any circumstances, but with the UN only if that could also be arranged.

The Rudd government came to office promising a return to close involvement by Australia with the UN. Rudd initiated the International Commission on Nuclear Non-proliferation and Disarmament (ICNND) and sought a seat for Australia on the UN Security Council. He withdrew the Australian troops from Iraq, Labor having opposed their presence there from the beginning of the Iraq War on the grounds that the UN Security Council did not authorise the invasion, which was in any case a diversion from the war that really mattered in the battle against terrorists; namely, the war against the Taliban insurgency in Afghanistan. Rudd therefore boosted the Australian military commitment to Afghanistan, increasing the number of Australian troops there from 1100 to 1550 in 2009. The Australians were part of the International Security Assistance Force, consisting mainly of North Atlantic Treaty Organization (NATO) forces, which the UN Security Council specifically authorised as a Chapter VII operation from 2001. Like Howard, Rudd was pro-American, seeing the United States as a force for good in the world, but unlike Howard, Rudd wanted to return Australia to its customary place as an advocate for the UN to play a central role in international security.

FURTHER READING

Australia and the Iraq War

Barker, Geoffrey, *Sexing it Up: Iraq, intelligence and Australia*, UNSW Press, Sydney, 2003. (Argues that John Howard, like Tony Blair, manipulated intelligence advice in order to justify his government's decision to join with the US in the invasion of Iraq.)

Bell, Roger, 'Extreme allies: Australia and the USA', in *Trading on Alliance Security: Australia in world affairs 2001–2005,* James Cotton and John Ravenhill, eds, Oxford University Press, Melbourne, 2007, pp. 23–52. (Perceptive analysis of Australia's participation in the Iraq War, set in the wider context of alliance and domestic politics under the Howard government.)

Doig, Allen, James P. Pfiffner, Mark Phythian and Rodney Tiffen, 'Marching in time: Alliance politics, synchrony and the case for war in Iraq, 2002–2003', *Australian Journal of International Affairs*, vol. 61, no. 1, 2007, pp. 23–40. (Argues that by mid 2002 the US, the UK and Australia had decided to wage war 'while insisting that no decisions on war had been taken', thereby undermining public trust in government.)

Australia and UN peacekeeping

Berry, Ken, *Cambodia—From Red to Blue: Australia's initiative for peace*, Allen & Unwin, Sydney, 1997. (An account of Australia's role in the negotiations leading to the Paris Accords that made possible the UN Transitional Authority in Cambodia, the largest UN peacekeeping operation ever undertaken. Far too detailed, but authoritative nevertheless.)

Breen, Bob, *A Little Bit of Hope: Australian force—Somalia*, Allen & Unwin, Sydney, 1998. (Australia's peacekeepers in the Horn of Africa.)

——*Mission Accomplished, East Timor: The Australian Defence Force participation in the International Forces East Timor (INTERFET)*, Allen & Unwin, Sydney, 2000. (The key role played by INTERFET in bringing security to East Timor.)

Horner, David, Peter Londey and Jean Bou, eds, *Australian Peacekeeping: Sixty years in the field*, Cambridge University Press, Cambridge, 2009. (Australian peacekeeping since 1947; covers the Middle East, Namibia, Cambodia, Somalia, Rwanda, Bougainville, Solomon Islands and East Timor, among others, and examines the role of the ADF, the AFP and NGOs; excellent.)

Londey, Peter, *Other People's Wars: A history of Australian peacekeeping*, Allen & Unwin, Sydney, 2004. (Useful narrative account of Australian peacekeeping from 1947 to 2001.)

Smith, Michael G. with Moreen Dee, *Peacekeeping in East Timor: The path to independence*, Lynne Rienner Publishers, Boulder, CO, and London, 2003. (The best and most detailed account of the military intervention and later UN peacekeeping operation in East Timor, by an Australian military officer who played a key role in both.)

The responsibility to protect

Bellamy, Alex J., 'The responsibility to protect—five years on', *Ethics & International Affairs*, vol. 24, no. 2, 2010, pp. 143–69. (Argues that R2P has failed to create political will against atrocities since 2005 but 'has proven useful as both a diplomatic tool and as a policy lens'.)

——'The responsibility to protect and Australian foreign policy', *Australian Journal of International Affairs*, vol. 64, no. 4, 2010, pp. 432–48. (Traces Australia's contribution to the development of the R2P doctrine.)

Evans, Gareth, *The Responsibility to Protect: Ending mass atrocity crimes once and for all*, Brookings Institution Press, Washington, 2008. (The former Australian foreign minister argues that there are limits to R2P, which is not a justification for military intervention but a tool for assisting weak states to avoid atrocities.)

Global Responsibility to Protect. (The leading print and online journal examining the principle of the responsibility to protect, its application in practice and its development as an international norm.)

Thakur, Ramesh, 'Developing countries and the intervention-sovereignty debate', in *The United Nations and Global Security*, Richard M. Price and Mark W. Zacher, eds, Palgrave Macmillan, New York, 2004, pp. 193–208. (An expert on UN peacekeeping points to the risks of accepting humanitarian intervention as a principle of international relations.)

The Responsibility to Protect: Report of the International Commission on Intervention and State Sovereignty, Department of Foreign Affairs and International Trade, Canada, 2001. (Founding document on the R2P doctrine as a guide to the international response to gross violations of human rights.)

Wheeler, Nicholas J., *Saving Strangers: Humanitarian intervention in world politics*, Oxford University Press, New York, 2000. (Examines 1990s interventions in Iraq, Somalia, Rwanda, Bosnia and Kosovo, and argues that a new conception of international society and its responsibilities has emerged.)

Websites

The International Coalition for the Responsibility to Protect: <www.responsibilitytoprotect.org>
UN Peacekeeping: <www.un.org/en/peacekeeping>

6

Defence and regional security

- Is the old debate between 'forward defence' and 'continental defence' still relevant to Australia's security?
- Does the ANZUS alliance with the United States continue to serve Australia's security interests?
- What has been the impact of the 'war on terror' on Australian military and security relations with the United States?
- Should the expectation that China will transform the strategic situation in East Asia play an important role in Australian defence thinking, or is it exaggerated?
- What is Australia's defence policy to 2030 as outlined in the 2009 Defence white paper? Is it justified under the circumstances?
- What is the significance for Australia of the Lombok Treaty?
- In what ways does Australia seek to enhance regional security in South-East Asia and the Pacific Islands?
- What would be the best defence policy for Australia?

Defence and security are interrelated. Security is an all-encompassing concept, referring to everything that contributes to the protection and wellbeing of a national population. Defence is the recourse to arms to protect national territory or advance national interests. Diplomacy, trade, investment, immigration, intelligence and political relations with other countries can, under certain circumstances, be just as important in creating the environment in which Australia is secure. Defence was just one element in Australia's security alongside the others in the 1990s. At a time when the focus of international diplomacy was shifting decisively towards economics, traditional Australian concerns with maintaining military power and protecting populations from attack seemed less urgent, and governments calculated that they could achieve as much for national security by diplomacy as by military means.

Defence has since regained a central role in security, in both popular thinking and official judgement. From the time of the East Timor intervention in 1999, and especially after the 11 September 2001 attacks on New York and Washington and the Bali bombings of October 2002, the Howard government spent more on defence, added to the numbers of defence personnel, made major decisions about future defence equipment and maintained forces abroad on a continuous basis. The Rudd government proved even more willing than Howard to spend money on defence. Howard made much of Australia's military exploits, seeing them as a source of national pride; Rudd did the same. The people of the Australian Defence Force, he said in 2009, 'are a world-class group of professionals. They are the most valuable capability of a modern defence force. Theirs is our nation's highest calling. Supporting them is one of our greatest responsibilities in safeguarding our nation's security.'[1]

This chapter will chart recent defence and regional security policy in Australia in order to clarify key issues at a time when the strategic environment is changing rapidly.

DEFENCE: FORWARD VERSUS CONTINENTAL

The Vietnam War of the 1960s and 1970s revived an old controversy about how to defend Australia already referred to in Chapter 2. On one side were those who favoured *forward defence*, the doctrine that Australia is best defended by sending troops to fight enemies far from its shores. The theory was this: Australian troops, too few to play a decisive military role by themselves, join the much larger forces of a powerful ally on a foreign battlefield, the ally is delighted they have come, Australia wins credit, and the whole operation enhances the probability that the ally will come to its aid at times of peril in the future. On the other side were those who favoured *continental defence*, the idea that Australia's military forces should be confined to the task of defending the continent itself, or the continent and its immediate maritime surrounds, and that Australia has no place involving itself in foreign wars. Historically, the Coalition parties were more closely identified than Labor with forward defence, and the emphasis in defence policy shifted one way and then the other according to which side was in government. The approach of the Rudd government, however, suggested a new bipartisan consensus had emerged on this issue. The Rudd government perpetuated, and even accentuated, the forward defence posture adopted by the Howard government, arguing that a narrow 'defence of Australia' approach would be an abdication of Australia's responsibility 'as a capable middle power that is able to contribute to global and regional security, including by way of military means'.[2]

Forward defence has been the more influential of the two doctrines. The idea of forward defence not only powerfully influenced Australia's military planners but seeped into the popular consciousness. Enemy forces have directly threatened or occupied Australian territory only once—during World War II—yet Australian troops have fought in numerous theatres of war at other times. None of the Australians who saw battle in World War I did so to protect Australian territory from invasion and most were in armies on the other side of the world, in Flanders, northern France, Turkey and Palestine. After World War II, Australians joined in a succession of East Asian conflicts, none of which placed Australian territory directly at risk. Governments could not point to any immediate danger to Australian territory because there was none. So they claimed Australia had to fight in Korea, Malaya, Borneo and Vietnam to help its great and powerful friends and to guarantee Australia's security in the long term. The emphasis was on fighting the enemy, or the potential enemy, in other people's countries rather than on Australian soil. The mentality of forward defence made Australia a warlike nation.

A number of developments undermined the rationale of forward defence at the end of the 1960s. The Americans grew disenchanted with the Vietnam War and with the whole idea of sending troops to land wars in East Asia. The US president, Richard Nixon, speaking in Guam in 1969, said America would no longer send ground forces for the defence of Asia-Pacific allies involved in regional wars. The Guam Doctrine, as it came to be known, invalidated one of the principal justifications for Australia's involvement in the Vietnam War—the expectation that a grateful America would feel obliged to come to Australia's aid in some future time of peril. While many Australians still thought of ANZUS as a firm promise of American military protection, Australian military planners knew from the start that things had fundamentally changed. From now on nothing was guaranteed, if indeed it ever had been. The Americans might come to Australia's aid in the event of a regional attack on Australian territory or they might not. Australia would have to learn to defend itself. At the same time the United Kingdom, once the greatest colonial and naval power in the Far East, withdrew its military forces from everywhere in the region east of the Suez Canal. All that was left of the British in the region, apart from Hong Kong, was a military agreement between Britain, Australia, New Zealand, Singapore and Malaysia called the Five Power Defence Arrangements (FPDA).

The logic of the new situation was for Australia to bring troops and defence assets back from South-East Asia and to shift quickly towards defending the continent, but a decisive shift away from forward defence was delayed for more than fifteen years after the Guam Doctrine. The Labor prime minister Gough Whitlam ended Australia's participation in the Vietnam War, withdrew an army garrison from Singapore and initiated a major reconsideration of defence policy. The 1976 Defence white paper leaned towards continental defence but Australia swung back to forward defence under the Coalition government of Malcolm Fraser (1975–83), especially after the Soviet Union invaded Afghanistan and Cold War tensions flared between the superpowers. Fraser thought the Soviet Union was an expansionist power which could be checked only by a strong America loyally supported by allies such as Australia. He increased Australian naval and air surveillance of the Indian Ocean, sending maritime patrol aircraft to bolster the Australian presence at Butterworth RAAF base in Malaysia, and he permitted the Americans to use Darwin for the transit of B-52 bombers. Fraser was convinced that the Soviets' naval base at Cam Ranh Bay in Vietnam threatened regional stability.

The Hawke Labor government did not share these fears. Instead Labor wanted a clear, coherent statement of the assumptions behind Australia's defence policy—one that would reflect its preference for more independence—and commissioned Paul Dibb to review 'the content, priorities and rationale of defence forward planning'. In 1986 Dibb produced the *Review of Australian Defence Capabilities*, the most thoroughgoing reconsideration of Australian defence since World War II.

Dibb questioned the most cherished beliefs about Australia's defence and security. The first was about threats. Many people, not least serving military personnel, believed Australia to be threatened by an uncertain international situation and even to be in potential danger of invasion. Dibb found Australia to be one of the safest countries in the world. Far from being at risk, Australia faced 'no identifiable direct military threat', a global war between the Soviet Union and the United States was 'most unlikely' and there was 'no conceivable prospect of any power contemplating invasion of our continent and subjugation of our population'.

The proponents of forward defence had always found a threat to Australian national security somewhere in the world, whether in the war in Vietnam, the Soviet invasion of Afghanistan or instability in the Middle East. Dibb urged a less melodramatic approach. He thought the threats that Australia actually faced were not on the other side of the world, were not about conquest and were not the ones for which the Defence Force was preparing itself. They were low-level military contingencies such as harassment of fishing vessels, illegal incursions into Australian coastal waters or terrorist raids on offshore oil rigs. He wanted defence planners to prepare for the minor threats that were likely rather than for major threats that were improbable.

The second belief Dibb questioned was about Australia's national security interests. These, he said, were difficult to define at a time when Australia faced no real threat. In any case these interests were of different kinds, dividing into those over which Australia had a degree of control and those over which it did not. The Defence Force could never do much to secure certain national security interests—preventing global nuclear war, for example, protecting Australian economic interests worldwide or even maintaining a 'favourable strategic situation in South-East Asia and the South Pacific generally'. Better therefore to recognise the considerable limits to Australian power and concentrate on those national security interests which the Defence Force could reasonably be expected to maintain—'the defence of Australian territory and society from threat of military attack' and 'the protection of Australian interests in the surrounding maritime environment'.[3]

The third belief questioned by Dibb was about the ANZUS alliance. Hawke was strongly pro-ANZUS and his government reaffirmed Australia's commitment to the alliance on coming to office in 1983. The majority of Australians supported him on this issue and believed, almost as an article of faith, that ANZUS was fundamental to Australian national security. Dibb was not anti-ANZUS but he approached it in a sceptical spirit. He said ANZUS was worth having because the costs for Australia were not high (hardly the enthusiastic endorsement Australians were used to hearing), and he underscored the point that the alliance was a promise of consultation, not a guarantee of help. Still, for political reasons, Australia could hardly withdraw and the alliance provided practical benefits for Australia in the form of military intelligence, technology transfer and equipment.

Dibb proposed a strategy of denial, a 'defensive defence' policy that would give low priority to the distant projection of military power. What mattered most was Australia's area of direct military interest, most of which lay to the north. Australia should focus on defending this area, defined as the Australian continent and its maritime approaches including the Timor, Arafura and Coral seas, the Tasman Sea and the closer parts of the Indian Ocean, in all some 10 per cent of the earth's surface. Australia should undertake this defence by means of layers of interlocking barriers capable of blocking the advance of an enemy, if not far out to sea, then closer, and if not there, then on Australian soil. Such a focus would entail a different force structure, with new submarines, frigates and patrol boats and with fighter squadrons but without an aircraft carrier or a large complement of tanks; and it would mean relocating parts of the Defence Force to the north and west of Australia where they were needed from the south-east where they were not.

Labor hesitated to embrace this novel approach in its entirety, choosing selectively from among Dibb's recommendations instead. The proposals Labor liked were, first, to move defence facilities and personnel to Australia's north and, second, to structure the Defence Force so that at least in theory it could defend Australia against conventional attack without help from outside. These were the key elements in Labor's new policy of defence self-reliance, which has remained Australian defence doctrine ever since. As the 2009 Defence white paper put it, 'the most effective strategic posture continues to be a policy of self-reliance in the direct defence of Australia, as well as an ability to do more when required ...'[4]

The Hawke government rejected continental defence in its pure form as a 'narrow concept'. The foundation of defence policy did not become the task of protecting a strictly defined and limited area of direct military interest close to Australia and within its borders. Instead the government contemplated using 'elements of the Defence Force in tasks beyond our area of direct military interest in support of regional friends and allies', and replaced Dibb's essentially defensive strategy of denial with defence in depth, a posture designed to confront an adversary 'with a comprehensive array of military capabilities, having both defensive and offensive components'.[5] No wholesale withdrawal of Australian defence assets or troops from South-East Asia occurred, nor was there any reduction in Australia's inventory of offensive strike weapons as Dibb proposed.

Hawke's Labor government gave defence policy coherence, direction and a fresh sense of priorities. The ADF became a force designed to defend the continent against an attack with conventional weapons without outside assistance, and most defence decisions were assessed against that criterion. Yet Labor's defence policy was a political compromise, not a radical reordering of defence arrangements. The shift was away from forward defence and towards defending the continent of Australia either in it or near it, but Hawke was no more willing than other prime ministers to confine the Defence Force to the immediate defence of Australian territory or to abandon the option of sending expeditions of Australian troops to overseas theatres of war whether near or far away. Hawke did not want to seem disloyal to Washington. He said the new defence policy was properly described as 'defence self-reliance within an alliance' and signified no slackening in Australia's commitment to ANZUS because Australia could not have self-reliance without the vital alliance that ensured a constant flow of intelligence and technology.

John Howard went to the 1996 election standing for a stronger ANZUS. He wanted Australia back in a closer military relationship with the United States, and he wanted a greater emphasis on forward defence. The Coalition rejected Labor's definition of Australia's region of primary strategic interest as confined to South-East Asia and the South Pacific, and proclaimed a much wider definition instead, one that found Australian strategic interests at stake everywhere from North-East Asia to South-East Asia, the South Pacific and even South Asian countries such as India. The Coalition also discarded Labor's emphasis on defensive defence and low-level threats. In its place came a new emphasis on forward projection of forces and strike capability, and the promise to upgrade high technology weapons systems including the F-111 and FA-18 fighter aircraft and the navy's guided missile frigates.

For financial reasons, both Labor and Coalition governments wanted fewer Defence Force personnel. Between the late 1980s and 1996 Labor reduced the size of the ADF from 69,000 to 57,000 military personnel and from 24,000 to 19,000 civilians. To begin with, the Howard government planned even deeper cuts, with a radical restructuring that would have left a force of just 42,500 but, under pressure from the service chiefs, it settled for 50,000. The ambitious tasks Howard had assigned to the ADF were to be achieved with smaller numbers. The number had returned to more than 55,000 by 2010.

DEFENCE POLICY UNDER THE HOWARD GOVERNMENT

Secrecy obscured the extent of Australia's return to forward defence under Howard. The classified version of *Australia's Strategic Policy*, not for public consumption, is said to have contained numerous references to forward defence operations and to Australian deployment alongside the United States in North-East Asia. When a regional security crisis arose, however, it was much closer to Australia, being just 400 kilometres across the Timor Sea from Darwin. As the situation in East Timor deteriorated in the early months of 1999, the government ordered the Defence Force to be ready to deploy considerable forces within 28 days. In the end, troops were deployed in just five days once the decision was made to intervene. The ADF responded swiftly and effectively, leading a multinational force with a UN mandate to restore security. East Timor—Australia's largest overseas military deployment since the Vietnam War—showed how quickly and seriously the regional situation for Australia could worsen, and how ready Australia needed to be for future interventions of this kind. Meantime, religious violence erupted in the eastern Indonesian islands of Ambon and Maluku; the province of Papua attempted to break away from Indonesia; Papua New Guinea (PNG) experienced civil disorder; and coups occurred in Fiji and Solomon Islands. All these countries and territories lie close to Australia. For the first time in decades, Australian defence policy was being made not in the vacuum of wondering what threats might arise, or on the basis of a routine response to American requests as in the Gulf War, but against a background of sending more than 5000 Australian troops to a neighbouring state.

The Howard government's Defence white paper, *Defence 2000: Our future Defence Force*, reiterated the familiar justifications for the American alliance: military cooperation with the United States gave Australia access to US military technology, and uniquely valuable opportunities to train and exercise; ANZUS was a part of a network of alliances that kept the United States committed to the defence of the Asia-Pacific region; and ANZUS promised American help in time of need. In practical terms Australia's close military relations with the United States dictated a high degree of 'interoperability' in military equipment, and in this way influenced Australian decisions about force structure and capability. As defined by Brendan Nelson, defence minister in the Howard government, *interoperability* is 'the structured effort by two or more countries in an alliance to ensure that their forces can operate together seamlessly. In practical terms this means things such as operating procedures, common communications links, common doctrine and standards, and compatible equipment.'[6] The need for interoperability with the Americans remains a central theme of Australian weapons acquisitions.

Events soon overtook the government's defence planning. In the wake of the 11 September 2001 attacks on New York and Washington the Howard government quickly invoked the ANZUS alliance, with its promise that treaty partners would come to each other's defence, and sent troops to assist the United States in the war on the Afghan Taliban regime that had sheltered Osama bin Laden's Islamic terrorist al-Qaeda movement. Then came the shock of 12 October 2002, when terrorists bombed nightclubs on the island of Bali in Indonesia, killing and injuring hundreds of innocent tourists. Among the dead were 88 Australians, with many others injured. Whether or not the terrorists targeted Australians in particular, it was reasonable to imagine they had. Australia, many thought, was now as much in the sights of the terrorists as the United States. When the United States appealed for help in invading Iraq and overthrowing the regime of Saddam Hussein, Australia joined the United Kingdom as one of only three allies who responded by sending troops to the war on Iraq in 2003. Like its allies, Australia claimed Iraq held stockpiles of weapons of mass destruction, which posed a serious risk to the rest of the world.

'We are in no doubt that the strategic landscape has changed', the government said in its *Defence Update* of 2003, and it identified global terrorism and weapons of mass destruction as creating 'renewed strategic uncertainty'. The assumptions of the 2000 Defence white paper were already seen as outdated. Instability in what the government called Australia's 'troubled region' now assumed new significance because of what it might portend for the spread of terrorism. Muslim fundamentalist groups in South-East Asia such as Jemaah Islamiyah were no longer irrelevant to Australian security, and neither was the collapse of government in Pacific Island countries such as Solomon Islands. In a world of terrorism, a failed state, the government thought, might one day become a base for terrorists. In the official view, the implications for defence of the new strategic uncertainty were these: the Defence Force was now less likely to be needed to defend Australia against conventional attack, but more likely to be called upon for operations in Australia's immediate neighbourhood, and with coalition partners in other parts of the world. There would be more Afghanistans and more East Timors.

The Bali bombings engendered a sense of threat in Australia, and the Howard government invoked that threat in explaining why it was sending yet more troops abroad, this time to restore order in Solomon Islands. Australian troops and police led a regional intervention force of more than 2000 troops and police who entered Solomon Islands in mid 2003. Within the space of four years the Howard government sent troops to four overseas destinations—East Timor, Afghanistan, Iraq and Solomon Islands—and was gaining a reputation for willingness to use the military instrument in the service of foreign policy. Between 850 and 1300 ADF personnel were in operational areas in Afghanistan,

Kyrgyzstan and the Persian Gulf from late 2001, and, although some were with-drawn from Afghanistan a year later, Australian troops returned to that theatre in 2005 and were there five years later. At the same time the government created a 'domestic terrorism response structure' to enable the Defence Force to deal with serious terrorist incidents on Australian soil. The Special Operations Command was formed in 2003, and included tactical assault groups of special forces units and the Incident Response Regiment, which was trained to deal with chemical, biological, radiological, nuclear or conventional explosive incidents both at home and in support of Australian forces overseas. The Howard government also used the Defence Force to prevent refugees from reaching Australian territory across its northern maritime approaches.

DEFENCE POLICY UNDER THE RUDD AND GILLARD GOVERNMENTS

By the time Labor was elected in 2007, hundreds of Australian troops were in Iraq, Afghanistan, East Timor and Solomon Islands, and a small number had been deployed briefly to Tonga following riots in 2006. Except in the case of Iraq, Labor shared the Coalition's view that keeping troops overseas was in Australia's national interest. And like the Coalition, Labor fully supported the ANZUS military alliance with the United States. ANZUS was a formal military alliance between three countries—Australia, New Zealand and the United States—until the mid 1980s, but the nuclear-free stance of New Zealand at that time led to a crisis in its relations with the US, which withdrew its security guarantee to New Zealand in 1986. The ANZUS Treaty has never been abrogated, merely suspended in the case of security relations between New Zealand and the US, and each year Australian and American leaders meet in AUSMIN, or the Australia–United States Ministerial Consultations. Australia cooperates closely with both New Zealand and the United States in military matters.

Fighting together in the 'war on terror' has given Australia more access to American intelligence, led to more Australians being placed in US military commands, and lent new prominence to the alleged need for interoperability between US and Australian military forces. Principles on interoperability were agreed at AUSMIN 2004, and they are beginning to take effect in joint training exercises by the two countries. The idea that interoperability is desirable also influenced the Rudd government's defence policy.

THE GOVERNMENT DECIDES UPON MILITARY EXPANSION

... The principal task for the ADF [Australian Defence Force] is to **deter and defeat armed attacks on Australia** by conducting independent military operations without relying on the combat or combat support forces of other countries. This means that the ADF has to be able to control our air and sea approaches against credible adversaries in the defence of Australia, to the extent required to safeguard our territory, critical sea lanes, population and infrastructure.

After ensuring the defence of Australia from direct attack, the second priority task for the ADF is to **contribute to stability and security in the South Pacific and East Timor**. This involves conducting military operations, in coalition with others as required, including in relation to protecting our nationals, providing disaster relief and humanitarian assistance and, on occasion, by way of stabilisation interventions.

The next most important priority task for the ADF is to **contribute to military contingencies in the Asia-Pacific region**, including in relation to assisting our Southeast Asian partners to meet external challenges, and to meeting our alliance obligations to the United States as determined by the Australian Government at the time. The strategic transformation of the region will mean that Australia should be prepared to make contributions—including potentially substantial ones—to such military contingencies in support of our strategic interests.

Finally, the ADF has to be prepared to **contribute to military contingencies in the rest of the world**, in support of efforts by the international community to uphold global security and a rules-based international order, where our interests align and where we have the capacity to do so.

As a result of these priorities, the ADF of 2030 will need to be a more potent force in certain areas, particularly undersea warfare and anti-submarine warfare (ASW), surface maritime warfare (including air defence at sea), air superiority, strategic strike, special forces, Intelligence Surveillance and Reconnaissance (ISR), and cyber warfare. It is the Government's judgement that these are the crucial areas which require particular attention to secure our unique strategic interests ...

Department of Defence, *Defending Australia in the Asia Pacific Century: Force 2030*, Canberra, 2009, p. 13.

As prime minister, Rudd commissioned a fresh statement of defence policy, which appeared in 2009 as *Defending Australia in the Asia Pacific Century: Force 2030*. The Rudd government's National Security Committee of Cabinet (NSC) met to discuss the central issues and provide strategic direction at each stage of the

2009 white paper's development. Unlike an earlier generation of Labor ministers in the Hawke and Keating governments, Rudd's ministers did not resist demands from some defence experts for a big build-up. In place of a focus on defensive defence, low-level threats and regional peacekeeping, they opted for 'offensive defence' and intensified key elements of Coalition defence policy; that is, forward projection of forces, strike capability, and high technology weapons systems.

Like the Coalition in 2000, Labor conducted community consultation through public meetings. Predictably, people said different things: many expected Australia to be strongly armed against attack, however remote that possibility might be; others wanted defence placed in a wider context of security that encompassed aid programs, diplomacy and the work of non-government organisations; and some reminded the government that the Defence Force would be increasingly called upon to offer disaster relief, humanitarian assistance and political stability in regional states. Having listened, the government could then do as it wished while claiming to have consulted the community.

The Rudd government introduced two new elements to Australia's defence planning. The first was to promise a new Defence white paper every five years, with the next due in 2014, and the second—optimistic in the extreme—was to save $20 billion by making savings and efficiencies in defence administration. A third element, introduced by Howard and perpetuated by Rudd, quarantined Defence from the ordinary operations of budgetary processes by guaranteeing that real spending would grow every year until 2030.

The Rudd government identified the principal task of the Australian Defence Force as being 'to deter and defeat armed attacks on Australia by conducting independent military operations without relying on the combat or combat support forces of other countries'. This statement reiterated 'self-reliance within an alliance', Australia's policy for the previous twenty years. The ADF's second priority task was 'to contribute to security and stability in the South Pacific and East Timor', a formulation echoing the 2000 Defence white paper while reflecting the experience of the years in between. This time the government talked of enhancing interoperability and coordination with civilian organisations, especially the Australian Federal Police, which had become Australia's key instrument in regional interventions to restore political stability.

Third in the list of priorities came 'contributing to military contingencies in the Asia Pacific region'—a familiar theme in Australian defence policy—but expressed this time in more urgent terms and on the basis of a new analysis of Australia's strategic situation. The central new idea in the Rudd government's defence thinking was that East Asia would be transformed strategically by the rise of China in the years to 2030. According to the white paper, Australia confronted a 'transformation of major power relations in the Asia-Pacific region', also described as a 'strategic transformation of the region over the period to 2030'. Said to be 'currently unlikely' in one part of the white paper, it was accepted elsewhere as a fact requiring an Australian response. And the response would be an unprecedented military build-up over twenty years: twelve submarines and 100 F-35 joint strike fighters together with new destroyers and frigates, cruise missiles, naval combat helicopters, early warning aircraft, armoured vehicles and enhanced cyber-warfare capabilities. The strategic transformation, according to the white paper, would arise from China's rising military power and rapid military modernisation, which would threaten the strategic primacy of the United States in East Asia.

The China question presented the government with a dilemma. On the one hand, China's vast appetite for resources underpins Australia's future prosperity; on the other hand, China's military power might one day match America's in Australia's part of the world. Should the government depict the rise of China as opportunity or threat? In the end, those who wrote the white paper argued both ways. 'In coming years', they said, 'China will develop an even deeper stake in the global economic system, and other major powers will have deep stakes in China's economic success. China's political leadership is likely to continue to appreciate the need for it to make a strong contribution to strengthening the regional security environment and the global rules-based order.' Elsewhere, they stressed that China would be the strongest Asian military power 'by a considerable margin', and that its military modernisation was more than might normally be expected even from a growing power. One side of the white paper's seemingly schizophrenic view of China was that it was a potential threat. This interpretation—contested by the white paper itself and speculative in nature—became the basis of the government's ambitious plans to arm Australia.

The fourth task of the Defence Force was to contribute to global security, and the government pointed to Australia's Afghanistan commitment as an example of such a contribution in action, in this case, alongside the Dutch, NATO and the Americans.

As a number of observers pointed out, *Defending Australia in the Asia Pacific Century: Force 2030*, the 2009 Defence white paper, was written as if defence policy is a silo remote from foreign policy, and it lacked the clarity and consistency of argument that characterised earlier defence white papers.

REGIONAL SECURITY

Governments differentiate between two kinds of security: global and regional. Global security may be defined as preventing war between the major powers. Regional security refers to keeping the peace within Australia's region, which is defined in different ways. Governments refer vaguely to Australia's 'wider region' and 'immediate region', leaving themselves room to manoeuvre, but generally speaking the wider region is South-East Asia and North-East Asia and the immediate region is PNG and the South Pacific.

With eleven countries—Indonesia, East Timor, Singapore, Malaysia, Brunei, the Philippines, Vietnam, Cambodia, Laos, Thailand and Burma—South-East Asia is home to 600 million people. North-East Asia consists of the emerging giant China, Japan, Taiwan, the far-east region of the Russian Federation, and the two Koreas, and is home to about a quarter of the world's population. The South Pacific is a region of 22 states and territories that stretch in a long arc across the Pacific Ocean from the Northern Mariana Islands in the north to French Polynesia and Pitcairn Island in the east. The total population is a mere 9.5 million, and only one country, PNG, has a population of more than 1 million. The rest are microstates or territories. But the proximity of these countries makes them important in any calculation of Australian national security. The island microstates depend heavily on foreign aid, much of which comes from Australia, and their long-term economic prospects—unlike those of most South-East Asian countries—are not promising.

Canberra considers political developments in both these parts of Australia's region to be critical to national security but has much greater influence over what happens in the tiny South Pacific, where Australia is a superpower, than in South-East Asia where it remains something of an outside player. As for North-East Asia, no part of the world matters more to Australian trade and economic prosperity, but Australia's influence there is marginal. China, Japan, Russia and the United States are the powers that will decide the fate of that region, and any Australian military involvement there would inevitably be as a minor ally of the United States.

Australia steadily moved closer to its South-East Asian neighbours diplomatically and militarily during the 1990s, though not as far as Australian governments wanted. For domestic political reasons, the Malaysian prime minister Mahathir Mohamad blocked Australia's full inclusion in regional affairs. He quarrelled with Paul Keating, opposed Australia over APEC, excluded

Australia from a forum of ASEAN and European Union leaders called the Asia-Europe Meeting, and declined to invite John Howard to a summit of regional leaders to mark the thirtieth anniversary of ASEAN in 1997. Not until Mahathir retired as Malaysian prime minister in 2003 did regional doors begin to open for Australia.

While Australia cannot be in ASEAN itself, Australia's representation at key regional organisations has grown in recent years. Australia is a founding member of the East Asia Summit (EAS), which is a forum for strategic dialogue among the leaders of the ten ASEAN states, together with those of China, Japan, India, the Republic of Korea, Australia and New Zealand, sixteen countries with half the world's population and, by some calculations, almost a third of its economic output. The US and Russia were due to join the EAS in 2011. Australia is also a founding member of the ASEAN Regional Forum (ARF), which has met each year since 1994. The ARF was the first diplomatic arrangement in modern South-East Asia set up to deal specifically with security matters. Over the years its membership has expanded to 27 countries—the ten ASEAN states, their major trading partners (the United States, Japan, China, Canada, India, South Korea, Australia, New Zealand and the European Union), three states from North-East Asia (Russia, Mongolia and North Korea), three from South Asia (Pakistan, Bangladesh and Sri Lanka), and two small developing countries close to Australia, East Timor and Papua New Guinea. The ARF has focused on confidence-building measures in disputed areas such as the South China Sea, coordination in disaster relief, and—since the emergence of terrorism as a regional threat—cooperation in counter-terrorism. In 2009 the organisation embarked on a plan to develop a capacity in preventive diplomacy; that is, initiating diplomatic intervention in advance of emerging security crises in order to ensure that they do not happen.

The East Asia Summit and the ARF are examples of diplomatic institutions that can add steadily to the security, stability and prosperity of the region that matters most to Australia economically. Through such institutions, and through a web of other treaties, initiatives and arrangements—multilateral and bilateral—Australia enhances both its security and its economic prospects. Enmeshment in diplomatic webs of this kind exemplifies a multidimensional approach to regional security. Australia does not rely for its security on military capability alone, but on diplomacy, economic links, development assistance, exchanges of people and ideas, and cooperation with regional states in dealing with terrorism, environmental threats, the drug trade, health problems and unregulated population flows, and defence is best seen in this wider context.

Defence links nevertheless matter for regional security. They not only foster cooperation between defence forces of different countries and create personal friendships between military officers across national borders, they also create transparency about military capabilities and intentions. The idea of multiplying Australia's South-East Asian defence links—as distinct from its diplomatic ones—goes back decades. Australia has bilateral defence arrangements with Singapore and Malaysia under the Five Power Defence Arrangements (FPDA), which originated in 1971 as a series of defence relationships between Australia, New Zealand, the United Kingdom, Singapore and Malaysia. The 2009 FPDA exercise, directed from Singapore's Changi Command and Control Centre, involved manoeuvres by the five nations in the South China Sea. Australia also conducts combined exercises with the military forces of Thailand, the Philippines and Brunei with frequent attachments, exchanges, study visits and training programs. Thai and Filipino soldiers joined the ADF as peacekeepers in East Timor. Australia's program of military cooperation, joint exercises and intelligence exchange with South-East Asian countries has expanded since the 1990s, and at one stage the Defence Force was exercising more frequently with South-East Asian countries than with the United States, though not on so large a scale. Australian governments realised in the 1990s that South-East Asian countries would become richer, stronger and technologically more advanced and would therefore be valuable as strategic partners. The approach was designed to match Australia's multiplying economic links with military ones.

Global terrorism lent new urgency to developing such links with Australia's regional neighbours. Australia hosted an ARF workshop on managing the consequences of a terrorist attack as early as 2003. The workshop dealt with issues such as search and rescue, treating mass casualties, and undertaking police investigations into a terrorist incident. At the same time Australia cooperated with Indonesia in establishing the Jakarta Centre for Law Enforcement Cooperation, which trains police from South-East Asian countries in the techniques of investigating, identifying and prosecuting terrorist suspects. In the view of the former Australian foreign minister Stephen Smith, Australia and Indonesia have had 'tremendous success against Jemaah Islamiyah, particularly in Indonesia'.[7] By 2010 Australia had signed counter-terrorism agreements with fourteen countries: Indonesia, the Philippines, Malaysia, Cambodia, Thailand, Brunei, Fiji, Papua New Guinea, East Timor, India, Pakistan, Afghanistan, Turkey and Bangladesh.

Indonesia

No South-East Asian country has preoccupied Australia's defence community so much over the past 50 years as Indonesia. With a population of 240 million, and a maritime border with Australia, Indonesia is critically important in any calculation of Australia's security interests. But Indonesia has proved a problematic partner in defence cooperation. In a dramatic departure from traditional defence policy, Australia signed a security agreement with Indonesia in December 1995. For eighteen months negotiators worked in secret on the pact, which the Labor prime minister Paul Keating announced shortly before the 1996 election hoping to lift his party's spirits, demonstrate his leadership and win votes. For the first time since 1951, when Australia signed the ANZUS Treaty with the United States and New Zealand, Australia entered into a binding security arrangement with a major foreign country. (The only other such arrangement is with PNG.) The agreement committed both sides to confer and cooperate on security issues, and 'to consult each other in the case of adverse challenges to either party or to their common security interests and if appropriate consider measures which might be taken either individually or jointly and in accordance with the processes of each Party'.[8]

The agreement did not survive Indonesia's humiliating withdrawal from East Timor. Four days before Australian troops entered the territory in 1999, the Indonesian government announced it was abrogating the agreement on the grounds that 'the attitude and actions of Australia on the questions of East Timor have not been helpful in the efforts to maintain bilateral relations with Indonesia'.[9] Reconstructing a defence and security relationship with Indonesia then became a matter of considerable strategic importance to Australia. The Bali bombings of 12 October 2002 were a tragedy for both Indonesia and Australia, and offered promise of renewed cooperation on security. The loss of over 200 lives at the hands of Muslim terrorists pointed to the shared interest of both countries in countering the rise of Islamic extremism, and Australian Federal Police were soon working productively with their Indonesian counterparts in infiltrating the Jemaah Islamiyah network and bringing perpetrators to justice in Indonesian courts.

Remarkably, given the depths to which relations had sunk, the Howard government succeeded in negotiating a new treaty with Indonesia in 2006. Called the Lombok Treaty, it came into effect in 2008 and marked a full return to a productive bilateral relationship. The treaty provides for cooperation on a wide range of issues: response to natural disasters; maritime and aviation security; law enforcement in areas such as people smuggling, money laundering, financing of terrorism, corruption, illegal fishing, cyber-crimes, and the drug trade; counter-terrorism 'including through rapid, practical and effective responses to terrorist threats and attacks; intelligence and information sharing; assistance to transport security, immigration and border control; and effective counter-terrorism policies and regulatory frameworks'. Speaking to the Australian Parliament on his visit to Canberra in 2010, Indonesian President Susilo Bambang Yudhoyono announced that there would be annual meetings of the two countries' foreign and defence ministers. Some observers, however, think that Australia could do more to reinvigorate Australia's relationship with Indonesia and that Australian governments have failed to realise the extent and importance of its democratic transformation. Hugh White, a former senior defence bureaucrat, told the ABC in 2010: 'We tend to cast ourselves in a heroic role of the liberators of East Timor, and Indonesia as a whole, the whole 240 million Indonesians, as the villains in the piece. In the end East Timor was liberated from Indonesian rule by Indonesia, by a decision of President Habibie as he then was.'[10]

The South Pacific

Lying directly north of Queensland across the Torres Strait and bordering Indonesia to the west, PNG is the South Pacific country that matters most to Australia. A former Australian territory, PNG is where thousands of Australians lost their lives fighting the Japanese in World War II. Australia's flag was lowered and PNG gained independence in 1975 but the relationship between the two countries has remained close. Thousands of Australians live in PNG, Australian companies have invested billions of dollars there and the country lies within Australia's area of direct military interest. For reasons of this kind Australia gives as much aid to PNG as to Indonesia—more than $450 million a year. Under the 1987 Joint Declaration of Principles, Australia must consult with PNG in the event of an armed external attack on its sovereign territory. The real threats to security, however, come from within the country rather than without.

Australia has much at stake in the political stability of its former colony. PNG is failing to achieve development for most of its people, and its small defence force has, in the past, been undisciplined and ineffective. With Australian assistance, the PNG Defence Force has been reduced in size and professionalised. It played an important role in ensuring the success of national elections in 2007.

But gaps in government authority remain. For more than a decade the government has been largely absent from Southern Highlands Province, whose natural gas reserves, now being developed by ExxonMobil, give it a key place in the country's economic fortunes. Law and order are tenuously maintained in the towns, and many Papua New Guineans receive few government services. In the 1990s Australia responded to these conditions by boosting support for the military and police, and by tying aid to specific projects and programs with an identifiable development outcome so as to avoid the frittering away of funds in corruption. Under the Strongim Gavman Program (Tok Pisin for 'strengthening or empowering government'), Australian public servants are posted to PNG government departments to strengthen performance on economic management and legal and judicial affairs. Far from diminishing, Australian involvement in PNG is likely to accelerate in coming years. A similar shift towards interventionism has occurred in Australia's policy towards the rest of the South Pacific.

For its own sake, Australia keeps close links with defence forces in PNG and the South Pacific, though Australia cancelled military cooperation with Fiji after the military coup there in 2006. One consequence was that Fiji military officers could no longer undertake courses at the Australian Defence College's Centre for Defence and Strategic Studies in Canberra, as they regularly did before the coup. Australia contends that Fiji is plagued by a military force given to illegal interference in the democratic process. Defence cooperation with other Pacific states includes not just training, exercising and exchanges, but also the Pacific Patrol Boat Project. Since the 1980s Australia has supplied many South Pacific island countries with patrol boats to police their exclusive economic zones. Under the Law of the Sea Convention of 1982, states may declare ocean waters extending 200 miles from their coasts as exclusive maritime territory, and may therefore control economic activities within that area. While all South Pacific countries have declared such zones, they are too small to exercise surveillance and authority over the zones effectively, in particular over fishing vessels seeking migratory tuna. Under the Pacific Patrol Boat Project, to which Australia is committed until 2027, Australia supplies and refits high-powered vessels which have the unique task of undertaking economic defence in peacetime, and has ADF personnel posted to the region as military advisers.

The South Pacific has its own multilateral regional security mechanism, the Biketawa Declaration, adopted by the sixteen member states of the Pacific Islands Forum in 2000 following the forcible overthrow of democratically elected governments in two member states, Fiji and Solomon Islands. The declaration provides for the forum to take a series of graduated steps in the event of security crises in member states, and was invoked by Australia and other forum countries in 2003, when they decided to intervene with a military and police force in Solomon Islands.

ASSESSMENTS

Australians have disagreed for generations about how best to make Australia secure. They have done so from the conscription referenda of World War I to the disputes over the Vietnam War in the 1960s and 1970s, the challenge to the American alliance in the 1980s and opposition to the war on Iraq in 2003. Familiar themes in this national debate appear and reappear—whether to rely on allies or self-defence, whether to fight abroad or only at home, whether to define Australia's region broadly or more narrowly, how much to depend upon diplomacy as compared with defence, and so on. The emergence of a new threat in the form of global terrorism has ensured that the debate about defence and security continues. That debate centres on four interrelated issues: the nature of threats to Australia's security, the likelihood of those threats, the character of security in the modern world and the way in which Australia should respond.

The intellectual crucible of that debate, some argue, is a 'strategic culture' of widely shared assumptions about a country's security and the best way to protect it. Some dissenters lie outside the strategic culture and object to any approach to national security which gives the military a significant role. In an era of economic interdependence, they contend, security should be organised on an interdependent basis, with countries cooperating to meet common threats rather than constructing national military systems against each other. If we think of the security of Australia in the broadest terms, then perhaps we might conclude that major investment in the environment, education and infrastructure—on a scale to match or outdo the investment now made in the ADF—matters more than spending on the military. The environmental degradation of the Australian continent and the destruction of rainforests in South-East Asia and the South Pacific might be a far greater risk to national security in the long term than invasion by a hostile power. The corollary is that Australia should scrap its offensive weapons systems and reduce its area of direct military interest.

Governments are in the business of prediction, and no more so than on issues of defence and national security. So they turn to a class of people called *defence planners*, who predict the future in order to enable governments to decide on defence policy. Those people, by training and environment, are pessimistic about what is going to happen. Their task is to warn of possible threats to national security, and when they sit down to think up threats and spend their professional lives discussing threats with their colleagues, they end up with a long list of things that conceivably might just happen. Alongside the planners are the public servants in the Department of Defence, DFAT, the Department of Prime Minister and Cabinet and associated organisations who put the final touches to a document such as the 2009 white paper after it has been emailed back and forth between the offices of Russell Hill, Canberra. Their task is to confer coherence on incoherent arguments, and soften the hard edges of policy with euphemism.

In the 1990s Australian planners stressed the uncertainty of the post–Cold War situation and liked to list potential flashpoints in East Asia. They pointed to the Korean peninsula, for example, where a decaying communist state and a rising but troubled capitalist one confronted each other across a demilitarised zone; to the Taiwan Straits, where China might have entered hostilities with Taiwan over the question of reunification; and to the Spratly Islands in the South China Sea, where five regional powers, including China, competed for territory potentially rich in sub-seabed oil and gas. More generally, military planners said ASEAN states were modernising weapons systems and spending more on defence than ever before, so we had to do the same. Some of those themes remained in the 2009 white paper. Now they worry as well about the rise of China, arguing that China will be the strongest Asian military power 'by a considerable margin'. Not only that, the modernisation 'appears potentially to be beyond the scope of what would be required for a conflict over Taiwan'.

Defending Australia in the Asia Pacific Century: Force 2030, the 2009 Defence white paper, envisaged a massive military build-up by Australia, though not immediately. The central recommendations for force structure and new weapons systems appear to have been driven, in large part, by domestic politics (the twelve new submarines were to be built in South Australia) and the need for interoperability with American forces in future deployments like those in Iraq and Afghanistan. The white paper's ruling theoretical assumption was that nation-states are armed against each other in a global anarchy, as they once were, rather than restrained by the multiplying interconnections of globalisation, as they now seem to be. And the focus on the state itself as the key organiser of armed conflict largely missed the central fact of modern warfare; namely, that it is principally initiated by non-state actors such as the Taliban or al-Qaeda.

The white paper also failed to place defence within the context of numerous other contributions to Australian national security, particularly the diplomatic work undertaken by the Department of Foreign Affairs and Trade, now seriously under-resourced by government. Some critics asked why diplomacy, the instrument supposed to sustain a global and regional web of relationships and cooperative arrangements favouring Australia, should receive only a twentieth of the funds allocated to defence. Australia, it seemed, would now be saddled with a defence build-up that would send a clear message to its neighbours to do the same.

A number of conclusions emerge from this analysis. First, defence policy changes slowly. The lesson many drew from Australia's participation in the Vietnam War was that forward defence did not make Australia more secure. That lesson became part of defence policy only in the late 1980s, then only partly, and has now been abandoned. Governments and defence bureaucracies tend to be in thrall to the assumptions of the past. A new strategic situation, characterised by global terrorism and asymmetric warfare, emerged in the late 1990s and was symbolised by the terrorist attacks on American cities in 2001. Australia began to respond to it in the defence updates of 2003 and 2005, but the 2009 Defence white paper returned to a preoccupation with the wars between states that are now a minor feature of global armed conflict. The Defence Force also changes slowly. If personnel numbers fall over a period of years, as they did in the 1990s, a further period of years is needed to replenish them. Decisions made now about submarines, fighters, destroyers, cruise missiles and cyber-warfare systems will have no significant effect on the capability of the ADF for as much as a decade.

Second, the least likely military threats determine defence policy far more than the most likely threats. Much of the Defence Force is structured and equipped on the assumption that a hostile power might one day attempt to attack Australia or its territories from the north, crossing the sea–air gap from the Indonesian islands to the Australian continent. The Rudd government saw 'the defence of Australia against direct armed attack' as in Australians' 'most basic strategic interest', and as the fulcrum on which defence policy should hinge. The main task of the Australian Defence Force, therefore, was to 'deter and defeat armed attacks on Australia by conducting independent military operations without relying on the combat or combat support forces of other countries'. A conventional invasion from the north is among the least likely military contingencies Australia might face. As Rudd pointed out in 2009, the contingencies for which the ADF is being prepared 'range from stabilisation operations and humanitarian and disaster relief to the more remote possibility of direct conflict'.[11] Yet that 'remote possibility' has a determining effect on Australia's defence planning.

Third, the most likely threats to security in the second decade of the twenty-first century do not require vast increases in military spending. Terrorism—a threat more likely than invasion—creates extreme asymmetry in military affairs. Countering it requires effort and energy by governments, but not an expanded military capability. That threat is best met with better information-gathering by intelligence agencies and quick action by state and federal police. Australia's proposed array of defence assets might be useful against an invading army, which is highly unlikely to come, but offers no protection against the more probable contingency of a suicide bomber wishing to trigger an explosion in a crowded city street. In the same way, regional deployments of Australian troops do not entail a large expansion of Australia's military forces or strike capability. The largest single deployment of Australian troops in recent times has not been to our northern borders to protect the country from invasion or even to Iraq and Afghanistan, but rather to East Timor at the head of INTERFET, 'a coalition of the willing' with UN authority.

Fourth, no Australian government dares to craft a defence policy without first taking into account the likely reaction of the Pentagon in Washington. The consequence is a focus on interoperability at the expense of rational Australian defence planning to meet real threats.

FURTHER READING

American alliance and Australian defence policy

Australian Journal of International Affairs, vol. 55, no. 2, July 2001. (A special issue devoted to the history and politics of the American alliance half a century after the signing of the ANZUS Treaty.)

Beeson, Mark, 'Australia's relationship with the United States: The case for greater independence,' *Australian Journal of Political Science*, vol. 38, no. 3, pp. 387–405. (The strategic relationship with the US 'commits Australia to policies that reflect America's global geopolitical priorities, but which may not be in keeping with Australian interests'.)

Cheeseman, Graeme, *The Search for Self-Reliance: Australian defence since Vietnam*, Longman Cheshire, Melbourne, 1993. (How defence policy changed, 1960s to 1990s.)

Grey, Jeffrey, *A Military History of Australia*, Cambridge University Press, Melbourne, 1999. (Chapter 11 analyses defence policy from Whitlam to Howard.)

Official reports and policy statements

Australia's National Security: A Defence Update, Canberra, 2003. (Coalition reconsiders defence strategy in the light of global terrorism and regional instability.)

Australia's Strategic Policy, AGPS, Canberra, 1997. (Coalition returns to a variant of forward defence.)

Counter Terrorism White Paper: Securing Australia, protecting our community, Department of Prime Minister and Cabinet, Canberra, 2010. (Focus is mainly domestic but covers Labor government's counter-terrorism cooperation with international partners.)

Defence 2000: Our Future Defence Force, Canberra, 2000. (Coalition plans to expand the Australian Defence Force over the next decade.)

Defending Australia: Defence White Paper 1994, AGPS, Canberra, 1994. (Labor looks towards South-East Asia.)

Defending Australia in the Asia Pacific Century: Force 2030, Canberra, 2009. (Labor plans large military build-up by 2030 but cannot decide whether China is friend or foe.)

The Defence of Australia 1987, AGPS, Canberra, 1987. (Labor embraces defence self-reliance.)

Transnational Terrorism: The threat to Australia, Canberra, 2004. (An official examination of the evolution of al-Qaeda, extremist-Muslim terrorism in South-East Asia, and Australia's strategy for countering the threat.)

Evaluations of defence policy

McAllister, Ian, *Public Opinion in Australia Towards Defence, Security and Terrorism,* ASPI *Special Report*, Issue 16, Australian Strategic Policy Institute, August 2008. (Examines popular perceptions of security threats, defence as an election issue, opinions on defence spending, attitudes to China and Indonesia and much else; excellent.)

Tubilewicz, Czeslaw, 'The 2009 Defence white paper and the Rudd government's response to China's rise', *Australian Journal of Political Science*, vol. 45, no. 1, 2010, pp. 149–57. (Finds the white paper's analysis of China flawed and contradictory; examines Chinese reaction.)

Walters, Patrick, 'The making of the 2009 Defence white paper', *Security Challenges*, vol. 5, no. 2, 2009, pp. 1–10. (How the white paper was prepared; what it says; and why it is extremely ambitious.)

White, Hugh, 'Strategic interests in Australian defence policy: Some historical and methodological reflections,' *Security Challenges*, vol. 4, no. 2, 2008, pp. 63–79. (Examines the notion of 'strategic interests', the debate over continental and forward defence, the assumptions of the 2000 Defence white paper and the question of what Australians want their armed forces to be able to do.)

Regional security

Advancing the National Interest: Australia's foreign and trade policy white paper, Canberra, 2003. (Includes regional security policy post-9/11.)

Ball, Desmond, *Presumptive Engagement: Australia's Asia-Pacific security policy in the 1990s*, Allen & Unwin, Sydney, 1996. (Regional security policy in the era of Labor's engagement with South-East Asia.)

Lovell, David, ed., *Asia-Pacific Security: Policy challenges*, Institute of Southeast Asian Studies, Singapore, and Asia Pacific Press, Canberra, 2003. (Examines Australian and Asia-Pacific security following 9/11, and includes a useful chapter by James Cotton on the evolution of Australia's regional security policy.)

Websites

ASEAN Regional Forum: <www.aseanregionalforum.org>
Australian Strategic Policy Institute: <www.aspi.org.au>
Department of Defence: <www.defence.gov.au>
Lowy Institute for International Policy: <http://lowyinstitute.org>
Strategic and Defence Studies Centre, ANU: <http://rspas.anu.edu.au/sdsc/index.php>

7

The nuclear challenge

- In what ways have recent developments in global politics undermined the argument for nuclear deterrence?
- What is meant by 'extended deterrence'?
- Is proliferation the most important nuclear threat to global security?
- What was the impact of the end of the Cold War on nuclear arms control?
- What is the implicit bargain contained in the Nuclear Non-Proliferation Treaty and has it been broken by the nuclear weapons states?
- How likely is nuclear terrorism?
- Are the main proposals of the International Commission on Nuclear Non-proliferation and Disarmament wishful thinking or are they practical steps towards making a safer world?
- To what extent did the Obama administration change the global nuclear situation?
- Why did the Rudd government sponsor the International Commission on Nuclear Non-proliferation and Disarmament?

Nuclear issues are less prominent in Australian foreign policy than they were a few decades ago. Yet this was the situation twenty years after the end of the Cold War:

> ...there are at least 23,000 nuclear warheads still in existence, with a combined blast capacity equivalent to 150,000 Hiroshima bombs. The US and Russia together have over 22,000, and France, the United Kingdom, China, India, Pakistan and Israel around 1,000 between them. Nearly half of all warheads are still operationally deployed, and the US and Russia each have over 2,000 weapons on dangerously high alert, ready to be launched immediately—within a decision window of just 4–8 minutes for each president—in the event of perceived attack.[1]

People think they are safe from nuclear attack because the United States and Russia have dramatically reduced their nuclear arsenals. But their reductions are incomplete. Control over nuclear weapons is in danger of slipping beyond the control of sovereign states. The threat of nuclear weapons to global security is as great as ever, and may be greater. And the need for global agreement on arms control is pressing.

As President Obama said in his Prague speech of April 2009, the Cold War has disappeared but thousands of nuclear weapons have not:

> In a strange turn of history, the threat of global nuclear war has gone down, but the risk of a nuclear attack has gone up. More nations have acquired these weapons. Testing has continued. Black market trade in nuclear secrets and nuclear materials abound. The technology to build a bomb has spread. Terrorists are determined to buy, build or steal one. Our efforts to contain these dangers are centered on a global non-proliferation regime, but as more people and nations break the rules, we could reach the point where the center cannot hold.[2]

Some say nuclear weapons are keepers of global peace. They have—it is argued—kept the general peace between the major powers since World War II, and were responsible for generating the security stasis of the Cold War from 1946 to 1990, when neither the Americans nor the Russians dared press the nuclear button. Speaking to the House of Commons in 1955 about the emergence of the hydrogen bomb, the British prime minister Winston Churchill said, '… it may well be that we shall by a process of sublime irony have reached a stage in this story where safety will be the sturdy child of terror, and survival the twin brother of annihilation'.[3] This is the argument for nuclear deterrence, accepted in practice not only by the United States but also by its allies, which see themselves as protected by 'extended deterrence'; that is, by the supposedly deterrent effect on potential enemies of the possibility that the United States would respond with nuclear weapons to an attack on an ally. A similar notion applies to Russia's nuclear deterrent, which applies to its allies in the Commonwealth of Independent States, that is, the successor states of the old Soviet Union.

Like previous Australian governments, the Rudd government was committed to stable nuclear deterrence as the ultimate guarantor of international security, and to US nuclear deterrence as the ultimate guarantor of Australia's national security. The government believes 'stable nuclear deterrence will continue to be a feature of the international system for the foreseeable future', and echoes Cold War nuclear doctrines that the purpose of possessing nuclear weapons is, paradoxically, so that they will not be used. In the 1970s strategists held that the mutual threat of annihilation, as long as it was credible, would produce a situation of 'stable deterrence' in which war would not occur because both sides would be too frightened to start it. Under such conditions, it was argued, nuclear peace could be assured for as long as the major nuclear weapons states such as the United States and the Soviet Union could convince potential aggressors that, if attacked, they would retaliate so destructively as to make the attack pointless. Meantime, the nuclear weapons states would renounce any intention of making a first strike. The Rudd government also believed in extended deterrence, another Cold War nuclear doctrine, which holds that allies of the United States shelter under its nuclear umbrella, and that adversaries are as deterred from attacking them as from attacking the United States itself. Extended deterrence, said the government, 'provides a stable and reliable sense of assurance and has over the years removed the need for Australia to consider more significant and expensive defence options'.[4]

The argument for nuclear deterrence, however, is far weaker than it was during the Cold War, and it is being questioned by its earlier advocates. In a famous 2007 letter to the *Wall Street Journal*, four leading Americans called for a world free of nuclear weapons. They were Henry Kissinger and George Schultz, US secretaries of state under Republican presidents in the 1970s and 1980s; William Perry, US Secretary of Defense in the 1990s; and Sam Nunn, a former chairperson of the US Senate Armed Services Committee. 'North Korea's recent nuclear test and Iran's refusal to stop its program to enrich uranium— potentially to weapons grade—highlight the fact that the world is now on the precipice of a new and dangerous nuclear era', they pointed out. 'Most alarmingly, the likelihood that non-state terrorists will get their hands on nuclear weaponry is increasing. In today's war waged on world order by terrorists, nuclear weapons are the ultimate means of mass devastation. And non-state terrorist groups with nuclear weapons are conceptually outside the bounds of a deterrent strategy and present difficult new security challenges.'[5] Deterrence, in other words, makes little sense in a world where the main nuclear threat comes either from states under unstable regimes or from terrorists who glory in their own martyrdom. The four Americans called for substantial reductions in the number of nuclear weapons held by nuclear-armed states and for a series of other measures designed to lay the groundwork for a nuclear-free world, and their call was repeated in 2009 by an international commission on nuclear weapons set up by the Rudd government.

The argument for *extended* nuclear deterrence is similarly weaker than it used to be. It has long been contended that if the allies of the United States were to begin to doubt the reliability of the American nuclear deterrent they would acquire their own nuclear weapons, making the world even less safe. But no one is proposing a sudden withdrawal of the American nuclear umbrella that might have such an effect. The proposals emanating from serious contributors to the arms control debate focus instead on reducing risks to humanity by means of gradual drawdowns in nuclear capability. The fundamental problem is that, over the long term, someone with control of nuclear weapons will use them. Nuclear deterrence cannot be relied upon to secure peace indefinitely. At some point nuclear deterrence will break down and the consequences will be catastrophic.

The maintenance of large nuclear arsenals, moreover, does nothing to solve the key nuclear problem of the early twenty-first century. This is not general nuclear conflict but proliferation: the spreading of nuclear weapons beyond the five states that originally possessed them, the original 'nuclear weapons states'— the United States, Russia, China, France and the United Kingdom. Nuclear threats now arise from other states that have acquired nuclear weapons, such as Israel, India, Pakistan and North Korea; from states that appear likely to develop nuclear weapons from a civilian nuclear energy program, such as Iran, which has been enriching uranium; and from terrorists, possibly assisted by a state, who might employ such weapons in a nuclear version of 9/11 or mount a radiological attack in which a conventional explosive blasts nuclear materials into the environment. The Internet has spread nuclear weapons knowledge, and a black market may exist in nuclear materials. In addition, climate change makes civilian nuclear energy—with its ultimate potential for weapons development— more attractive to governments seeking to reduce carbon emissions.

Looking back, we can identify three periods in the history of nuclear weapons. In the first period, from 1945 to 1962, the political leaders of the United States and the Soviet Union approved the development of ever more destructive weapons systems and means of delivery, moving quickly from atomic to hydrogen bombs and from bombers to intercontinental ballistic missiles, yet without fully appreciating that, by any rational calculation, these weapons could never be used in warfare. The second period began with the Cuban missile crisis of 1962, when the world came closer to wholesale destruction than ever before, and it ended with India's nuclear tests of 1998, marking the beginning of the breakdown of the non-proliferation regime. Stability characterised most of this period: the 'number of nuclear weapons deployed declined dramatically; a test ban entered into force; several states voluntarily surrendered their weapons; and many other industrialised states effectively froze their potential weapons capabilities'.[6] The exception was the brief return of nuclear tension in the first half of the 1980s in what is called the Second Cold War. We live in the third period, which threatens further proliferation and a return to the terrible uncertainties of the first.

THE SECOND COLD WAR AND THE 1990S

A revived nuclear arms race between the United States and the Soviet Union in the early 1980s fed worldwide fears that the superpowers might go to war with nuclear weapons, and triggered the emergence of anti-nuclear sentiment, especially in Europe but also in Australia. Labor governments of the time responded with an activist policy on arms control and disarmament. Arms control is a process that seeks to limit the development, testing and deployment of weapons without abolishing them altogether. Disarmament seeks total abolition of weapons by international agreement and an end to nuclear deterrence.

Australia has a history of opposing nuclear tests, especially those in the South Pacific, which was the site of American and British tests (1946–63), and then of tests conducted by the French (1966–96). France tested in the atmosphere until 1974, spreading radioactive contamination on the islands of the South Pacific and throughout the Southern Hemisphere. When Labor took office under Bob Hawke in 1983, it negotiated the South Pacific Nuclear-Free Zone Treaty under which regional states undertook not to test nuclear weapons in their territory, not to help other countries wishing to test such weapons anywhere, not to make or possess nuclear weapons, and not to station nuclear weapons on their soil. Almost all the states of the Pacific Islands Forum signed the treaty and by doing so drew attention to the fact that France, with three Pacific territories, was alone in using the region to test and develop nuclear weapons.

The South Pacific Nuclear-Free Zone Treaty was an example of Labor's 'qualified nuclearism', a compromise between the anti-nuclearism of the peace movement and the pro-nuclearism of the Coalition.[7] The treaty did not prohibit the Americans' existing or potential nuclear activities in the South Pacific. It said nothing about the testing of missiles, the export of uranium, the presence of American C3I (command, control, communications and intelligence) facilities, the movement of nuclear-armed surface vessels, submarines and aircraft through the region or nuclear ship visits to regional ports. At the time the Americans did not appreciate Hawke's efforts on their behalf and did not like the nuclear-free zone. The US defense secretary Caspar Weinberger, visiting Australia in 1986, thought the zone would assist the Soviets. The United States refused to sign the protocols to the treaty for another decade. Taking their cue from the Americans, the Coalition, which at that time was in opposition under John Howard, opposed the nuclear-free zone, saying the treaty undermined American military strength in the Pacific and helped to 'upset the global balance through contributing to a weakening of the West's nuclear alliance'.[8] Yet the nuclear-free zone treaty was a success for Labor in political terms. It provided a focus for island anti-nuclearism, captured the middle ground of Australian opinion, symbolised the region's opposition to French testing and was universally accepted in the long run. The treaty showed what an imaginative government could do to translate popular nuclear-free aspirations into practical politics.

When Jacques Chirac succeeded François Mitterrand as French president in 1995 he announced that France would conduct a final series of Pacific nuclear tests. Most Australians were outraged. French tests united public opinion. A Newspoll opinion poll taken soon after France's announcement showed 89 per cent of respondents 'strongly against' French nuclear testing in the Pacific, 6 per cent 'partly against' and only 1 per cent in favour. To be against French nuclear testing in Australia in 1995 was to be entirely respectable. Organisations as diverse as Greenpeace, the ALP, the Liberal Party, Westpac bank, the Royal Australasian College of Physicians and the Body Shop openly opposed France's resumption of testing. Australia froze defence cooperation with France, recalled the Australian ambassador for consultations, prohibited all French military aircraft and naval vessels from entering Australia and placed a ban on all military training with France. Australia then played an active role in the international negotiations leading to the UN adoption in 1996 of the Comprehensive Nuclear Test Ban Treaty (CTBT), which prohibits 'any nuclear weapon test explosion or any other nuclear explosion'.

Prime Minister Paul Keating (1991–96) set up the Canberra Commission on the Elimination of Nuclear Weapons in 1995. Keating was driven both by conviction and electoral considerations. He wanted a nuclear-free world and in the approach to the 1996 election he hoped to capitalise on the anti-nuclear mood of Australians following France's nuclear tests in the Pacific. Commission members included Michel Rocard, a former prime minister of France, Robert McNamara, who was American Secretary of Defense in the 1960s, and a one-time chief of the British defence force, Field Marshal Lord Carver. They advocated a nuclear-free world. Any use of nuclear weapons, they said, 'would be catastrophic. The proposition that nuclear weapons can be retained in perpetuity and never used—accidentally or by decision—defies credibility. The only complete defence is the elimination of nuclear weapons and assurance that they will never be produced again.'[9] The commission recommended, as a first step, that the five nuclear weapons states commit themselves unequivocally to eliminate nuclear weapons. The practical steps to be taken after that included taking nuclear forces off alert status, removing warheads from missiles and ending deployment of non-strategic nuclear weapons.

Meantime, the end of the Cold War stopped the nuclear arms race between the United States and the Soviet Union. Progress in arms control after 1987 was breathtaking by comparison with anything that had been achieved in the previous 30 years. Reagan and Gorbachev removed from Europe an entire class of nuclear weapons: the Soviet and American intermediate-range nuclear missiles. The Strategic Arms Reduction Talks treaties, START I and START II, together with other agreements of the 1990s, took the same logic further. Russia and the United States reduced their deployments of strategic weapons by about two-thirds, abandoned strategic weapons with multiple warheads, removed short-range and tactical nuclear weapons from their navies and cut the number of submarine-launched ballistic missiles, usually regarded as vital to nuclear deterrence. At the same time all nuclear weapons were removed from the former Soviet republics of the Ukraine, Belarus and Kazakhstan. At independence in 1991, Ukraine possessed thousands of nuclear weapons as well as cruise missiles and intercontinental ballistic missiles (ICBMs), yet they gave up all of them in return for American and Russian financial assistance. The START verification regime—the system established to ensure that each side could be sure the other was abiding by its treaty obligations—was the most intrusive in the history of nuclear arms control and allowed Russian and American experts on to each other's national territory. Similar progress followed the 2002 US–Russian Strategic Offensive Reduction Treaty (SORT), which required each side to lower the number of strategic nuclear warheads even further to between 1700 and 2200 by the end of 2012.

ARMS CONTROL, DISARMAMENT AND NUCLEAR TERRORISM

Prime Minister Kevin Rudd revived Australia's activism on nuclear issues. Together with Japan, Australia set up the International Commission on Nuclear Non-proliferation and Disarmament in 2008 in order to breathe new life into

KEVIN RUDD, PRIME MINISTER, ON THE NUCLEAR THREAT, 2008

... In the past decade, the world has not paid adequate attention to nuclear weapons. There have been nuclear developments that we have had to confront—like North Korea's nuclear program and the danger it poses to the region; as well as Iran's continued nuclear ambitions. And there has been some thinking about new ways to counter the threat of weapons proliferation. Australia and Japan were both founding partners in the Proliferation Security Initiative (PSI). And Australia and Japan cooperate closely on export controls in the Nuclear Suppliers Group (NSG). These help to support the cornerstone of the global effort to eliminate nuclear weapons—in particular the Nuclear Non-Proliferation Treaty (NPT).

But there has not been the same focus on the danger of nuclear weapons that we saw at the height of the Cold War. In some ways that is understandable—nuclear weapon stockpiles have come down a long way since their peaks in the 1980s. The two main nuclear powers, our shared ally the United States and Russia, have negotiated a series of treaties that have cut the number of nuclear weapons. And South Africa and Ukraine have shown that it is possible for countries that have nuclear weapons to eliminate them. We no longer live with the daily fear of nuclear war between two superpowers.

But nuclear weapons remain. New states continue to seek to acquire them. Some states including in our own region are expanding their existing capacity. Hiroshima reminds us of the terrible power of these weapons. Hiroshima should remind us that we must be vigilant afresh to stop their continued proliferation. And we must be committed to the ultimate objective of a nuclear weapons free world.

The cornerstone of the global nuclear disarmament efforts remains the Nuclear Non-Proliferation Treaty (NPT). It is a treaty that is grounded in the reality of the existence of nuclear weapons, but with a firm goal of their eventual elimination. It is a treaty that, by any historical measure, has helped arrest the spread of nuclear weapons—particularly given the proliferation pressures that existed across states in the 1960s when the treaty was negotiated.

But 40 years later the treaty is under great pressure. Some states have developed nuclear weapons outside the treaty's framework. Some, like North Korea, have defied the international community and have stated that they have left the treaty altogether. Others like Iran defy the content of the treaty by continuing to defy the International Atomic Energy Agency—the agency assigned to give the treaty force.

There are two courses of action available to the community of nations: to allow the NPT to continue to fragment; or to exert every global effort to restore and defend the treaty. Australia stands unambiguously for the treaty. I accept fully that we have a difficult task ahead of us. But I believe Japan and Australia working together can make a difference in the global debate on proliferation ... I announce today that Australia proposes to establish an International Commission on Nuclear Non-Proliferation and Disarmament, to be co-chaired by former Australian foreign minister Gareth Evans ...

Kevin Rudd, 'Building a Better World Together', Speech at Kyoto University, 9 June 2008, <http://pmrudd.archive.dpmc.gov.au/node/5755>.

negotiations over the globe's nuclear future. The commission hoped to build an international consensus on key arms control issues in order to ensure that the 2010 Nuclear Non-Proliferation Treaty (NPT) Review Conference would achieve more than its predecessor in 2005. The joint chairpeople of the commission were two former foreign ministers, Gareth Evans and Yoriko Kawaguchi. The commissioners included a former prime minister, Gro Harlem Brundtland of Norway; a former foreign minister, Ali Alatas of Indonesia; a former head of state, Ernesto Zedillo of Mexico; and a former defence minister, William Perry of the United States, as well as military strategists and disarmament experts from around the world. The commission argued that nuclear threats posed as grave a problem to humanity as climate change, and with more immediately disastrous effects.

The commission said the international community should seize the opportunity created by a new and favourable political climate. Barack Obama made major changes to the nuclear posture of the United States in the first year of his presidency. He undertook to negotiate with the Russians on further cuts in deployed strategic weapons, he promised to push for US ratification of the Comprehensive Nuclear Test Ban Treaty, and he altered the US position on negotiations for a fissile material cut-off treaty, making a successful outcome more likely. Both Barack Obama's United States and Dmitry Medvedev's Russia wanted progress on arms control and disarmament. A good first step, according to the commission, would be for the United States and Russia to agree on further large reductions in the deployment of strategic nuclear weapons in a follow-on treaty from START. Strategic weapons include land-based ICBMs with a range of 5500 kilometres or more, submarine-launched ballistic missiles (SLBMs) carried by nuclear submarines, and heavy bombers with a range of 10,000 kilometres or more carrying bombs, air-to-surface missiles and cruise missiles. The warheads (or bombs) carried on all these missiles are thermonuclear; that is, they would produce a thermonuclear explosion many times the size of the bomb exploded at Hiroshima in 1945.

Nuclear doctrine should also be changed, said the commission. Nuclear doctrine is the official rationale given by states for their possession of nuclear weapons. The American nuclear doctrine inherited by President Obama was one of strategic ambiguity, leaving open the possibility that the United States might use nuclear weapons in response to any kind of attack, whether nuclear, conventional or terrorist. The commission called on the United States to adopt a doctrine declaring that the sole purpose of possessing nuclear weapons is to deter nuclear attacks on the United States or its allies, and called for other nuclear-armed states to do likewise. In similar vein the commission urged nuclear-armed states to issue assurances, backed by a Security Council resolution, that they would not use nuclear weapons against non-nuclear members of the NPT.

The commission urged states to negotiate an early end to inherently dangerous force postures. Nuclear force posture refers to the way states deploy nuclear weapons, and how ready they are to use them at a moment's notice. In 2010, twenty years after the end of the Cold War, about 3000 nuclear weapons held by the United States, Russia, France and Britain remained on hair-trigger alert, ready to be launched as soon as warning was received. The perpetuation of this 'launch-on-warning' posture gave leaders between four and eight minutes to determine whether a threat was genuine, a computer malfunction, or a flock of birds, and to decide whether to respond with a nuclear attack.

A dangerous paradox inherent in dependence on nuclear weapons, and long recognised by strategists, is that nuclear defence undermines nuclear deterrence. Any effective form of defence against nuclear attack, such as a missile defence system, removes mutual vulnerability and the incentive not to use nuclear weapons in a first strike. That is why the Rudd government opposed the unilateral development of missile defences by any country, including the United States. Such defences, the government said, weaken 'the deterrent value of the strategic nuclear forces of the major nuclear powers, and especially the viability of their second strike capabilities'.[10] As the commission argued, 'mutual deterrence depends on each side being vulnerable to retaliation from the other, and that mutuality breaks down if one side has significantly greater capability to defend against a retaliatory strike'.[11] The aim of a program of nuclear arms control, therefore, should be to reduce states' nuclear defences so as to maintain their vulnerability. Strategic ballistic missile defences, the ultimate destabilisers of deterrence, should therefore be severely limited, according to the commission, even if theatre ballistic missile defences were permitted to grow.

On the question of proliferation, the commission confronted the reality that Israel, India and Pakistan have nuclear weapons and are not members of the NPT. They should, it thought, be brought into the fold by means of arms agreements that would run parallel to those of the NPT and, if they respected those agreements, be given access to nuclear materials for civilian purposes. In a similar way, the commission recommended that the Bush administration's Proliferation Security Initiative, under which states cooperate in interdicting suspected shipments of nuclear materials, should be brought within the UN system as a neutral organisation rather than remaining outside it as a US-led program.

Except for North Korea, which conducted nuclear tests in 2006 and 2009, the world has observed an informal moratorium on nuclear testing since the Indian and Pakistani tests of 1998. In effect, the 1996 Comprehensive Nuclear Test Ban Treaty created a global norm against which nuclear testing violations are measured, even though that treaty has not yet become international law. By 2009 most states (182) had signed the treaty and Australia was among the 151 countries which had also ratified it. More than 200 monitoring stations and laboratories have been established around the world as part of the treaty verification process. The CTBT can come into force only when the 44 states designated in Annex 2 of the treaty ratify it. They include Russia, the United Kingdom and France, which have ratified, but there is also a long list of countries that have not—the United States, China, Egypt, Indonesia, Iran, Pakistan, Israel, Iraq and North Korea. Of these the most important is the United States, where the Senate voted against ratification in 1999, falling far short of the 67 votes required. If the US Senate were to change its mind, China and Indonesia would probably follow suit, but ratification by the remaining Middle East and South Asian states appears unlikely in present circumstances. North Korea under its erratic family dynasty is unpredictable. Ratification may matter less in practice, however, than international practice. Without coming into force, the treaty has nevertheless hindered nuclear proliferation by sending a signal about global opinion on a key nuclear issue.

Nuclear-armed states do not threaten Australia, and the effectiveness of extended deterrence is unlikely to be tested. But what about nuclear terrorists, whom American nuclear weapons would not deter? The theory of deterrence, after all, is based on the presupposition that states are rational actors that put their self-preservation first, and would therefore decline to initiate a nuclear exchange if they knew it would lead to their own destruction; whereas a suicide nuclear terrorist would operate under no such constraint and might even see a nuclear 9/11 as fulfilling God's will. French police arrested a French-Algerian scientist working at the European Organization for Nuclear Research (CERN) in 2009, charging him with membership of a terrorist group.[12] Some say a terrorist group might acquire a nuclear weapon in the midst of the chaos that would surround the collapse of a nuclear-armed state such as Pakistan. A Pakistani scientist called A.Q. Khan, the father of the country's nuclear weapons program, was found to have provided nuclear weapons technology to Libya, Iran and North Korea in what amounted to a personal network of proliferation, fuelling the suspicion that a similar flow of Pakistani assistance might one day go to a terrorist group. The security of Pakistan's nuclear arsenal is a particular concern of the United States. What might happen, for example, if the Taliban, which is fighting a war against the Americans, the Australians, NATO forces and others in Afghanistan, were to seize control of Pakistan? Or if the Pakistani army, whose officers and ordinary soldiers have long been exposed to fundamentalist Islamic ideas, were to split, permitting a group of officers to gain control of nuclear assets? The Americans have responded by working closely with the Pakistani army and spending large amounts of money to improve nuclear security. The Americans might—in an emergency—intervene directly to ensure that Pakistan's nuclear weapons do not fall into enemy hands.[13]

Yet how likely is nuclear terrorism? Formidable obstacles, both political and technical, face any non-state group of extremists wanting to execute an act of nuclear terrorism, such as detonating a nuclear bomb. States, the only organisations with the wealth, authority and expertise to acquire nuclear weapons, are jealous of their nuclear monopoly and highly unlikely to assist a non-state group to become a nuclear-armed competitor. The political collapse of a nuclear state is unlikely to offer terrorists access to nuclear arms, because weapons are so carefully protected with elaborate locks and, as the supreme expression of military power, might well remain under guard even in chaotic circumstances. If a stateless group were to steal or buy fissile material, they would require industrial capacity to build a usable nuclear device and would need to maintain secrecy about the project over months and even years. The conspiracy would dwarf that of 9/11, and would almost certainly come to the notice of intelli-

NUCLEAR TERRORISM

Thus far terrorist groups seem to have exhibited only limited desire and even less progress in going atomic. This may be because, after brief exploration of the possible routes, they, unlike generations of alarmists on the issue, have discovered that the tremendous effort required is scarcely likely to be successful.

It is highly improbable that a would-be atomic terrorist would be given or sold a bomb by a generous like-minded nuclear state because the donor could not control its use and because the ultimate source of the weapon might be discovered.

Although there has been great worry about terrorists illicitly stealing or purchasing a nuclear weapon, it seems likely that neither 'loose nukes' nor a market in illicit nuclear materials exists. Moreover, finished bombs have been outfitted with an array of locks and safety devices. There could be dangers in the chaos that would emerge if a nuclear state were utterly to fail, collapsing in full disarray. However, even under those conditions, nuclear weapons would likely remain under heavy guard by people who know that a purloined bomb would most likely end up going off in their own territory, would still have locks, and could probably be followed and hunted down by an alarmed international community.

The most plausible route for terrorists would be to manufacture the device themselves from purloined materials. This task requires that a considerable series of difficult hurdles be conquered in sequence, including the effective recruitment of people who at once have great technical skills and will remain completely devoted to the cause. In addition, a host of corrupted co-conspirators, many of them foreign, must remain utterly reliable, international and local security services must be kept perpetually in the dark, and no curious outsider must get consequential wind of the project over the months or even years it takes to pull off. In addition, the financial costs of the operation could easily become monumental.

Moreover, the difficulties are likely to increase because of enhanced protective and policing efforts by self-interested governments and because any foiled attempt would expose flaws in the defense system, holes the defenders would then plug.

John Mueller, *The Atomic Terrorist*, 30 April 2009. Paper prepared for the International Commission on Nuclear Non-proliferation and Disarmament, <www.icnnd.org/research/Mueller_Terrorism.pdf>.

gence agencies. And as Los Alamos research director Stephen M. Younger has argued, uranium is 'exceptionally difficult to machine' while 'plutonium is one of the most complex metals ever discovered, a material whose basic properties are sensitive to exactly how it is processed'.[14]

'Dirty bombs', or radiological weapons that spread fissile materials by means of a conventional explosion, would be easier to make and present a more likely risk. Yet, terrible as it would be, the explosion of such a bomb even in a large city would result in mass disruption rather than mass destruction. The international community has in any case been acutely aware of this possibility since 9/11 and is responding. The UN adopted the International Convention for the Suppression of Acts of Nuclear Terrorism in 2005, providing for states to cooperate in detecting, preventing, suppressing and investigating acts of nuclear terrorism. Together with the International Atomic Energy Agency's (IAEA's) Code of Conduct on the Safety and Security of Radioactive Sources (2000), strengthened in 2003, the convention is an attempt to keep track of nuclear materials around the world by requiring governments to keep national registers and report losses. Australia is numbered among the countries that have programs to assist governments to manage radioactive materials. The United States and Russia announced their Global Initiative to Combat Nuclear Terrorism (GICNT) in 2006 during the G8 Summit in St Petersburg, with the aim of enhancing the ability of governments around the world to identify nuclear terrorist threats and respond to them. Seventy-six countries belonged to GICNT by the end of 2009. Potential terrorists must now take into account the emerging science of nuclear forensics, which allows experts to track the origin of bombs and the way they are made.

THE NUCLEAR NON-PROLIFERATION TREATY (NPT)

The risk of proliferation was recognised from the beginning of the nuclear era, and the response of the international community was one of the more successful multilateral treaties ever negotiated: the Nuclear Non-Proliferation Treaty (NPT), which came into effect in 1970. By 2009, 188 states were parties to the treaty, leaving just four that were not: Israel, India, Pakistan and North Korea. The NPT is a kind of bargain between two kinds of countries, the five original nuclear weapons states on the one hand and all other countries that sign it on the other. As the name suggests, the non-proliferation treaty is meant to stop nuclear weapons from spreading beyond the five core states while committing nuclear weapons states to disarm in the long run. In return for renouncing nuclear weapons, the non-nuclear states receive an intangible benefit—the promise of eventual nuclear disarmament—and a more concrete set of rewards in the form of help in developing peaceful nuclear energy with uranium supplied under an international safeguards system administered by the IAEA. The NPT has succeeded in creating an international norm against nuclear proliferation, and has encouraged numerous states to abandon nuclear weapons research. Four states have given up their weapons—Ukraine, Belarus, Kazakhstan and South Africa. The problem of 'loose nukes' troubled US policymakers after the end of the Cold War, and the United States, through its 'cooperative threat reduction' programs, oversaw the destruction of old nuclear weapons and nuclear materials in the former Soviet Union. NPT members have reached further agreements—on trade in uranium, for example—aimed at preventing proliferation. But the NPT is an inherently unequal treaty, giving privileged status to some states over others. The original nuclear weapons states have not kept their side of the bargain. They have reduced their arsenals while remaining in possession of thousands of weapons. Their appeals to other states not to acquire nuclear weapons appear hypocritical, and their actions undermine the international norm.

Under the original articles of the NPT of 1970, member countries agreed to meet after 25 years in order to decide whether the treaty would be extended indefinitely or extended only for a fixed period. That meant a conference in 1995, the NPT Review and Extension Conference, and the 175 member states that attended agreed to extend the treaty indefinitely. The 2000 conference resulted in an 'unequivocal undertaking' by the original nuclear weapons states 'to accomplish the total elimination of their nuclear arsenals' in an agreed thirteen-step process. But the United States disavowed this undertaking once Bush became president and the United States experienced terrorist attack. The United States and Russia have since said they will keep nuclear weapons indefinitely and they, as well as China, are modernising their nuclear forces. No agreement could be reached at the 2005 conference, not even on the text of a final document.[15]

Alexander Downer declared Australia's 'unwavering support for the NPT's prohibition against the spread of nuclear weapons' in 2005.[16] In doing so he appeared to be reaffirming the position on nuclear proliferation held by both sides of politics since the 1970s; namely, that the best route to containing the spread of nuclear weapons was multilateral and through UN processes. The Howard government welcomed the CTBT in 1996. Downer said Australia could be proud of the result, having led international action to save the treaty. The Howard government also condemned the nuclear tests by India and Pakistan in 1998 and suspended bilateral defence links with both countries in response. But after 9/11 Howard and Downer grew equivocal about multilateral solutions to proliferation, including the NPT. They wanted to reassure Bush that they were the closest of American allies, and they thought terrorists might acquire nuclear weapons. The Bush administration embarked on its own, unilateral response to proliferation in the form of the Proliferation Security Initiative, a 'coalition of the willing' who would come together to interdict the movement of weapons of mass destruction. Australia joined the American-sponsored initiative, which had 95 participant member states by 2009. On the one hand, Australia reaffirmed 'the value of the NPT' and agreed 'with other states that previous agreements should not be rolled back simply because the US wished it to be so'.[17] On the other, it backed the Americans' anti-proliferation regime outside the NPT.

Howard was caught between a desire to side with Bush and a bipartisan tradition of Australian support for the NPT. The conflict arose again when the United States decided in 2005 to sidestep the NPT in order to supply India with equipment and technology for its civilian nuclear program. India is not a member of the NPT. Australia has always exported its uranium only to NPT members, in accordance with the requirements of the Nuclear Suppliers Group, which was founded in 1974 for the specific purpose of preventing trade of this kind on the grounds that it might foster nuclear proliferation. Visiting India in 2006, Howard upheld Australia's traditional no-supply policy. But he did so without enthusiasm, and by August 2007 he had abandoned it altogether, announcing his government would approve uranium sales to India, a nuclear weapons state outside the framework of international nuclear law. The issue divided the Coalition and Labor, and the Rudd government quickly restored Australia's old policy of non-supply after being elected a few months later. The policy remained throughout the Rudd government, even though the Nuclear Suppliers Group, pressed hard by the United States, made an exception of India in 2008, permitting nuclear trade in return for Indian undertakings not to share nuclear technology or carry out further nuclear tests.

By the time nations gathered for the NPT Review Conference in 2010, a succession of American initiatives had changed the political atmosphere and increased the chances of a positive outcome. First, the Obama administration concluded a new arms control agreement with Russia on strategic weapons, the ultimate hardware of nuclear deterrence during the Cold War. Under the New START Treaty signed in Prague in April 2010, the United States and Russia agreed to significantly reduce their strategic arms within seven years, with a limit of 1550 warheads each, 74 per cent lower than the 1991 START Treaty, and a combined limit of 800 ICBM launchers, SLBM launchers, and heavy bombers carrying nuclear weapons, of which 700 could be deployed. The treaty lasts until 2020 and provides for an intrusive verification regime including short-notice on-site inspections by each side of the other's weapons and extensive exchange of information.

Second, President Obama modified the nuclear posture of the United States. Under the new policy, membership of the NPT became a source of security, because the United States pledged not to use or threaten to use nuclear weapons against any NPT member state; and even if such a state were to use chemical or biological weapons against the United States or its allies or partners, the United States would not respond with nuclear weapons but rather with 'a devastating conventional military response'. The Obama administration also undertook not to develop new nuclear warheads, nor to test nuclear weapons, but to seek the ratification and entry into force of the Comprehensive Nuclear Test Ban Treaty. The new nuclear posture reflected the new global situation, shifting the focus from nuclear deterrence between states to preventing nuclear terrorism and proliferation, and in particular directing attention towards Iran and North Korea, states that remain defiantly outside the non-proliferation regime. 'For the first time', President Obama said, 'preventing nuclear proliferation and nuclear terrorism is now at the top of America's nuclear agenda, which affirms the central importance of the Nuclear Non-Proliferation Treaty'.[18]

Third, President Obama convened the Nuclear Security Summit, which was the largest gathering of world leaders in the United States since World War II and included Hu Jintao of China, Yukio Hatoyama of Japan, Manmohan Singh of India, Nicolas Sarkozy of France and Angela Merkel of Germany. Australia did not send its prime minister, Kevin Rudd, but the Minister for Defence John Faulkner instead. The problems confronted by the summit were the existence of more than 200 tonnes of plutonium and highly enriched uranium in a variety of countries, the fact that thefts of these materials had already occurred, and the need to prevent them falling into the hands of terrorist groups. The summit communiqué reaffirmed the following:

> ... the fundamental responsibility of States, consistent with their respective international obligations, [is] to maintain effective security of all nuclear materials, which includes nuclear materials used in nuclear weapons, and nuclear facilities under their control; to prevent non-state actors from obtaining the information or technology required to use such material for malicious purposes; and emphasise the importance of robust national legislative and regulatory frameworks for nuclear security.[19]

Leaders agreed to facilitate all forms of nuclear security and to meet again in 2012. Participant countries also made national commitments. Russia pledged to stop producing plutonium, for example; the Ukraine, to remove all highly enriched uranium by 2012; and Australia, to ratify the International Convention on Suppression of Acts of Nuclear Terrorism. (Two months before the summit Australia had blocked three shipments of unidentified materials to Iran in case they were used to help develop Iranian nuclear weapons.)

Fourth, in the interests of transparency, President Obama released newly declassified information on the American nuclear stockpile, revealing that the United States had 5113 warheads, 75 per cent fewer than in 1989 and 84 per cent fewer than at the height of the Cold War in 1967.

The NPT Review Conference was a moderate success. Altogether, 189 states took part, making the conference one of the largest multilateral conferences ever conducted. The advantage of such inclusive multilateralism is that it is representative—virtually the whole world was there—and is therefore able to influence global norms on issues such as nuclear testing and nuclear security. The disadvantage is that decisions on which everyone can agree are modest in scope. In New York,

THE UNITED STATES REVEALS THE EXTENT OF ITS NUCLEAR STOCKPILE

The United States is releasing newly declassified information on the U.S. nuclear weapons stockpile. Increasing the transparency of global nuclear stockpiles is important to non-proliferation efforts, and to pursuing follow-on reductions after the ratification and entry into force of the New START Treaty that cover all nuclear weapons: deployed and non-deployed, strategic and non-strategic.

Stockpile. As of September 30, 2009, the U.S. stockpile of nuclear weapons consisted of 5,113 warheads. This number represents an 84 percent reduction from the stockpile's maximum (31,255) at the end of fiscal year 1967, and over a 75 percent reduction from its level (22,217) when the Berlin Wall fell in late 1989. The below figure shows the U.S. nuclear stockpile from 1945 through September 30, 2009.

Warhead Dismantlement. From fiscal years 1994 through 2009, the United States dismantled 8,748 nuclear warheads. Several thousand additional nuclear weapons are currently retired and awaiting dismantlement.

Non-Strategic Nuclear Weapons. The number of U.S. non-strategic nuclear weapons declined by approximately 90 percent from September 30, 1991 to September 30, 2009.

US Department of Defense Fact Sheet, *Increasing Transparency in the U.S. Nuclear Weapons Stockpile*, 3 May 2010.

NPT member states reaffirmed the basic bargain of the NPT and called for every effort to be made to prevent the proliferation of nuclear weapons. They recognised the contribution made to non-proliferation by nuclear-free zones, including those in the South Pacific, Africa and Central Asia, and called upon India, Israel and Pakistan to accede to the NPT. They deplored nuclear testing by North Korea and called upon its regime to abandon all nuclear weapons. They urged states to 'improve their national capabilities to detect, deter and disrupt illicit trafficking in nuclear materials throughout their territories', and agreed that the Conference on Disarmament in Geneva should begin negotiating a treaty prohibiting the production of fissile material for use in nuclear weapons, in other words a fissile material cutoff treaty. The NPT conference called on all Middle East states to work towards a regional nuclear-free zone, and the United States, the United Kingdom, Russia and the UN Secretary-General said they would co-sponsor a conference on the issue in 2012.[20] If such a conference were to occur, it would mean that Iran, Lebanon, Saudi Arabia and Syria would, for the first time, have to acknowledge Israel's right to exist by virtue of sitting with Israel at an international meeting. The 2010 conference reached agreement on a final statement, resumed the global conversation about the danger of nuclear weapons and restored the multilateral nuclear arms control process.

Realists might interpret these affirmations and calls for action as 'motherhood' statements with little meaning. Liberal internationalists, on the other hand, saw them as evidence of a strengthening global norm against nuclear testing, the production of fissile material and nuclear proliferation. The Australian government under Kevin Rudd belonged squarely in the liberal internationalist camp on this issue. Foreign minister Stephen Smith welcomed the outcomes of the 2010 conference and contrasted it with that of 2005, generally regarded as a failure. He pointed to the constructive role Australia played by working with Japan to organise the International Commission on Nuclear Non-proliferation and Disarmament. He said Australia had 'a long and proud record of activism and achievement on nuclear non-proliferation and disarmament', and he was right.[21] On the other hand, the Rudd government did not endorse the International Commission's objective of reducing the number of nuclear weapons in the world to 2000 by 2025, and reaffirmed 'the value to Australia of the protection afforded by extended nuclear deterrence under the US Alliance. Under this, as long as nuclear weapons exist, we can rely on US nuclear forces to deter nuclear attack on Australia'.[22] Like earlier Australian Labor governments, the Rudd government simultaneously supported nuclear arms control and extended nuclear deterrence.

ASSESSMENTS

Labor governments since the 1980s have given Australia an effective role in arms control and disarmament. But political circumstances and public opinion have changed in the meantime. Nuclear questions held a special urgency during the Cold War, never more so than when the possibility of global nuclear war between the Soviet Union and the United States re-emerged in the early 1980s and the spectre of nuclear annihilation once again haunted the imagination of human-kind. In an atmosphere of renewed global tension, an articulate minority of Australians wanted to know why their country played host to US military facili-ties, supported the American nuclear deterrent, endorsed the deployment of new American missiles in Western Europe, permitted nuclear-armed warships to enter its ports, and participated in the nuclear fuel cycle by exporting uranium. In short, they wanted to know why Australia was so closely enmeshed in America's nuclear strategies. Echoing an old argument about Australia's foreign policy, they called on the government to make Australia nuclear free, to press internationally for arms control and to assert independence by decoupling the country from the nuclear threat. The anti-nuclear purists of the 1980s gave expression to a commu-nity concern, less radical than theirs but more widely shared, that nuclear war threatened Australia and the government should be doing something about it. Labor ministers believed the government needed to meet such concern halfway in case anti-nuclear sentiment undermined broad community backing for the American alliance. It was a short step, they thought, from saying 'I am against nuclear weapons' to saying 'I am against ANZUS, which is a nuclear alliance'.

Three conditions underlay Labor's earlier activism in arms control: public opinion aroused against nuclear weapons by a sense of threat; a government party that, when pushed, liked the idea of Australia advocating arms control internationally; and foreign ministers committed to achieving success in the field of arms control and disarmament. Gareth Evans championed multilateral arms control as the kind of niche Australia should be seeking to fill with its new middle-power 'niche diplomacy'. By that he meant that Australia, while too small to play a role across the whole range of international issues, could never-theless enhance its stature by devoting diplomatic resources to a few key issues such as nuclear and chemical arms control.

The arms control activism of the short-lived Rudd government had a quite different origin, which lay in the personal commitments of Kevin Rudd himself. By the time he became prime minister, Australians no longer worried about the nuclear threat. The French had long since stopped testing nuclear bombs in the South Pacific, the Cold War that propelled the nuclear arms race was a thing of the past, and relations between the United States and Russia were no longer antagonistic. Most people thought terrorism and climate change were more serious perils than nuclear war. For Rudd, however, nuclear proliferation was an issue on which Australia could demonstrate its credentials as an activist middle power, and on a visit to Japan in 2008 he toured the museum at Hiroshima—site of the world's first nuclear attack—and announced that Australia would work with Japan to establish the International Commission on Nuclear Non-proliferation and Disarmament (ICNND).

Rudd had elite support in taking this initiative. Former Liberal prime minister Malcolm Fraser joined with the former chief of the Australian Defence Force General Peter Gration and former army chief Lieutenant-General John Sanderson, among others, in offering to foster bipartisan public backing for the ICNND. In a letter to Rudd, they wrote: 'Unless the world's official nuclear states commit to the obligations implicit in Article 6 of the non-proliferation treaty and work to bring the nuclear weapon states outside the treaty with them, we believe that more and more countries will acquire nuclear weapons. This is one of the very important reasons total nuclear disarmament is so vital, but it is only one.'[23] This time, however, mass public support for the government on nuclear arms control was missing, and the impetus to act came, as it usually does in foreign policy, from the executive.

Yet the ICNND report had no impact on Australia's nuclear policies or on its attitude to those of the US. They remained the same. The conclusion must be that Rudd commissioned the report without intending to change policy but simply in order to contribute to the global conversation about nuclear weapons and remind Australians that his government belonged to the Labor tradition in foreign policy. The episode was one of middle-power activism by Australia but with a limited outcome.

FURTHER READING

The Second Cold War and the 1990s

Parliamentary Research Service Current Issues Brief No. 47, 1994–95, *Raison d'Etat and Popular Response: The resumption of French nuclear testing in the South Pacific*, Canberra, 1995. (History of French nuclear testing and Australia's response.)

Pugh, Michael C., *The ANZUS Crisis, Nuclear Visiting and Deterrence*, Cambridge University Press, Cambridge, 1989. (Focus on New Zealand and its breach with the US over nuclear visiting.)

Arms control, disarmament, nuclear terrorism and the Nuclear Non-Proliferation Treaty

Cirincione, Joseph, *Bomb Scare: The history and future of nuclear weapons*, Columbia University Press, New York, 2007. (History and theory of nuclear weapons with proposals for dealing with the proliferation problem.)

Cotton, James, 'The Proliferation Security Initiative: Legality and limitations of a coalition strategy', *Security Dialogue*, vol. 36, no. 2, 2005, pp. 193–211. (Origins of the Bush administration's PSI initiative, which Australia supported, its limitations, and its applicability to the case of proliferation of weapons of mass destruction by North Korea.)

Evans, Gareth and Yoriko Kawaguchi, *Eliminating Nuclear Threats: A practical agenda for global policymakers*, Report of the International Commission on Nuclear Non-proliferation and Disarmament, 2009. (Report of the Commission organised by Australia and Japan; detailed, informative, realistic and an excellent starting point for understanding contemporary nuclear issues, especially proliferation.)

Freedman, Lawrence, *Deterrence*, Polity Press, Cambridge, 2004. (A short study by a leading scholar examining the rise and decline of deterrence as a doctrine, the problem of assuming states to be 'rational actors', and the role of deterrence post-9/11.)

Hanson, M. J., 'Arms control', in *An Introduction to International Relations*, R. Devetak, A. Burke and J. George, eds, Cambridge University Press, Cambridge, 2007, pp. 155–66. (Arms control, including nuclear arms control, in the context of international relations theory.)

O'Neil, Andrew, 'Shifting policy in a nuclear world: Australia's non-proliferation strategy since 9/11', in *Australian Foreign Policy in the Age of Terror*, Carl Ungerer, ed., UNSW Press, Sydney, 2008, pp. 74–100. (Examines Australia's traditional non-proliferation strategy and how it changed under the Howard government after 9/11.)

Stockholm International Peace Research Institute, *SIPRI Yearbook 2010: Armaments, disarmament and international security*, Stockholm, 2010. (Annual survey covers all important developments in military expenditure, arms production, world nuclear forces, nuclear arms control and non-proliferation.)

The Non-Proliferation Review, vol.17, no. 1, 2010. (Includes a special section on the dynamics of nuclear disarmament and the future of the non-proliferation regime.)

Parliament

Joint Standing Committee on Treaties, *Report 106, Nuclear Non-Proliferation and Disarmament*, Canberra, September 2009.

Websites

International Atomic Energy Agency: <www.iaea.org>
International Commission on Nuclear Non-proliferation and Disarmament: <www.icnnd.org>
UN Office for Disarmament Affairs: <www.un.org/disarmament>

8

Intervention and state building

- In what ways did 9/11 and the Bali bombings change the strategic context of Australian policy towards fragile states in its region?
- Why has state building in regional countries become an objective of Australian foreign policy?
- Why did the Howard government change Australia's policy on East Timor?
- What caused the secessionist war in Bougainville? How was peace achieved?
- Is the Regional Assistance Mission to Solomon Islands a justified case of state building by Australia and other countries or an act of imperialism against a small neighbouring state?
- What are the circumstances under which armed intervention in a sovereign state is legitimate?
- How did Australia respond to the Fiji coups of 2000 and 2006?
- What are the origins of the discourse of 'failed states'? Does this discourse serve the interests of small countries in Australia's immediate region or not?

The arc of islands that lies across the top end of Australia has preoccupied Australia's foreign policymakers in recent years more than their modest populations might seem to justify. Papua New Guinea has a population of about 7 million, East Timor not much more than 1 million, Fiji 840,000, Solomon Islands 550,000, and Tonga a mere 100,000. Why, then, do they matter so much to Australia? The answer is both general and particular. All states must be concerned with events in their neighbourhood. Peaceful and stable neighbours, such as Australia and New Zealand, create a beneficial strategic and economic environment for each other. Unstable neighbours can threaten the security of more fortunate countries in their midst, undermine prospects for prosperity, and destabilise whole regions. As it happens, Australia is a rich country located next door to the developing world, and is inevitably caught up in the complex politics of countries where internal security, effective government, and orderly political transitions cannot be taken for granted. The fate of small weak states, moreover, has assumed new strategic importance for Australia since the emergence of a continuing terrorist threat in Indonesia. In the view of successive governments, a weak or failed state close to Australia could be a haven for terrorists just as Afghanistan was for al-Qaeda, as well as being a conduit for drugs, disease and refugees.

Australia's closest neighbours to the north, north-east and north-west are poorer than Australia, less endowed by history and culture with internal cohesion, and more likely (though not certain) to experience political instability. Indonesia, though now a democracy, has experienced long periods of authoritarian rule punctuated by violent political upheavals. East Timor was subject to repressive Indonesian rule between 1975, when Indonesia invaded, and 1999, when Australia led an intervention force to ensure that independence was achieved. After a long and bloody struggle, East Timor finally achieved independence as a new nation in 2002. Papua New Guinea experienced a secessionist war in the 1990s when the island of Bougainville fought to break away as a separate state. Solomon Islands suffered a breakdown of law and order and a collapse of effective government following a coup in 2000. Serious riots in Tonga in 2006 destroyed part of the capital Nuku'alofa. A few weeks later, a coup in Fiji, the second in six years, overthrew the elected government and installed a military commander, Voreqe (Frank) Bainimarama, as prime minister. He entrenched his power in 2009 by dismissing all judges, muzzling the media, and abrogating the constitution.

This chapter examines political turbulence in these five political entities—East Timor, Bougainville, Solomon Islands, Fiji and Tonga—and Australia's evolving policy response in each case.

A TURBULENT REGION

A secessionist movement is one that wants to secede, or break away, from a larger state with the intention that the territory it claims will itself become a new state. The two regional secessionist movements that have most affected

Australia were in East Timor and Bougainville. East Timor was a province of Indonesia from 1975 to 1999. Bougainville is now an autonomous province of Papua New Guinea. Both have been parts of larger states, and fought to become independent nation-states. The origins of secessionism lie to a large extent in what happened at the time of decolonisation, the process by which a foreign colonial government withdraws in favour of a local independent one. The withdrawing colonial power differed—Portugal for East Timor, Australia for PNG—and so did the circumstances of withdrawal, but the incoming political and economic order triggered secessionism in both cases. The consequence has been violence and political instability in countries which share maritime borders with Australia.

Secessionists in the new states of Africa, South-East Asia and the Pacific—those that have come into existence only since World War II—usually point to the fact that their territory became part of a new state against their will. European colonisers drew the borders that define most countries of the former colonial world. The governments of new states inherited those borders at independence. Not infrequently, the borders were drawn without regard for the popula-tions enclosed within them or divided by them. These borders are legacies of arrangements between the colonial powers in the nineteenth century, have been confirmed at independence, and have given rise to secessionist movements by peoples who have resented being included in new states controlled by those they have regarded as foreigners.

State failure describes a political situation where government ceases to function effectively, or is hijacked by a small group of people for themselves, and where law and order breaks down in favour of control by those who are armed. Those with guns get what they want, while the rest cower in fear. Under such circumstances people have no authority to protect them and must depend upon themselves for security. For various reasons, Solomon Islands moved from state weakness to serious instability in 2000, after a militia composed of people from one island in the Solomon Islands group seized control of the government and police force. To stop the disorder and reconstruct the state, Australia intervened in 2003 at the head of a regional intervention force called the Regional Assistance Mission to Solomon Islands (RAMSI). Order remained fragile nevertheless. Riots following the 2006 elections destroyed parts of the capital Honiara, and Australia, having withdrawn troops, sent them back again to restore stability. Australia remains committed to a long-term reconstruction of government in that country.

Fiji poses a different security problem. Fiji is a military dictatorship rather than a weak state. For the past 40 years, ever since independence, politics in Fiji has been a delicate balancing act between the two major ethnic communities, punctuated by successive political crises in which coups overturn elected governments. The Fiji military, meanwhile, has expanded in size and broken free of civilian control, seizing government at will. The present Fiji prime minister, Frank Bainimarama, who is also commander of the military forces, claims to have seized power in order to transcend Fiji's ethnic conflict but, just as plausibly, he could have seized power for its own sake.

Howard intensified Australia's engagement with the South Pacific and East Timor, while Rudd and Gillard followed in his footsteps. The official position was that 'a porous, underdeveloped and insecure region can increasingly feed instability, inhibit development and pose a threat to Australia's national security'.[1] Under Howard, Australia gave more aid, sent more advisers, employed more consultants, commissioned more reports, and demanded more accountability in island countries than ever before as part of an ambitious project to remake the region in the image of good governance, and it continues to do so. The new element in Australian policy is armed intervention—which Australian governments justify as both humanitarian and cooperative—aimed at restoring law and order for the sake of human security, and agreed to beforehand by sovereign island governments seeking foreign assistance. Australia's policy also reflects changes in international definitions of sovereignty, a concept whose strict meaning was being questioned in the 1990s by those who were appalled by human rights abuses in Rwanda, Sierra Leone, Somalia, and the former Yugoslavia. A turning-point was the decision by NATO to bomb Yugoslavia in 1999, when the United States and its European allies intervened to stop Serb forces from driving Kosovar Albanians from Kosovo. Since then many countries, though not all, have accepted that sovereignty is not absolute, but contingent on governments meeting basic obligations towards their people. The new doctrine is sometimes called *sovereignty as responsibility*. In the absence of responsibility, it is argued, there can be no sovereignty and therefore no legal bar against the armed intrusion of outside states seeking to protect people from harm.

State building—the business of constructing the full apparatus of modern government in fragile states—is seen as one of Australia's tasks in foreign policy, and planned for by the Australian Defence Force, the Australian Federal Police, AusAID and other government organisations in what has become a 'whole-of-government' exercise. In order to coordinate activities in state building and peacekeeping, the Rudd government established the Asia Pacific Civil–Military Centre of Excellence in 2008. The 2009 Defence white paper predicted that 'many South Pacific island states and East Timor will continue to be beset to some degree by economic stagnation and political and social instability' and foresaw 'security problems of the kind to which Australia may need to respond directly with appropriate forms of humanitarian and security assistance, including by way of ADF deployments'.[2]

The idea that Australia might intervene in nearby small states is not new. Political instability in Fiji, Vanuatu and Papua New Guinea in the late 1980s prompted the Hawke government to raise the possibility that Australia might intervene militarily in the region 'in unusual and extreme circumstances'. Hawke's foreign minister, Gareth Evans, said Australians 'should not be embarrassed about using the military capability we possess, with prudence and sensitivity, to advance both Australia's and the common security of the region'. But the situation quietened and no interventions occurred. The peacekeepers Australia sent to Bougainville in 1998 carried no arms and were there to maintain a peace already agreed upon. Even Australia's armed intervention in East Timor in 1999 appeared to be a special case, not a precedent. When the Solomon Islands government asked Australia to intervene in 2000, following a breakdown of law and order, the Howard government said no.

The threat of global terrorism, however, changed the strategic context of Australia's foreign policy. After 9/11 the United States and other Western powers saw Afghanistan as a failed state where an absence of effective government had allowed al-Qaeda to flourish. Policymakers in Canberra began to discern a link between state failure and terrorism, to see fragile states in Australia's own region as threats to national security, and to describe Solomon Islands as just such a state. From 2003 Australia's regional security policy, at least as far as nearby small island states were concerned, was embedded in a discourse of failed states and characterised by a new activism. Howard said he knew he was engaging in a change in policy. In earlier times Australia might have tolerated the presence of a failed state in its region, and remained content with supplying a mix of mediators, peace monitors and aid experts as palliatives. In an era of international terrorism, however, such an approach began to seem complacent. Terrorists, after all, had found havens in failed states elsewhere, such as Afghanistan and Somalia. They might, in time, be drawn to the South Pacific for the same reason. John Howard told the ABC interviewer Kerry O'Brien in 2003, 'we are dealing here with the potential of a failed state. And it is not in Australia's interest for a country like the Solomon Islands to fall over. It would then become potentially a haven for drug running, money laundering, terrorism … it is in Australia's interests to have stability in the Pacific area and particularly amongst the small island states.[3] Since then Australia has repeatedly deployed soldiers and police to the South Pacific and East Timor in response to riots, political instability and the breakdown of law and order.

EAST TIMOR

For almost a generation East Timor was at the centre of the debate about the morality of Australia's foreign policy, from the time Indonesia invaded in 1975 to the dramatic days of 1999, when the East Timorese finally voted for their own independence. However, what followed the national referendum was a campaign of targeted destruction carried out by militias with the backing of the Indonesian military forces. Many people believed Australia had betrayed East Timor over the years by failing to intervene in support of its independence, and were relieved when the Howard government—under the pressure of events— ordered Australian troops across the Timor Sea at the head of an international intervention force which stopped the killing and created the conditions for the country's transition to independence. To understand why Australia accepted East Timor's incorporation into Indonesia for so long, and why it then reversed that policy, we need to examine how the territory came to be swallowed up by its much larger neighbour.

Timor is a rugged, mountainous island lying 430 kilometres north-west of Darwin. For centuries, Timor was occupied by two European colonial powers: the Dutch in the west and the Portuguese in the east. West Timor became part of the new Indonesian republic when the Indonesians expelled the Dutch and declared their independence in 1945. But the dictators who ruled Portugal until the 1970s did not accept that Portuguese overseas territories in Africa and Asia had any right to independence. East Timor remained an overseas province of Portugal, a tropical backwater of Empire with a population of about 680,000 by the 1970s.

Then events in Portugal changed everything for the East Timorese. A group of military officers staged a democratic revolution and overthrew the dicta-torship in Lisbon in April 1974. They announced a new deal for Portuguese overseas territories, one that recognised their right to self-determination. East Timorese political parties, previously illegal, quickly appeared. The two main party groupings were the conservative UDT (Timorese Democratic Union) and the left-wing Fretilin (Revolutionary Front for an Independent East Timor), both of which favoured independence for East Timor. A small third party called for integration with Indonesia. Indonesia soon launched *Operasi Komodo*, a secret campaign of propaganda, disinformation and subversion designed to sow dissension among the East Timorese and bring about the kind of political turmoil that would justify Indonesian intervention. The East Timorese were divided in any case and obliged the Indonesians by fighting a brief, two-week civil war in August 1975, causing refugees to flee across the border to West Timor as well as by sea to Darwin.

Fretilin emerged victorious from the war and declared an independent East Timor on 28 November 1975, only to confront Indonesian forces within days of the declaration. The invasion, which began on 7 December 1975, ranks as one of the more brutal military campaigns of modern times. Indonesian soldiers shot civilians, looted houses and demanded women and girls whom they then raped. They killed about 2000 people in the capital Dili in the first week, putting tens of thousands to death in the months that followed. No one knows how many East Timorese died from bullets, bombs, starvation and disease. Estimates of loss of life in the first four years of Indonesian occupation range from a tenth to a third of the 1975 population of about 680,000. Whatever the true figure, all agree that Indonesia's invasion was pitiless, caused the deaths of scores of thousands of people at the very least and fundamentally dislocated East Timorese society. Not surprisingly, the invasion also gave rise to a secessionist or independence movement.

For as long as Suharto remained in power, East Timor complicated and frustrated attempts by Australian governments to cultivate good relations with Indonesia. Many Australians saw the Suharto regime as dictatorial, repressive and untrustworthy. Each side of the Australian debate about East Timor exasperated the other. Critics said East Timor revealed the hypocrisy of Australia's claim to take a consistent foreign policy approach to human rights abuses. Some saw ministers and diplomats as the instruments by which Australia betrayed the East Timorese people and failed to prevent attempted genocide. They said Australia sacrificed the East Timorese for the sake of good relations between Canberra and Jakarta, and for the oil and gas of the Timor Sea. Governments, both Labor and Coalition, replied that Australia did all it could for the East Timorese through aid and diplomacy, given the wider diplomatic context which no government could responsibly ignore.

In the end, economic turmoil shook the Suharto regime to its foundations and opened political space for East Timor. As part of a general loss of international confidence in South-East Asian economies, the financial markets moved suddenly against the Indonesian currency in 1997, producing a massive devaluation of the rupiah against the US dollar and causing the closure of a large number of Indonesian banks. The International Monetary Fund intervened with funds to enable Indonesia to meet its international obligations, in particular its debts to foreign banks, but imposed a price that destabilised the country. The Indonesian government was required, under the terms of the rescue package, to remove government subsidies on key commodities (all except rice), ensuring that prices would rise fast just as millions lost their jobs. Sporadic riots broke out early in 1998, culminating in a massive riot in the capital Jakarta in May, when mobs killed more than 1000, mainly ethnic Chinese, in an orgy of looting and burning. After 32 years as president, Suharto was forced to resign in favour of his vice-president, B.J. Habibie, a former engineer with an international outlook and a desire to leave his mark on history.

President Habibie signalled a new approach to East Timor within weeks of taking office, promising to consider giving the territory a special status and releasing East Timorese prisoners. Soon afterwards Australia undertook a consultation exercise with East Timorese leaders in order to gauge the way events were likely to develop, and began to review its entire East Timor policy in the light of the rapid changes taking place. To solve the East Timor problem, after all, would be to remove the main barrier to good relations with Indonesia, and by the end of 1998 the Howard government had refashioned Australia's policy on East Timor. Before the policy shift was made public, Howard wrote a letter to his Indonesian counterpart, suggesting that the East Timorese should eventually be able to participate in an act of self-determination, after a period of years. During this time the Indonesian government would have the chance to persuade them to stay as part of the Indonesian republic.

Habibie, a mercurial man given to sudden bursts of enthusiasm, was in no mood to wait for the East Timor issue to fester. 'Why should we remain a captive of East Timor?' he asked his adviser Dewi Fortuna Anwar. 'Why don't we just let them go if they no longer want to stay with us?'[4] He announced, to general surprise, that Indonesia would allow the East Timorese to vote on whether they wanted to stay as part of the country or leave and become independent.

Howard's letter was the initial element in Australia's intervention over East Timor. Others soon followed, as Australia became deeply involved in UN initiatives, first to organise and observe an internationally acceptable act of self-determination, then to intervene militarily to restore order, and subsequently to govern the territory and maintain security during its transition to independence as a new state. Darwin became the staging point for the United Nations Mission in East Timor that oversaw and organised the act of self-determination in August 1999, and Australia supplied it with helicopters, aircraft, vehicles, medical kits, rations and office accommodation as well as personnel. When the East Timorese voted overwhelmingly for independence, pro-Indonesian militias ran amok and East Timor descended into anarchy. Australia evacuated most of the UN personnel to Darwin in a series of dramatic rescue operations. Then the international community decided to intervene, and Australia led the intervention force.

The first Australian soldiers entered the East Timorese capital of Dili on 20 September 1999, five days after the UN authorised the establishment of the International Force in East Timor (INTERFET) to restore peace and security. Australia's commitment of troops to East Timor was easily its largest since the Vietnam War, 5500 of INTERFET's peak strength of 11,500, and enjoyed widespread support from the Australian public. INTERFET included Western military contributions from Canada, Britain, New Zealand, Portugal and the United States, as might have been expected. More surprising was the fact that Australia was able to persuade South-East Asian countries—Thailand, Singapore, the Philippines and even Malaysia—to be involved and to give INTERFET the legitimacy of being partly Asian. INTERFET was short-lived but highly successful, and paved the way for a comprehensive UN transitional administration in East Timor, protected by UN peacekeepers, to oversee the path to independence between 2000 and 2002. By this time Australia had fewer troops on the ground, about 1500, but they were still the largest national peacekeeping contingent, and 440 Australians remained there as part of the UN peacekeeping force in 2004.

The international community, believing East Timor's problems were solved, had largely withdrawn by 2006. Australia called almost all its troops home, the UN police force was down to 26 and foreign forces numbered just 40. But a serious political crisis erupted when the military commander dismissed half his soldiers, the so-called *petitioners*, in April of that year. Violence broke out in Dili between soldiers and police, while youth gangs of mostly *loromonu* (westerners) rampaged through the city burning houses owned by *lorosae* (easterners), throwing rocks and shooting at will. The disturbances killed at least 38 people, forced 100,000 people out of their homes, 30,000 of them into makeshift refugee camps, and continued even after the 1200-strong

'CO-OPERATIVE INTERVENTION': JOHN HOWARD SENDS TROOPS BACK TO EAST TIMOR, 2006

Since I made my statement to the House the National Security Committee of Cabinet met again after Parliament Question Time, and subsequently I've had some further briefings from my department and defence and ONA. It's quite clear that the situation in Dili has deteriorated since I made my statement, and there are widespread reports of a very chaotic situation. The airfield has been secured by the advance detachment of some 130 commandos. Given the deteriorating situation, we will go ahead without any conditionality, and the 1,300 will be in place in a very short order. But I'm not going to commit myself to a number of hours, but they will certainly be in place very quickly. And the fact that we did prepare in advance for this possibility means that they can get there very quickly. HMAS *Adelaide* is already in Dili harbour. The finer details of the working arrangements of the deployment will be worked out with the authorities in East Timor after all the forces have arrived.

They have a very clear mission, it's a very orthodox mission, and they will operate in accordance with appropriate Australian national policy for rules of engagement. They essentially are to assist the authorities in East Timor in the restoration of security, confidence and peace, and re-establish and maintain public order, and the ADF personnel will take whatever action is necessary to give effect to that, including assisting in the provision of security and safety to people and property and the suppression of violence and intimidation. In other words, they will be there to secure the peace and to take what action is needed. They won't be there, of course, to take sides. And the preliminary reports indicate that the presence of the Australian forces has been warmly welcomed by the people of Dili. They will of course have, as part of their mission, the evacuation of Australia and other approved foreign nationals, and to audit an account for the location of weapons that belong to different groups within East Timorese society.

During the Cabinet meeting this afternoon I spoke to the Secretary General of the United Nations, Mr Kofi Annan, who rang to express his gratitude for what Australia was prepared to do. He himself had spoken to the president and prime minister of East Timor, and they clearly wanted security to be maintained in order to be restored. The Secretary General also indicated to me that he would be sending his personal representative into East Timor, and that will be Mr Ian Martin, who was his personal representative in East Timor way back in 1999, and he is very well versed in the area, and his presence will be very welcome to both the prime minister and the president.

'John Howard Holds Press Conference on East Timor Engagement', 25 May 2006, ABC PM program transcript, <www.abc.net.au/pm/content/2006/s1647641.htm>.

International Stabilisation Force (ISF) and a large force of UN police arrived to restore order. Australia led the ISF, initially with 925 troops, New Zealand assisted, and Malaysia sent troops as well. During the crisis one military officer, Major Alfredo Reinado, deserted and fled into the hills with a band of followers. Hundreds of other former soldiers also remained at large until promises of government compensation for their service persuaded most of them to surrender early in 2008. At this point Reinado was shot dead by a soldier guarding the home of East Timor's president, José Ramos-Horta, who was out jogging. When he came home, Ramos-Horta was himself shot by one of Reinado's men and had to be evacuated to Darwin for hospital treatment. The attempted assassination of the president was world news, and the East Timorese government responded by imposing a curfew, placing the army and police under joint command, and obtaining the surrender of the last remaining rebel soldiers.

In an arrangement that echoed INTERFET, the ISF supported but was not part of the UN Integrated Mission in Timor-Leste (UNMIT), which has been given a succession of mandates by the UN Security Council since it was formed in 2006. Australia preferred to operate this way rather than come under direct UN command. Australian soldiers in East Timor worked to professionalise the East Timor armed force, the F-FDTL (Falintil-Forças de Defesa de Timor-Leste), while Australian police train the PNTL (Policia Nacional de Timor-Leste), and Australian aid personnel and other public servants worked on AusAID projects throughout the country.

Once again Australian troops and police found themselves maintaining order in a neighbouring fragile state. They did so with the support of most Australians and both major party groupings. But their deployment raised a key issue that has haunted the debate about East Timor since the 1970s: now that intervening in neighbouring states where necessary had become Australian policy, was Australia destined to act as East Timor's permanent security guarantor?

Such a role—desirable though it may be on security and humanitarian grounds—has considerable potential to damage the Australian–Indonesian relationship, especially if that relationship should come under strain for other reasons.

BOUGAINVILLE

The origins of Bougainvillean secessionism lie in the colonial history of PNG, and in the international border drawn in 1899 between the German and

British parts of Solomon Islands. Today the islands of Bougainville and Buka, geographically in the Solomons, are politically within the sovereign territory of Papua New Guinea.

Geologists discovered a vast deposit of copper in the Panguna Valley in central Bougainville in the 1960s and the Australian administration permitted Bougainville Copper Limited, an Australian company, to mine on highly favourable terms via the *Mining Bougainville Copper Agreement Act 1967*. Secessionist sentiment was stirred by the high profits recorded by the Australian company Bougainville Copper Limited in the first years after production began in 1972. After all, Bougainvilleans thought, why should they share their wealth with other people in islands to the west just because inherited colonial borders happened to place Bougainville inside the new state of PNG? In 1974, not long before independence in September 1975, PNG renegotiated the agreement with the mining company so as to ensure that a large stream of revenue flowed from the Bougainville copper mine into the coffers of the new national government, which became a minority owner of the enterprise. The idea was to subsidise the development of the whole country from the proceeds of a single massive mine. By the time the mine shut down in May 1989, the national government had received 63 per cent of the revenue generated by the mine, the provincial government 4.8 per cent and the local landowners themselves, who had lost land and seen pollution of the air, water and soil, 0.2 per cent. The rest went to shareholders other than the government. Even though Bougainville as a province benefited disproportionately from mine revenues, local landowners were poorly compensated and many Bougainvilleans saw the distribution of resources as unfair. The 1974 agreement was a recipe for secessionism in a new state with uncertain authority over a remote, resource-rich province.

The impetus for the secessionist rebellion that started in 1988 came from landowners directly affected by the copper mine, and specifically from a younger group of landowner activists who demanded massive compensation for losses of land and damage to the environment. When they failed to receive satisfaction they launched attacks on mine property, sparking a cycle of violence that brought police and then the PNG Defence Force to Bougainville. The secessionists organised a guerilla force called the Bougainville Revolutionary Army (BRA), closed the mine, rejected a government peace package and launched a war of independence. After further fighting the BRA declared Bougainville independent in May 1990, whereupon the national government blockaded the island and cut off medical supplies, fuel and telecommunications links. Schools closed, living conditions worsened, diseases flourished and avoidable deaths proliferated. No one knows how many people died directly or indirectly as a result of the war but they number at least 5000, maybe 10,000 and possibly many more. Tens of thousands of people found refuge from the fighting in government care centres. From 1990 armed conflict ebbed and flowed on Bougainville. Peace settlements were reached repeatedly only to collapse soon afterwards. To complicate matters, some Bougainvilleans were organised in resistance forces opposed to the BRA. The conflict became a civil war not only within PNG but also within Bougainville itself. The war was fought on a much smaller scale than secessionist wars in Indonesia but it brought poverty and suffering to what was once PNG's most prosperous province and it destabilised PNG economically and politically.

Australia's response was to back PNG with civil and military aid and to call for a negotiated solution. The copper mine accounted for 37 per cent of PNG's foreign exchange earnings and 19 per cent of government revenues when rebels forced its closure. PNG faced an immediate economic emergency equivalent to the sudden loss by Australia of all coal and iron ore exports. Australia gave an extra $20 million in civil aid, doubled military assistance and backed loans from multilateral aid donors such as the World Bank. Australia also supplied four Iroquois helicopters in Bougainville on condition that they not be used as gunships, though in fact they were used for precisely that purpose. Australian military aid was part of a wider strategy to equip PNG with the means of ensuring internal security.

After eight years of fighting the Bougainville Civil War became a political crisis for PNG and a security problem for Australia. A group of 71 mercenaries arrived in PNG in 1997, sent there by a British company that specialises in mercenary operations, Sandline International. They were said to be military trainers, employed to enhance the skills of government troops fighting secessionists on the island of Bougainville. Howard and his advisers were alarmed. Here was a group of hired killers, mostly South Africans with experience of wars in Africa, coming to the South Pacific to settle a problem which in Australia's view had no military solution. One man with good reason to object to the Sandline mercenaries was the commander of the PNG Defence Force, Brigadier-General Jerry Singirok. Their arrival, after all, was a sign that the government had no faith in his soldiers. In what became known as the St Patrick's Day mutiny, he intervened to stop his men cooperating with the mercenaries and ordered all army barracks sealed before any new campaign in Bougainville could commence. He then went on national radio and called on the prime minister to resign. When the prime minister, Sir Julius Chan, dismissed him, demonstrations and riots erupted in PNG's capital Port Moresby and other towns, indicating support for Singirok and dissatisfaction with the government. As looters took advantage of the situation, Australia placed troops in Townsville and Richmond on alert to evacuate thousands of Australians from the country if order disintegrated. Howard then sent three emissaries to tell the PNG prime minister that Australia would curtail aid unless he changed course. He could not afford to ignore them. Australian aid was one of the lifelines that kept Papua New Guinean governments afloat. So the PNG government agreed to suspend the mercenary contract and the mercenaries were flown out of the country.

Ironically, the 'Sandline affair' created an opening for peace in Bougainville by dramatising the potential security risks the war was creating for the whole region. New Zealand, seen by all sides as neutral, brought the parties together at a series of peace talks in 1997. In an imaginative piece of diplomacy, the New Zealand foreign minister, Don McKinnon, calculated that agreement was most likely to be achieved by a process that allowed for Melanesian ways of making peace; that is, by consensus, with as many stakeholders as possible, and without the pressure of a tight deadline. So New Zealand flew no fewer than 280 Bougainvilleans to an airforce base and, after lengthy negotiations in these culturally congenial circumstances, they eventually agreed to lay down their arms.

More than 5000 troops and civilians from Australia, New Zealand, Vanuatu and Fiji served as unarmed peacekeepers in Bougainville over the six years of peace monitoring that ended in 2003. They oversaw the ceasefire, the repatriation of displaced villagers, the reconciliation of former enemies, the disposal of weapons and the return of government services. Peace enabled people to move around the island, to send their children to school and to receive medical treatment once again. Many Bougainvilleans have made peace with each other following traditional customs of compensation and reconciliation, though a few rebels with guns remain. The PNG government has amended the country's constitution to give Bougainville an autonomous status, and will allow Bougainvilleans to vote in a referendum on independence in 2015. An election for president of the autonomous PNG province of Bougainville in 2010 returned John Momis, a long-time political leader and one of the architects of PNG's constitution. Peace now appears to have come permanently to Bougainville.

FIJI

Most Australians think of Fiji as a good place to go for a holiday in the sun, not one where politics looms large. With a population of just 840,000, Fiji seems too small to matter. Yet they are wrong. Politics in Fiji is hard fought and political divisions run deep. While small by world standards, Fiji is nevertheless the giant in the South Pacific region east of Papua New Guinea, where every other country is even smaller, and it is therefore the centre for an intricate array of regional and international institutions that serve not just Fiji but all the other small island countries as well. When security is threatened in Fiji, the South Pacific as a whole suffers. That is why Australia keeps a watching brief on political developments in Fiji, and why Australia reacts when elected governments are overthrown, as they often are.

As in East Timor and Bougainville, the origin of Fiji's political problems lies in history. Here, though, the past has bequeathed a different legacy to the present, not artificial national borders or forced incorporation into a neighbouring state but rather the difficulty of governing a country with two large ethnic communities that were deliberately kept apart during the colonial period, and which now possess distinctly different senses of identity. The two communities are the indigenous Fijians, the original occupiers of the land, and the descendants of Indians brought to work on the sugar plantations by the British a century ago. Many indigenous Fijians have never accepted the majoritarian logic of liberal democracy, by which the party that wins the greatest number of votes has the right to form government. They fear that by those rules Indians might win power and take their land. They still see Fiji as a country in which the Indians are guests, who might deserve to be tolerated but who do not have the right to govern. When Indians happen to succeed in occupying the government benches in parliament, they do not last long. A military coup in 1987 led by an army officer, Sitiveni Rabuka, overthrew a newly elected government consisting of both Fijians and Indians within months of its election. Rabuka's coup seriously weakened Fiji, which until then had been easily the best governed and most prosperous South Pacific country. Scores of thousands of Fiji's brightest and most highly skilled citizens, mostly of Indian origin, sought a better life elsewhere and the country lurched into declining efficiency and lacklustre economic performance. With the old constitution overthrown, a new one emerged, so transparent in its design to keep indigenous Fijians permanently in power that the international community refused to endorse it. Rabuka, by now the prime minister, therefore agreed to yet another constitution, one which restored the balance between the two communities and was closer to Western liberal democracy.

This new constitution of 1997, combined with a new electoral system, delivered an unexpected result at the elections of 1999. Fiji suddenly had its first Indian prime minister, Mahendra Chaudhry, leading a Fiji Labour Party government. For a year the country simmered. Then on 19 May 2000 a group of civilians, led by a Fijian called George Speight and assisted by a rebel army contingent, marched into parliament and seized the parliamentarians, whom they kept hostage for the next 56 days. The army intervened, deposed the president, abrogated the constitution, imposed a curfew and maintained a loose cordon around the parliament while parleying with the rebels. When the hostages were finally released, the army arrested hundreds of rebels. But the army did not restore the deposed Indian prime minister. Instead, an unelected government under an indigenous Fijian prime minister, Laisenia Qarase, came into office with army approval.

Fiji appeared to re-establish a stable democracy under Qarase, whose party won the 2001 election. But Qarase had no control over the military forces, which increasingly asserted an independent role. The military commander Frank Bainimarama turned against his protégé Qarase, and acted as if the constitution, which gave authority over the military forces to the government, no longer applied. From 2004 onwards Bainimarama engaged in open and continuous public criticism of the government, threatening coups, opposing legislation and purging his force of constitutionalist officers who might block the way to another coup. When the government won another election—in 2006—the scene was set for military intervention, which came on 6 December, when Bainimarama declared on radio that the military, which had 'observed the concern and anguish of the deteriorating state of our beloved Fiji', had, therefore, 'taken over the government as executive authority in the running of the country'. Bainimarama became president and later prime minister of a country that was under military rule for the third time in less than twenty years.

Bainimarama entrenched his coup in April 2009. Outraged by a Fiji Court of Appeal judgment that had the effect of ruling his coup illegal, he dismissed all judges, abrogated the constitution, declared a 'New Legal Order', expelled foreign journalists and imposed strict censorship by posting soldiers and police in media offices. He released soldiers found guilty of coup-related crimes including murder, a signal to his men that they could act with impunity. He militarised the governing of Fiji, replacing civilians with military officers throughout the bureaucracy. He gave himself control of police, prisons, immigration, justice, the postal service, airports and fisheries, and put his own non-military appointees in charge of key institutions such as the Reserve Bank. Where previous coup leaders had merely overturned elections, Bainimarama destroyed the key institutions that underpin democracy such as free media, freedom of speech, freedom of association, an independent and impartial judiciary, and a legal profession that can operate independently and according to law. Under his New Legal Order, Fiji became an oppressive military dictatorship in the middle of a region of direct strategic importance to Australia.

SOLOMON ISLANDS

Solomon Islands prompted a change in Australia's foreign policy, this time on the broader issue of intervening in the South Pacific. Ever since most of the South Pacific nations became independent in the 1960s and 1970s, Australia has been careful to respect their sovereignty and avoid any appearance of interference in their internal affairs. Following a period of political turbulence in the region in the late 1980s, the Hawke Labor government had sought to define the circumstances under which Australian military intervention might occur in the South Pacific, but the judgement of successive governments was that those circumstances had never arisen. Even when the beleaguered government of Solomon Islands appealed for Australia to send troops or police to restore order in 2000, Australia said no. Yet by July 2003 John Howard was announcing a reversal of Australia's traditional approach, and Australian troops and police were disembarking in the Solomon Islands capital Honiara at the head of a regional intervention force, the Regional Assistance Mission to Solomon Islands, sent to restore order and reimpose effective central authority in the small island nation. Crowds of grateful Solomon Islanders cheered Howard as his car drove through the streets of Honiara a few weeks later.

To understand this second Australian military intervention in a neighbouring state, we need to ask what went wrong in Solomon Islands. A Melanesian archipelago lying to the east of PNG, Solomon Islands is a former British colonial territory which became independent in 1978. Preparation for the transition to a Westminster system of government was rushed, and Solomon Islands faced daunting problems of national political cohesion as soon as it had raised its own flag. Solomon Islanders speak more than 80 languages, and they identify far more closely with their own language speakers and with kin than with wider political groupings such as the nation. Under these circumstances, Westminster democracy proved a weak basis for effective government and national unity. The economy, too, was undeveloped at independence, with most people depending on gardens, fishing and cash crops for survival, and the country turned to exporting tropical timber as the route to development. The Asian timber companies that invested in Solomon Islands, however, steadily undermined the integrity of government institutions by bribing government officials to permit unrestrained logging of the country's virgin tropical forests with minimal payment of tax. By the mid 1990s corrupt politicians were permitting so many tax remissions to timber companies that government income was falling as log exports were rising. The government was bankrupting the country.

Meantime, people were migrating from other islands to the capital of Honiara on Guadalcanal Island, drawn by the bright lights and chance for wage employment at the government centre. Many of them came from the nearby island of Malaita, and the Malaitans became competitors with local Guadalcanal people for land and government jobs. None of this might have mattered if the Solomon Islands economy had provided a degree of prosperity for the rapidly growing population of young people in a country that has one of the world's highest birthrates. But it did not. Urbanised young men, in particular, with no jobs and no prospects, were potential recruits for whatever political movement might arise. This tinderbox of grievances burst alight in 1998, when Guadalcanal militants began a campaign of murder and arson to force the Malaitans off their land and out of their island. A ragtag army of Guadalcanal militants armed with shotguns and .22 rifles emerged, and called itself the Isatabu Freedom Movement. In 1999, declaring a state of emergency, the government repatriated thousands of Malaitans to their home island in an effort to bring peace.

The situation worsened in 2000. The Malaitans formed their own militia called the Malaita Eagle Force (MEF), which raided the police armoury for high-powered weapons and finally overthrew the constitutionally elected government, replacing the prime minister with one of their own choosing. As the MEF, in cooperation with many of the police, tightened its grip on the capital and began to distribute government funds to supporters, fighting intensified and looting became widespread. Many Solomon Islanders fled Honiara, and Australia sent a naval vessel to evacuate Australian citizens. Major commercial enterprises such as the Gold Ridge mine stopped operating. After further disorder and loss of life, Australia organised a peace conference between the two warring parties in Townsville. The Townsville Peace Agreement of October 2000 provided for militant factions to surrender their weapons under the supervision of the International Peace Monitoring Team, and to give the militants a new role by appointing them as special constables on the government payroll. Many ex-militants, however, decided to retain their high-powered weapons. No one could stop them. The police force, now consisting mainly of Malaitans, was part of the country's problem, periodically intimidating the government into giving them 'compensation' or special payments, and doing nothing to stop the gangs of thugs who stole, raped and murdered as they pleased. The Australian diplomat who led the regional intervention force into Solomon Islands, Nick Warner, later recalled the country as it was in mid 2003:

> . . . imagine a country where hospitals, schools and clinics have simply ceased to function for a lack of funds, imagine a country where public servants go weeks without pay—not surprisingly, some turn up to work, but many do not—imagine roads that are literally falling apart, public thoroughfares that are the preserve of drunks and thieves. Then, to complete the picture, add to the mix guns, ethnic tensions, rogue police, corrupt politicians and business people, and armed criminals.[5]

Solomon Islands was becoming a failed state.

The Regional Assistance Mission to Solomon Islands (RAMSI) began as a police operation with military backing, led by Australia and with a force from nine South Pacific countries, consisting of 1700 military personnel. Within a few months, the mission proved strikingly successful in disarming and arresting militants, destroying thousands of seized weapons, and removing criminal elements from the police force. The sheer size and power of the force, at least by Solomon Islands' standards, discouraged armed resistance, and Australia was soon able to withdraw many soldiers. With law and order re-established, the mission moved to the more difficult task of rebuilding the institutions of government. Civilians from Australian government departments occupied leading positions in the justice system, the ministry of finance and elsewhere, attempting to reconstruct an efficient bureaucracy that could deliver services to the Solomon Islands people.

Even a state-building mission on the scale of RAMSI, however, could not create stability overnight, as the Solomons elections of 2006 showed. As soon as a new prime minister appeared before the crowd at Parliament House, people shouted abuse at him, accusing him of corruption. Within hours rioters were burning police vehicles, torching Chinese businesses, and swirling through the capital Honiara in a fury of destruction. They continued to riot into the next day when the Pacific Casino Hotel was also burnt down. The mission's police force having failed to maintain order, Australia sent 120 soldiers and 30 police, with more joining them from New Zealand and Fiji. The affair arose in part from

A SOLOMON ISLANDER ON WHY AUSTRALIA INTERVENED IN HIS COUNTRY

Australia's willingness to lead the Pacific Islands Forum regional intervention into Solomon Islands cannot be understood by looking at what happened in Solomon Islands alone. It is also necessary to examine changes in the global security discourse, especially approaches to the war against international terrorism. Australia became an important player through its partnership with the United States and Great Britain.

The decision to lead the regional intervention force into Solomon Islands was a 'preemptive strike' to prevent the threat of terrorist attack on Australia, its citizens, and its interests in the region. Canberra became interested in Solomon Islands only when it became an important piece of Australia's foreign policy 'jigsaw puzzle.'

The intervention was justified by the 'failing state' discourse, which argued that the Solomon Islands state was collapsing and prone to being used by terrorist organizations. The decision was made easier because of Canberra's long-term negative representation of the Pacific Islands, and its perception of its role as leader, protector, and superior arbiter of regional affairs.

Foreign intervention, while useful in the short term, does not offer an easy solution to internal problems. It might create a quasi-functioning state that is able to restore order and serve the interests of the intervening forces, but it often does not address the underlying causes of civil unrest, nor can it build long-term peace.

Moreover, in the Solomon Islands case, the focus on the state, while important, must not be allowed to overshadow other entities that could contribute positively to peace building and nation rebuilding. It is necessary to restore not only a functional state but also relationships between people.

Finally, for intervention to be successful it must cultivate a capacity for positive change within the country; otherwise it reinforces a culture of dependency. The role of the intervening force must be one of *facilitating* positive development rather than *dictating* it. In Solomon Islands, Australian interests and discourses must not be privileged over those of Solomon Islanders. If that happens Solomon Islanders will continue to say 'letem olketa ramsi kam stretem'—wait for ramsi to come and fix it.

Tarcisius Kabutaulaka, 'Australian foreign policy and the RAMSI intervention in Solomon Islands', *Contemporary Pacific*, vol. 17, no. 2, 2005, pp. 302–3.

the way the Westminster system works in Solomon Islands, where voters elect a collection of individuals to parliament rather than two or three tightly organised parties, and those individuals then choose the prime minister in a process that involves numerous bribes and inducements. Powerful social forces are also at work. The Solomon Islands population has a large cohort of young people, mostly unemployed. Alienated young men were prominent among the rioters.

By 2010, however, RAMSI could point to successes. A 2009 opinion survey of more than 5000 Solomon Islanders found that 88 per cent supported the presence of RAMSI in their country. Government revenues were growing. People were better off: GDP grew from US$815 per person in 2004 to US$1268 in 2009. Order had been restored by the 300 members of the Participating Police Force, drawn from across the Pacific and backed by troops from Australia, New Zealand, PNG and Tonga. A Truth and Reconciliation Commission was endeavouring to heal the wounds of conflict. RAMSI and Solomon Islands had agreed on a Partnership Framework to measure progress in improving law and justice, economic governance and government administration. And the 2010 Solomon Islands election was conducted peacefully. No Australian government has set a deadline for withdrawal.

TONGA

Tonga, a Polynesian group of islands east of Fiji, had a long history of political stability until 2006. Ruled over by its royal family, and with a population of just 100,000, Tonga seemed tranquil. But Tonga was not a democracy. Under its 1875 constitution, the monarch had enormous powers, appointing ministers and forming governments at will, while the common people had little say. These quaint arrangements worked well for more than a century but as more and more Tongans obtained education, or moved abroad for work, popular pressure for reform and accountability grew. Some Tongans thought the royal family was enriching itself at their expense, and resented the Economic and Public Sector Reform program, which widened salary inequalities and privatised public enterprises. Public servants went on strike for six weeks in 2005, crippling the economy. Demonstrators held protest marches, and made unprecedented demands for democratic reform. Then on 16 November 2006, referred to by Tongans as '16/11', rioters burnt much of the central business district in the capital Nuku'alofa.

Once again, Australia sent troops and police to a Pacific Island country. Fifty ADF personnel and 34 AFP officers went to Tonga on a brief deployment until security was restored. The affair showed that Australia would intervene even in small Pacific states threatened with a breakdown of law and order. And as the reconstruction of the capital commenced in 2009, under Chinese supervision and funded by a loan from Beijing, the authorities in Canberra were also reminded that China was a rising power in a region they have traditionally regarded as under Australian influence. After the unrest of 2006, Tonga moved towards greater democratisation, which the Tongan pro-democracy movement had been advocating since the early 1990s. A 2010 law expanded popular representation in the country's parliament, and the 2010 elections were the first to return a majority of people's representatives. The new arrangements curbed the powers of King Siaosi Tupou V, who was crowned in 2008, and they seemed likely to return Tonga to its customary political stability.

AUSTRALIA'S RESPONSE

Australia's response to political instability in the small developing countries and territories to its north raises three key issues. The first is Australia's changed course on East Timor. The second relates to Australia's approach to the South Pacific and East Timor, and the third to its non-intervention in Fiji.

For many years and under governments of both persuasions, Australia supported Indonesia over East Timor. Yet Australia struck out on a new course in 1998 and in the end became principal midwife to the birth of East Timor as a new state in 2002, doing what governments in Canberra for the previous 25 years had vowed never to do. How did this happen? Why did Australia's approach change? And how fundamentally did it change?

Australian policy changed, above all, under the pressure of events over which it had no control. Governments were right about one thing during the years of domestic controversy over East Timor: nothing Australia did would solve the basic problem. Only developments in Indonesia would make a difference. And so it proved. A new future for East Timor became possible only because of the political repercussions of Indonesia's economic downturn in the late 1990s and the forced resignation of President Suharto. As the pace of change quickened in Indonesia, events carried Australia along. Canberra had no alternative but to adapt. At the end of 1998 Australia was cautioning Indonesia against haste in determining East Timor's ultimate political status. By mid 1999 Australia was deeply involved in preparing for the popular consultation. By the end of 1999 Australia had 5500 troops in the territory and was committed for years to come to support East Timor's independence as a microstate bordering Indonesia. The entire episode is a reminder of the extent to which foreign policy can be driven by external developments over which Australia has little influence.

Australia's initial shift in 1998 was, in any case, not a total reversal of previous policy. During the years of controversy about Australia's approach to East Timor, Australian policy had ambiguous elements. For a long time the policy diverged little from the lines laid down by Gough Whitlam in the 1970s: support for Indonesia and sympathy for the East Timorese. Sympathy took the form of humanitarian and development aid for East Timor arranged in consultation with the Indonesian authorities. Soon after the 1991 Dili Massacre, for example, Labor agreed to a $30 million aid package for East Timor over five years. Australian governments walked a tightrope on East Timor, balancing public opinion against the Indonesian relationship and hoping people would not be scandalised by fresh outrages in the province. The Keating Labor government eventually came to accept self-determination for East Timor as a theoretical possibility. Gareth Evans ventured criticism of the military presence in East Timor in his last years as foreign minister, urging the Indonesians to reduce the troop presence and consider a special status for the province. He also gave Australia's support to East Timor talks between the foreign ministers of Indonesia and Portugal organised by the UN Secretary-General, as did his successor Downer. Before 1998 Labor and Coalition alike called for fewer soldiers, more respect for human rights and greater autonomy for the East Timorese. Pulled one way by Jakarta and the other by public opinion, governments tried to please everyone. Australia recognised the right of the East Timorese to self-determination and the status of East Timor as a non-self-governing territory, yet at the same time recognised Indonesia's sovereignty and benefited materially from that recognition through oil and gas from the Timor Sea.

Even after Habibie became president, Australia would have preferred East Timor to remain part of Indonesia if that could have been accomplished with the consent of the East Timorese. Australia feared an immediate vote on East Timor's political status would lead to a premature and precarious independence that would eventually be a regional security problem. Indeed, the whole purpose of Howard's 1998 initiative was to suggest to the Indonesians how to delay a vote on self-determination. Australia wanted a vote years into the future, after the Indonesians had had the opportunity of convincing the East Timorese of the merits of remaining within their country. As Howard wrote:

> ... the advice I am receiving is that a decisive element of East Timorese opinion is insisting on an act of self-determination. If anything, their position—with a fair degree of international support—seems to be strengthening on this.

It might be worth considering, therefore, a means of addressing the East Timorese desire for an act of self-determination in a manner which avoids an early and final decision on the future status of the province ... The successful implementation of an autonomy package with a built-in review mechanism would allow time to convince the East Timorese of the benefits of autonomy within the Indonesian Republic.[6]

In explaining Australia's 'historic policy shift on East Timor', Downer emphasised that Australia envisaged an act of self-determination taking place 'at some future time, following a substantial period of autonomy'.[7] What Canberra had in mind was an arrangement like that made by France for its Pacific territory of New Caledonia, where a final referendum on independence was delayed first for ten years and then for a further fifteen. For reasons of his own, Habibie ignored Australia's advice and chose instead to proceed to a referendum that allowed for immediate independence. These subtleties, however, were not appreciated by Australia's Indonesian critics who blamed Australia for dismembering their country, and who interpreted subsequent events, when Australia sent military forces to East Timor, as proof of Australia's anti-Indonesian designs.

Those who were at the heart of policy discussions in Canberra disagree about what happened. Looking back, Howard and Downer say they foresaw and welcomed the prospect of an independent East Timor from the time Habibie agreed to a referendum, but could not say so publicly for fear of derailing the Indonesian initiative. According to the journalist Paul Kelly, they actively backed the independence of East Timor. Hugh White, who was then Deputy Secretary for Strategy in the Department of Defence, has a different recollection.[8] He recalls the Howard government having no clear commitment to independence, but rather being driven along by events, which were increasingly in the direction of independence in the months up to the referendum. By this interpretation, once INTERFET and the UN had secured East Timor's independence, and the sending of Australian forces proved popular, Howard and Downer claimed they favoured it from the start. Either way, the events of 1999 changed Australia's relations with East Timor permanently, as well as damaging Australia's relations with Indonesia for a number of years.

Australia's policy on the oil and gas resources of the Timor Sea—the less publicised side of the issue—changed little throughout the turmoil. Australia and East Timor reached an accommodation on access to those resources in the 2002 Timor Sea Treaty, which favoured East Timor less than the Howard government claimed. Australia, it is true, made one major concession by providing that East

Timor should get 90 per cent of oil and gas revenues from what is called the Joint Petroleum Development Area, instead of the 50 per cent that previously went to Indonesia. Over 30 years that resource might be worth as much as US$10 billion to East Timor. But oil and gas also come from parts of the Timor Sea under Australian jurisdiction, and Australia is not willing to agree that the median line—halfway between the two coastlines—is the maritime border between the two countries. If it were, East Timor would receive much greater revenues. Indeed, Australia fears that, if the border dispute were taken to international bodies to decide, the arbitrators would rule in favour of the median line or something like it. For that reason Australia quietly withdrew in 2002 from consent to any decisions on maritime boundaries made by the International Court of Justice or under the UN Law of the Sea Convention. As a major aid donor to East Timor, Australia could negotiate bilaterally over the maritime boundary from a position of strength, but would be in a weaker position before an international tribunal. Critics accused Australia of taking the lion's share of sub-seabed resources in the Timor Sea at the expense of the poorest and newest country in South-East Asia.

The second issue is Australia's approach to the South Pacific and East Timor and its shift towards an active policy of intervention. The Howard government's response to the very different political situation in Bougainville belonged to a long tradition of policy towards the South Pacific, one that offered involvement, cooperation and assistance to the island nations but respected their sovereignty and stopped short of intervening directly in the way they governed themselves.

Australia was embroiled in the Bougainville conflict and at times imposed heavy diplomatic pressure on the PNG government but it did not seek to take over that government. From the time the rebels in Bougainville declared war on PNG in 1989, Australia sided with the PNG government and provided military assistance because it did not want to encourage the fragmentation of an already weak state. PNG always matters in Australian foreign policy because it is strategically located across the Torres Strait, and has strong ties of trade, investment and defence with Australia. When the Sandline affair created an opportunity for peace in 1997, Australia was ready to take it, working closely with New Zealand and making use of the New Zealanders' neutral, outsider status in the Bougainville issue. Australia organised meetings of the parties, provided the major resources for a regional peace-monitoring group and paid the hefty bill for reconstructing Bougainville after years of armed conflict and destruction.

Solomon Islands was a first case of Australian intervention in the Pacific Islands, and represented a policy shift towards more in the future. Where the terrorist threat had figured importantly in the justification for intervening in Solomon Islands in 2003, the Howard government increasingly emphasised other, more traditional threats to Australian and regional security. Howard said in 2007:

> Instability in the South Pacific is harmful to the societies affected. It also undermines our interests. It reduces our ability to protect the approaches to Australia; it undermines our development assistance efforts; and it feeds people smuggling, illegal immigration, drug trafficking and money laundering that can jeopardise all Australians. In addition to our national interests, our relative size and prosperity give us a moral responsibility to help our neighbours. And our international allies and partners rightly expect it of us. For all these reasons my government decided in early 2003 on a major shift to a more active, robust and where necessary interventionist policy approach in our region. In doing so we consciously put aside the rather disinterested—and failed—policy of earlier years.[9]

The Howard and Rudd governments saw the South Pacific states as too small and poorly governed to be left to themselves. 'The events of the last few months in Solomon Islands', Downer said in 2003, 'have naturally led the Australian government to re-examine how we can best support the development efforts of our other South Pacific neighbours. We are not willing to stand back and watch regional neighbours descend into instability.'[10]

In the case of Papua New Guinea, Australia sent teams of experts to work alongside their local counterparts in central parts of the government, including law and justice agencies, economic and finance departments, immigration services, customs, border control and aviation safety. The country faced major challenges, with a growing population, declining economy and an HIV epidemic. The Howard government was careful to call this initiative by the polite title of 'Enhanced Cooperation Program', but it amounted to a partial recolonisation of Australia's former territory.

The third issue is Australia's non-intervention in Fiji. Having adopted an interventionist policy in the Pacific, why did Australia decline to intervene in Fiji in order to restore democracy? Fiji presented the Howard and Rudd governments with a perplexing foreign policy problem. Armed intervention in Solomon Islands was possible only because that country's government invited its neighbours to intervene, ensuring that Australia did not breach the UN Charter. Such a solution was out of the question in Fiji, where the government was in the hands of a military force determined to retain power and where many people welcomed the coup. In a show of force, the Howard government sent three warships to evacuate Australian citizens at the time of the 2006 coup, but the deployment was probably counterproductive, enabling Bainimarama to rally his soldiers behind him and against the foreign threat. All Australia could do was to condemn the coup, reduce aid, sever military links and impose smart sanctions, such as travel bans on those accepting high positions in the new regime, while working behind the scenes diplomatically to find a way through the impasse. Australia gave support, for example, to mediation efforts by the Commonwealth.

Some said Australia should accept the situation in Fiji. Bainimarama, they argued, wanted to transcend Fiji's racial divisions, reform the electoral system to remove its racial bias, and remake the country as a genuine democracy on the Western model. He was a strong man with good intentions, and Australia should back him, not oppose him. While Australia shunned Fiji, they said, China was offering development assistance, investment and trade, and enhancing its South Pacific influence at the expense of Fiji's traditional allies. The argument convinced neither Howard nor Rudd. Where the apologists for Bainimarama saw a benevolent dictator, Australia saw a military man willing to destroy Fiji's democratic institutions and abuse human rights for the sake of his own power. His talk of future democracy, in Canberra's view, was merely a justification for an illegal seizure of political authority. Everything in Australia's democratic traditions, foreign policy experience and regional interests pointed towards isolating the Fiji dictatorship rather than tolerating it.

Wider foreign policy considerations inevitably influenced Australia's response. Regionally, the Australian government thought it vital to adhere to democratic principle. The Biketawa Declaration, adopted by all sixteen member states of the Pacific Islands Forum in 2000, enshrines a regional norm in favour of democracy. Under Biketawa, Pacific Island countries are committed to democratic processes and institutions, including the peaceful transfer of power, the rule of law and the independence of the judiciary, all of which Fiji flouted. Having pushed for Biketawa in the first place and consistently urged the virtues of democracy upon island governments, Australia could hardly abandon them for the sake of better relations with a military dictator.

Similarly, Australia had no wish to abandon the international norm in favour of democracy. This norm may not be universal, given China's rise, but the international community supports it widely. These days, the leader of a coup in a small developing country faces international pressure to return to democracy as soon as his troops are on the streets. US law requires American presidents to suspend aid to countries where coups have occurred. The European Union (EU) imposes democratic conditionality on its aid and trade dealings with the 79 member states of the Africa, Caribbean and Pacific group to which Fiji belongs. Bainimarama's coup had the effect of blocking EU funds that were to have assisted with restructuring Fiji's sugar industry. Australia joined New Zealand, the UN, the United States, the Commonwealth, the EU and the Pacific Islands Forum in condemning Bainimarama's coup in 2006 and his abrogation of the constitution in 2009. The Commonwealth and the forum suspended Fiji's membership when promised elections failed to materialise.

ASSESSMENTS

Western advanced countries, led by the United States, have embraced the idea of state building in the developing world ever since US forces invaded Afghanistan in 2001, when Washington blamed the weakness of the Afghan state for enabling al-Qaeda to organise the attacks of 9/11. The Obama administration argues that building the state in Afghanistan is the main reason why American, NATO and other forces are fighting the Taliban there. Similarly, Australia frames its approach to near neighbours in the broader context of the war on terrorism. Australia sees fragile states as potential threats, with the security forces given key roles in the response. Yet fear of terrorism alone does not explain Australian policy. Australia worries that an unstable Pacific could be a conduit for drugs, small arms and illegal immigrants, and that corruption in Pacific countries subverts and weakens Australia's aid program.

The interventions in East Timor and Solomon Islands brought together the Australian Defence Force, the Australian Federal Police, AusAID and other elements of the Australian public service in a joint project of restoring law and order while building the state. On a much smaller scale, a similar initiative took soldiers and police to Tonga. Yet building the state in Australia's neighbourhood is dauntingly difficult. Melanesia, the region that includes Solomon Islands and Papua New Guinea, is home to hundreds of languages and local identities. The numerous village communities of these countries traditionally considered themselves independent and acted towards each other as if located in an international system, not in a single state. Colonial rule was short-lived, lasting less than a hundred years in both countries, and was experienced for only a few decades by the large populations of the PNG Highlands, which came under government only after World War II. The state left behind by the colonisers at independence was modern in design and modelled on Western institutions, but weak in reach and without roots in Melanesian culture. Papua New Guineans and Solomon Islanders have since adapted the state to their purposes, but not strengthened it or rendered it more effective in delivering services to citizens. Australia's state-building efforts rest on the assumption that building state capacity is largely a technical matter, requiring Australians to fill gaps in the state apparatus—regularising procedures, establishing accountability, ensuring that government decisions are implemented, and training locals. Australia can hardly do otherwise in what are, after all, sovereign states accepting foreign assistance, not latter-day colonies. The barriers to success, however, are more political than technical, and there is no early prospect of radical political trans-formation in the small states of Australia's region.

Fiji demonstrates the limits of intervention as a policy response to regional instability, and its dangers if taken too far. Intervention in Fiji by Australia would be highly counterproductive. The policy makes sense as a series of specific responses to particular regional challenges, but not as a general response applied indiscriminately, and it runs the risk of degenerating into a claim that Australia has the right to interfere at any time in the affairs of its small neighbours. Australia's state building is not in some 'ideal ethical realm' beyond politics.[11] Australian state builders are political actors themselves, empowering some people at the expense of others, and influencing political outcomes. That is why the whole idea of state building, however humanitarian in motive, remains contested, and why Australia's policy of regional intervention may not endure.

FURTHER READING

Global context

Chandler, David, *Empire in Denial—the politics of state-building,* Pluto Press, London, 2006. (A critical evaluation of state building as a new form of Western intervention in developing states, highly intrusive but portrayed as humanitarian.)

Chesterman, Simon, *You, the People: The United Nations, transitional administration, and state-building,* Oxford University Press, Oxford, 2004. (A history of UN participation in complex peace operations and state building; includes East Timor.)

Smith, Michael, 'Military intervention and humanitarian assistance', *Global Change, Peace & Security,* vol. 20, no. 3, 2008, pp. 243–54. (Argues that human security should be a pillar of Australian strategic policy, and that Australia should work more closely with the UN on integrated peace operations.)

East Timor

Cotton, James, *East Timor, Australia and Regional Order: Intervention and its aftermath in South-east Asia*, Routledge, London, 2004. (East Timor as an issue in Australian foreign policy since the 1970s with a focus on the 1999 intervention and peacekeeping.)

——'Timor-Leste and the discourse of state failure', *Australian Journal of International Affairs*, vol. 61, no. 4, 2007, pp. 455–70. (A theoretical and comparative analysis of the extent to which we can say East Timor is a functioning state or should expect it to be so.)

East Timor in Transition 1998–2000: An Australian policy challenge, Department of Foreign Affairs and Trade, Canberra, 2001. (The official account of East Timor's ballot on independence, the violent aftermath, and the international intervention led by Australia; highly informative and readable, with key documents.)

Goldsworthy, David, 'East Timor', in *Facing North: A century of Australian engagement with Asia. Volume 2: 1970s to 2000*, Peter Edwards and David Goldsworthy, eds, Department of Foreign Affairs and Trade and Melbourne University Press, Melbourne, 2003, pp. 216–57. (The East Timor issue in Australian foreign policy, 1975–99.)

Greenlees, Don and Robert Garran, *Deliverance: The inside story of East Timor's fight for freedom*, Allen & Unwin, Sydney, 2002. (A revealing account of East Timor's bloody transition to independence, and of the part played in these events by Australia.)

International Crisis Group, *Resolving Timor-Leste's Crisis, Asia Report No. 120*, 10 October 2006. (Detailed account of the 2006 crisis, its causes and consequences.)

Lowry, Bob, *After the 2006 Crisis: Australian interests in Timor Leste*, Australian Strategic Policy Institute, Strategic Insights 38, November 2007. (A clear statement of Australian interests, including oil and gas, together with an explanation of the 2006 crisis.)

Martin, Ian, *Self-Determination in East Timor: The United Nations, the ballot, and international intervention*, Lynne Rienner Publishers, Boulder, CO, and London, 2001. (The UN Secretary-General's Special Representative in East Timor for the popular consultation describes the work of UNAMET, the conduct of the ballot and the subsequent intervention by international forces.)

Report of the United Nations Independent Special Commission of Inquiry for Timor Leste, Geneva, 2 October 2006. (The Commission interviewed more than 200 witnesses in compiling this authoritative account of the 2006 crisis.)

White, Hugh, 'The Road to INTERFET: Reflections on Australian strategic decisions concerning East Timor, December 1998–September 1999', *Security Challenges*, vol. 4, no. 1, pp. 69–87. (Argues that Australia 'completely failed to achieve the strategic objectives it had set itself at the start of 1999'.)

Bougainville

Alley, Roderic, *The Domestic Politics of International Relations: Cases from Australia, New Zealand and Oceania*, Ashgate, Aldershot, Hampshire, and Burlington, VT, 2000. (Chapter 4 examines the war and the 1997 breakthrough in peace negotiations.)

Regan, Anthony, 'Causes and course of the Bougainville conflict', *Journal of Pacific History*, vol. 33, no. 3, 1998, pp. 269–85. (An excellent explanation of the reasons for the war in Bougainville.)

——*Light Intervention: Lessons from Bougainville*, United States Institute of Peace Press, Washington DC, 2010. (The peace process from the 1990s to 2010, with lessons to be drawn for peacebuilding interventions elsewhere; excellent.)

——'The Bougainville intervention: Political legitimacy and sustainable peace-building', in *Intervention and State-Building in the Pacific: The legitimacy of 'co-operative intervention'*, Greg Fry and Tarcisius Kabutaulaka, eds, Manchester University Press, Manchester, 2008, pp. 184–208. (Argues that the regional intervention in Bougainville succeeded because it 'was not seen as imposed from outside, but rather as part of a locally initiated and controlled process'.)

Fiji

Fraenkel, Jon and Stewart Firth, eds, *From Election to Coup in Fiji: The 2006 campaign and its aftermath*, Asia Pacific Press, Canberra and IPS Publications, Suva, 2007. (Comprehensive survey of the 2006 Fiji elections, with addendum on the military coup.)

Fraenkel, Jon, Stewart Firth and Brij Lal, eds, *The 2006 Military Takeover in Fiji: A coup to end all coups?*, ANU E Press, Canberra, 2009. (Detailed examination of the 2006 coup, including the role of the military, the media, religious organisations, the labour movement, the legal profession and political parties.)

Solomon Islands

Australian Strategic Policy Institute, *Our Failing Neighbour: Australia and the future of Solomon Islands*, Canberra, June 2003. (The semi-official report that charted a new course for Australia in Solomon Islands.)

Barbara, Julien, 'Antipodean statebuilding: The Regional Assistance Mission to Solomon Islands and Australian intervention in the South Pacific', *Journal of Intervention and Statebuilding*, vol. 2, no. 2, 2008, pp. 123–49. (RAMSI in a global context; argues that apolitical interventions are impossible.)

Dinnen, Sinclair, 'Winners and losers: Politics and disorder in the Solomon Islands, 2000–2002', *Journal of Pacific History*, vol. 37, no. 3, 2002, pp. 285–98. (The best explanation of why law and order collapsed in Solomon Islands.)

Dinnen, Sinclair and Stewart Firth, eds, *Politics and State-Building in Solomon Islands*, Asia Pacific Press and ANU E Press, 2008. (Examines the 2006 crisis, its impact on Solomon Islanders and the Chinese minority, and how the Regional Assistance Mission responded.)

Fraenkel, Jon, *The Manipulation of Custom: From uprising to intervention in the Solomon Islands*, Victoria University Press, Wellington, 2004. (Perceptive explanation of the country's descent into disorder, with a focus on how politicians used custom for their own ends.)

Fry, Greg and Tarcisius Kabutaulaka, eds, *Intervention and State-Building in the Pacific: The legitimacy of 'co-operative intervention'*, Manchester University Press, Manchester, 2008. (Authoritative survey setting Australian-led intervention in a global context.)

Moore, Clive, *Happy Isles in Crisis: The historical causes for a failing state in Solomon Islands, 1998–2004*, Asia Pacific Press, Canberra, 2004. (Argues that the crisis 'principally related to inequitable economic and political development, not to ethnic tensions or separatist insurgency'.)

Tonga

Maclellan, Nic, *Pomp and privatisation: Political and economic reform in the Kingdom of Tonga*, The Australian Centre for Peace and Conflict Studies, Occasional Papers Series, No. 13,

March 2009. (Wide-ranging survey of Tonga's political and social situation, including the 2006 riots and the constitutional reform process.)

Websites

Pacific Islands Report (regional news online): <http://pidp.eastwestcenter.org/pireport>
State, Society and Governance in Melanesia Program, ANU:
    <http://rspas.anu.edu.au/melanesia>
UN Integrated Mission in Timor-Leste: <http://unmit.unmissions.org>

PART III

Economy

9

Globalisation and the global financial crisis

- What was the essence of the Bretton Woods system as it applied to (a) international movements of capital, and (b) international trade?
- What is Keynesianism?
- Why did the long boom after World War II end?
- What were the key economic reforms made by the Hawke and Keating governments? Did they achieve their objectives?
- What were the causes of the global financial crisis of 2008?
- Why did Australia survive the global financial crisis better than most other advanced economies?
- What problems remain in the post-GFC global economy?
- In what way does the new prominence of the G20 as an institution of global economic governance reflect a changing global economic order?
- Has Australia become too dependent on China for its prosperity?

The national economy decides whether we get a job, how much we are paid and how many of life's opportunities we have the chance to enjoy. Australians, like the people of other Western industrialised societies, have long held governments responsible for the fate of the national economy. Governments proclaim their ability to manage the economy successfully and voters decide periodically whether they have done so or not. Week by week during the political cycle from election to election, journalists track key economic indicators such as unemployment and the growth rate; government ministers respond by emphasising successes and overlooking failures; and Opposition shadow ministers argue that the government's policy is not working. The party contest is principally fought over national economic issues.

Many people do not realise how much the international economy also affects us all. The national economy, after all, is part of a much larger network of economic relationships that embraces the globe itself. Australian mining companies and primary producers sell their products to the rest of the world. Australian companies trade with, borrow from and invest in overseas companies. Foreign companies invest in Australia and remit profits abroad. Foreign banks lend money to Australian companies and governments and are repaid with funds earned in Australia. Foreign tourists and students spend funds earned abroad here, and their spending counts as part of Australia's export income. The issues raised by this complex web of financial and commercial transactions between Australians and foreigners may appear purely economic but are inevitably political. The international economy has a decisive influence not only on Australia's prosperity, but also on how that prosperity is distributed among Australians. International economic issues are therefore a high priority on Australia's foreign policy agenda.

The interconnection of national and international economies raises fundamental questions: How important is the international economy in creating the conditions for Australia's economic success or failure? What has been Australia's response to the growing integration of economic activities worldwide? To what extent have foreign and domestic economic policy become intertwined? What caused the global financial crisis and why did Australia survive it better than most advanced economies? What was Australia's foreign policy response to that crisis? These are the questions this chapter addresses. The chapter begins with the 1980s and 1990s, when the foundations of Australia's contemporary economic enmeshment with the rest of the world were laid.

THE RISE AND FALL OF BRETTON WOODS

In order to understand Australia's place in the international economy we must begin with the international economic order established after World War II by the United States and Britain. Meeting at a town in New Hampshire called Bretton Woods, American and British economists reached agreement in 1944 on the key issues that would determine the way the international economy worked when the war ended. At the top of their priorities was the question of international finance. The conference delegates were determined to avoid the mistakes of the 1930s, when international trade declined and tens of millions of people in the industrialised economies were thrown out of work. One of the causes of the

Great Depression, they believed, was the fact that prewar exchange rates between different national currencies were not fixed but allowed to float according to the market. The result had been erratic flows of capital from country to country as international financiers sought quick profits. What was needed instead were two things: government regulation of the movement of capital from one country to another, and fixed but flexible exchange rates which, by creating much greater predictability for businesses, would encourage international trade.

In order to enable countries to maintain fixed exchange rates, the Bretton Woods Agreement set up the International Monetary Fund or IMF to gather contributions from member states and then lend money back to them if they encountered temporary balance-of-payments difficulties. The idea was to enable countries to continue importing even when, for a while, they had run out of the foreign funds to do so. In this way, it was hoped, international trade would flourish. At the same time governments would have freedom to stimulate their economies in order to create full employment without having to be constantly concerned about the reaction of foreign exchange markets.

The other central issue in the management of the international economy was trade. During the 1930s many countries increased tariffs in order to protect employment, with the result that international trade slumped and all countries were worse off. The United States, which emerged from World War II as the world's wealthiest and most powerful country, was determined this should not happen again. Instead, international trade should be liberalised and countries encouraged to reduce levels of protection in the interests of all. Liberalised trade was especially to the advantage of the United States, at that time the world's leading manufacturing and technologically advanced power. The postwar agreement on trade, drawn up in 1947, was called the General Agreement on Tariffs and Trade or the GATT, referred to briefly in Chapter 2 and in detail in Chapter 10. Its basic principle was non-discrimination. All member states of the GATT agreed that if they offered any advantage or concession in trade to another member state, they would offer it to all. In this way, and through a series of further GATT negotiations on lowering tariffs, restrictions on international trade would gradually be dismantled.

The essence of the postwar international economic order was that trade would be liberalised while finance came under stricter international super-vision. These arrangements, which lasted until the early 1970s, are often known as the Bretton Woods system. In many ways the system did not develop as origi-nally planned. Rather than being a multilateral monetary order, it became an

American one in which the US dollar emerged as the world's reserve currency and America became banker to the world. When Europe proved too impoverished to pay for imports in the first years after the war, the United States decided to encourage the international circulation of goods and money by injecting US$18 billion into European economies in the form of aid under the Marshall Plan, which was established by its Foreign Assistance Act of 1948. Similar amounts of American dollars brought the Japanese economy to life as well, and American military expenditures around the world stimulated global economic growth. The American government stood behind the world currency, guaranteeing that US dollars could be converted to gold at the rate of US$35 an ounce.

While this system was not the one envisaged at Bretton Woods it worked for a while in much the same way. The dollar was as good as gold, and other currencies such as the Australian pound were converted into dollars at fixed rates controlled by governments. Governments regulated and restricted the international movement of capital. At the same time the GATT turned out to be a brilliantly successful device for encouraging international trade, which boomed as never before. The Kennedy Round of GATT negotiations in the 1960s, for example, achieved an across-the-board tariff cut of 35 per cent on about 60,000 products worth about US$40 billion. Australia remained protectionist but benefited from the global economic upswing as trade was liberalised.

The Bretton Woods system under American management produced high and stable economic growth in Western industrialised economies during the 1950s and 1960s. Unemployment virtually disappeared, inflation remained low and Western governments successfully used Keynesian methods to manage their economies. The term *Keynesian* comes from John Maynard Keynes, an English economist who pioneered the idea of using government intervention to moderate the booms and slumps characteristic of capitalism. Governments could maintain full employment, Keynes argued, by accumulating surpluses in good economic times and running deficits in bad ones, and by controlling interest rates so as to subdue or stimulate economic activity. Australia in these years employed just such techniques to keep economic growth high and unemployment low, and shared its long boom with all other Western industrialised economies.

The international long boom, and with it the good times in Australia, came to an end in the early 1970s. For a variety of reasons, the Bretton Woods monetary arrangements collapsed. International finance began to escape the disciplines imposed by governments. Despite controls imposed by governments, banks and other financial organisations started to move capital more rapidly and in greater quantities from country to country. For the first time in the postwar period governments discovered that the international mobility of capital—the speed with which money could be moved around the world—was now great enough to influence domestic interest rates. Monetary policy—the control or influencing of interest rates by governments—began to be a less certain way of encouraging economic growth, and governments began to lose one of the key instruments of Keynesian demand management. Governments wanting to stimulate demand and increase employment by reducing interest rates found that, as soon as interest rates fell, capital was moved abroad to countries where higher rates were being paid. The system of fixed exchange rates also came under pressure as governments found they could not intervene effectively to maintain the value of national currencies because the international money markets outmatched them in financial power.

To add to the problems of the international monetary order, the United States paid for the Vietnam War and for the new social programs of President Lyndon Johnson's 'Great Society' without increasing taxes. In effect, America paid its debts to the rest of the world in dollars that were no longer worth as much as before. America's Vietnam War and Great Society were paid for by international inflation. As creditors took out insurance by swapping their dollars for gold and people's faith in the dollar waned, America's gold reserves fell dangerously low. Finally, President Richard Nixon acted by announcing that from 15 August 1971 the US dollar would no longer be convertible into gold. His intervention marked the end of the Bretton Woods system which had worked so well and it initiated a long period of instability in international monetary arrangements. That instability is with us still, and it was seen in the sudden collapse of international confidence in the economies of Thailand, Indonesia, Malaysia and South Korea in 1997, and the global financial crisis of 2008. The liberalisation and deregulation of international finance since the 1970s have proven to be inherently destabilising, just as they were before the Great Depression of the 1930s.

The first oil shock compounded the economic problems emerging in the early 1970s. The Organization of Petroleum Exporting Countries (OPEC) dramatically raised the price of oil in 1973. Countries such as Libya and Saudi Arabia wrested control of the oil industry from the seven Western companies that dominated world oil production and then did what the companies had done: they restricted production in order to keep up the price. This time, however, the price quadrupled in a year, sending shock waves through every

Western economy, including Australia, and effectively transferring a sizeable chunk of Western resources to the oil-producing countries. All advanced countries, and most others, are crucially dependent on oil for energy. Suddenly the energy needed to run an industrialised economy cost much more than before. As governments struggled to adjust, inflation shot upwards. Prices in Australia rose by an average of 14.2 per cent each year from 1974 to 1977, more than four times the rate at which they were rising a few years before.

THE ECONOMY: A NEW DIRECTION FOR AUSTRALIA

Australia's economic problems persisted under Malcolm Fraser's Coalition government (1975–83). These were years of high inflation, low growth and increasing unemployment, ending in disastrous economic circumstances which propelled Labor back into power under Hawke in 1983. After a short-lived recovery at the end of the 1970s, Australia in 1979 confronted a second series of OPEC oil price rises which triggered a general Western recession and undermined international demand for Australian exports. At 6 per cent of GDP or gross domestic product, Australia's current account deficit in 1981–82 was the highest for 30 years. In other words, Australia's net payment to foreigners for goods and services was considerably greater than the income received by Australian companies and residents from abroad. By the time Fraser was defeated, more people were out of work than at any time since the Depression.

Australia's growth rate between 1972 and 1982 (2 per cent a year on average) was no longer enough to sustain full employment. By comparison, certain economies in North and South-East Asia grew by leaps and bounds during those years—Hong Kong by 9 per cent; and South Korea, Singapore and Taiwan by 8 per cent each. These four economies repeated that growth performance in the following decade (1982–92), and in the process transformed themselves into models that commanded world attention.

The centre of world manufacturing production was shifting from Europe and the United States towards East Asia. Singapore, for example, lifted its living standards in one generation from those of the Third World to those of the First World. Though Japan was later to slump, its economy grew on average twice as fast each year as Australia's for the period 1972–92. A mature economy like Australia's, people said, ought to be able to do the same. No one yet foresaw the explosion of economic growth in China that would follow the reforms initiated by Deng Xiaoping in 1978, but in time it would confirm the economic rise of East Asia.

Everyone agreed that something was fundamentally amiss in the Australian economy. But what was it? Which combination of things was undermining growth? People were less agreed on these questions. Some said Keynesian economic management should continue in modified form, while others, including the more influential economists in the English-speaking world, lost faith in the old Keynesian consensus.

The economists argued that regulated economies no longer produced prosperity and that governments had to get out of the way and give more room to the free market. Instead of creating growth, they said, government intervention in the economy merely produced stagnation and inflation simultaneously, the phenomenon in industrialised countries known as *stagflation*. The new ideas, that were introduced in Chapter 2 and called *neo-liberalism*, were a return to beliefs that determined economic policies before the Depression, though they came in more sophisticated form. By the time Hawke became prime minister these ideas had become the new conventional wisdom of economists in the Treasury, the most powerful part of the federal bureaucracy, and the new Labor treasurer Paul Keating was a ready convert. In time, much of Canberra's policy-making community came to share the new faith in post-Keynesian policies, and it still does, though that faith has been shaken by the global financial crisis.

The neo-liberals' first target of criticism was the government's regulation of financial markets and control of the exchange rate. Deregulating the banks and financial sector of the economy was not a new idea—the Campbell Report, the product of the Financial System Inquiry into Australia's financial structuring, recommended along these lines to the Fraser government in 1981—but no one thought a Labor government would be the first to take action in this field. Yet in December 1983, without consulting the party, Hawke, Keating and a few ministers made their most important decision in thirteen years of Labor government. They decided to float the Australian dollar and abolish controls over the movement of capital in and out of Australia. Soon afterwards the government removed interest rate ceilings on most bank loans, opened Australia's doors to sixteen foreign banks and cancelled key restrictions on foreign investment. The floating of the dollar, a technical issue as far as most Australians were concerned, had far-reaching ramifications for the Australian economy.

The second target of criticism was Australia's highly regulated labour market. Strong trade unions and a centralised wage-fixing system acted together, the neo-liberals said, to generate wage increases that reduced Australia's international competitiveness and added to inflation, as happened in the last years of

KEYNESIANISM VERSUS NEO-LIBERALISM

Keynesianism is the term given to the ideas and policy prescriptions of the English economist John Maynard Keynes. Most Western industrialised countries followed Keynesian economic policies after World War II, and all Australian governments, whether Coalition or Labor, were Keynesian governments until the 1980s.

The aim of Keynesianism was twofold—to create full employment and to sustain a welfare state, in which governments provided benefits to people in need. The way governments achieved this aim was by managing demand through fiscal policy (taxes) and monetary policy (credit). When a recession threatened, governments lowered taxes and eased credit; when the economy boomed, they raised taxes and tightened credit. Keynesians believed governments should regulate economies in order to protect people from the volatility of pure free markets.

Keynesianism in any particular country, however, could work only as long as the international economy was also regulated. Keynes believed that governments should control the movement of capital from one country to another; without such controls, the international financial markets would be able to prevent governments from creating full employment, and would cause sudden crises when they withdrew capital. Controls of this kind were part of the Bretton Woods system which ended in 1971.

Neo-liberalism is the term given to the ideas and policy prescriptions of the economists who oppose Keynesianism, and who have determined economic policy in Australia since the early 1980s. All Australian governments, Labor or Coalition, have been neo-liberal in economic policy to a greater or lesser extent since 1983. Neo-liberalism is sometimes called 'economic rationalism' in Australia.

Neo-liberals believe the route to prosperity lies in a radically minimal role for government and in embracing the free market in almost every area of economic life. In most circumstances, governments should not regulate labour markets or seek to influence wages by law, they should not own business enterprises, and they should not protect industries through tariffs (taxes on imports). All these things, in the neo-liberal view, are almost always better left to the free market.

At the international level, neo-liberals think financial markets work best without—or with a minimal level of—government regulation or government control of the exchange rates of national currencies.

The old debate between the two approaches to managing capitalist economies returned when the global financial crisis of 2008 exposed the deficiencies of neo-liberalism and governments everywhere adopted Keynesian approaches to stimulating economic growth in order to avoid a depression.

the Fraser government; like the financial market, the market in labour needed to be made more flexible if Australia was to compete on world markets. Labor, whose historic ties were with the unions, gave much less ground on this part of the neo-liberal agenda. In any case, the Hawke government had a better idea, one that did not leave wages purely to the market yet at the same time restrained them in the interests of Australian competitiveness. This was the Prices and Incomes Accord, negotiated at the start of Hawke's years as prime minister and renegotiated periodically up to the defeat of Keating in 1996. Under the accord, unions traded off wage increases against improvements in the 'social wage', such as Medicare and other welfare benefits, and gained higher wages in return for more flexible work practices and higher productivity. Not until the Howard government passed new industrial relations legislation in 1996 could the neo-liberals claim a victory, and the victory was not assured. The government backed the stevedoring company Patrick in 1998 when it sacked all waterside workers in the Maritime Union of Australia in an attempt to de-unionise the waterfront, but Patrick's scheme misfired. Thousands of Australians mobilised in support of the workers, and the courts ruled against the company. The Howard government's next attempt to apply neo-liberal principles to the labour market came with the policy called Work Choices, which came into effect in 2006 and proved so unpopular that Labor's opposition to it helped Rudd win government in 2007. The Rudd government dismantled Work Choices in favour of a more regulated approach, Fair Work Australia, which offered greater protections to employees. For a century many Australians have believed the bargaining relationship between employer and employee to be inherently unequal, the corollary being that wages should be regulated rather than left to the market.

The third target of criticism was the supposed inefficiency of government business enterprises. For this the neo-liberals prescribed competition, privatisation (selling public enterprises) and corporatisation (allowing public enterprises to be run as if they were private). These proposals struck at the heart of traditional Labor beliefs and sparked sharp debate within the ALP but the Labor government adopted them in the end, announcing thoroughgoing competitive reforms in its March 1991 statement 'Building a competitive Australia'. The government's process of 'microeconomic reform' aimed to make Australia efficient by world standards, particularly in the government enterprises that construct and supply the country's infrastructure of energy, transport and communications. Labor established an interstate electricity grid to encourage competition between suppliers, licensed Optus to compete in telecommunications with the state monopoly Telstra, sold

QANTAS, the Commonwealth Bank and the Commonwealth Serum Laboratories to private shareholders, corporatised Australia Post and gave it a customer focus, insisted on more open pricing policies by public monopolies, and commissioned a report on national competition policy. Australia's federal and state governments largely accepted the recommendation of the 1993 Hilmer Report, the National Competition Policy Review, that private businesses should have a much freer hand in competing with government enterprises. According to the Industry Commission, a stronghold of neo-liberalism in economic policy, the Hilmer reforms would be worth an annual gain in Australia's gross domestic product of 5.5 per cent if they were all implemented. Labor, which was not the traditional free enterprise party, joined the Coalition in seeing competition as a way of making Australia prosperous. The Coalition later privatised Telstra by selling shares to the public.

The fourth target was tariff protection. For most of its history as a federation, Australia has imposed very high tariffs on imports in order to protect domestic manufacturing and employment. Manufacturing output and employment grew in fits and starts, with rapid advance in the decade before World War I, the 1920s, World War II, and the long boom from the late 1940s to 1973. By then Australia was counted among the highly industrialised countries of the world. Yet Australia was an industrialised country with a difference. It made goods for a small home market with few economies of scale and did not export manufactured goods in any significant quantity. Australia's exports were primary commodities—wool, wheat, meat, iron ore, other metal ores and coal—leaving the economy vulnerable to sudden fluctuations in price and to long-term decline in the terms of trade. From the 1950s the terms of trade moved against Australia as they did against all countries that specialised in exporting primary commodities. In the global market, primary commodities tended at that time to be worth less over the long term compared with manufactures. One economist estimated that in the three decades to the mid 1980s Australia had to increase exports by 2 per cent each year simply in order to pay for the same volume of imports. The China boom reversed that trend in the first decade of the twenty-first century, with the terms of trade moving in favour of Australia as commodity prices rose.

The country was a good farm and quarry but needed to be a good factory and service provider in order to check the slide into economic marginalisation. Australia's way of industrialising behind tariff walls and for a domestic market left industry inefficient and productivity low, and from the mid 1960s successive governments wrestled with the problem of restructuring Australian industry so as to make it competitive in world terms. Apart from Whitlam's 25 per cent across-the-board tariff cut in 1973, governments took no action on protection and restructuring until Hawke was elected ten years later. The question was a politically sensitive one because Australians in protected industries naturally regarded lower tariffs as a threat to jobs.

Under Hawke and Keating, the ALP—which had long defended protection as vital for employment—oversaw a quiet revolution in Australia's economic relationship with the rest of the world. Beginning in 1983, the government began to cut import quotas and tariffs significantly, first on steel and tele-communications products, chemicals and plastics, then on cars and finally on almost every manufactured import. In a reversal of Australia's traditional policy, Labor reduced maximum tariff protection for most industries to 15 per cent by 1992 and 5 per cent by 1996. Financial deregulation created the conditions for this fundamental change of direction on tariffs. Global demand for primary commodities fell in 1985, and the Australian dollar fell with it, making Australian exports cheaper and giving the government a unique opportunity to reduce tariffs at a time when the exchange rate was providing another form of protection. Urged on by Treasury and academic advisers, the government then continued down the path towards free trade in the belief that only in this way would Australian manufacturing industry be restructured, revitalised and made competitive. With some exceptions, the Howard, Rudd and Gillard governments continued Australia's move towards free trade.

Key reforms in foreign and domestic economic policy help to account for Australia's success in meeting the competitive challenges of a globalising world over the last 25 years: floating the dollar, deregulating the financial markets, bringing flexibility (to a greater or lesser extent) to the labour market, privatising government enterprises, and embracing free trade. These were all initiated by the reforming Labor governments of Bob Hawke and Paul Keating, adopted by the Coalition government under John Howard, and retained by Labor under Rudd and Gillard. In part for this reason, and also because China created a boom in Australian exports, Australia has enjoyed impressive economic growth since the mid 1990s, better than has occurred in most other advanced industrialised countries.

THE GLOBAL FINANCIAL CRISIS

In neo-liberal economic theory, free markets are supposed to do a better job of delivering economic growth and prosperity than governments, which should therefore leave markets, including financial markets, largely unregulated. This was the theory that drove American economic policy from the Reagan administration of the 1980s onwards and inspired the chairman of the US central bank, the Federal Reserve, from 1987 to 2005, Alan Greenspan, who believed the banking industry in the United States should be left free of government regulation. But, as he admitted in 2008, he was wrong, and it was the global financial crisis that proved him wrong.

Booms and busts have characterised capitalism ever since it emerged as a global economic system in the nineteenth century. The biggest bust in history was the 1929 New York stock market crash, which triggered the Great Depression. No one who knew economic history should have been surprised by the global financial crisis of 2008 or by the recession it caused in the United States and Europe. After all, the nature of capitalism—its dynamism, inequality, injustice, expansion and contraction—has been at the centre of political and economic theory since the time of Karl Marx. And, since World War II, the governments of advanced, industrialised countries, recognising the problem, have endeavoured to counteract the boom-and-bust cycle of capitalism through 'counter-cyclical' economic policies such as adjusting interest rates and government spending.

Despite all this, few foresaw the global financial crisis, such was the collective amnesia of a generation that had come to expect never-ending economic growth as its birthright. The bankers and stockbrokers whose decisions precipitated the global financial crisis thought they knew the answer that eluded their predecessors, and that this time, capitalism—disciplined by the free market—would prosper indefinitely. Beneath them, however, powerful structural forces were influencing the global capitalist economy everywhere, especially in the United States, and creating the conditions for a sudden and potentially catastrophic shock to the financial system.

The key force, and one that remains, is debt. As the historian Niall Ferguson has pointed out, we live in an age of debt.[1] Since the 1970s, companies, banks, governments and individuals in the United States and Europe and, to a lesser extent, in Australia have borrowed on an unprecedented scale, leaving a 'debt overhang' that now has to be repaid.

This colossal debt originated in a number of ways. Some are technical. In the 1970s and 1980s young American bankers invented new ways of packaging debt; in other words, new ways of lending money and attracting investors who wanted to profit from loans made by others. The first invention was the 'mortgage-backed security', which was a way of getting lots of people to take on the debts of homeowners who had taken out mortgages. The second invention was to divide packages of mortgages into different levels of risk: the riskiest paid the highest rate; the less risky paid less; and so on. In essence, mortgage-backed securities were a way in which the banks could offload their debts on to someone else by persuading others that they were profitable investments. At the same time, 'pension funds' emerged in the United States and Europe as major investors. Superannuation—saving for retirement—became more popular, and the pension funds accumulated huge pools of money seeking good returns and creating the incentive for the development of increasingly artificial methods of investment. Alongside the pension funds came the 'hedge funds', whose speculative operations went largely unregulated by governments. A shadow system of banking that lay beyond the control of governments arose alongside the normal system of banking in New York, London and elsewhere and accounted for more and more of the world's financial transactions.[2]

Political changes also helped to cause an explosion of debt in the United States and Europe. A new consensus on economic policy emerged in Britain and the United States in the 1970s and 1980s and influenced governments everywhere. Economists discarded the old Keynesian consensus in economic policy, which had been directed at maintaining full employment through regulation and government intervention, and embraced a neo-liberal approach in which the free market was to be allowed to determine the fate of the economy. That meant deregulating the banks and financial markets, which from now on would be free to operate with minimal government supervision. The Clinton and Bush administrations in the United States, spanning the years 1993 to 2009, both deregulated banks in ways that allowed them to borrow funds far in excess of previous limits. Australian governments, Labor and Coalition, were more conservative, and kept a tighter hold on what banks were allowed to do. John Howard's treasurer, Peter Costello, for example, established the Australian Prudential Regulation Authority in 1998 as the principal instrument for government regulation of banks, credit unions, building societies, insurance and the superannuation industry.

In this same period the Chinese saved while the Americans, Japanese, Europeans and Australians borrowed and spent. The saving and borrowing were two sides of a dangerous global imbalance. China has consistently run up gigantic balance-of-payments surpluses since the 1990s, mainly because Chinese companies sell so much to the rest of the world. The Chinese government has invested much of that money by lending it to the American government; that is, by buying US government bonds. So the effect of Chinese saving was to ensure a plentiful supply of money in the US economy and to prop up American spending by keeping interest rates low, far lower than they would normally have been. There were other reasons why American interest rates were unusually low in the first years of the twenty-first century. The so-called *dot.com bubble*, a period of speculation in Internet stocks, burst in 2000 and caused a short-lived recession, to which the American central bank, the Federal Reserve, responded by cutting interest rates. The Federal Reserve took similar action in response to the terrorist attacks of 11 September 2001 in order to maintain business confidence, with the result that interest rates in the United States in 2003 fell to their lowest level since the 1960s. People and institutions could borrow money virtually for free, contributing to an upward spiral of speculation in real estate and stocks. All that easy money, underwritten by borrowings from China, fuelled a classic real estate boom, in which the price of houses rose for years before finally collapsing. Between 2000 and 2005 the average house price in the United States rose by 50 per cent despite very low inflation. People felt rich, borrowed back more money against the equity held in their properties and went on a spending spree for consumer goods that boosted the American economy. In effect, China lent the Americans the money to buy the cheap Chinese goods that filled American stores.

Compounding the problem in the United States were the banks and other financial institutions lending, directly or indirectly through many intermediaries, to people who wanted to buy a house but could not afford to repay the loan. These so-called *sub-prime loans* were made to millions of people whose income and financial resources made them bad risks. More than US$1.1 trillion of the US$3 trillion in mortgages written in the United States in 2006 were made either to people who were too poor to repay or to people whose income had not been checked by the lender. The reason this could happen was that those who were lending the money were able to offload their debt on to others in the form of mortgage-backed securities and other financial instruments. The technical elaboration of the business of lending—so complicated that many bank CEOs later admitted they did not understand what their own institutions were doing—created a gap between lender and borrower that removed or diminished the normal risks of lending. In the language of economics, risk became dangerously underpriced. Almost the entire banking industry in the United States and the United Kingdom was now in the grip of the mania that accompanies financial booms, in which it is in everyone's interest to believe that the boom will continue indefinitely, and the normal checks were missing. The ratings agencies, such as Standard & Poor's, Moody's and Fitch, had the task of determining risk and creditworthiness of banking institutions and investments, and should have sounded the alarm, but they were compromised by their connections with Wall Street and continued to give reassuring triple-A ratings to banks that were, in fact, dangerously exposed to a cascade of debt once the boom began to unravel.

Not surprisingly, the American housing boom began to crash, starting in 2007, and the economy began to falter. As house prices fell and people defaulted on their mortgage payments, unemployment rose. Unpaid debt rippled through the economy. By early 2008 the financial system became affected, and when the large Wall Street investment banking company Bear Stearns appeared likely to collapse, the US government arranged for banking giant JPMorgan Chase to take it over. It did so at a small fraction of Bear Stearns's previous share value. But the real crisis did not come until 15 September 2008, when the US government allowed the investment bank Lehman Brothers to go bankrupt. At that point all confidence in the financial system was lost. For a few days it looked as if the entire global financial system would fail, with banks afraid to lend to anyone, even to other banks. Credit suddenly dried up.

If governments had done nothing, another Great Depression would have ensued. In the 1930s, before Keynes, governments believed that they should cut spending, not increase it, in the face of financial crisis, with the result that by 1933 three-quarters of household mortgages in the United States were in default. People could not pay them, and the economy ground to a halt with a massive rise in unemployment. This time governments intervened on a massive scale to use the resources of the state to bail out failing financial institutions and to put money in the hands of consumers. By early 2009 the US government had made guarantees to the US financial sector worth US$12.7 trillion—a staggeringly gigantic sum—and spent over US$4 trillion, with about US$750 billion going straight to Wall Street. The reason the government had to intervene was not just that the banks were 'too big to fail', but also that they were 'too interconnected' to fail; that is, they were truly global institutions and would have brought down the global financial system with them.

The governments of the advanced economies, including Australia, and of emerging economies such as China, all followed the American example, spending huge amounts of money to ensure that the system did not collapse. These were the so-called *stimulus packages* that were believed to have saved the global economy and, in some cases, such as the United Kingdom, they involved nationalising banks and converting them temporarily into state-owned enterprises. Until 2008, policies of this kind were anathema to most economists. The prevailing view, an expression of the ruling neo-liberal philosophy in economics, was that free markets tend towards equilibrium and are self-correcting. This view was shown to be false beyond all doubt, because it was governments that had to intervene to rescue the financial markets from their own inherent tendency to boom and bust. Strictly speaking, markets are self-correcting, but only at enormous social cost. If governments had done nothing, banks and financial institutions that had taken too many risks would have gone bankrupt. There would have been a depression, at least in the United States and Europe, and the system would eventually have reconstituted itself on a different basis. In the world of real politics, however, no government could contemplate presiding over a depression that would create mass unemployment and potentially last for a decade.

The crisis left two substantial problems in its wake. The first was a heightened risk of sovereign debt default, meaning that governments might be unable to pay their debts. The stimulus packages, necessary as they were to avert depression, left some governments dangerously indebted. Iceland was the first to default, and doubts were later raised over the ability of a number of countries in the eurozone, notably Greece, Spain, Portugal and Ireland, to meet their obligations. France and Germany responded in 2010 with financial guarantees meant to restore confidence in the economies and the currency of the European Union, but uncertainty over Europe's economic future remains. The US government was also highly indebted, though not on the scale of some European countries. Some people say the US government has borrowed so much money that even the United States risks sovereign debt default, but the Americans are more likely to print money and create inflation in order to pay their way out of the crisis over the coming decade. Governments in the United States, Europe and Japan faced a thorny problem by 2010: should they act early to restrain spending in order to pay off debt and risk returning to recession, or spend more to avoid recession and risk default?

The second problem was 'moral hazard'. The largest investment banks and financial institutions now know that governments will rescue them with taxpayers' funds in order to avert a disaster for the financial system as a whole, and their business strategies are likely to reflect that belief. The disciplining influence of going bankrupt has been minimised, increasing the chances that the entire episode will be repeated in due course.

AUSTRALIA AND THE GLOBAL FINANCIAL CRISIS

The global financial crisis affected Australia immediately. Stocks fell, business confidence evaporated and a few large companies failed, among them Babcock & Brown, Allco Finance and ABC Learning. The Rudd government acted quickly and decisively to avert recession. The government guaranteed retail bank deposits up to $1 million in order to avoid the possibility of a run on the banks, and gave money to people in two stimulus packages, with the objective of maintaining retail spending. Australians who completed their tax returns were posted a cheque for $900. Billions of dollars were spent building new classrooms, libraries and other additions to the nation's public schools. The federal and state governments offered generous incentives to first-home buyers in order to avert a real estate crash, and the Reserve Bank, which is independent of governments, cut interest rates by 4.25 per cent. Australia experienced a slowdown in economic growth but not a recession, and the rise in unemployment was less than the government predicted.

Australia survived the global financial crisis better than most other advanced economies for a number of reasons. First, the financial sector was more regulated in Australia than in the United States or the United Kingdom. The Howard government inherited and maintained Paul Keating's 'four pillars' banking policy whereby no major bank can take over any other of the big four banks. The Australian Prudential Regulation Authority, established in 1998, regulated the financial sector. Second, the Howard government paid off government debt and was committed to surplus budgets, leaving the Rudd government able to spend money to stimulate the economy without borrowing excessively. Third, China underwrote the prosperity of the Australian economy: China's gigantic stimulus package indirectly boosted the Australian economy; and the minerals boom driven by Chinese demand merely paused for a year before resuming its former growth.

Kevin Rudd thought the global financial crisis discredited neo-liberal economic doctrines and proved that the free market needs the state in order to work properly. He wrote:

> With the demise of neo-liberalism, the role of the state has once more been recognised as fundamental. The state has been the primary actor in responding to three clear areas of the current crisis: in rescuing the private financial system from collapse; in providing direct stimulus to the real economy because of the collapse in private demand; and in the design of a national and global regulatory regime in which government has ultimate responsibility to determine and enforce the rules of the system.[3]

Australia and the G20

The formal institutions of global economic governance are the World Bank, the IMF and the World Trade Organization (WTO). Among other things, they deliver, manage and shape globalisation. The World Bank and the IMF are across the street from one another in Washington, symbolising American dominance of this process. But there are also informal institutions of global economic governance—groups of advanced economies that meet regularly to coordinate policy, and global meetings of political and business leaders such as the one held at Davos in Switzerland each year. The global financial crisis has had the effect of thrusting to prominence another informal institution, the G20, as a way of achieving maximum policy coordination by the world's largest economies.

Rudd addressed the UN early in the crisis and called for a global response. He foresaw the need to coordinate that response through a broadly representative group of states with economies big enough to produce a global effect. Formerly this would have been the G7—consisting of France, Germany, Italy, Japan, the United Kingdom, the United States and Canada—which had informally performed the function of global economic governance since the 1970s, or the G8 as it became with the addition of Russia in the 1990s. But the root of the problem was in these very G8 countries, since the global financial crisis had originated in the United States and spread quickly to the United Kingdom and Europe. They represented the global economy of the late twentieth century, not the global economy of the early twenty-first century. The major emerging economies of China, India and Brazil were not included.

What was needed to coordinate the response of countries to the global financial crisis was a broader and more inclusive group of economies. Rudd wanted the G20 to be recognised as the key informal institution of global economic governance, and he played a key role in urging the Americans to accept it. The G20 includes not only the countries of the G8 but also Argentina, Brazil, China, India, Indonesia, Mexico, Saudi Arabia, South Africa, South Korea, Turkey, the European Union—and, crucially for Rudd, Australia. The group, which first met in the late 1990s in response to the East Asian financial crisis, is drawn from all continents and represents two-thirds of global population and 90 per cent of global GDP. The Americans were not hard to convince, having decided they needed a counterweight to the European voices that dominated discussions in the G8, and they were happy to let Rudd make the case for the G20. According to David McCormick, Under-Secretary for International Affairs in the US Treasury,

'Australia had the horsepower to put into the fray, to drive analysis, direct policy discussion ... and was more in line with the US on the substance of how we thought a regulatory reform agenda should move forward. We were interested in Australia playing a more prominent role.'[4]

With his formidable command of argument and detail, Rudd mounted a campaign for the G20 that included numerous phone calls to national leaders and a direct appeal to President Bush himself. Rudd pointed out that the G20, unlike

KEVIN RUDD, PRIME MINISTER, ON THE G20

We're here in Pittsburgh for the G20 Summit, to continue working on our combined response to the worst global recession in three-quarters of a century. The challenges before us are clear. The global economy remains fragile, significant economic risks remain and there still remain risks of global economic setback. The full impact of this global economic recession will be felt for some time through rising unemployment in Australia, and around the world. Australia, of course, is doing much better than most other economies in the world in the face of this recession, but it would be absolutely foolish at this point to make the mistake of thinking that the global economic crisis is over.

What have we achieved so far through the G20? The G20 has played a critical role in breaking the fall of the global economy, which set in after the Lehmans collapse about one year ago. The G20 has delivered unprecedented coordinated action to deal with the ensuing global recession, including a $5 trillion injection in stimulus into the global economy, more than $1 trillion injected into the international financial institutions to restore confidence and guard against future financial difficulties within particular jurisdictions. Thirdly, agreements to reform and reshape the nature of the global financial regulatory system. And fourthly, an historic agreement to resist protectionist measures to avoid a tariff war, something which has broken out in times past when great times of economic difficulty have prevailed.

The G20 has emerged as a key body for economic cooperation. I have long argued that the G20 must remain an important body for strengthening the global economy into the future. The G20 provides Australia with a voice in the decisions of the management of the global economy, which directly affects us—a seat at the top table for the first time, which we have not had before at Head of Government level, and a table where the decisions on the future of the global economy are taken.

Joint doorstop interview with the Prime Minister and the Treasurer, Carnegie Mellon University, Pittsburgh, 25 September 2009.

some of the smaller groupings being proposed, included the Muslim nations of Indonesia, Saudi Arabia and Turkey, and—most important of all—brought China and its regional partners into a representative global forum. Bush called a meeting of the G20 in November 2008, and it now assumed a new importance in world affairs. Meeting in London and Pittsburgh in 2009, the G20 designated itself 'to be the premier forum for our international economic cooperation', and agreed on a joint program of stimulus packages designed to stabilise financial markets, revive international trade, resist protectionism, restore confidence and prevent global output from contracting. G20 leaders acted in the knowledge that the alternative might well be another Great Depression, when a lack of global policy coordination produced the opposite result. The G20 meeting in Toronto in 2010, meeting as the global economy began to recover, committed advanced economies to halve their government deficits by 2013 in order to rein back the debts incurred by stimulus spending.[5] Australia seemed likely to do much better and return to a budget surplus by 2013, but most other G20 countries faced years of austerity if they were to meet this goal. Whether the economic coordination agreed on by the G20 would revive the fortunes of the global economy remained to be seen. Pessimistic observers predicted that a second global financial crisis would follow the first.

The new prominence of the G20 shows that the global financial crisis had the effect of rebalancing international power relations in favour of China and other emerging economies such as India and Brazil. The Pittsburgh G20 meeting acknowledged that the relative weight of IMF members had 'changed substantially in view of the strong growth of the dynamic emerging market and development countries' and agreed to increase the influence of those countries in the organisation, as well as increasing their voting power in the World Bank.[6] At the same time the G20 offered the United States and China a means of dealing with each other on economic issues and exerting considerable sway over the global economy within the legitimising framework of a multilateral institution. The G20, said Rudd in Pittsburgh, 'provides Australia with a voice in the decisions of the management of the global economy, which directly affects us—a seat at the top table for the first time, which we have not had before at Head of Government level, and a table where the decisions on the future of the global economy are taken'.[7] Australia's membership will be distinctly in the national interest for as long as the G20 remains effective, and Rudd's diplomatic crusade to enhance the G20's role in global economic governance may come to be seen as his greatest achievement in foreign policy.

ASSESSMENTS

Under conditions of globalisation, high rates of economic growth tend to be accompanied by widening inequalities of wealth and income and longer hours of work as the labour market becomes more 'flexible'. That was, in particular, the experience of the United States, where real wages have stagnated since the 1980s while profits soared until the global financial crisis. The Australian experience has been somewhat different. Inequality has grown, but real wages have risen since the 1990s, and the majority of Australians have enjoyed rising prosperity. A sizeable minority, however, have benefited marginally, if at all, from a growing economy. Globalisation has changed the modern state, including Australia, in fundamental ways. Countries now compete more aggressively for shares of the world market. They are becoming 'competition states' in which governments calibrate policies according to international standards. The highest efficiency of ports, railways, aviation and telecommunications in one location on the globe, for example, becomes the 'international best practice' that all other states seek to emulate for the sake of their own export industries. The logic of the competition state is that if one country's corporate taxes are higher than another's, then the higher taxes will be reduced in order to discourage firms from moving offshore; wages in one country will adjust to competition from labour elsewhere; and the state becomes a mechanism to transmit international forces rather than shelter people from them.

Hawke and Keating accepted some of this logic but not all. The government reduced corporate taxation and restrained wages through the Prices and Incomes Accord but, on the other hand, introduced workforce training programs and targeted welfare. Howard accepted more of the competition state agenda, including policies of labour flexibility resisted by Labor, but at the same time acted conservatively to ensure that the financial sector of the economy was properly regulated. Having inherited the fundamental economic reforms and opening up of Australia to the global economy enacted by Hawke and Keating, Howard and his treasurer Peter Costello were able to maintain them without surrendering effective government supervision of the economy. The Reserve Bank, meanwhile, was accepted by all governments from Keating onward as independent from the government of the day, and reached its own decisions on setting interest rates. The judgement of economists and central bankers rather than short-term political expediency now determined monetary policy, as Howard discovered to his cost when the Reserve Bank increased interest rates—

and therefore the cost of home mortgages—in the months before the 2007 federal election. The result has been a broadly bipartisan solution to managing Australia's open economy, one that combines the foundation of the free market with Reserve Bank independence and a degree of government regulation that proved its value in the global financial crisis. Underpinning this success has been the China boom, which has filled the coffers of government from the profits of resource companies.

The global financial crisis revealed the limitations of the global shift from governments to markets since the 1970s. As Geoffrey Underhill points out, a 'market is a political device to achieve certain outcomes, conferring relative benefits on some and costs on others in both political and economic terms; it is, in essence, a political institution that plays a crucial role in structuring society and international politics'.[8] Markets are efficient allocators of resources in many circumstances but they necessarily redistribute wealth and create inequality even as they generate economic growth, and they require regulation to work properly. Unsurprisingly, wealthier people tend to like the market whereas poorer people seek the protective, regulatory and redistributive intervention of government. For this reason the entire debate about neo-liberalism, market solutions, competitiveness, free trade and global economic governance—usually conducted in the technical language of economics—is actually a debate about who should benefit most and who least from the political arrangements of society. When people argue about economics, they are invariably arguing about politics as well.

Ideologically, the global financial crisis has undermined the case for neo-liberal economics, at least in its purest form, and strengthened the case for government regulation and intervention.

FURTHER READING

The global economy

Held, David and Anthony Grew, eds, *The Global Transformations Reader: An introduction to the globalization debate*, Polity, Cambridge, 2nd edn, 2003. (Part IV of this excellent collection is on the global economy.)

The economy: A new direction for Australia

Capling, Ann, Mark Considine and Michael Crozier, *Australian Politics in the Global Era*, Addison Wesley Longman Australia, South Melbourne, 1998. (Part I deals with

Australia's transition from Keynesian nation-building up to the 1970s to neo-liberal globali-sation and financial deregulation in the 1980s and 1990s.)

Jennett, Christine and Randal G. Stewart, eds, *Hawke and Australian Public Policy: Consensus and restructuring*, Macmillan, Melbourne, 1990. (Labor policy in the 1980s.)

Kelly, Paul, *The End of Certainty: Power, politics and business in Australia*, Allen & Unwin, Sydney, rev. edn, 1994. (How Hawke and Keating opened Australia to the global economy.)

Pusey, M., *Economic Rationalism in Australia: A nation building state changes its mind*, Cambridge University Press, Sydney, 1991. (A critique of neo-liberal economics as a political project.)

The global financial crisis

Gamble, Andrew, 'The political consequences of the crash', *Political Studies Review*, vol. 8, 2010, pp. 3–14. (Argues that stimulus packages worked to save the global economy from collapse 'but at the cost of creating serious problems of adjustment for the future'.)

Garrett, Geoffrey, 'G2 in G20: China, the United States and the world after the global finan-cial crisis', *Global Policy*, vol. 1, no. 1, 2010, pp. 29–39. (Argues that 'China and the US are committed to embedding their bilateral diplomacy in multilateralism, with the G20 as their preferred vehicle'; examines the place of the G20 in global economic governance.)

Kindleberger, C., *Manias, Panics, and Crashes: A history of financial crises*, 5th edn, John Wiley and Sons, Hoboken, NJ, 2005. (A history of financial manias and crashes since the tulip bulb bubble in the Netherlands in 1636.)

Taylor, Lenore and David Uren, *Shitstorm: Inside Labor's darkest days*, Melbourne University Press, 2010. (Readable account of how the Rudd government dealt successfully with the global financial crisis and its threat to the Australian economy.)

Website

Global Policy (journal with focus on global economic governance):
<www.globalpolicyjournal.com>

The politics of international trade

- Why did the GATT system falter in the 1970s?
- What has the Cairns Group achieved and what are the obstacles it faces?
- Why are bilateral free trade agreements often called bilateral preferential trade agreements?
- Why did the Howard government conclude a free trade agreement with the United States?
- Does modern free trade undermine national sovereignty?
- What are GATS and TRIPS?
- Why have negotiations in the Doha Round of the WTO achieved so little?
- Why is Australia a quarry and mine for the world, just as it was in the 1960s? Why has the pattern of Australian trade not changed more?

Trade plays a vital role in making a country rich or poor. Trade is an intensely political issue because states depend for survival on importing key resources and maintaining access to overseas markets. When states have a great need to import a vital commodity, such as oil, they are prepared in the last resort to exercise force to ensure that supplies are not cut off, as a coalition of countries did in the Gulf War of 1991. Iraq had occupied Kuwait and its oilfields, a major source of oil for the industrialised world. Going to war is an extreme example of a phenomenon that commonly takes a more moderate form in international affairs—the politicisation of trading relations. The tendency of states to protect themselves in trade is inevitable; yet, if each acts according to its own immediate interest, all are likely to be worse off. That is one reason why so much diplomatic effort has been expended in the last 60 years in attempting to reach international arrangements that benefit all by encouraging global trade. Yet complete free trade in the contemporary international economy implies a loss of national autonomy which many fear, and in recent years trade agreements have intruded increasingly on issues of culture, social policy and national identity. In a globalising world, trade agreements are instruments of global governance policed by international institutions far removed from democratic control. Trade has become more political than ever.

Australia's place in international trade became more precarious in the last quarter of the twentieth century. By the 1980s Australia was significantly less competitive in world terms, unable to export goods and services in the quantities and at the prices needed to sustain traditional prosperity. Australia's exports grew year by year but not as fast or as profitably as those of many other countries, and its share of world trade fell between 1953 and 1989 from 2.6 per cent to 1.3 per cent. Alarmed by the decline, the Hawke government took action to improve Australia's performance as a trading nation. Hawke responded to international competition by putting the resources of his government behind the national task of selling more to the rest of the world, and by encouraging the diversification of the Australian exports. He reorganised the foreign policy bureaucracy so as to put trade and the economy at the centre of Australia's diplomatic efforts, and he employed Australia's diplomats on two major trade initiatives designed to improve Australia's exporting prospects. The Hawke government decisively cut tariffs. The result was that Australia's exports surged during the 1990s and early 2000s, more so than for a century, and at the same time services and manufactured goods joined the traditional agricultural and mining commodities as major contributors to the country's export income. Some believed the social costs of this transformation to be too high, but free trade certainly appeared to be delivering increased Australian competitiveness and higher growth rates. When the global financial crisis delivered a body blow to the global economy in 2008 and 2009, Australia was one of the few OECD (Organisation for Economic Co-operation and Development) countries not to suffer a recession.

TRADE LIBERALISATION

Trade liberalisation can occur in three different ways: unilateral, bilateral and multilateral. Australia embraced unilateral liberalisation under Whitlam, Hawke and Keating when it reduced tariffs on imports without requiring any other country to do so. Economists who favour free trade argue that unilateral trade reform of this kind is always in a country's interest because of the advantages it brings in cheaper prices, regardless of what other countries might do. Bilateral liberalisation occurs when two countries agree to favour the imports of the other, and is not regarded by free trade purists as 'free trade' at all, because it discriminates against third countries. Multilateral liberalisation occurs when more than two countries—in practice many more; in fact all the major players in the global trading system—agree to reduce trade barriers simultaneously and without discrimination against any of the countries in the agreement. The conventional wisdom has been that Australia has most to gain from multilateral trade liberalisation. This is for two reasons: Australia is a small player without much influence, and its agricultural exports face trade barriers that can be reduced only by multilateral agreement worldwide.

Labor's strategic vision for Australia in the 1980s and 1990s was pro–free trade, pro-unilateral and pro-multilateral. The Hawke and Keating governments believed the best hope for Australia—an isolated advanced economy highly dependent on foreign trade—lay in cutting tariffs unilaterally and supporting a multilateral global trading system in which the same rules applied to all players. The Howard government was less enthusiastic about free trade and multilateralism, and more in favour of a degree of protectionism together with bilateral trade deals with particular countries. Soon after coming to office, Howard froze planned tariff reductions on motor vehicles as well as textiles, clothing and footwear, delaying further action until 2005. The Howard government negotiated bilateral free trade agreements with Singapore, Thailand and the United States, and opened negotiations for further agreements with other countries. The Rudd government, while rhetorically in favour of the multilateral trade agenda, maintained the emphasis on bilateral trade agreements.

THE GATT

The General Agreement on Tariffs and Trade, or the GATT, was established under American sponsorship in the late 1940s as a way of ensuring that the world did not repeat the mistakes of the 1930s. During the Great Depression, countries tried to protect employment by raising tariff barriers against the products of other countries, only to find that everyone was poorer because world trade declined. The way past this problem, according to the architects of the GATT, was for countries to agree to reduce tariffs simultaneously and multilaterally. If all acted at the same time, no one would be worse off, and if all extended the same reductions to everyone else, trade in general would flourish.

Originally meant to be a temporary arrangement while a better one was devised, the GATT became permanent. The GATT's central principle was non-discrimination, enshrined in the 'most-favoured-nation' rule which required that 'any advantage, favour, privilege or immunity granted by any contracting party to any product originating in or destined for any other country shall be accorded immediately and unconditionally to the like product originating in or destined for the territories of all other contracting parties'.[1] This rule ensured that the GATT would constantly promote a greater liberalisation of trade on a multilateral basis.

The GATT was a political compromise from the start, full of exceptions. One such exception was the discriminatory trading bloc, such as the British Commonwealth and the European Common Market, which gave trade preferences to members and raised tariffs against outsiders. Another was trade in services, not covered by the original GATT and far less important in the 1940s than it was to become later. A third was trade in agriculture, specifically exempted from GATT rules so that the United States could subsidise American farmers and protect them from imports. In time this exemption was to allow Western European countries to develop elaborate and expensive systems of subsidising their farmers too, eventually on a scale that far exceeded that of the Americans. By 1990, the countries of the European Community (EC) were subsidising their agriculture at a cost of US$133 billion a year, the US was paying US$74 billion and Japan was not far behind with subsidies worth US$59 billion.

Like other institutions of the Bretton Woods era, the GATT worked well until the 1970s. Successive rounds of multilateral negotiations, involving scores of countries and lasting for years at a time, succeeded in fostering international trade on an unprecedented scale. Tariffs fell and prosperity grew, especially in advanced industrialised countries, whose merchandise trade grew by more than four times between 1963 and 1973. Japan and Germany leapt from ruin to abundance in a generation, not least because they took advantage of the boom in global trade founded on GATT agreements.

In the 1970s, however, the GATT system faltered. Countries had been happy enough to cut tariffs and other barriers to trade when times were good, but in the 1970s things began to go bad. The collapse of Bretton Woods meant that some major countries moved from fixed to floating exchange rates, and that in itself slowed trade; OPEC massively increased the price of oil, causing rapid price inflation in the advanced economies; Western European countries began to turn inward to protect their own industries; and, as we have seen, the long boom came to an end. After 1973 governments around the world confronted growing lines of unemployed and, in democratic countries, faced elections where people wanted to know how they would be protected from losing their jobs. Cutting tariffs, as the Whitlam government discovered, became a political liability because people blamed unemployment on lower levels of protection from foreign competition.

A tariff, which is a tax on something that crosses a national frontier, is only one way of restricting trade; as the most visible trade barrier, it is the easiest to identify. Other barriers can be just as effective in preventing the free flow of goods and services between countries. Subsidies to producers are an example of such barriers because they enable countries to gain access to markets by selling below cost. During the 1970s and 1980s such barriers began to affect a form of trade already protected and outside the GATT: trade in agriculture. Under the Common Agricultural Policy of the EC, governments subsidised farmers so handsomely that they accumulated huge surpluses of sugar, wheat, butter, poultry and other products. People spoke of Europe's 'butter mountain' and 'wine lake', put there not by the laws of supply and demand but by governments responding to voters. The original idea had been to maintain traditional farming communities and ensure food security within Europe, but with tonnes of food to dispose of and no one to eat it, the EC turned to the export business. Between 1976 and 1982 the EC's agricultural exports more than doubled, threatening US dominance and provoking American retaliation. In principle, the Americans stood for a free market in agriculture but they responded to the Europeans with export subsidies of their own, particularly on wheat and other grains.

Australia was caught in the crossfire as the EC and the United States fought a trade war over access to markets for agricultural produce. The Americans subsidised wheat exports to overseas markets which traditionally bought grain from Australia. At the same time Australia encountered obstacles in selling beef to Japan. Under pressure from the Americans the Japanese reached bilateral agreements that gave preference to American over Australian beef. Australia, we should remember, was hardly a model of free trade itself. While Australia did not subsidise agricultural exports, it imposed high tariffs on manufactured goods coming from Europe and the United States. Australia wanted, and still wants, to remodel international trade in its own national interest, which would be served by genuinely competitive access to overseas markets for agricultural products.

Problems of this kind thrust economics to prominence in Australian foreign policy. Hawke signalled the change by appointing an economist, Stuart Harris, as head of the Department of Foreign Affairs in 1984. Three years later Labor amalgamated the Department of Foreign Affairs and the Department of Trade in a major restructuring operation which involved over 5000 public servants, the majority of them in overseas diplomatic or trade missions. The new Department of Foreign Affairs and Trade (DFAT) now included Australia's experts on multilateral trade negotiations, and integrated trade with political work in its geographic sections. Since then, bureaucrats in DFAT have been responsible to two ministers, the Minister for Foreign Affairs and the Minister for Trade, and trade negotiations have been a central responsibility for the department.

THE WORLD TRADE ORGANIZATION (WTO)

Since 1995 the GATT has been institutionalised in the form of a new body called the World Trade Organization (WTO) with a permanent secretariat in Geneva, a court to adjudicate trade disputes and the task of administering the 28 agreements reached in the Uruguay Round. The WTO is much more than the mere successor to the GATT, and its trade agreements deal with much more than the word 'trade' might suggest. WTO agreements now cover trade in a whole range of intangibles that constitute a growing part of global production in services such as banking, insurance, tourism, telecommunications, sport, education and legal advice. Services are now estimated to account for about 70 per cent of production and employment in OECD countries. The WTO has extended international protection to copyright and trademarks in books, films and music as well as intellectual property rights.

WTO trade rules are legally enforceable in the 153 states that are now members of the organisation, and are part of a web of international arrangements that promote globalisation. Most important of all, many WTO trade agreements intrude directly into what used to be regarded as the sovereign affairs of states in matters of national economic policy, social protection and cultural independence. If trade is to be free, after all, and if trade includes investment and services, then countries might be required by a WTO agreement to surrender the controls previously exercised over foreign investors, or abandon a government monopoly in the delivery of services to citizens. Free trade in its modern form impinges on national sovereignty. For this reason, and in order to take advantage of the WTO dispute settlement system, DFAT includes a WTO Trade Law Branch in its Office of Trade Negotiations.

THE CAIRNS GROUP

Two problems worsened for Australia in the mid 1980s. The politicisation of agricultural trade threatened exports and foreign debt suddenly rose. Unless something was done, the government feared, Australia faced Third World status. When the April 1986 current account figures showed a sharp deterioration of Australia's trading position, Treasurer Paul Keating told John Laws on Sydney radio that Australia was living beyond its capacity to meet obligations by $12 billion a year. He was speaking over the phone from the kitchen of a function hall. In a hypothetical context, he talked of a 'banana republic'. The press seized upon the phrase as Keating's prediction for Australia and the scene was set for a media scare about the country's economic vulnerability.

In this crisis atmosphere the Hawke government devised a major trade initiative which came to be known as the Cairns Group. The United States, Japan and the EC—the states and trading blocs doing best in a politicised trading environment—were strong. They could use their strength to gain access to markets. To take one example, the United States, which had underwritten the defence of Japan since World War II, was in a good position to persuade the Japanese to increase the quota for grain-fed American beef imports. The Americans could use their political predominance for economic ends. Smaller countries such as Australia lacked influence, could not achieve much bilaterally and would gain most from changing the multilateral rules, those that applied to a large number of states. That meant changing the GATT and in particular removing the exemption on agricultural trade. Once agricultural trade came under the GATT there would be a mechanism to ensure that access to markets was fair to all rather than skewed in favour of the strongest or the most subsidised.

Since Australia could not hope to change the GATT by itself the answer was to build a coalition of countries in a similar position; that is, of small and middle powers with efficient agricultural sectors struggling to compete against subsidised exports. Each on its own could achieve little; together, they might make a difference to the outcome of the round of GATT negotiations due to start in 1986. That, at least, was Australia's hope when it invited agricultural producing countries to a conference of 'fair traders' at the Queensland town of Cairns in August 1986, just weeks before the first meeting in Uruguay of what became known as the Uruguay Round of the GATT. The thirteen nations were the most diverse of any group of states with which Australia has allied itself on a major foreign policy issue. Canada and New Zealand were obvious inclusions, but after them came five Latin American states (Argentina, Brazil, Chile, Colombia and Uruguay), four from South-East Asia (Indonesia, Malaysia, the Philippines and Thailand), one South Pacific microstate (Fiji) and one country from Eastern Europe, at that time still in the Soviet bloc (Hungary). Membership of the coalition owed nothing to Cold War considerations and everything to pressing national interests in trade. Its diversity pointed to a new confidence in Australian foreign policy making as well as a new emphasis on trade in international diplomacy. Over the years two states have left the Cairns Group (Fiji and Hungary), while seven others have joined, among them Pakistan and Peru. The Cairns Group now comprises Argentina, Australia, Bolivia, Brazil, Canada, Chile, Colombia, Costa Rica, Guatemala, Indonesia, Malaysia, New Zealand, Pakistan, Paraguay, Peru, the Philippines, South Africa, Thailand and Uruguay.

The major players in the GATT negotiations—the United States, the EC and Japan—took the Cairns Group seriously for two reasons. One was the group's importance in global agricultural trade. Together, the fourteen countries, with Australia leading, accounted for almost twice as much of the world's agricultural exports as the United States (26 per cent compared with 14 per cent), and in this respect were not far short of the EC (31 per cent). The other was the technical and intellectual competence of the Cairns Group bureaucrats who prepared the background papers and assembled the complex arguments advanced in international meetings. The GATT multilateral trade negotiations were probably the most complicated ever conducted by the international community. They involved numerous countries, 116 in total, and a wide variety of intricate technical issues. After the first five years of the Uruguay Round the package of reforms agreed upon was 440 pages long, and the round continued for more than two years after that. Under these circumstances, many smaller countries lacked the professional expertise needed to mount convincing negotiating arguments. The two countries with such expertise in the Cairns Group were Australia and Canada, with Australia leading the way because it was more committed to the issue. The government mobilised the considerable resources of DFAT to advance the case, anticipate objections, develop negotiating strategies and identify interim goals. The Cairns Group possessed the bureaucratic ability to argue its case effectively.

This exercise in coalition building worked, although the Cairns Group's influence in the Uruguay Round should be placed in context. On trade matters, as on all others, the great powers dominate the international system. The United States, the EC and Japan made the critical decisions and determined the shape of the new GATT. But the Cairns Group played a vital role in giving prominence to the agriculture issue in the early years of the Uruguay Round and developing negotiating positions that permitted agreement between the Americans and the Europeans. The group wanted lower tariffs, less domestic support for farmers, an end to export subsidies and special arrangements for less developed countries. When the Uruguay Round was finally concluded in April 1994 a version of this agenda had been achieved, with specific commitments to cut protection levels, reduce export subsidies and enforce rules against using minimal risks to human, animal or plant health as excuses for blocking trade in agricultural products. Above all, agricultural trade was made part of the GATT system, a lasting benefit for Australia.

The Cairns Group did not dissolve at the end of the Uruguay Round. Instead, it has become a permanent third force after the United States and the EU in international agricultural diplomacy, checking that countries keep their promises and trying to maintain the momentum towards free trade in agriculture in the latest round of global trade negotiations known as the Doha Round, also called the Doha Development Round to suggest that it will enhance the economic prospects of developing countries. Progress has been slow, however. The main goal of the Cairns Group—to bring free trade to global agriculture— is central to the conclusion of the Doha Development Round of the WTO, the GATT's successor. So far, however, the group has been frustrated with the failure to conclude. The Doha Round negotiations, having begun in 2001, were continuing in 2010 without hope of speedy resolution. At its meeting in Uruguay in 2010, the Cairns Group looked forward to the Doha Round delivering the elimination of all export subsidies on agriculture by 2013, but such an outcome seems unlikely. With its 153 member states, the WTO is an even more unwieldy mechanism for achieving diplomatic agreement than was the GATT at the time of the Uruguay Round.

Rural exports, with wheat, wine, meat and wool topping the list, are not as important to Australia as they once were. In 1988–89 they were worth 27.3 per cent of exports, and by 2008–09 that proportion had dropped to 10.3 per cent. Australia would nevertheless benefit from more freedom in global agricultural trade, because its rural exports are still being sold into the world's most protected markets, where high tariffs and subsidies distort the free flow of goods. The subsidies are of two types: domestic subsidies paid to producers and export subsidies designed to reduce the price of goods artificially. For political reasons, the main one being the lobbying power of farmers in the EU, the

THE CAIRNS GROUP

The formation of the Cairns Group was one of the successes of Australian foreign policy in the 1980s. Each of the nineteen countries of the group has three things in common with the rest—it is a significant exporter of agricultural products, it is too small by itself to influence international rules about agricultural trade, and it is at the mercy of the 'majors'. The majors are the US and the EU, which import and export agricultural products on a large scale, and Japan, which is an important market for exports from elsewhere. Together, members of the Cairns Group account for one-third of global agricultural exports.

Apart from their interest in agricultural trade, the Cairns Group countries are remarkably diverse, being drawn from Oceania, South-East Asia, North America, Latin America and Africa, with most being developing countries. The Cairns Group is an issue-specific coalition.

When the Cairns Group came into existence in 1986, agricultural trade still occurred outside the framework of trading rules enshrined in the GATT. Smaller countries suffered from the subsidies, tariffs and quotas which kept the Japanese market virtually closed and which enabled the Europeans and Americans to sell their agricultural produce at artificially low prices.

The aim of the Cairns Group was to change this situation, so that GATT rules would embrace agricultural trade and begin opening it to market forces. In this way countries like Australia would gain greater access to overseas markets and on a fairer basis.

The Group achieved this aim, but global agricultural trade remains highly protected. Special protection for agriculture arises in part from the political influence of farmers in the US, the EU and Japan, and in part because agriculture sustains rural communities and tends to be regarded by governments as more than just an economic activity.

The Cairns Group has much left to do if global trade in agriculture is to be fully liberalised. Having put agricultural trade on the multilateral agenda of the WTO, the Cairns Group is committed to achieving liberalisation of that trade in the Doha Round of WTO negotiations which began in 2001, above all by securing commitments from the majors to remove tariffs and subsidies. The Doha Round of negotiations remained unfinished in 2010, however, and seemed unlikely to be hastened to conclusion by the advanced industrialised countries experiencing unemployment as a result of the global financial crisis.

The member countries of the Cairns Group are Argentina, Australia, Bolivia, Brazil, Canada, Chile, Colombia, Costa Rica, Guatemala, Indonesia, Malaysia, New Zealand, Pakistan, Paraguay, Peru, the Philippines, South Africa, Thailand and Uruguay.

United States and Japan, global trade in agriculture is likely to remain distorted by subsidies, even though opening the markets of the rich world to the agricultural exports of developing countries would do more than anything else to redress global inequalities.

ASIA-PACIFIC ECONOMIC COOPERATION (APEC)

Australia's global trade initiative under the Hawke government was the Cairns Group; its regional trade initiative was APEC, the Asia-Pacific Economic Cooperation forum announced by Hawke in a speech in South Korea in January 1989. Hawke had pressing reasons to push for an Asia-Pacific regional trading arrangement. He could not be sure that the Uruguay Round of the GATT would be successfully negotiated; if GATT were to fail, Australia's next best alternative would be to be part of an economic grouping in its own region. He feared the emergence of major trading blocs from which the Australian economy would be excluded—in Europe, North America and East Asia. He wanted a dramatic foreign policy move to show he was taking action to enhance Australia's future prosperity. In line with the recommendations of the neo-liberals, Hawke sought to lock Australia into international free trade agreements that would give the government arguments against industries complaining about lower tariffs. As the American economist Paul Krugman pointed out, international trading regimes 'are intended at least as much to protect nations from their own interest groups as they are to protect nations from each other'.[2] Finally, Hawke could see long-term security advantages for Australia in binding the diverse countries of the Asia-Pacific into a cooperative arrangement which might serve to dampen regional tensions.

Australia hosted the first APEC meeting in 1989, bringing together twelve Pacific rim countries—the United States, Canada, Japan, South Korea and the six member states of the Association of Southeast Asian Nations (ASEAN) together with Australia and New Zealand. Rhetoric flowed copiously at that meeting, where member states promised to recognise the diversity of the region, participate in open dialogue and consensus, and advance common interests to achieve mutual benefits. Noble sentiments but not much else characterised APEC in the early years. Keating brought new energy to making the case for APEC and pushed for a summit meeting, which took place in Seattle in 1993, an occasion that gave new international prominence to APEC and brought together more Asia-Pacific heads of government than at any time since 1966. The summit meeting, which has been followed by annual summits since, showed that APEC could be useful for security as well as economic cooperation. Australia hosted the APEC summit in 2007, when a draconian security cordon was placed over Sydney's central business district in order to ensure the safety of the visiting world leaders.

The 1994 meeting of APEC, held in Indonesia, adopted what is called the Bogor Declaration. This committed the region's advanced industrialised countries, including Australia, to free and open trade and investment by 2010, with the developing countries following suit by 2020. APEC leaders decided in 1997 to include Russia, Vietnam and Peru. Shortly before this happened, the Howard government warned that 'too rapid an expansion of APEC's membership could substantially inhibit its capacity to achieve its ambitious trade and investment liberalisation goals'.[3] The warning proved correct. With 21 members including Russia, APEC extends from Mexico and Peru across the Pacific to Russia's border with Eastern Europe, and is so large and diffuse as to risk losing the ability to act decisively. The APEC countries are not a 'region' like the EU or NAFTA (United States, Canada and Mexico), and since APEC output is roughly 50 per cent of global output they are better thought of as half the world. APEC has the world's three biggest economies—those of the United States, Japan and China—but those countries disagree on many issues with each other and with the other big player, Russia. As a result, APEC has lost much of its former effectiveness. Member states have come to value it less for trade liberalisation than for its annual leaders' summit where they can discuss other issues. APEC's tagline or slogan, however, remains 'Advancing free trade for Asia-Pacific prosperity'.

BILATERAL FREE TRADE AGREEMENTS, GATS AND TRIPS

In the late 1990s the Howard government began to abandon the multilateral route to trade liberalisation and to explore the potential of bilateral trade agreements with particular countries such as Singapore, Thailand and the United States. The decline of APEC as a force for trade liberalisation through open regionalism was one reason. Another was the fiasco of the December 1999 WTO meeting in Seattle, where the authorities declared a state of emergency after tens of thousands of anti-globalisation protesters took to the streets, forcing the collapse of plans for a new global round of multilateral trade negotiations.

Most important of all, though, were the signals that Australia would continue to be excluded from East Asia's key regional trade and diplomatic arrangements.

Australia had never sought membership of the ASEAN or claimed to be a South-East Asian country but worked actively to be admitted into ASEAN Plus Three. If Australia were invited to participate in ASEAN Plus Three, Alexander Downer said in 2000, 'we'd be happy to do so'.[4] Nothing eventuated. At the same time Japan and South Korea, longtime supporters of the multilateral trade agenda, began to move towards regional and bilateral trade arrangements.

The Howard government thought Australia was being systematically excluded from East Asia's preferential trade arrangements and should therefore negotiate preferential trade arrangements of its own with trading partners who wished to cooperate. Australia would continue to play a part in multilateral trade negotiations through the WTO but at the same time would work towards bilateral free trade agreements. The first two, which came into effect in 2003, were with Singapore and Thailand. A third, potentially much more significant free trade agreement was reached with the United States in 2004 requiring approval by the US Congress and legislation by the Australian Parliament before it could come into effect. During the negotiations the government predicted great benefits, claiming that a free trade agreement with the United States 'that removed all barriers and harmonised standards could produce net economic welfare gains of about $40 billion, shared almost evenly between both countries, over 20 years'.[5]

Critics pointed to political realities. The American farm and steel lobbies wield great influence in Washington, much more than Australia does, and American governments periodically yield to the pressure by raising tariffs and subsidies. A free trade agreement with the United States that removed all barriers, critics said, would never happen. As the weaker party in the negotiations Australia would be unable to drive a hard bargain, and trade barriers were likely to remain firmly in place against Australian exports of goods such as wool, sugar, grain, beef, steel and dairy products, precisely the products that Australia most wanted to sell to America. These critics were proved correct. Under the agreement, the United States kept strong protection against imports of Australian beef, dairy products and sugar while at the same time gaining a much freer hand in investment, services and intellectual property. Australian agriculture, which was supposed to emerge the winner from the agreement, ended up with minor gains at most. The beef industry would have to wait eighteen years, for example, before gaining full access to the American market. Overall, the limited agreement that emerged from the negotiations has not stimulated much economic growth in Australia. Growth has come, instead, from China.

Howard wanted the free trade agreement with the United States for political reasons, and saw it as symbolising the closeness of the Australian–American relationship. At the same time he initiated free trade negotiations with other countries such as Malaysia and Japan. But his most important legacy came in the form of negotiations for an ASEAN–Australia–New Zealand free trade area, which eventually came into effect under the Rudd government in 2010, covering twelve countries with a combined population of 600 million. The ASEAN–Australia–New Zealand Free Trade Agreement (AANZFTA) includes provisions covering not just trade in goods and services, but also investment, intellectual property, the movement of business people and e-commerce. Under the agreement,

THE ASEAN–AUSTRALIA–NEW ZEALAND FREE TRADE AGREEMENT (AANZFTA)

This agreement is between Australia, the ten ASEAN countries — Brunei Darussalam, Cambodia, Indonesia, Laos, Malaysia, Myanmar, the Philippines, Singapore, Thailand and Vietnam — and New Zealand. It came into effect in 2010. The agreement covers about one-fifth of Australia's two-way trade in goods and services and encompasses a region of 600 million people.

ARTICLE 1 OBJECTIVES

The objectives of this Agreement are to:
(a) progressively liberalise and facilitate trade in goods among the Parties through, *inter alia*, progressive elimination of tariff and non-tariff barriers in substantially all trade in goods among the Parties;
(b) progressively liberalise trade in services among the Parties, with substantial sectoral coverage;
(c) facilitate, promote and enhance investment opportunities among the Parties through further development of favourable investment environments;
(d) establish a co-operative framework for strengthening, diversifying and enhancing trade, investment and economic links among the Parties; and
(e) provide special and differential treatment to ASEAN Member States, especially to the newer ASEAN Member States, to facilitate their more effective economic integration.

From the Agreement Establishing the ASEAN–Australia–New Zealand Free Trade Area, <www.dfat.gov.au/trade/fta/asean/aanzfta/aanzfta.pdf>.

Australia has removed all tariffs on imports from South-East Asian countries, which will themselves lower their tariff protection on most Australian-sourced imports over time. The agreement is typical of a modern free trade agreement in including provisions on services. It allows greater access for Australian accountants, architects, engineers, lawyers and bankers to certain South-East Asian markets, for example, and binds all ASEAN countries to permit 'level playing field' competition from foreign suppliers of telecommunications services. The Rudd government signed a similar agreement with Chile in 2009. Free trade will apply to all merchandise trade between Chile and Australia by 2015.

Concluding a bilateral free trade agreement with China has proved more difficult. Negotiations began in 2005 and the fourteenth round took place in 2010, with talks to continue. Yet Chinese demand is so buoyant, and its impact on Australian prosperity so positive, that a trade agreement would add only marginally to the advantages China gives Australia. The central fact is China's economic transformation. As Kevin Rudd pointed out in 2010:

> The change in China since the reform and opening era began in 1978 cannot be denied. The figures tell the story. First, after two decades of growth of around 10 per cent per year, China has become the second largest economy in the world. It is the world's largest exporter of manufactured goods, and the third largest exporter of all goods and services. It is also now the world's second-largest car market after the United States. This year, in the aftermath of the worst global economic downturn since the Great Depression, China continues to be the principal engine of global economic recovery—a fact highlighted by the International Monetary Fund in recent days. Only a decade ago, this would have been unimaginable. Three decades ago, it would have been seen as sheer fantasy. We have all been beneficiaries of China's remarkable performance.[6]

Globalisation—the ever-increasing integration of economies across territorial borders—is the force that lies behind the push for free trade, whether that is negotiated multilaterally or bilaterally. Globalisation is characterised by huge increases in flows of capital across the world, rapid growth in trade, the emergence of new kinds of trade in services, a technological revolution in communications that makes the globe itself the site of operations for major companies, and the growing influence almost everywhere of market forces. Nowadays the free trade agenda is not only about reducing tariffs. Free trade negotiators talk a lot about harmonisation, compatibility and mutual recognition, meaning that member countries of free trade agreements will eventually do things much the same way economically. Customs procedures, product standards, laws relating to investment, the enforcement of property rights, trade regulations: all these, in the vision of the WTO, will one day closely resemble each other across the globe. In a future free trade world, economies will be closely coordinated in the interests of investors, and governments will cooperate, for example, to keep company taxes at similarly low levels so as to encourage investment. The WTO, then, exists to promote high levels of integration, harmonisation and coordination between countries in economic matters. Australia has so far enthusiastically supported these goals.

The two major multilateral agreements that focus on this side of free trade are the General Agreement on Trade in Services (GATS) and the Agreement on Trade-Related Aspects of Intellectual Property Rights (TRIPS). Australia wanted a GATS agreement and worked effectively for it during the Uruguay Round by deploying skilled and knowledgeable diplomats in a complicated area of negotiations. GATS was originally supposed to create a multilateral free trade agreement that would make virtually the whole world a market for services from any country, whether those services were in finance, insurance, telecommunications, health, education, publishing, shipping or film and television. GATS was more limited when finally agreed upon because countries worried about their national interests. While Australia might welcome new investors in telecommunications, for example, it did not want to open the door to foreign doctors or sign the death warrant of the Australian film industry by permitting unfettered competition from Hollywood. In the end GATS became a way of enabling countries to list the services sectors where they would liberalise while maintaining exemptions elsewhere. Under GATS, Australia offers market access on a non-discriminatory basis in numerous sectors but not in the politically sensitive areas of cultural and audiovisual services, and only in a highly limited way in health and education.

TRIPS has become more contentious than GATS. The impetus to the TRIPS Agreement came mainly from the United States, whose corporations stood to gain most from protecting and enforcing intellectual property rights, such as patents and copyright, in areas such as computer hardware and software, pharmaceuticals and film. No longer would it be possible, the United States hoped, for governments and companies in developing countries to manufacture cheap generic drugs rather than importing American brand-name ones or to copy software without paying for it. TRIPS went even further and attempted to privatise biological life itself by enabling internationally enforceable patents to be placed on seeds, for example, and genetic material. The effect of TRIPS is to transfer resources from developing countries, which mostly import rather than export intellectual property, to the developed world in the United States and Europe, and is an example of how globalisation in some forms enriches some at the expense of others. Unsurprisingly, the US government is a strong supporter of TRIPS, which benefits its pharmaceutics, biotechnology, information technology and media industries among others. Australia, increasingly an exporter of intellectual property, supports TRIPS.

TRIPS exemplifies the intrusive nature of contemporary free trade. Some say that to continue down the path of integrating with the global economy is to surrender the capacity of future governments to decide the fate of the Australian people. International agreements will predetermine government policy in so many areas of economic life that elections will become irrelevant and people will be powerless to change what really matters. The aim of WTO harmonisation, for example, is to reach a point where countries act jointly in domestic economic policy. International comparisons will become central, national aspirations peripheral.

ASSESSMENTS

The rationale for economic integration is to achieve the most efficient deployment of resources in producing wealth. The Australian economy grew more quickly as it became more integrated into the global economy in the 1990s and 2000s, productivity rose and efficiency increased. Yet in the 30 years since Australia embarked on its journey to globalisation, many Australians have experienced precisely what such a major reorientation might be expected to produce: greater job insecurity, increased surveillance by employers in the workplace, a new dependence on part-time employment, and a growing sense that democratic elections make no difference to the prospects of ordinary people. Many Australians have benefited but some have been pitchforked into an underclass that is permanently excluded from full-time employment. The proponents of a globalised, free trade Australia might well be right about the stimulus this fundamental change of direction has given to the economy—higher growth rates appear to suggest that—but the fear is that a globalised Australia where only efficiency matters will be less identifiably Australian, less democratic, less equal and more ravaged by environmental degradation. Australians will no longer be citizens but merely employees and consumers in the global economy. Efficiency is only one criterion against which the success of a society can be measured. Some say other criteria matter more, such as national identity, democratic responsiveness, social equality and environmental preservation, all of which should be balanced against efficiency rather than subordinated to it.

Such arguments once enjoyed little currency in the major political parties. Labor's ministers tirelessly preached international competitiveness and were supported by the Coalition parties when they were in opposition. Once in office, however, the Coalition proved sensitive to anti-globalisation sentiment, which was especially strong in the rural heartlands of the National Party. From the start, the Howard government spoke with two voices. One voice championed APEC, the WTO, the multilateral trading regime and the promise of further integration into the global economy. The other voice talked about national interests, and linking the Australian economy with the United States, as much for security as for prosperity. The Howard government delayed the move towards free trade in motor vehicles, as well as textiles, clothing and footwear, fearing an electoral backlash, and secured GATS exemptions in the politically sensitive areas of the media, education and health. By the time Rudd became prime minister, the entire project of globalisation was in question because of a deepening financial crisis that originated in the United States, and a new concept—globalisation with regulation, which he championed—was beginning to emerge. But free trade remained an integral part of globalisation with regulation, and the Rudd government sought trade opportunities wherever they could be found, whether multilaterally in the Doha Round, plurilaterally in AANZFTA or bilaterally with China, Japan and other trading partners.

Three conclusions can be drawn from considering Australia's trade policy. First, Australian diplomacy is now as much about economics as politics. Foreign affairs are seen as a terrain where government and the private sector work hand in hand, the assumption being that Australia as a whole will benefit. Winning international markets for Australian business has become one of DFAT's major objectives.

Second, Australia's response to globalisation has been broadly bipartisan since the 1980s, during which time Australia has undertaken a historic shift from protectionism to free trade. The major parties agree that trade liberalisation opens new markets overseas and that the country's future lies in free trade and economic integration with the Asia-Pacific. The consequence of decisions made in the 1980s can be seen in the growth of Australian trade since then, and in the integration of the Australian economy into East Asia. By 2009, six out of Australia's top ten trading partners were countries from Asia, its top five export markets were China, Japan, India, South Korea and the United States, and its top five import sources were China, the United States, Japan, Singapore and Thailand. The free trade agreement with New Zealand and ASEAN adds to East Asia's economic importance to Australia. Exports and imports in 2009—a bad year because of the global financial crisis—were nevertheless worth four times more than in 1989, and trade was worth almost half Australia's GDP. The driving force lay in the demand for coal and iron ore, whose export value grew almost sixfold from 1999 to 2009, from $12 billion to $69.4 billion.

Australia's trading pattern is not quite what the proponents of free trade envisaged. Australia was supposed to become the clever country by virtue of opening its economy to the world, and to export services and 'elaborately transformed manufactures' in large quantities. While education, tourism and professional services now rank among Australia's top ten exports, coal, iron ore, gold and crude petroleum are far more important. Australia is still a quarry and mine for the rest of the world, as it was 40 years ago. Still, most observers count the move to free trade as a success.

Third, the peak in multilateral trade reform has passed. For as long as that reform favoured the most powerful actors on the world trading scene—the United States, the European Union and Japan—liberalisation proceeded apace. Such liberalisation, after all, benefited exporters in the rich world specialising in high technology, services and intellectual property. But the Doha Round of WTO trade negotiations aimed to bring similar liberalisation to agricultural trade, where most rich countries (though not Australia) had interests to protect in the form of highly subsidised agriculture. Many people in the United States blame loss of jobs in manufacturing on unfair competition from China, and the United States has led a new trend towards bilateral trade deals. As a consequence, barriers to Australian agricultural exports are likely to remain for many years to come.

FURTHER READING

Australia and international trade

Australian Journal of International Affairs, vol. 62, no. 2, 2008. (Issue is devoted to articles on Australian trade policy in an era of regional preferential trade agreements.)

Capling, Ann, *Australia and the Global Trade System*, Cambridge University Press, Cambridge, 2001. (The only comprehensive history of Australian trade policy since World War II; includes chapters on the Cairns Group, GATS and the shift to bilateralism.)

Garnaut, Ross, 'An Australia–United States Free Trade Agreement', *Australian Journal of International Affairs*, vol. 56, no. 1, 2002, pp. 123–41. (Argues against the FTA with the US, in part on the grounds that it is about preferential trade, not free trade.)

Ravenhill, John, 'Australia and the global economy', in *Trading on Alliance Security: Australia in world affairs 2001–2005*, James Cotton and John Ravenhill, eds, Oxford University Press, Melbourne, 2007, pp. 192–212. (Covers the growth of bilateralism, the Australia–US free trade agreement, APEC and the WTO.)

The Cairns group

Cooper, Andrew F., Richard A. Higgott and Kim Richard Nossal, *Relocating Middle Powers: Australia and Canada in a changing world order*, Melbourne University Press, Melbourne, 1993, Chapter 3. (Australia's role in the Cairns Group initiative.)

Asia-Pacific Economic Cooperation (APEC)

Keating, Paul, *Engagement: Australia faces the Asia-Pacific*, Pan Macmillan Australia, Sydney, 2000. (Chapter 5: the former prime minister on his role in advancing APEC and Asia-Pacific free trade.)

Ravenhill, John, *APEC and the Construction of Pacific Rim Regionalism*, Cambridge University Press, Cambridge, 2001. (A detailed, technical account of the evolution of APEC and why it lost relevance.)

Tracy, Noel, 'The APEC dilemma: Problems along the road to a new trade regime in the Pacific', in *Middling, Meddling, Muddling: Issues in Australian foreign policy*, Richard Leaver and Dave Cox, eds, Allen & Unwin, Sydney, 1997, pp. 142–59. (Early doubts about the effectiveness of APEC.)

GATS and TRIPS

Arup, Christopher, *The New World Trade Organization Agreements: Globalizing law through services and intellectual property*, Cambridge University Press, Cambridge, 2000. (Legal analysis of GATS and TRIPS, showing how they intrude on national sovereignty.)

Websites

APEC Secretariat: <www.apec.org>
The Cairns Group: <www.cairnsgroup.org>
World Trade Organization: <www.wto.org>

PART IV

Issues in foreign policy

The global environment

- What are the principal global environmental problems?
- What is a 'framework convention'?
- Why did the Howard government decline to ratify the Kyoto Protocol and why did the Rudd government proceed to ratify it?
- Why did the Rudd government fail to legislate an emissions trading scheme?
- Why was it easier to achieve global agreement on the depletion of the ozone layer than to achieve global agreement on climate change?
- Why did the Copenhagen climate change conference achieve less than many people hoped?
- In what ways are state sovereignty and the protection of the global environment in conflict?
- In what way do global environmental issues challenge commonplace assumptions about the purpose of Australian foreign policy?

A new consciousness of the place of humankind in nature has arisen since the 1970s. At a time when our numbers are increasing exponentially and our demands on nature are greater than ever before, we have become aware that we live in nature and not just from it. We are beginning to realise that we are waging war on the natural environment which is our only habitat. We burn fossil fuels at a rate that appears likely to cause global warming and destabilise climatic patterns. We plunder the oceans for fish. We destroy the tropical rainforests and drive numerous other kinds of life to extinction. We release substances that deplete the ozone layer in the atmosphere, our only protection against serious injury from the ultraviolet rays of the sun. Humankind has become dominant on earth, and our activities are not only shaping the landscape but affecting the atmosphere, the oceans, the forests and non-human life in ways that might ultimately threaten our own survival.

Global population has risen sharply over the last 200 years and now stands at almost 7 billion, increasing by 87 million a year. For most of human history fewer than 500 million people have populated the planet but by 2050 the world will be home to 9 billion people, whose numbers will have grown in just twenty years by more than the entire world population at the beginning of the twentieth century. Most of the increase is taking place in developing countries in Asia, Africa and Latin America and, because so many people there are still young, population growth has a momentum that will continue well into the twenty-first century. Between 2006 and 2020 the population of Africa will have grown from 943 million to 1.2 billion, and that of Asia and the Pacific from 3.6 billion to 4.2 billion.

At the same time, people the world over are embracing the Western mode of development, which depends upon ever-increasing consumption of energy, exploitation of natural resources and pressure on the environment. Western-style capitalism has transformed China from a vast zone of underdevelopment into the world's second largest economy in just 30 years, with rapid growth continuing and raw materials drawn there from all over the world. Economic growth, the overriding aim of governments and business corporations everywhere, cannot continue indefinitely without encountering the limits imposed by nature itself. Many scientists argue that humankind is already reaching those limits. Rapidly rising population and the triumph of industrialisation are combining to cause a problem which some think is serious but manageable and others fear is an apocalyptic environmental crisis.

Almost all global environmental problems derive from pollution or depletion of the atmosphere, water, land and life forms.

One category of air pollution takes dramatic form. The return of sunlight to the Antarctic each spring causes a chemical reaction which depletes levels of ozone (O_3), a gas that plays a vital role in protecting the earth from the destructive effects of ultraviolet radiation. The chemical reaction is between ozone and chlorine atoms of human origin, produced by the worldwide emission of chlorofluorocarbons, halons and certain other gases in industrial solvents, styrofoam, air conditioners, refrigerators, spraycan propellants and fire extinguishers. The scientists' predictions of further depletion in ozone levels proved correct, although stratospheric ozone levels are now stabilising. If the depletion of the ozone layer had been allowed to continue, it would have caused higher rates of skin cancer, more eye disease, suppression of the human and animal immune systems, damage to plants, and possible destruction of aquatic ecosystems because of the effect of ultraviolet radiation on phytoplankton, the foundation of the food chain in the oceans of the world.

If the most pessimistic scientific predictions prove true, melting of ice is likely to cause a general rise in ocean levels over the next 50 years, to inundate low-lying coastal areas all over the world and to make atoll countries in the Pacific and Indian oceans uninhabitable. Most scientists believe that global warming already influences climate and weather in some parts of the world. They argue that hurricanes have recently been of unprecedented force and that world weather is becoming less stable. They point to the increased frequency and severity of the El Niño southern oscillation, in which vast areas of warm water move from one side of the South Pacific to the other, producing serious drought in parts of Australia, Papua New Guinea and Indonesia when the warmth is in the eastern Pacific.

Water pollution is accelerating. The runoff of industrial waste on every continent comes in the form of toxic chemicals, radioactive waste, silt from topsoil or sewage and fertilisers that cause huge algal blooms. This detritus of industrial civilisation is polluting the oceans and seas that cover 70 per cent of the earth's surface. Accidents occur in ocean drilling for oil, as happened in 2010 when a British Petroleum deep sea oil well blew in the Gulf of Mexico, contaminating the surrounding coasts. Smaller, enclosed seas such as the Baltic, the Black, the Caspian and the Mediterranean are being contaminated, coral reefs in many parts of the tropics are disintegrating, and fish stocks are falling as commercial fishing becomes more efficient, making use of sophisticated detection methods and gigantic nets and longlines. The oceanic populations of a large number of fish species have seriously declined and are likely to decline further.

Land is also being polluted and depleted. The most serious case of land pollution is around Chernobyl in the Ukraine, where a nuclear reactor melted down in 1986 and contaminated the surrounding countryside with radioactive fallout and debris, forcing 100,000 people to evacuate the area permanently and causing a long-term increase in cancers among the population. Industrialisation everywhere causes less dramatic but nonetheless damaging land pollution, which takes the form of toxic runoff from mining, landfills and waste disposal. Land depletion is also taking place. Certain kinds of modern agriculture cause soil erosion on a massive scale, estimated by the UN to be the equivalent of losing 70,000 square kilometres of productive farmland every year. All over the world the rain washes topsoil into rivers and the sea, and the wind blows it away. In effect, some intensive forms of agriculture are gradually stripping the planet of the topsoil in which much of our food is grown. Irrigation in many places is proving to be a technology that increases agricultural production temporarily, only to degrade the land in the long run by increasing underground water levels and creating salination, a serious problem in some parts of Australia. One expert estimate is that a fifth of the world's 250 million hectares of irrigated land is now significantly degraded.

Human beings are depleting non-human life on the planet in a number of ways, above all through desertification and deforestation. Semi-arid lands across the globe, especially in Africa, are becoming deserts largely devoid of plant and animal life as human populations press harder on their margins by overcropping, overgrazing and cutting brush and trees for fuel. Deserts expand as natural forests diminish in both tropical and temperate climates. Forests not only absorb carbon dioxide and emit oxygen, they also influence climate, purify water sources and are home to much of the planet's life. Humankind had destroyed half the world's tropical forests by 1991. The destruction continues, especially in the tropical rainforests of South-East Asia, the South-West Pacific and the Amazon Basin, though it appears to be slowing. The UN Food and Agriculture Organization's 2009 report *State of the World's Forests* estimated that the annual rate of global deforestation fell from 8,868,000 hectares a year in the 1990s to 7,317,000 hectares a year between 2000 and 2005. Asia and the Pacific actually added 3 million hectares of forest between 2000 and 2005, mainly because of a high rate of reafforestation in China.

No one knows how many species of plants and animals there are. We only know that they number millions and are the legacy of hundreds of millions of years of evolution. We are rapidly reducing their number, in some cases even before we know of an individual species' existence, by polluting and depleting nature and above all by clear-felling tropical rainforests. Generally speaking, biodiversity—the number of species in an ecosystem—increases from higher latitudes to lower and is at its peak near the equator. Tropical rainforests are believed to harbour half of all species of life on earth. Many biologists believe human-induced loss of biodiversity is a serious environmental problem, even a crisis, which might rebound unfavourably on human populations in the future by depriving us of species differentiation vital to our survival.

THE INTERNATIONAL RESPONSE

Popular consciousness that we depend on the global environment dates from the late 1960s and early 1970s, when citizen groups in the United States and Canada such as Friends of the Earth, the Sierra Club and Greenpeace began to mobilise public opinion against human threats to the environment. At the level of states, the 1972 UN Conference on Human Environment was a turning-point, though its focus was on regional (not global) environmental problems such as the movement of air pollution across national boundaries. It led to the formation of the UN Environment Programme, contributed to rising aware-ness among governments of the environment and proposed a concept now central to international environmental diplomacy, 'sustainable development', which seeks to reconcile economic growth with environmental protection and has been defined as 'development that meets the needs of the present without compromising the ability of future generations to meet their own needs'. The pace of environmental activism by governments and non-government organ-isations quickened during the 1980s. The *Global 2000 Report*, commissioned by the Carter administration in the United States, warned that the world in 2000 would be 'more crowded, more polluted, less stable ecologically, and more vulnerable to disruption than the world we live in now' and correctly predicted loss of forests, desertification, depletion of soil and increased pollution of air and water if existing trends continued. The Brundtland Report of 1987, *Our Common Future*, was the outcome of four years' work by an international commission on the environment and development and argued that govern-ments everywhere had to make sustainable development their first priority. Greenpeace became adept at confronting polluters, whalers and other threats to the environment in ways that attracted media attention, the World Wildlife Fund (WWF) campaigned against species loss, numerous groups fought to save the forests, and environmentalism became a force in the electoral politics of a number of industrialised countries, including Australia.

Climate change, the key environmental problem of the twenty-first century, also emerged as an issue in the 1970s and 1980s. At that time most people thought climates would remain much the same from year to year. But research by the World Meteorological Organization in the 1970s began to undermine this commonsense understanding. The World Meteorological Organization held a number of conferences on greenhouse gases and climate. One of these, the 1985 Villach conference in Austria, reached the conclusion that 'in the first half of the next century a rise of global mean temperature could occur which is greater than any in man's history', and called for limits on the emission of greenhouse gases.[1] The 1980s were the hottest decade recorded and the United States experienced a severe drought in 1988. Many people suspected climate change was already occurring. These events, together with the Villach findings, the Brundtland Report and concerted lobbying by climatologists and environmental groups, prompted governments to form the Intergovernmental Panel on Climate Change (IPCC) in 1988. The panel's task is to act as a global scientific authority on global warming and its findings are central to all international negotiations over climate change. Spurred on by the IPCC's 1990 report, the UN General Assembly initiated negotiations for an international agreement on the atmosphere.

One hundred and sixty-five countries signed the UN Framework Convention on Climate Change in 1992 and it came into force in 1994. The convention aims to stabilise greenhouse gas concentrations at a level that will 'prevent dangerous anthropogenic interference with the climate system'; in other words, one that will stop changes to global climate induced by human activities. The Intergovernmental Panel on Climate Change has compounded the sense of urgency in a series of reports based on scientific observation of the planet's climate system. The 2001 report pointed to clear evidence of increasing temperatures. The scientists predicted adverse impacts on human populations caused by more floods and extreme weather events and they identified glaciers, coral reefs and atolls, polar and alpine ecosystems and tropical forests as especially vulnerable to climate change.

The 2007 IPCC report concluded that warming of the climate system was 'unequivocal, as is now evident from observations of increases in global average air and ocean temperatures, widespread melting of snow and ice and rising global average sea level', and it pointed to the fact that eleven of the twelve years between 1995 and 2006 were among the twelve warmest years since 1850. Most of the observed increase in global average temperatures, according to the report, was 'very likely due to the observed increase in anthropogenic GHG concentrations', in other words, the result of greenhouse gases produced by humankind. The report predicted a loss of biodiversity on the Great Barrier Reef and in the Queensland wet tropics by 2020 and increased drought and fire in southern and eastern Australia.[2]

Uncertainties remain but the balance of evidence is this: human beings are affecting global climate. By 2100, unless something is done now, global temperatures will have risen by between 2.4 and 6.4 degrees Centigrade. Climate changes will affect global food supplies and human health, mostly for the worse, and could cause widespread forest dieback. We could stabilise the concentration of CO_2 in the atmosphere immediately, but only by reducing CO_2 emissions by up to 70 per cent, a change that would disrupt modern industrial civilisation, and if we are to stabilise greenhouse gas concentrations at twice preindustrial levels we will eventually have to cut emissions to half what they are now. Even if immediate stabilisation were possible, the climate would continue to warm and the sea levels to rise for centuries.

The climate change convention was one of a number of outcomes of the UN Conference on Environment and Development (or Rio Earth Summit), held in Rio de Janeiro in 1992. The summit gave expression to a rising tide of concern about the impact of humanity on the planet. Delegations came from 178 countries, including Australia. The Rio Earth Summit did not change the world or even significantly check pressure on the environment, but it put environmental protection on the international diplomatic agenda, and set a process in train. The UN organised a string of global environmental conferences after Rio, on population, fisheries, small island states, chemical safety, human settlements, biological diversity, climate change and desertification, and from them and other meetings came a series of international environmental agreements, among them the Convention on Biological Diversity (1992), the UN Convention to Combat Desertification (1994), the Kyoto Protocol on Climate Change (1997), the Rotterdam Convention on Prior Informed Consent Procedure for Certain Hazardous Chemicals and Pesticides in International Trade (1998), the Cartagena Protocol on Biosafety (2000) and the Stockholm Convention on Persistent Organic Pollutants (2001).

OZONE AND THE MONTREAL PROTOCOL

Scientists at the University of California pointed in 1974 to a chain of events which linked chlorofluorocarbons, or CFCs—apparently harmless chemicals in everyday use—to a threat to life. Rather than breaking down quickly as many gases do when released into the atmosphere, CFCs retain their chemical structure and move upwards to the stratosphere. They remain there for decades or even centuries, slowly breaking down in the worst possible way by releasing large amounts of chlorine. Since one chlorine atom destroys tens of thousands of ozone molecules, the loading of the stratosphere with chlorine even in tiny amounts reduces the ozone layer that shields the earth from destructive UV-B lightwaves. Scientists in the 1970s could not prove that ozone was being destroyed high above the earth but they correctly predicted that observations would one day vindicate them. Environmentalists persuaded some governments to act. The US Clean Air Act of 1977 gave authorities the power to regulate substances which could be expected to affect stratospheric ozone and soon afterwards the US government banned the use of CFCs as aerosol propellants in many kinds of spraycans. Canada, Norway and Sweden—countries where environmentalists were well organised—followed the American example, but ozone depletion was yet to become a public issue in Australia.

The ozone issue presented the international community with a new challenge, which was how to respond to an unproven but plausible scientific theory which made dire predictions. If governments banned certain chemicals and the theory were shown to be false they would look foolish, but if they did nothing and the theory were true they would have failed to stop a catastrophe. We now know that atmospheric chlorine increased from a concentration of 0.6 parts per billion before industrialisation to three parts per billion by 1985, and that chlorine has destroyed a small but measurable part of the ozone layer, but these things were not known in 1981 when the United Nations Environment Programme took the first steps towards an international agreement to protect the ozone layer.

The 1985 Vienna Convention for the Protection of the Ozone Layer (VCPOL), the outcome of those early negotiations, shows that many states were initially sceptical about damage to the ozone layer. The idea that human beings could be profoundly affecting the global ecosystem seemed fantastic to all but the experts. In keeping with this scepticism, the VCPOL provided for research cooperation and required states to take 'appropriate' steps 'should it be found' that human activities threatened the ozone layer. The convention did not specify the meaning of 'appropriate'.

The VCPOL was one of a new generation of international agreements called *framework conventions*, which have since proved especially suitable for environmental matters. The typical framework convention does not demand much of governments that sign it, at least to begin with. The aim is rather to gain agreement in general terms that something needs to be done, and to establish a negotiating procedure that can revise the original convention as necessary, especially if scientific evidence points to more urgent action. Framework conventions are flexible instruments that allow for future protocols or amendments to be negotiated in the light of emerging knowledge. Often the protocols are more important than the original convention.

In the case of ozone, the 1987 Montreal Protocol on Substances that Deplete the Ozone Layer matters far more than the Vienna convention to which it is attached. Under the Montreal Protocol, states agreed to freeze or reduce the production and consumption of certain CFCs and halon gases by certain dates. The agreement was the first recognition on a global level that humankind had gone too far in modifying the environment and that even apparently minor modifications such as trace gases could have global effects. The impetus for states to agree came from scientific findings released in 1986. A major international study coordinated by the National Aeronautics and Space Administration (NASA) in the United States found that key CFC concentrations had doubled in the atmosphere in just ten years and that human populations in the Northern Hemisphere could be dangerously exposed to ultraviolet radiation by the second half of the twenty-first century. The negotiators who met in Montreal in 1987 made modest progress to begin with, agreeing to control just eight chemicals, whereas almost one hundred are now controlled.

Scientists reached even more alarming conclusions soon afterwards. Not only was ozone actually thinning but it was thinning faster than expected, and the atmosphere had lost as much ozone by 1988 as the Montreal negotiators assumed would be lost by 2050. The Ozone Trends Panel confirmed a British discovery that ozone levels over Antarctica were falling sharply each spring with the return of sunlight after the darkness of the Antarctic winter. Measurements of ozone made at Britain's Halley Bay Research Station showed a steady decline in ozone levels each October since the mid 1970s. By the mid 1980s the 'ozone hole' covered an area larger than the United States, with losses of as much as 95 per cent in the ozone layer in some places. These findings set the scene for a dramatic tightening of the Montreal Protocol and for cooperation from major chemical companies such as the American multinational DuPont, the largest CFC producer, which undertook to stop making all CFCs and halons by 2000. Under further revisions countries agreed not just to reduce the use of ozone-eating gases but to phase them out by 2000 and to phase out others not covered by the original protocol. By 2007, twenty years from the signing of the Montreal Protocol, the 191 signatory states had cut consumption of ozone-depleting substances by 95 per cent and the developing countries among them by 72 per cent.

Scientific evidence now points to the success of these measures, as the loss of ozone in the upper atmosphere slows. Full recovery is expected by 2050.

According to ozone scientists reporting in 2006, the 'total combined abundances of anthropogenic ozone-depleting gases in the troposphere continue to decline from the peak values reached in the 1992–1994 time period' and the 'current best estimate is that global (60°S–60°N) ozone will return to pre-1980 levels around the middle of the 21st century, at or before the time when stratospheric abundances of ozone-depleting gases return to pre-1980 levels'.[3]

AUSTRALIA AND THE GLOBAL ENVIRONMENT

Australia had a reputation in the early 1990s for being pro-environment. The Labor government appointed an Ambassador for the Environment in 1988, sent experts to the Intergovernmental Panel on Climate Change, passed the *Ozone Protection Act 1989*, committed Australia to stabilise greenhouse gas emissions at 1988 levels by 2000 and acted quickly to design a strategy for protecting Australia's biodiversity. Labor set up the Environment Assistance Programme in 1989 to help poorer countries meet the short-term costs of environmental protection. To do this, said Gareth Evans, was to 'put our money where our mouth is'. He depicted Labor's positive approach as part of Australia's good international citizenship, and spoke of the 'need for Australia to be at the forefront of international cooperation on the environment'.[4] Labor particularly pleased environmentalists by backing a whale sanctuary in the Southern Ocean.

The Hawke Labor government's most striking achievement in environmental diplomacy was to help achieve a 50-year ban on mining and oil exploration in Antarctica. The 1959 Antarctic Treaty prohibits military use of the region and sets it aside for scientific research but says nothing about minerals. When oil companies turned their attention to Antarctica after the 1973 OPEC oil shock, interested states began talking about a possible minerals regime for the region; that is, a system of rules to govern mining and oil extraction. No companies were in Antarctica, and governments called in 1977 for a voluntary moratorium on exploration and exploitation while they negotiated an agreement. Years later, this agreement emerged in the form of the 1988 Antarctic Minerals Convention, which would have allowed companies to prospect and exploit the mineral resources of Antarctica under certain conditions.

The international community fully expected the Minerals Convention to come into effect after the usual period needed for ratification but two Antarctic Treaty countries broke ranks and withdrew support in 1989. Australia and France said they wanted mining banned rather than regulated and the Antarctic declared a wilderness reserve rather than the world's last mining and oil-drilling frontier. The Australian and French governments were courting green votes and were receptive to the well-organised campaigns of environmental non-government organisations, which regarded the Minerals Convention as a disaster. And they were responding to wider public opinion, inflamed against oil-drilling by the Exxon Valdez incident in March 1989, when an American oil tanker ran aground in Alaska and discharged vast quantities of oil on the shores of Prince William Sound. Television around the world showed fish, seals and birds struggling to survive in a dramatically polluted environment.

By taking the lead Australia and France compelled other Antarctic Treaty governments to decide whether they were for or against mining in the Antarctic, and gradually won more and more allies. The Soviet president, Mikhail Gorbachev, committed his country to back Australia, and Malaysia sponsored a UN resolution calling for Antarctica to be declared a World Park free of mining. Negotiations began for a new and comprehensive environmental agreement known as the Madrid Protocol, which was adopted in 1991 and came into force in 1998. The protocol designates the Antarctic 'a natural reserve, devoted to peace and science' and effectively prohibits any activity related to mining for 50 years.

Non-government organisations played a vital role in overturning the Minerals Convention and replacing it with a ban on Antarctic mining. Greenpeace International dramatised environmental issues from its Antarctic research base set up in 1987. Greenpeace reported on the Antarctic at first hand and sent its ship to monitor the environmental performance of the countries that ran all the other research bases. As Lorraine Elliott has argued, neither non-government organisations nor states could have changed the Antarctic Treaty regime on their own: the non-government organisations needed states to shape what is, after all, an agreement between governments; and states needed non-government organisations to mobilise public opinion in favour of saving the Antarctic. Gareth Evans made just this point in 1991, when he commended the efforts of Lynn Goldsworthy, political coordinator for the Greenpeace International Antarctic Campaign. Evans pointed out that 'Greenpeace and other environmental groups played a large part in creating an atmosphere back in 1989 in which the Government found it relatively easy—domestically at least—to support a mining ban in Antarctica'.[5]

The Howard government agreed with Labor on a number of environmental issues, especially whaling and fisheries, and participated in the multilateral environmental process where, in the official view, it served Australia's national interests. Australia under the Howard government joined New Zealand in proposing another whale sanctuary in the South Pacific, stretching south of the equator across the region from Papua New Guinea to French Polynesia. Australia under the Howard government continued to have an Ambassador for the Environment, to contribute to the Global Environment Facility and to participate in the UN Commission for Sustainable Development. It also ratified the Rotterdam Convention on Prior Informed Consent Procedure for Certain Hazardous Chemicals and Pesticides in International Trade and the Stockholm Convention on Persistent Organic Pollutants.

Climate change was the issue that threw doubt on the Howard government's environmental credentials. The official position was that Australia should be allowed to increase greenhouse gas emissions, not cut them, and the government achieved this outcome at the 1997 Kyoto climate change conference, where 39 developed countries committed themselves to reaching greenhouse gas targets by 2012 in an agreement known as the Kyoto Protocol to the UN Framework Convention on Climate Change. In effect, nations undertook to be releasing agreed levels of greenhouse gases by that year so as to begin the process of averting possible global climatic catastrophe sometime later in the twenty-first century. Most countries said they would reduce emissions below 1990 levels. Led by the Minister for the Environment, Senator Robert Hill, the Australian team at Kyoto were tough negotiators for their government's position. Hill knew the credibility of the final agreement would be diminished unless all advanced countries signed, and so he threatened that Australia would withdraw unless his team got what it wanted. His tactic worked. Together with Iceland and Norway, Australia was one of just three countries specifically allowed to increase greenhouse gas emissions by 2012, in Australia's case by 8 per cent over 1990 levels. In the tiring all-night session that ended the conference, Australia gained an extra concession, one that includes land clearing in calculating Australia's contribution to greenhouse gases at the 1990 level. This is known as the *Australian clause*. Not cutting down trees as fast as before was counted as a carbon credit for Australia. As the rate of land clearing slowed, more room was left for Australia's smokestack industries to pump gases into the atmosphere, and Australia's gross emissions, not including forests, leapt by 30 per cent between 1990 and 2007. The prime minister greeted the news from Kyoto as a victory for Australian diplomacy, seeing the outcome as a victory for Australian jobs.

The Kyoto Protocol allowed Australia to increase greenhouse gas emissions but Howard's Australia joined the United States as one of only two developed countries that refused to ratify it. The US president, George W. Bush, like his predecessor Bill Clinton, thought ratification of Kyoto might damage the American economy for no good purpose given that China and India were free to increase greenhouse gas emissions. Howard's objection was also economic: population was growing much faster in Australia than in many OECD countries, especially European ones; Australia relied more heavily than most other industrialised countries on agriculture and mining, both of which produce greenhouse gases; Australia was a large exporter of coal, oil and gas; Australia would therefore bear excessive economic burdens if it were to ratify Kyoto. Paradoxically, the government then committed itself to voluntarily reaching 108 per cent of 1990 emission levels by 2012, the same Kyoto target it condemned as economically damaging. The government seemed caught between pro-Kyoto lobbying by environmentalists and some sections of business on the one hand and anti-Kyoto lobbying by the fossil fuel and aluminium industries on the other.

The Kyoto Protocol came into force in 2005, and 190 countries had either signed or ratified it by 2010. The protocol's significance does not lie in what it has done to abate the emission of greenhouse gases. On average the cuts in emissions promised by Kyoto amount to an average of 5 per cent for industrialised countries by 2012, yet cuts of 60 to 80 per cent are needed by 2050 in order to stabilise emissions and avert the worst consequences of climate change.[6] Not only do the emissions targets under Kyoto demand little of the advanced industrialised states—the so-called Annex 1 Parties—but they are not being met except by the European Union. Nothing much has changed in the planet's atmosphere as a result of the Kyoto Protocol, whose real significance lies in pointing the way toward future global action. Kyoto was the world's first attempt to deal with climate change by international agreement, and sets a precedent to limit greenhouse gas emissions on a larger scale in the future—that is all.

In its final term, 2004–07, the Howard government attempted to counter claims that it was not doing enough for the environment. Predictions of climate change seemed vindicated as the rains failed across south-eastern Australia, the bush burnt, cities imposed water restrictions and state governments commissioned desalination plants. The Asia-Pacific Partnership on Clean Development and Climate was the government's answer to the Kyoto Protocol, an environmental 'coalition of the willing' rather than a global, multilateral treaty. The partnership brought together four of the world's top five coal producers, six countries that together accounted for half the world's greenhouse gas emissions, and the two largest emitters, the United States and China. But the Asia-Pacific

Partnership or APP had no mandatory targets and made no international commitments: it was purely voluntary, and depended for its success on the willingness of business to adopt technologies that, in the short run at least, would be more expensive than existing ones. A second initiative was the Global Initiative on Forests and Climate, which began with a $30 million contribution by Australia to the Kalimantan Forests and Climate Partnership. This initiative sought to preserve 70,000 hectares of peat land forests on the island of Borneo and to plant as many as 100 million new trees. And a third was the Australia–China Joint Coordination Group on Clean Coal Technology.

Kevin Rudd became prime minister in 2007 with an approach to climate change quite different from that of his predecessor. Rudd sought to 'tackle the risks climate change poses to our planet, and especially to the health, lifestyle and livelihoods of our children' and to do so by making Australia a leading participant in global efforts to check greenhouse gas emissions.[7] He rejected the argument that Australia would damage itself by accepting internationally agreed limits on emissions, and depicted action on the issue as a vital national interest, staking his political reputation on combating climate change. His first foreign policy acts as prime minister were to attend the UN Bali Climate Change Conference and to ratify the Kyoto Protocol, signifying Australia's support for the UN's multilateral climate process in the lead-up to the 15th Conference of the Parties at Copenhagen in 2009.

The British government meanwhile commissioned an economist, Nicholas Stern, to report on climate change. The 2007 Stern Review on the economics of climate change concluded that the scientific evidence for human-induced climate change was overwhelming and demanded 'an urgent global response'. If the international community acted quickly, Stern said, disaster could still be averted, but action needed to be taken by all countries, rich and poor. In particular, Stern called for emissions trading so as to make possible a transition to low-carbon economies; cooperation on research and development of new low-carbon technologies; action to reduce the loss of forests; and international funding to enable developing countries to adapt.

Rudd asked Ross Garnaut, an economist and former Australian ambassador to China, to write a similar report, the 2008 Garnaut Climate Change Review. Less optimistic than Stern, Garnaut described climate change as a 'diabolical policy problem' and one on which international cooperation faced serious obstacles, above all in the interest that states have in letting other states bear most of the burden of cutting greenhouse gas emissions. He thought

CLIMATE CHANGE: A DIABOLICAL PROBLEM AND A SAVING GRACE

Climate change is a diabolical policy problem. It is harder than any other issue of high importance that has come before our polity in living memory. Climate change presents a new kind of challenge. It is uncertain in its form and extent, rather than drawn in clear lines. It is insidious rather than (as yet) directly confrontational. It is long term rather than immediate, in both its impacts and its remedies. Any effective remedies lie beyond any act of national will, requiring international cooperation of unprecedented dimension and complexity. While an effective response to the challenge would play out over many decades, it must take shape and be put in place over the next few years. Without such action, if the mainstream science is broadly right, the Review's assessment of likely growth in global greenhouse gas emissions in the absence of effective mitigation tells us that the risks of dangerous climate change, already significant, will soon have risen to dangerously high levels.

Observation of daily debate and media discussion in Australia and elsewhere suggests that this issue might be too hard for rational policy making. It is too complex. The special interests are too numerous, powerful and intense. The time frames within which effects become evident are too long, and the time frames within which action must be effected too short.

But there is a saving grace that may make all the difference. This is an issue in which a high proportion of Australians are deeply interested. A high proportion of Australians say that they are prepared to pay for mitigation in higher goods and services prices. Most of them say that they are prepared to pay even if Australia is acting independently of other countries. There is a much stronger base of support for reform and change on this issue than on any other big question of structural change in recent decades, including trade, tax and public business ownership reform. People in other countries, to varying degrees, seem to share Australians' interest in and preparedness to take action on global warming.

Public attitudes in Australia and in other countries create the possibility of major reform on emissions reductions, despite the inherent difficulty of the policy problem.

Ross Garnaut, *The Garnaut Climate Change Review. Final Report.* Cambridge University Press, Port Melbourne, 2008, pp. xviii–xix.

Australia had more at stake in climate change than any other developed country, and that radical reduction of emissions globally was in Australia's interests. He recommended that Australia support an international agreement on holding atmospheric concentrations at 450 parts per million of CO_2 and

CO_2 equivalent gases, and, if international agreement was reached, should commit itself to reducing emissions by 25 per cent by 2020 and 90 per cent by 2050. If no agreement was reached, Australia should make an unconditional offer to reduce emissions by 5 per cent from 2000 levels by 2020.

The key to global action on climate change is for states to coordinate domestic policy with international agreement. If climate change is to be checked, states need to establish emissions targets and ways of reaching them—through a tax on carbon, for example, or an emissions trading scheme accompanied by a cap or limit on how much greenhouse gas can be produced. Rudd followed Garnaut in promising a conditional reduction of 25 per cent below 2000 levels by 2020 if the international community reached a global agreement to stabilise greenhouse gas levels at 450 parts per million or lower, and 60 per cent below 2000 levels by 2050. His instrument for achieving these targets was an emissions trading scheme, which he called the Carbon Pollution Reduction Scheme. Rudd promised that Australia would be strongly engaged in the UN multilateral process and he expected his scheme to be law by the time he represented Australia at the Copenhagen climate change conference in 2009. Instead, the Coalition parties replaced their leader Malcolm Turnbull, who supported Rudd's scheme, with Tony Abbott, who did not. That meant the measure could not pass the Senate even though it had been passed by the House of Representatives. Even a modest proposal to reduce emissions, it seemed, would face fierce political resistance in Australia, a country heavily dependent on fossil fuels for power at home and exports abroad; and climate change scepticism grew in direct proportion to the threat that people saw to their economic wellbeing in any reduction of emissions.

The Copenhagen conference, which fell far short of expectations, showed the political difficulties of achieving global agreement on an issue that goes to the heart of the modern economy. The conference did not reach a binding global agreement on cutting greenhouse gases; it set no firm date by which global emissions would fall and dropped the target of 50 per cent fall in emissions by 2050; it did not indicate how different countries would share the burden of mitigation; it reached no long-term understanding on assistance to developing countries; it did not replace the Kyoto Protocol with a new agreement, as Australia wanted; and its aspiration to keep the increase in global temperature to no more than 2 degrees Celsius disappointed the small island states, which wanted no more than 1.5 degrees Celsius in order to avert inundation by rising seas. Environmentalists considered Copenhagen at best a diplomatic failure and at worst a disaster for the planet. Others were more optimistic. They pointed out that the Copenhagen Accord, for the first time, commits both developed and developing nations, including China, to achieve reductions in greenhouse gas emissions. Agreement on checking climate change might be weak, they said, but there is a process under way that will end with an agreement that is both global and binding.

The Rudd government, strongly behind the UN process before Copenhagen, had doubts about it afterwards. Penny Wong, climate change minister, talked about pursuing all channels 'in the UN and beyond to help forge global action' and attended the US-led Major Economies Forum on Climate and Energy, an alternative climate change coalition, in 2010.[8] In similar vein the Rudd government initiated the Global Carbon Capture and Storage Institute to undertake research on the holy grail of Australia's coal industry, a technology that would store carbon emissions underground. Before Copenhagen Rudd spoke of the 'overwhelming need for Australia to tackle the great challenge of our generation', but after it, his government's emissions reduction target was so modest it would do nothing either to stop climate change or inspire action by other states. As for the emissions trading scheme that had done much to define Rudd as a reforming prime minister, he opted to defer it until 2013 rather than take it to voters again in the 2010 election, a decision that undermined his credibility and contributed to his replacement by Julia Gillard. Australia's official policy in 2010 was to commit itself unconditionally to a 5 per cent emissions reduction on 2000 levels by 2020, as Garnaut suggested, and not to offer any more until a strong and verifiable global agreement was in place.

ASSESSMENTS

Why has global action so far succeeded in meeting the challenge of ozone depletion in the atmosphere, but not succeeded on the more important challenge of human-induced climate change?

Global action on the thinning of the ozone layer succeeded for a number of reasons. Politicians accepted the science, even though the evolution of scientific understanding came to reveal the need for much tighter controls than were first envisaged. Sceptics about ozone depletion did not exist, whereas they abound on the issue of climate change. The key players in the production of ozone-depleting substances, centred on the American chemicals industry, were small in number and were persuaded to change direction for the sake of the planet even though CFCs were widely used in everything from pillows, mattresses and car dashboards to refrigerators, air conditioners and dry-cleaning agents. Together with other CFC manufacturers organised in the Alliance for Responsible CFC Policy, the DuPont chemical company supported global controls on the use of CFCs from 1986, transforming the prospects for reaching an effective global agreement. The design of the Montreal Protocol as a diplomatic instrument eased the way to agreement: the protocol included an adjustment provision which enabled countries to agree on new controls without having to refer them to lengthy processes of ratification by signatory states. And the protocol provided for an environmental multilateral fund designed to enable developing countries to meet their obligations to reduce the use of ozone-depleting substances. In the 2009–11 triennium the Multilateral Fund, to which Australia is a contributor, spent US$490 million to assist developing countries in making the transition to non-ozone-depleting substances.

Like ozone depletion, climate change is a problem of potentially immense and fateful proportions, but unlike it, climate change resists solutions based on global cooperation. The reasons for this lack of progress are widely recognised. First, there is the problem of delayed effects. Climate change now being created by global emissions will not happen on a truly dangerous scale for decades, and yet politicians are being asked to transform the energy base of their national economies—and upset interest groups and voters—now.

Second, climate change exemplifies the so-called *free-rider* problem in international agreements. Every country would benefit from lessening or avoiding climate change, whether they restrict their emissions of greenhouse gases or not, so governments will be tempted to let other countries bear a disproportionate share of the burden. This is particularly so with Australia, which has a high per capita rate of greenhouse gas emissions but accounts for less than 2 per cent of global emissions. If the rest of the world were to cut their emissions and Australia were not to do so, Australia would still benefit from the impact on global climate change.

Third, acting on climate change entails a direct assault on the modern industrialised economy, which is heavily dependent for growth on fossil fuels. An effective global agreement on climate change would transform the energy base of the modern economy. Such a revolution may well take place in the twenty-first century, but it is unlikely to be driven by an international agreement; instead, major states are likely to shift the energy base of their economies for reasons of national self-interest, including fear of climate change.

The fourth problem is enforcement. To be effective, any global agreement on climate change would need to be enforced in a situation where states have powerful incentives to avoid enforcement and misreport emissions.

Finally, and fundamentally, competing national interests divide the international community over climate change. Governments think about the global ecosystem from the perspective of their own political survival. The Howard government's 2003 white paper on foreign policy, for example, emphasised that Australia's response to global environmental problems would be determined 'by our unique national interests' and that Australia 'might choose to stand aside from particular multilateral environmental agreements'. The Rudd government's 2009 Defence white paper canvassed the possibility that disruption caused by climate change in Australia's 'immediate neighbourhood', if not solved by economic assistance, might lead to the use of the Australian Defence Force 'to deal with any threats inimical to our interests'.[9]

Developing countries see global warming as a problem created by the developed world. They resist curtailing their own industrialisation just when general prosperity is in sight for the first time in history. The developing countries use less energy and emit less fossil CO_2 than the developed countries but are generating more and more of the planet's greenhouse gases as industrialisation proceeds, as is already clear from the serious air pollution in many Chinese cities. Not having created the problem, developing countries want aid and technology in return for agreeing to the environmental demands of the rich world. The split between developed and developing countries was at the core of the failure of the 2009 Copenhagen summit. China led a group of developing countries that favoured a continuation of the Kyoto Protocol rather than an entirely new agreement, because Kyoto required the developed countries to bear most of the burden of climate change.

A split also exists between different kinds of developing countries. The Organization of Petroleum Exporting Countries, led by Saudi Arabia, has done much to slow progress in global climate change negotiations over the years because of its influence within the G-77, a group of more than 130 developing countries, and its fear that effective measures to cut emissions would reduce the price of oil.[10] China and India want fast industrial growth. At the other end of the spectrum, the Alliance of Small Island States wants strong action to forestall global warming because of the direct threat to their low-lying land. Some Pacific Island countries, for example, are increasingly concerned about the possible consequences of climate change for their very existence. The Tuvalu ambassador to the UN, Afalee Pita, told the UN Security Council in 2007:

Ocean warming is changing the very nature of our island nation. Slowly our coral reefs are dying through coral bleaching, we are witnessing changes to fish stocks, and we face the increasing threat of more severe cyclones. With the highest point of four metres above sea level, the threat of severe cyclones is extremely disturbing, and severe water shortages will further threaten the livelihoods of people in many islands ... our livelihood is already threatened by sea level rise, and the implications for our long term security are very disturbing. Many have spoken about the possibility of migrating from our homeland. If this becomes a reality, then we are faced with an unprecedented threat to our nationhood. This would be an infringement on our fundamental rights to nationality and statehood as constituted under the Universal Declaration of Human Rights and other international conventions. But Tuvalu is not alone in facing the threats of climate change, many millions of people will suffer the effects. The world has moved from a global threat once called the Cold War, to what now should be considered the 'Warming War'. Our conflict is not with guns and missiles but with weapons from everyday lives—chimney stacks and exhaust pipes.[11]

Tuvalu's precarious geographical situation—nine low-level atolls in the middle of a rising Pacific Ocean—became a powerful symbol at the Copenhagen summit of the plight of small island states. By proposing that major emerging economies should accept legally binding commitments to cut greenhouse gas emissions, an initiative thwarted by China, India, Saudi Arabia and other large developing countries, the Tuvalu delegation at Copenhagen showed that the developing world is far from united on climate change and is itself contributing to the problem.

If the planet itself is threatened by the activities of humankind, how can any country claim to possess the sovereign right to act as it wishes within national borders? This question points to the inherent conflict between the sovereignty of states and the protection of the global environment. The conflict is one that will be resolved only when states identify their own national interests with a healthy global ecosystem, as appears to have happened when they were shocked into taking strong action over ozone. The ozone issue suggests that states do not act until there is impending disaster, observable or scientifically proven. The response to uncertainty, however, should not be inaction. That, at least, is the conclusion reached by governments at the Rio Earth Summit, which adopted the principle that for the sake of the environment 'the precautionary approach shall be widely applied by states according to their capabilities. Where there are threats of serious or irreversible damage, lack of full scientific certainty shall not be used as a reason for postponing cost-effective measures to prevent environmental degradation.'[12] By this view, the risk of doing nothing—given the potential danger—is greater than the risk of taking measures which later prove unnecessary.

The global environment in general is unique as a foreign policy problem. We depend on scientists to identify key problems and tell us whether they are being solved or not. Without science, we would not know that climate change is a potential threat, and we would be less aware of the possible consequences of losing forests, polluting oceans and creating deserts. Yet science is an evolving form of knowledge, based on hypotheses tested over time against evidence. Scientists disagree about hypotheses until the evidence is firm, and they particularly disagree about predictions that depend on models with numerous variables. That is why the Intergovernmental Panel on Climate Change continues to give percentage probabilities to its predictions.

The global environment challenges commonplace assumptions about progress and the purpose of foreign policy. Australian governments routinely assume that economic growth is desirable for Australia, for our major trading partners and for the world as a whole. They regard a higher economic growth rate as better than a smaller one, more trade as better than less, and a booming economy—whether global, regional or national—as better than a depressed one. Governments see the central purpose of foreign policy as being to enhance Australia's long-term economic prospects, so that more Australians will have jobs, incomes and the capacity to consume in the future. Governments find the national interest in economic success and are inclined to resent global environmental controls. Yet in the long run Australian and all other governments might achieve more for the security of their people by shifting economies to renewable sources of energy, leaving the old-growth forests intact and even abandoning the entire project of achieving economic growth. For the moment, though, such a paradigm shift in the way political leaders think is inconceivable.

FURTHER READING

The environment in political theory and international relations

Benedick, Richard Elliott, *Ozone Diplomacy: New directions in safeguarding the planet*, Harvard University Press, Cambridge, MA, 1992. (Ozone negotiations by a participant.)

Campbell, Kurt, ed., *Climatic Cataclysm: The foreign policy and national security implications of climate change*, Brookings, Washington DC, 2008. (Argues that climate change could undermine the national security of the US.)

Carter, Neil, *The Politics of the Environment: Ideas, activism, policy*, Cambridge University Press, Cambridge, 2001, Chapter 9, 'International environmental politics'. (A perceptive analysis of the place of environmental issues in international relations.)

Eckersley, Robyn and Andrew Dobson, eds, *Political Theory and the Ecological Challenge*, Cambridge University Press, Cambridge, 2006. (Examines the implications of the global environmental crisis for political ideologies, understandings of the state and concepts of justice.)

Elliott, Lorraine M., *The Global Politics of the Environment*, Palgrave Macmillan, 2nd edn, 2004. (Covers international diplomacy from Rio to Johannesburg, and the prospects for successful global environmental governance.)

Global Environmental Politics. (Scholarly journal devoted to examining the interaction of environmental change and global political forces.)

Stern, Nicholas, *The Economics of Climate Change: The Stern Review*, Cambridge University Press, Cambridge, 2007. (The British report that confirmed climate science and called for global action to combat climate change.)

The environment in Australian foreign policy

Alley, Roderic, *The Domestic Politics of International Relations: Cases from Australia, New Zealand and Oceania*, Ashgate, Aldershot, Hampshire, and Burlington, VT, 2000. (Chapter 3 analyses Australia's climate change policy before and after Kyoto.)

Elliott, Lorraine, 'Pragmatism, prosperity and environmental challenges in Australian foreign policy', in *Trading on Alliance Security: Australia in world affairs 2001–2005*, James Cotton and John Ravenhill, eds, Oxford University Press, Melbourne, 2007, pp. 213–28. (Places the Howard government's environmental foreign policy in a theoretical and global context.)

Elliott, Lorraine M., 'Improving the global environment: Policies, principles and institutions', *Australian Journal of International Affairs*, vol. 61, no. 1, March 2007, pp. 7–14. (Examines the way global environmental politics works, and why the institutions need strengthening.)

Garnaut, Ross, *The Garnaut Climate Change Review: Final report*, Cambridge University Press, Cambridge, 2008. (Key climate change report commissioned by the Rudd government, recommending that Australia participate fully in reaching a global solution.)

Stevenson, Hayley, 'Cheating on climate change? Australia's challenge to global warming norms', *Australian Journal of International Affairs*, vol. 63, no. 2, June 2009, pp. 165–86. (Compares the climate change policies of the Howard and Rudd governments, and points to the political influence of Australia's economic dependence on resource exports.)

Websites

Australian policy on climate change: <www.dfat.gov.au/environment/climate>
CSIRO climate change site: <www.csiro.au/science/Climate-Change.html>
Department of Climate Change and Energy Efficiency: <www.climatechange.gov.au>
Greenpeace Australia Pacific: <www.greenpeace.org/australia>
Intergovernmental Panel on Climate Change: <www.ipcc.ch>

Foreign aid

- What are the UN Human Development Index, the Development Assistance Committee and the Millennium Development Goals?
- Why did the Cold War and decolonisation lead to an expansion of foreign aid?
- Where does Australia's official development assistance go, and why does it go there rather than somewhere else?
- Why do countries give aid to other countries?
- Does foreign aid produce development in developing countries?
- How should Australia improve its foreign aid program?
- In what way does the Australian foreign aid program reflect Australia's wider foreign policy goals?
- In what ways did Australian foreign aid change under the Rudd government?

Australians are collectively among the world's most fortunate peoples, with ready access to the elements of a good life—food in abundance, clean water, sanitation, medical care, housing and education. Australians live in a high-income country with low infant mortality, high life expectancy, low levels of adult illiteracy, universal access to education, universal health care and so on. The UN human development index (HDI) measures social and economic indicators of this kind, and ranks countries accordingly. Australia always comes high on the index, and was second out of 182 countries in 2009.

Australia's regional neighbours are far less fortunate. We tend to think of East Asia as booming economically and therefore prosperous. The countries of East Asia have enjoyed far higher rates of economic growth than any other part of the world for decades, and most have recovered from the global financial crisis of 2008. Yet outside Japan and the four Asian tiger economies (Singapore, Hong Kong, Taiwan and South Korea), only a small minority of people in East Asia enjoys a Western standard of living of the kind taken for granted by Australians. China has lifted hundreds of millions of people out of poverty since the 1970s in what is the most significant contribution to global development by any country in the world. Yet at least 800 million Chinese, 175 million Indonesians and 65 million Vietnamese wrest a meagre living from the land as peasants and rural labourers in conditions that Australians would regard as poverty, and millions of others do the same elsewhere in the region. If we focus on the countries of South-East Asia, we find they must all travel a long road before reaching Australian standards of living, with the exception of the city-state of Singapore and oil-rich Brunei. Malaysia did best on the 2009 UN HDI (66), followed by Thailand (87) but the rankings for Vietnam (116), Indonesia (111), Cambodia (137) and East Timor (162) point to considerable development challenges. Except for East Timor, the 25 countries at the bottom of the human development index are all in Africa.

As for the South Pacific, many of us think of it as a place where nature is abundant and no one needs to work. The image of the islands as paradise, as old as the European discovery of Polynesia in the eighteenth century, maintains its grip on the Western imagination. Yet reality differs from image here too. All independent countries of the region have much lower standards of living than Australia. All receive foreign aid and most need it to survive as viable modern states. In Solomon Islands (135), Vanuatu (126) and Papua New Guinea (148), the least developed countries in the region, most people live from the land in rural villages and are extremely poor by Australian standards. PNG is a country where, pro rata, ten times as many children die in infancy as in Australia, 300 times as many women die in childbirth and HIV/AIDS is rampant.

When people think of foreign aid, they think of people in rich countries such as Australia giving to people in poor countries such as Cambodia. In fact, foreign aid is much less straightforward. Australia's aid is part of a larger international phenomenon in which governments of some countries provide assistance to governments of others. Almost every country is involved in the aid business either to give or receive and a few, such as China, do both. Australia is among the 24 richest industrialised countries that belong to the OECD's Development Assistance Committee or DAC, but is far from being the most generous. Australia's development assistance in 2010–11 was 0.33 per cent of

AUSTRALIA INCREASES ITS FOREIGN AID

Australia in 2010 was a less generous donor than 30 years before, judged by aid as a proportion of the country's gross national income (ODA/GNI ratio), though more generous in absolute terms. The Howard government increased aid in its last few years, and the Rudd government increased it even more—to 0.33 per cent of GNI in the last Rudd budget. The Rudd and Gillard governments promised a swift and unprecedented increase to 0.5 per cent of GNI by 2015, with a focus on the Millennium Development Goals.

Year	Constant 2009–10 prices	ODA/GNI ratio
1980–81	$1957.7m	0.37%
1990–91	$2048.8m	0.31%
2000–01	$2236.3m	0.24%
2010–11	$4170m	0.33%

Source for table: *Budget. Australia's International Development Assistance: A Good International Citizen*, 11 May 2010, p. 68.

gross national income, in proportionate terms a third of the aid given by the top donor, Sweden (1.12 per cent), in 2009. The OECD statistics for 2009 show that after Sweden, in order of generosity, come Norway (1.06 per cent), Luxembourg (1.01 per cent), Denmark (0.88 per cent), the Netherlands (0.82 per cent), Belgium (0.55 per cent), Finland (0.54 per cent), Ireland (0.54 per cent) the United Kingdom (0.52 per cent), Switzerland (0.47 per cent), France (0.46 per cent) and Spain (0.46 per cent).[1] Total DAC aid to developing countries in 2009 was US$119.6 billion, a considerable flow of resources but dwarfed by the gigantic sums mobilised in the rich world to avert a collapse of the global financial system in 2008, when the US government spent US$183 billion of taxpayers' money bailing out just one insurance company, American International Group or AIG.[2] DAC coordinates the flow of development assistance to about 150 states and territories, ranging from 'least developed', such as Afghanistan, Cambodia and Solomon Islands, to 'other low income countries' (Ghana, PNG, Vietnam), 'lower middle income' (India, Indonesia, Thailand), and 'upper middle income' (Malaysia, South Africa, Cook Islands). Some countries that give aid, such as

China, Saudi Arabia, Taiwan and Poland, are not members of the Development Assistance Committee. South Korea was admitted to membership in 2010.

Foreign aid, an invention of the second half of the twentieth century, influences relations between states everywhere. At a UN summit in 2000, 189 countries, including Australia, adopted the Millennium Development Goals, which commit the international community to reaching a series of development goals and targets. The goals are to eradicate extreme poverty and hunger, achieve universal primary education, promote gender equality and empower women, reduce child mortality, improve maternal health, combat HIV/AIDS, malaria and other diseases, ensure environmental sustainability and develop a global partnership for development. Within that framework, the UN specifies targets to be reached by 2015, such as reducing the mortality rate of children under five by two-thirds of the 1990 level, halving the proportion of people without access to safe drinking water, halving the proportion of people whose income is less than one US dollar a day, and making primary school education universally available. One goal—to improve the lives of at least 100 million slum dwellers—is set to be reached by 2020. Under the Rudd government, achievement of the Millennium Development Goals became a key criterion for measuring the success of Australia's aid program.

ORIGINS OF FOREIGN AID

The origins of foreign aid lie in America's response to the devastation of Western Europe after World War II. European countries were shattered, their economies were in ruins and their people were unable to buy the manufactures which the Americans were so good at producing. So the United States decided to apply Keynesian ideas of demand management internationally and to revive European economies with massive infusions of aid. The Americans calculated that they would need to bring prosperity to Europe, the major market for their exports, in order to create lasting prosperity at home. From 1948 to 1952 they transferred US$13.6 billion in economic assistance to France, Britain, West Germany, Italy, the Netherlands and elsewhere, and a further US$7.8 billion in military assistance. Those sums, worth much more in dollar terms today, transformed Western Europe's economic prospects and underpinned the economic miracle that propelled West Germany from poverty to wealth in twenty years. Marshall Plan aid was a triumph of American foreign policy and a key cause of the long boom in Western industrialised economies after World War II.

Foreign aid flourished in the political climate of the Cold War. The Americans sent aid in the 1950s not only to non-communist Europe but also to pro-American allies in the Middle East and East Asia such as Turkey, Japan, South Korea, Taiwan and the Philippines with a view to strengthening America's global strategic position against the Soviet Union and China. American policymakers realised from the start that aid could be a weapon in the armoury of foreign policy. Governments whose economies and military forces depended on American aid would be highly likely to do America's bidding, welcome American investment and ally themselves with the United States in the global confrontation with communism. US aid during the Cold War, worth about US$400 billion between 1945 and 1990, reflected US national interests in both form and direction. A sizeable proportion came as military assistance to the armed forces of friendly states, and aid in general went to the countries that mattered most in containing communism. Almost half America's aid in the late 1960s, for example, went to South Vietnam. Under the Reagan administration in the 1980s, when Washington feared an extension of communist influence in Central America, aid flowed to pro-American El Salvador and to rebels against left-wing Nicaragua. On the other side of the Cold War divide the Soviet Union sent aid to pro-Soviet regimes in countries such as Vietnam, Afghanistan, Ethiopia, Cuba and Mongolia.

Decolonisation hastened the spread of aid in the 1960s. Most colonial powers rushed to assist former colonies after independence. Aid went where it would maintain the political influence and economic connections of the aid giver: Dutch aid to Indonesia, British aid to Britain's former colonies in Africa and Asia, especially India, Australian aid to PNG, French aid to the French-speaking countries of West Africa such as Ivory Coast, Senegal, Mali, Morocco and Cameroon, and so on. The end of the Cold War created a new kind of aid recipient among states—not with a developing economy like those of Asia, Africa and Latin America, but with a transition economy in the process of changing from command to market—as they moved from communism to capitalism. Transition countries joined the queue of states getting aid from the West, and *official aid*, as it was known, flowed to Belarus, Bulgaria, the Czech Republic, Estonia, Hungary, Latvia, Lithuania, Poland, Romania, Russia, the Slovak Republic and Ukraine.

Foreign aid is an inescapably political phenomenon, given by governments for political reasons. In a few exceptional cases such as Sweden, those reasons are to satisfy strong domestic demand for aid to help the poor of the Third World, but the political logic of aid in most donor states does not lead in such a clearly

humanitarian direction. Most governments give aid because it confers influence, offers strategic advantages, wins international prestige, builds commercial
contacts and opens the way for national companies that wish to invest in
recipient states. The ability to give aid is the mark of a successful economy, as
Japan demonstrates. Japan graduated rapidly in the 1960s from receiving to
giving, trebling aid between 1970 and 1990 and briefly surpassing America as
a donor. For this reason—and because aid smooths the way for investment—
some countries such as China both give and receive aid. Australia and many
other countries give aid to China, for example, while China gives aid to the
developing world, especially to Africa. These days the world's largest aid donors
are the United States, France, Germany, the United Kingdom and Japan, though
the French inflate their figures by including assistance to their own overseas
territories in the Caribbean, Pacific and elsewhere.

Most aid donors concentrate on countries in a particular region. As aid
has grown, the major donors have divided the developing world between
themselves—Japan becoming the leading donor to East Asia, the United States
to part of the Middle East (Israel and Egypt) as well as Latin America, France to
francophone Africa, Saudi Arabia to the Islamic states of the Middle East, and
Germany to Eastern Europe. Australia is not a major donor in global terms
but conforms to the general pattern of specialising in assistance to a particular
region: three in every four of its bilateral aid dollars go to East Asia, Papua New
Guinea and the South Pacific.

We live in a world of rich and poor, and many Australians respond gener-
ously to appeals for help. We might be tempted to think that government aid
is like the aid given by private agencies; that is, given to help the poor beyond
Australia's shores and to offer them the food, clothing, shelter, medical care and
clean water which we take for granted. By this view, Australian governments give
aid in order to lend a helping hand to the less fortunate overseas and to redress
global inequality. Some might think these facts alone explain Australia's foreign
aid program, and that governments, like individuals, give aid for humanitarian
reasons. Governments are keen to convey that impression. 'First and foremost',
Gareth Evans wrote as Labor foreign minister, 'Australia's aid effort is founded on
the commitment of the Australian population to basic humanitarian concerns—
the desire to help alleviate poverty, hunger and suffering wherever it occurs'.
His Coalition successor Alexander Downer aimed to 'strengthen the overriding
humanitarian focus of Australia's aid program'. Stephen Smith, foreign minister
in the Rudd and, for a short time, Gillard governments, and Bob McMullan,

Parliamentary Secretary for International Development Assistance, described the aid program in 2010 as one that reflected Australian generosity and enhanced Australia's reputation as a good international citizen.[3] Australia's foreign aid is less humanitarian, less generous and more political than governments claim, as we can see by examining where aid goes and what it is.

WHERE AID GOES

At the simplest level, that of where aid goes, Australia's development assistance program is not purely or even primarily humanitarian. If it were—if the guiding principles of the program were to send aid where people needed it most—the bulk of Australian aid would go to the least developed countries of Africa and South Asia such as Angola, Congo, Ethiopia, Tanzania, the Sudan and Bangladesh, which depend overwhelmingly on aid as a source of external financing. Yet the top five recipients of bilateral Australian aid in 2010–11 were Indonesia, PNG, Solomon Islands, Afghanistan and Vietnam. With the exception of Afghanistan these are countries that need aid but not as desperately as the poorest countries. In 2010–11 Samoa received almost twice as much Australian aid as India, which has a population 5000 times greater. That is because regional countries matter more to Australia, strategically and in some cases economically. Afghanistan is an exception in being a long way from Australia, but it is where AusAID works alongside the Australian Defence Force and it is regarded as strategically important because of Australia's military participation in attempting to defeat the Taliban insurgency. If humanitarian concerns were paramount, aid would change in volume and direction according to the needs of the poor globally. In fact, governments change aid according to the strategic or economic situation confronting Australia, and the direction of aid reveals Australia's foreign policy priorities.

The government's 2009 Defence white paper argued that, apart from the defence of Australia from armed attack, Australia's 'most important strategic interest is the security, stability and cohesion of our immediate neighbourhood, which we share with Indonesia, Papua New Guinea, East Timor, New Zealand and the South Pacific island states'.[4] Seventy-six per cent of aid that could be attributed to specific countries in the 2010–11 Budget went to PNG, the South Pacific, and East Asia (mostly South-East Asia); Africa received 7 per cent and South Asia 8.6 per cent (mainly Pakistan, India, Bangladesh, Sri Lanka, Nepal, Maldives and Bhutan), with the remainder going to the Middle East and South and Central America.

In the official view, aid underpins the security of Australia. The government decided to intensify aid efforts in Australia's immediate neighbourhood, especially in PNG and the South Pacific, after the Bali bombings. Australia's sharpened focus on the Pacific, according to the government, arose from a 'strengthened realisation that a porous, underdeveloped and insecure region can increasingly feed instability, inhibit development and pose a threat to Australia's national security'.[5] As a result, Australian aid to PNG increased by one-third in 2004–05, and aid to the South Pacific more than doubled, with much of the money paying for the reconstruction of government in Solomon Islands. Concern about the security of Australia's regional neighbours remained, with $1.245 billion, almost 30 per cent of the entire aid budget, going to just four countries in the 2010–11 financial year—Indonesia, PNG, Solomon Islands and East Timor.

Governments also direct aid according to economic opportunity. Aid to South-East Asia grew in the 1990s, reflecting the region's growing importance in Australian trade and investment. Indonesia comes first, but Vietnam, Cambodia and Laos have also become major recipients of Australian aid, amounting to more than $200 million a year. Similar calculations underlie Australia's long-established aid program to China, which is now worth about $37 million a year. In countries like these, Australia hopes to reap commercial rewards in the form of government contracts, a welcome for Australian investment and access for Australian exports.

We should not be surprised by the direction and concentration of Australian aid flows. Donor states such as Australia serve their own interests when they give money away. In any case, aid programs require broad public support at home if they are to endure, and aid is an easy political target. Pauline Hanson's One Nation Party, for example, called for an end to all Australian overseas aid on the grounds that the money would be better spent on Australians rather than foreigners, an argument likely to be more widely echoed at times of domestic economic difficulty. As shadow finance minister, Nationals Senate leader Barnaby Joyce raised similar concerns about Australian foreign aid in 2010, suggesting that funds going to the World Bank should be redirected to reduce food costs in Australia. Governments therefore need to be able to justify expenditure abroad in terms that find ready acceptance in the community.

WHAT AID IS

Foreign aid in its broadest sense includes both military and economic assistance. A large part of America's foreign aid during the Cold War—37 per cent of the US$279 billion disbursed abroad in the period 1962–89, for example—took the form of military grants and loans which were aimed at bolstering friendly regimes in the Middle East, East Asia, Latin America and Western Europe. Australia also gives military aid through the defence cooperation program, mostly in the form of training the armed forces of neighbouring countries in South-East Asia and the South Pacific. Military assistance does not count as part of Australia's official overseas aid program.

When foreign ministers talk of Australia's aid program, they are referring to 'official development assistance', 85 per cent of which is administered by a government agency called AusAID (Australian Agency for International Development). AusAID is an agency within DFAT, and its task is to advise the minister on policy, to plan and supervise aid projects, and to liaise with others in the aid business such as foreign governments, non-government organisations and development banks. Aid must be sponsored by government and its principal objective must be to promote economic development and welfare in order to count as official development assistance as defined by the OECD.

Official development assistance may take the form of loans as well as grants but loans must have a significant concessional element such as a lower interest rate or extended repayment period. Australia's official development assistance in 2010–11 took the form of $2.655 billion in bilateral aid or government-to-government 'country programs' and another $967 million in multilateral aid or 'global programs' (contributions to development banks, UN agencies, refugee programs, funding of volunteers, emergency relief and so on). Australia's aid program is 'whole-of-government', meaning that different government departments from the Treasury to Customs and the Attorney-General's Department engage in activities defined as providing official development assistance. These other departments accounted for an additional $336 million of the aid budget and the Australian Centre for International Agricultural Research for $68 million. With other elements the aid budget totalled $4.439 billion, a record amount, even adjusted for inflation, but it represented a smaller proportion of gross national income than Australian aid up to the mid 1980s. The Rudd government, however, claimed it would increase Australian aid by 2015–16 to 0.5 per cent of GNI, a level not matched by any Australian government in the previous 40 years.

Non-government organisations (NGOs) such as Care Australia, World Vision Australia, Oxfam Australia, Caritas Australia and Australian Volunteers International also deliver aid in humanitarian relief and development projects.

Governments have realised that well-managed NGOs can sometimes do a better job than themselves, especially in small-scale projects, emergency assistance and situations where an official Australian presence would be politically sensitive. So governments channel a small proportion of aid money through such private organisations, $69 million in 2010–11 to more than 40 Australian NGOs working in the developing world. These funds—government funds to NGOs, not money raised in public appeals—also qualify as part of Australia's official development assistance.

People think of aid as consisting mainly of help for the victims of emergencies such as wars, ethnic conflicts, earthquakes and hurricanes. Like all significant donor states, Australia sends refugee and humanitarian relief around the world, most of it channelled through either NGOs such as the International Committee of the Red Cross or UN agencies such as the World Food Programme, the UN High Commissioner for Refugees and the UN Central Emergency Response Fund. Australian assistance of this kind pays for food aid and for those who are suffering from natural disasters. Australia also delivers humanitarian relief bilaterally, as it did after the 2009 Samoan tsunami, which swept away villages on the south coast of the island of Upolu. Australia sent an RAAF C-130 Hercules aircraft with emergency supplies such as tents, tarpaulins and water containers, and assisted with the clean-up.

Emergency and refugee relief is truly humanitarian but represents under 7 per cent of Australia's aid in a typical year. The other 93 per cent, far less publicised, is meant not for immediate relief but for long-term development. Australia does lots of different things with aid. A random survey of Australian aid would reveal projects rebuilding village halls and health facilities in Indonesia's Aceh province following the destruction wrought by the 2004 tsunami;

AUSTRALIA ASSISTS SAMOA AFTER THE 2009 TSUNAMI

A year after a devastating tsunami washed away his home on Samoa's south coast, Alataua Tavana from the village of Saleaumua now has a new home and with it, new hope.

Alataua, his wife Noela, six children and young grandson survived the tsunami, but lost their home and all their belongings. During the past year, the family's home has been rebuilt by Caritas Samoa, supported by AusAID, and the family soon hopes to move in for good. It has been challenging for the family to return home given the trauma of their experience, but they're keen to move on with their lives.

'We are lucky to have this new home and one day soon, when we forget about the sea and the wave, we will return to this home,' said Alataua. 'We thank Caritas and AusAID for all their help.'

Alataua is one of the 70 families from seven villages along Samoa's south coast that now have a new home, thanks to the Caritas Samoa tsunami rebuilding project. The project has also worked to provide clean drinking water, return children to school and train youth and church leaders in counselling.

Director of Caritas Samoa, Puletini Tuala, said that initially, the Caritas efforts were on rebuilding homes in Poutasi, Saleaumua and Satitoa villages, but in agreement with the Ministry of Works, other priority areas were also identified.

'As the new homes were being built, we also focused on the wellbeing of people affected. This was very important to help people deal with the disaster,' Ms Tuala said. 'We helped nearly 500 children return and more than 500 youth and church leaders from 16 villages took part in special counselling and training to help their communities deal with the trauma of the tsunami.'

Australian High Commissioner to Samoa, Matt Anderson said that Australia's support to Caritas reflected a genuine desire to help all Samoan families affected by the tsunami.

'The Australian funding went where it was most needed—to build new homes for those who lost everything in the tsunami, to get children back to school and to monitor their mental health and wellbeing,' Mr Anderson said.

The support to Caritas was just part of Australia's support to Samoa in the wake of the tsunami in September 2009. More than 3,500 people were affected by the tragedy, many losing their homes and livelihoods and 143 people, including five Australians, perished.

The first Australian emergency response teams arrived in Samoa less than 24 hours after the tsunami, providing support in two critical areas—treating the injured and searching for survivors. Teams performed 101 surgical operations and 1,060 emergency department treatments.

In the days after the tsunami, eight Australian Defence Force emergency flights delivered more than 30 tonnes of disaster and emergency relief supplies. In November 2009 the Royal Australian Navy's HMAS *Tobruk* delivered another 188 tonnes of relief supplies.

Australia has provided $12 million to help Samoa following the tsunami.

AusAID, *Samoa—One Year After the Tsunami*, <www.ausaid.gov.au/hottopics/topic.cfm?ID =9002_1866_7431_9313_5586>.

supporting Indonesia's program to improve maternal and neonatal health in Nusa Tenggara Timur province; assisting Tuvalu, Vanuatu, Fiji, Samoa, Solomon Islands and Tonga in reducing their vulnerability to climate change by funding the replanting of coastal mangroves and strengthening disaster preparedness; assisting Cambodia to rehabilitate people injured by landmines; and working with Electricity of Vietnam to increase the capacity of electricity distribution in that country. Among many other programs, AusAID funds Australian Youth Ambassadors, young Australians who work on short assignments of up to a year with an NGO, government agency, company or community organisation in a developing country in the Asia-Pacific region. Some youth ambassadors find the experience so rewarding that they learn the language, immerse themselves in the culture, and later return to the region.

The government categorises aid by 'sector'. Apart from humanitarian and emergency relief, the key sectors are governance, education, infrastructure, health, rural development and environment. The governance sector of aid is the largest. By improving governance, AusAID means making public sectors in developing countries work more effectively, strengthening legal systems and law enforcement, developing civil society, fostering better economic and financial management, and bolstering democratic systems of government. The World Bank defines *governance* as 'the manner in which power is exercised in the management of a country's economic and social resources for development'. The end of the Cold War coincided with the discovery by the World Bank that development is not just a technical process that will respond to inputs such as development assistance, but a political process. The World Bank and aid donors now saw lack of good institutions and lack of good governance as the key barriers to economic growth and human development in the developing world. These days aid donors want good governance and they want to make the foreign governments that receive their aid less corrupt and more efficient, effective, accountable, transparent and responsive. Australia has initiated hundreds of governance-related programs and initiatives since the 1990s. They take the form of public sector reform, legal and judicial reform, strengthening institutions of accountability such as ombudsmen and parliamentary oversight bodies, and making recipient countries familiar with Australia's democratic system of government.

In one sense, good governance is unarguably desirable because it represents an approach to government and public administration that is efficient, accountable, transparent and responsive to the public. But, as preached to the developing world by aid donors such as Australia, good governance also means adopting market-oriented policies, embracing free trade and permitting the free flow of foreign investment, and is a way of extending globalisation and economic integration. Like human rights, good governance is an idea with roots in Western individualism and subject to similar criticism on culturally relativist grounds. Critics of the prominence given to the good governance agenda in the Australian aid program have argued that it depends upon Western assumptions about how people should rule each other and how they should balance individual rights and responsibilities with communal ones. The contention that Western-style good governance is the only sure route to economic growth is also contestable because of the success of China, where, so far at least, authoritarian government has delivered a rapid and continuous rise in prosperity.

Critics of aid may be found at all points of the political spectrum. On the right there are those such as the economist Helen Hughes, who sees aid to Pacific countries, for example, as the problem rather than the solution. She thinks the billions of dollars Australia has poured into the Pacific Islands since 1970 have prevented them from achieving economic growth. Aid, she believes, creates perverse incentives for economic development, because it goes to governments, and therefore encourages irresponsibility by political leaders, boosts public sectors at the expense of private investment, and generates the corruption that undermines development. 'The way that aid is being given to countries like Haiti or Timor-Leste or close to home the Solomon Islands', she told an ABC interviewer in 2010, 'keeps in power corrupt governments which otherwise would not be in power'.[6] On the left, organisations such as AID/WATCH campaign against what they call *boomerang aid*, which returns to the pockets of the Australian consultants, companies and public servants who win AusAID contracts, rather than reaching the poor who need it most. They say the aid program makes excessive use of Australian consultants, who fly in to a developing country, spend a couple of weeks there, and fly out again without taking time to understand the situation. In the middle are organisations such as the Australian Council for International Development (ACFID), the summit body of development NGOs, which campaigns for Australia to give more aid but to do so in more effective ways. ACFID welcomed the Rudd government's climate change adaptation programs for the Pacific, Indonesia, East Timor and elsewhere, for example, but said they should not be defined as 'official development assistance' because they might divert spending from aid that contributes to reaching the Millennium Development Goals.[7]

On a global scale, many have argued that the developing world would benefit far more from lower trade barriers than from more aid. The wealthy

OECD countries impose high protection on agriculture, and it is unlikely to be much reduced in global trade negotiations. The Doha Round of WTO trade negotiations, initiated in 2001, were meant to be the 'development round' that would finally achieve a significant reduction in agricultural protection in the rich world, but they were continuing in 2010 with no end in sight and fading hopes for a successful outcome. Yet agricultural products are typically the main exports of developing countries, who must therefore sell at lower prices into the markets of the rich world. Generally speaking, this trade-versus-aid critique does not apply to Australia, which pays almost no subsidies to its agricultural sector and is reducing trade protection of all kinds.

DOES AID PRODUCE DEVELOPMENT?

To ask whether aid produces development is to ask too crude a question. Clearly, aid alone cannot produce development, which is the outcome, above all, of efficient government providing public services from a secure revenue base and creating the conditions for large-scale investment in a modernised economy. Aid may, however, enhance the prospects of development. As far as Australian aid is concerned, PNG and the South Pacific microstates are good test cases of whether aid enhances those prospects. These countries depend on Australian aid more than anywhere else, they are small enough for the aid to make a difference and their fate matters to Australia.

In response to scepticism about the effectiveness of Australian aid in the Pacific, the Rudd government introduced a new framework for the delivery of assistance to the island countries in 2008. Since then progress towards achieving the Millennium Development Goals has become the criterion by which development is measured, and Australia has negotiated bilateral Partnership for Development Agreements with Pacific countries as a mechanism to ensure that, in return for assistance, island governments would improve governance and commit to better infrastructure, health and education. Eight Pacific countries—PNG, Samoa, Solomon Islands, Kiribati, Vanuatu, Nauru, Tuvalu and Tonga—had signed partnerships for development by 2010. Under the 2009 Cairns Compact on Strengthening Development Coordination in the Pacific, Pacific countries examine each other's progress on development.

PNG was the first Pacific country to sign a Pacific Partnership for Development. The record of Australian aid in PNG seems to suggest that aid does little to improve development prospects. PNG is a country where corruption is common, government is becoming less effective and the rule of law is deteriorating. The situation for many Papua New Guineans, especially rural villagers, was worse in 2010 than when Australia left in 1975. Roads were in worse repair, malaria and TB more prevalent, the health system in decline, crime more threatening, urban unemployment greater, government services fewer, and HIV/AIDS was an epidemic. In the Southern Highlands the writ of the national government hardly ran at all. Some Australian aid consultants, sent by AusAID to Port Moresby, feared for their safety. They spent their time in hotels and ventured out only to go to work and return home before dark, paying Papua New Guineans to refuel their cars at service stations rather than risk a carjacking by doing it themselves.

Papua New Guinea does not depend on aid as much as countries of similar size in Africa, where the average small developing country receives 10 per cent of its GDP in the form of aid. Aid accounts for 5 per cent of GDP in Papua New Guinea and much of it comes from Australia, which plans to increase the flow of development assistance from $457 million in 2010 to about $650 million by 2015. The problem with Australian aid to PNG, however, is that too much of it is in the form of 'technical assistance'; that is, advisers, consultants and other support personnel whose task is to 'build capacity' in the public sector and in the delivery of services such as health and education. Australian advisers cannot prevent corruption in public service departments, their initiatives are often abandoned after they leave PNG, their high rates of pay drain the aid budget, and they do not stay long enough in the country to make a difference. Kevin Rudd conceded in 2009 that too much money was 'consumed by consultants and not enough money was actually delivered to essential assistance in teaching, in infrastructure, in health services on the ground, in the villages'.[8] A mid-level public servant sent by AusAID to work in a government department in Port Moresby, for example, could expect to earn $400,000 a year and a mid-level consultant $340,000 in a country where a local graduate's initial annual salary was only $6000. A 2010 review of Australian aid to PNG pointed as well to the weak institutional structure in which consultants were working: PNG managers are often not committed to reform; the public service is politicised; poorly trained people occupy senior positions; politicians and senior public servants do not respect the rule of law; there is limited enforcement of accountability; and political leaders are not committed to improving the situation. The country's gross domestic product (GDP) has grown steadily in the last decade, but GDP per capita has not changed because the population is growing so fast. At the same time, inequality intensifies. The elite are becoming richer and ordinary Papua New Guineans remain poor. In fact, PNG's ranking on the UN human development index has fallen steadily in recent years.

The record of development in PNG must be set in historical and cultural context. PNG entered independence without an educated middle class to administer the new state efficiently. Vital technical and managerial skills were in short supply. The country's political traditions, formed over generations in small-scale village societies, were certain to lead to corruption by the elite and have done so. Traditionally, the leaders of PNG's hundreds of small societies amassed wealth for distribution among kin, and their power depended upon manipulating this patronage system successfully. Not surprisingly, patronage characterises the modern system of government in PNG as well, and politicians tend to think of public resources not as belonging to the nation as a whole but as wealth to be channelled to their particular *wantoks* or kinsfolk. Particularist loyalties are strong, and national loyalties are weak, as might be expected in a country of more than 800 language groups with no common history beyond being colonised by outsiders. The form in which Australian aid first came to PNG—as a block grant to the annual Budget rather than as targeted aid for specific development purposes—also encouraged corruption and inefficiency. Australia and PNG agreed in 1989 to replace budget support with 'program aid' targeted at particular areas, and gradually implemented the shift during the 1990s. Since 2001, Australian aid to PNG has been to activities such as education, health, law and justice, infrastructure and private sector development in what is called a *sector-wide approach* which, in effect, means greater Australian control of the way money is spent by the PNG government.

Even in this least promising case, few would argue that PNG, as the recipient country, would have been better off without aid. The outcome of decades of official development assistance might be disappointing but the alternative would have been worse, both for the Papua New Guineans and for Australia. A collapsing PNG economy might well have encouraged not just secessionism in Bougainville, but the general disintegration of Australia's closest neighbour. In any case, PNG's growth prospects are now being transformed by major resource investments, in particular ExxonMobil's $15 billion LNG project, which from 2014 will supply Japan, Taiwan and China with liquefied natural gas exported by tankers from Port Moresby. The project will more than double the country's GDP and will reduce its reliance on aid. PNG already depends much less on Australian aid than at independence in 1975 and the PNG prime minister

Michael Somare has even talked of phasing it out altogether. If that were to happen, Australian aid might be seen as having given PNG the bridge it needed over a number of decades to achieve development. On the other hand—and this seems more likely—the resource projects might enrich a few at the expense of the many, and Australia might need to continue delivering development assistance to PNG in order to secure the country's stability.

In two cases, Solomon Islands and Nauru, Australia is giving aid not so much to enhance the prospects of development as to avert national collapse. As we have seen, the decline of government in Solomon Islands was so complete that Australia—together with regional allies—has effectively undertaken the task of restoring a state to working order. That task, begun in 2003, was continuing in 2010 and costing Australia more than $200 million a year with no deadline set for a withdrawal. The Australian Federal Police, Treasury and Customs are all involved in state building alongside AusAID. Here too the task is daunting. One Australian Youth Ambassador for Development, Kate Higgins, worked in a Solomons community development program funded by AusAID from 2005 to 2007. Seeking to explain why Australia's attempt to 'build capacity'—to transfer skills and strengthen institutions—tended to be ineffective, she pointed to the divide between the expatriates and the locals:

> The first obvious reason for this divide is physical—the environments in which most Solomon Islanders and most expatriates live. In Honiara expats live on the ridges overlooking the beautiful neighbouring islands of Nggella and Savo, while the locals fight the immensely inflated rent prices to find houses in the valleys below. Expats drive huge four wheel drives, which loom above the myriad of local taxis, while most locals walk and *stori* along the road. The road was where I learned the basics of the Solomon Islands. Besides being an opportunity to build relationships with people at work, walking became my way of getting to know what was going on in Honiara, of improving my Pijin and gaining greater understanding of the culture. When walking to work, I invariably answered the same questions over and over again such as, 'where was I from?' and 'how many brothers and sisters did I have?' Through these questions I learned what Solomon Islanders value. I developed a sense of the surroundings and the places from which people had come.[9]

Most Solomon Islanders welcome the Australian presence and the assistance it brings, but gaps in standard of living, understanding and experience between Australians and Solomon Islanders undermine the effectiveness of the venture. Government aid programs mean sending well-paid Australians to poor countries where their standard of living separates them from most people. The gulf between rich and poor—the occasion for aid in the first place—is replicated in the circumstances of its delivery.

Nauru, an independent republic of just 12,000 people, is an even more extraordinary case of development failure. A small island with rich deposits of phosphate, Nauru entered independence in 1968 with a mining industry that promised to make every Nauruan rich. For 25 years it was the 'Kuwait of the South Pacific', with accumulated phosphate royalties amounting to more than $1 billion, and with extensive real estate investments in Australia and elsewhere. Nauru did not need aid, and Australia did not give it, apart from annual compensation for the rehabilitation of the worked-out phosphate lands that had once provided Australian farmers with an endless supply of cheap fertiliser.

Nauru, however, proved to be poor at husbanding its wealth. The national airline, Air Nauru, flew to numerous destinations for years at a huge loss, and corruption seriously undermined the country's public finances. The government borrowed heavily against the security of overseas investments, eventually reaching the edge of bankruptcy. Nauru became a transit point for billions of dollars generated by Russian crime syndicates, and documents surrendered by the Nauruans to the US government pointed to the tiny island state as a shelter for large amounts of illegal money from many countries. By 2001 Nauru was so desperate for cash that it agreed to host one of Australia's immigration detention centres, set up by the Howard government after the *Tampa* affair to prevent refugees from reaching the Australian mainland, and by mid 2002 more than 1000 refugees, mainly Afghanis and Iraqis, were detained on the island. The Howard government wanted a Pacific solution, and the Nauruans wanted aid. A deal was struck, with Australia giving Nauru a special additional grant of $13.5 million in the 2004–05 Budget. Since then Australia has intervened to restore order to public finances and to ensure that the Nauruan people continue to receive basic government services. Australians assist the Nauru government in drawing up its annual Budget, Australia funds the position of Secretary of Health and Director of Education, while the Australian Federal Police and the Attorney-General's Department support the police force, the judiciary and the Ministry of Justice. Australia's involvement in the affairs of Nauru is so considerable as to resemble a return to the days before independence in 1968 when Australia was the administering authority. As in Solomon Islands, the Australian aid program is part of a multi-agency intervention aimed at restoring the state.

The development situation in the rest of the South Pacific is better than in PNG and Solomon Islands, with longer life expectancy, higher rates of adult literacy and more access by more people to clean water, for example. Yet aid has not obviously succeeded in producing development here either. Apart from Fiji, which is the only South Pacific country with a sizeable and diversified export economy, the microstates all receive large amounts of Australian aid per capita. Some of this aid goes to island governments, and some to regional organisations such as the University of the South Pacific, the Pacific Community, and the Forum Secretariat which coordinates the development efforts of the member states of the Pacific Islands Forum. Australia is only one among a number of major aid donors to the region, which has traditionally received more aid per head than anywhere else in the world, in most cases amounting to well over a fifth of gross domestic product (GDP) and in some, to over half. The record of most South Pacific states in economic growth is less impressive, however, than that of their neighbours in East Asia or even of comparable microstates in the Indian Ocean and the Caribbean.

Economists puzzle over the 'Pacific paradox', in which large aid flows fail to produce significant economic growth, and are inclined to turn to the latest fashion in economic theory for an explanation. Australia has been prescribing neo-liberal economic policy as a cure for the ills of the South Pacific for many years. A 1993 report by the National Centre for Development Studies in Canberra, *Pacific 2010*, summarised the new orthodoxy in Australian thinking about the region. *Pacific 2010* predicted that unless island governments changed course their people faced a nightmare of rising populations, falling living standards, decaying schools, urban squalor and unemployment. According to the World Bank and the Australian government, Pacific Island countries should reduce their public sectors, cut tariffs, encourage private enterprise, allow maximum freedom to foreign investors and embrace free trade so as to become more competitive in a globalising economy. Australia embraced this new hard-headed approach to South Pacific aid policy in 1994, when the Minister for Pacific Island Affairs Gordon Bilney told Pacific Island governments that they had to embrace competition and the pursuit of comparative advantage in the global market.

Australia has preached a neo-liberal message to Pacific countries ever since. The 2006 white paper on aid argued that the small Pacific states would perform better if they were integrated with the global economy, and in 2009 Australia and other countries of the Pacific Islands Forum began negotiations for a regional trade and economic agreement called PACER (Pacific Agreement on Closer Economic Relations) Plus, which aims to achieve a single regional market for goods and services, and a wholesale liberalisation of investment. Critics think Australia, with its diversified and sophisticated economy, would stand to benefit much more from regional free trade than Pacific countries, which would lose tariff revenues while their small manufacturing sectors disappeared under the impact of foreign competition. Australia belongs to a wider international aid system that links official development assistance with the free market solutions of the World Bank, the International Monetary Fund, the World Trade Organization and regional banks such as the Asian Development Bank. Aid and the free market go hand in hand, and Australia, like other aid donors, identifies globalisation as one of the guiding themes of the aid program. Politicians in aid-dependent countries know they must sing the right tune if they wish aid to continue, and in the South Pacific they speak liberally of 'improving the attractiveness of the foreign investment regime', 'right-sizing the civil service', 'focusing on the needs of the private sector', 'reducing public sector subsidies', 'meeting benchmarks in the reform process', 'promoting integration into the world economy', 'enabling public enterprises to operate on commercial principles', 'improving the business environment', 'achieving effective private/public sector partnerships' and 'adopting measures to reduce infrastructure, service and energy costs for the business sector'.

Yet fast economic growth in the South Pacific is proving elusive. Pacific Island economies fail to grow fast for a number of reasons. Some are geographical and meteorological. The islands are spread over vast distances of ocean, transport between them is expensive, and they are remote from world markets. Most suffer from periodic cyclones which destroy cash crops and interrupt exports. The fundamental reasons for the slowness of South Pacific growth are more subtle, however, and more difficult to incorporate into economic theory. Let us consider a few examples.

First, some Pacific Island politicians tend to measure the success of aid differently from aid experts in Canberra. Politicians in small, aid-dependent economies may be inclined to use aid to give people jobs in the public service, to fulfil obligations to kin and to win prestige. Their political horizons may be local and traditional. They may not particularly care whether the people to whom they give jobs perform efficiently, nor may they be interested in achieving international competitiveness. In short, they may hold values that stress community over capitalist efficiency.

Second, Australian aid funds might be spent in ways that appear effective in Canberra but achieve little in the islands. Typically, an expert organises a 'workshop' on some aspect of public policy or good governance, accommodation is booked at a good hotel, and public servants and NGO representatives spend two or three days listening to lectures and joining discussions. The island participants are happy to be there because they have time off work. They say the words the expert wants to hear, and the expert returns to Canberra to write a report on the success of the exercise. Encountering smiles and agreement all round, the expert believes this has been a receptive audience, not realising that people were acquiescing mainly to avoid giving offence. A few months later a report appears, and AusAID is able to record a further step along the road to development. All sides are pleased to have been involved, yet little has changed in the way services are delivered, expenditure is accounted for, or corruption is checked.

Third, whole parts of the Australian aid program—the commitment to good governance, for example—are based on questionable assumptions about political behaviour under different cultural conditions: that Pacific Islanders share Western beliefs about individualism, for example, that they vote for policies rather than along lines of ethnic or kin loyalty, or that civil society organisations are on the right side of history. The reality of island cultures is usually quite different, and it is hardly surprising that deep cultural forces, rather than external forces, should be the major shapers of island societies. 'Kinship economics' based on obligations to relatives, for example, remains strong in every Pacific Island country and is fundamentally at odds with individualistic and entrepreneurial success in business. The Pacific Islander who establishes a business is often under pressure to distribute wealth to others following the logic of pre-capitalist economic systems.

Fourth, Pacific Island societies pose questions about how development should be defined. Many Islanders remain substantially outside the monetised economy, especially in Melanesia, and their work in gardens and fishing is not counted as part of economic growth even though experts agree that they are highly productive. As the Ni-Vanuatu commentator Ralph Regenvanu argues:

[In traditional economics] ... the simple act of leasing and clearing a piece of land would add to Vanuatu's GDP—and therefore count as positive 'development of the economy'—because the lease of the land, the hire of the bulldozer and the chainsaw, the purchase of the fuel to run them and the payment of labour can all be counted in cash. What would not be counted in cash would be the loss of gardening land and access to bush resources for the children of the land-holding family for at least two generations; the cutting down of ancient trees and the clearing of bush that provides habitat for wildlife and holds the rainwater in the ground; the pollution of the air, land and water with fuel and chemicals; the destruction of cultural sites important to identity; the weakening of the natural sea barrier resulting from removal of sand ...[10]

Kinship groups, not individuals, own most land in the South Pacific and island governments do not permit foreigners to buy it. Aid experts tend to see this non-individual system of land ownership as a major barrier to development in the Western sense because it prevents individuals from using land as collateral for bank loans and discourages foreign investors. Yet the system of land owner-ship also gives most Islanders access to the means of subsistence and serves as an informal, kin-based system of social security. That is why grinding, landless poverty of the kind encountered in sub-Saharan Africa or South Asia is rare in the region. AusAID concedes that social indicators such as infant mortality and life expectancy have improved in many South Pacific countries despite their modest economic performance, and attributes this in part to the strength of the subsistence economy in the region.

PNG and the South Pacific show that aid does not automatically produce Western-style development in poorer countries with non-Western cultural traditions. Capitalism, it turns out, is not just an economic system but a cultural one as well. If island governments were fully to embrace the Western version of development they might undermine the unrecognised form of traditional development that already exists. Monetised, individualised, export-oriented development of the kind recommended by aid agencies might not be in the long-term interests of Pacific Islanders whose kinship networks have so far protected them from the extreme poverty characteristic of many parts of Africa, South Asia or rural East Asia.

We may recognise aid for what it is—a flow of resources that does not always enhance development prospects—without concluding that it should be abolished. Australia's aid will not save the world from poverty, nor will it propel nearby countries to prosperity, but it has prevented the collapse of PNG as a modern state and enabled the microstates of the South Pacific so far to sustain a higher standard of living than that experienced in many parts of the Third World. In the process, aid has contributed to the political stability of the region.

ASSESSMENTS

Aid reflects Australian foreign policy. As Australia discovered the potential of East Asia, a greater proportion of aid went there, up from a third in the mid 1980s to two-fifths in the late 1990s. Then, with the emergence of instability in the South Pacific, more aid was directed to that region from 2003 onwards. As the economy moved to the centre of foreign policy in the 1990s, aid became increasingly commercialised, only to shift later to a focus on governance as security issues multiplied. And when Australia recognised climate change as a foreign policy issue, funding for climate change adaptation projects was incorporated into the aid budget. Australia's wider foreign policy goals include achieving closer economic and military ties with South-East Asian countries, gaining access to emerging markets in East Asia, and ensuring that weak states in PNG and the South Pacific do not compromise regional security. The terrorist threat prompted new aid initiatives. Where once Australian aid to the APEC Forum focused exclusively on trade, it now boosts counter-terrorist capabilities in APEC developing countries. Aid to Indonesia and the Philippines includes anti-terrorist assistance, and police are being assigned to PNG and South Pacific countries as part of a wider project meant to deter terrorists and transnational criminals from entering the region.

Aid cannot be separated from Australia's wider foreign policy goals, from relations with regional countries and from domestic politics. Whatever governments might say, aid is diplomacy by other means. Aid is not a simple and unconditional transfer of food, medicines and expert help from the rich of the world to the poor but a complex and politicised activity undertaken by governments for a range of domestic and foreign policy reasons. Aid is about much more than helping poor people in developing countries.

FURTHER READING

Sachs, Jeffrey, *Common Wealth: Economics for a crowded planet*, Penguin, London, 2008. (A noted development economist argues that wealthy nations can transform the lives of the world's poorest people.)

Australia's aid policy

AusAID, *One Clear Objective: Poverty reduction through sustainable development. Report of the Committee of Review 1997*, Canberra, 1997. (The Simons Report, which guided Australia's aid policy under the Howard government.)

——*Australian Aid: Promoting growth and stability*, Canberra, 2006. (White paper on the Australia's aid program following Howard's promise that aid would double by 2010.)

Australian Journal of International Affairs, vol. 62, no. 3, September 2008. (Includes a special section devoted to the impact of neo-liberal ideas on the Australian aid program.)

Hameiri, S., 'Risk management, neo-liberalism and the securitisation of the Australian aid program', *Australian Journal of International Affairs*, vol. 62, no. 3, September 2008, pp. 357–71. (Identifies a shift towards a more security-focused and interventionist aid policy.)

Kilby, Patrick, 'Australian aid: Dealing with poverty?', *Australian Journal of International Affairs*, vol. 61, no. 1, 2007, pp. 114–29. (Critical analysis of the 2006 white paper, suggesting economic growth alone is not enough to reduce poverty.)

Review of the PNG–Australia Development Cooperation Treaty (1999), Canberra, 19 April 2010. (How Australian aid works in PNG; critical of dependence on highly paid consultants.)

Websites

Aid Watch: <www.aidwatch.org.au>

Australian Agency for International Development: <www.ausaid.gov.au>

Australian Council for International Development: <www.acfid.asn.au>

Global Economic Governance Programme, Oxford: <www.globaleconomicgovernance.org>

Oxfam Australia: <www.oxfam.org.au>

UN Development Programme: <www.undp.org>

UN World Food Programme: <www.wfp.org>

World Vision Australia: <http://trans.worldvision.com.au/default.aspx>

13

Human rights

- Why is the concept of sovereignty central to the debate about human rights?
- How do advocates of human rights respond to objections to the idea of human rights?
- In what way are universality and culture at odds in the debate over human rights?
- What is the International Bill of Rights and what kinds of rights does it proclaim?
- What steps have Australian governments taken to demonstrate their human rights credentials? In what way do Coalition and Labor governments differ on the issue of human rights in foreign policy?
- What part is played by human rights in relations between Australia and China?
- How should Australia respond to human rights abuses in foreign countries?
- Why is there an inevitable tension between human rights and foreign policy?

Iran executes people by stoning them to death; until recently the generals in Myanmar kept Aung San Suu Kyi, the pro-democracy leader who won democratic elections there in 1990, in continuous detention; the Zimbabwe government holds people in prison without trial; and Fiji muzzles the media. These are all practices Australia condemned in 2010 in statements to the UN Human Rights Council, and those condemnations are examples of Australia's participation in the international human rights system.

The modern concern for human rights arose from World War II and the Nazi Holocaust, when a European state exercised domination over the individual to the point of systematically exterminating millions of citizens. Disregard and contempt for human rights, the UN General Assembly said, 'have resulted in barbarous acts which have outraged the conscience of mankind' and it proceeded to define such rights in the 30 articles of the Universal Declaration of Human Rights of 1948.[1] In effect, the international community accepted that individuals as well as states were its concern and that it should endeavour to protect individuals from states under certain circumstances. The impetus to protect human rights faltered during the decades of the Cold War, as countries assessed each other's human rights not according to what they were but on ideological grounds, and on the basis of governments' support for one side or the other. The United States and the Soviet Union overlooked the sins of allies and emphasised those of enemies. The end of the Cold War, however, created the possibility of a more even-handed approach, and the human rights institutions of the United Nations became more active than ever before. At the same time global television began to convey graphic depictions of human rights abuses around the world and to create a new global awareness of human rights issues.

Australia became part of this global movement to protect human rights. Labor governments ratified the key UN human rights treaties, implemented them and made Australia a more active advocate of human rights internationally. In parliament the Joint Standing Committee on Foreign Affairs, Defence and Trade established the Human Rights Sub-Committee in 1991 with the task of publicising human rights issues, conducting inquiries and making recommendations to government. Australians began to expect prime ministers and foreign ministers on official visits to, say, China, Vietnam or Indonesia to raise human rights issues with their hosts and to report on the observance of international human rights standards there. Australia's enthusiasm for the UN side of this endeavour ended with Labor's defeat in 1996 but returned under the Rudd government elected in 2007. From the start, John Howard was sceptical about the UN human rights system and portrayed UN criticism of his government's human rights record as interference in Australia's internal affairs. For a while he withdrew Australia from full participation in UN human rights mechanisms. The Rudd government, on the other hand, reinvigorated Australia's UN engagement on human rights and sought to ensure that Australian legislation complied more than ever before with the core UN human rights treaties. Rudd promised to establish a joint parliamentary committee on human rights.

This chapter aims to clarify the meaning of 'human rights', to explain their place in international law, to suggest that governments use them for political purposes, and to show how they play a political role in Australian foreign policy.

WHAT ARE HUMAN RIGHTS?

The idea of human rights pits one principle against another: the rights of states against the rights of individuals. Let us consider the rights of states first. To understand their importance we have to consider the history of the international system. No centralised government existed in the Europe of the Middle Ages. People were bound by a patchwork of different obligations to different authorities rather than by the rule of any single one. The state we know is a European invention, emerging first in Italy in the fourteenth and fifteenth centuries, when the horizontal ties of rulers and ruled across territories were gradually transformed into vertical relationships organised exclusively within separate territories. The Roman Catholic Church, focus of a political authority that had once spanned Christendom, lost its secular powers to kings, princes, dukes and townspeople over a long period of time and for many reasons, but principally because of the Protestant Reformation of the sixteenth century. Once the Protestants effectively challenged the power of Rome, the secular rulers of territories had a free hand to enhance their own power and to proclaim a new principle of non-interference in each other's affairs.

The origins of an idea that has since exercised enormous influence on international relations—sovereignty—may be found in the 'non-interference' that became vital once Europe was split between states professing competing versions of the Christian faith. The sovereign states of the sixteenth century recognised no superior authority within their borders and, four centuries later, states still claim sovereignty over populations living within the borders of discrete areas of the world's land surface. Sovereignty may be defined for our purposes as constitutional independence, or the possession of supreme legal authority within a territorial area.

Sovereignty is central to the debate about human rights. Governments and diplomats have always valued the freedom from interference and the freedom from embarrassment that the idea of sovereignty provides. The 'morality of states' is a concept that arises from sovereignty. By this view states, not individuals, have rights internationally, because whatever small amount of justice exists comes from the order states impose internally and between themselves. A 'states system' embodying such order emerged in early modern Europe. This system was a structure of state interactions which owed its form first of all to the claim by each state to do what it liked in pursuing its interests and, second, to the rules and conventions which gradually came to influence states' behaviour. These conventions included practising permanent diplomacy, keeping resident embassies in foreign states, calling peace conferences to settle wars, and limiting the methods by which war was fought. International law, including international human rights law—unenforceable but acting as a moral restraint on governments—has its origins in such agreed practices.

The idea of human rights lies in the Western political tradition going back to the Greek Stoics and to Cicero with his idea of a universal natural law that applied equally to Rome and Athens, and it was echoed in the universal moral doctrines of Christianity. The starting point of human rights in the modern era is the late eighteenth century and the proclamations of the American and French revolutions. The politicians of both these revolutions—drawing on the writings of philosophers such as Locke, Montesquieu and Rousseau—espoused the idea that individuals came before communities, and that the moral claims of individuals came before those of the state represented by the monarchy. What had gone wrong with society, according to French revolutionary doctrine, was that kings had not observed the 'natural rights of man' which could be derived from reason.

The 'natural rights' of the eighteenth century have become the human rights of the twenty-first century, and these Western-derived rights have in turn become global, enshrined in numerous UN treaties and accepted at least for show by many governments. The idea of human rights ultimately rests on the view that states are contrivances that frustrate the natural community of humankind, and that the moral claims of individuals as members of that community are superior to the moral claims of states. At its most extreme, this view sees the state as a positive evil that obstructs rather than creates justice for individuals.

The objections to the idea of natural or human rights are of four main types—conservative, Marxist, relativist and realist—and each is echoed in modern debates about human rights in foreign policy.

The conservative objection to the idea of human rights was best expounded by Edmund Burke, the most articulate opponent of the French Revolution. Such natural rights, according to Burke, were like trumps in a card game— they would always win. Burke thought politics should be about compromise and adjustment to circumstances whereas the natural rights proclaimed by the French revolutionaries were moral absolutes introduced into the political arena. They heightened political animosities while preventing reasonable agreements, led to fanaticism and were pretexts for 'pride, ambition, avarice, revenge, lust, sedition'.[2] In other words, people would give the name 'natural right' to everything they wanted knowing that the new label imparted extra political leverage. Burke said there were no natural rights, only those rights which everyone agreed existed by virtue of custom and inheritance.

The Marxist objection to the idea of human rights is that natural rights are merely an ideological attempt by the propertied class to make its wealth and privileges acceptable to the poor and property-less. Marx wanted a society of individual freedom but he thought that could come not by proclaiming individual rights but only through community.

The relativist objection to the idea of human rights is that moral claims cannot be universal because they derive from different cultural contexts, each with a particular set of values. We cannot preach to other countries, the relativists say, because each has its own unique cultural tradition and sense of what is right and wrong. Relativism implies tolerance of diversity, a disinclination to tell other countries what to do, and an acceptance of culture, whereas the assertion of universal human rights implies a critique of culture. As Mary Nyangweso Wangila points out, 'cultural relativism contradicts the basic premise of the human rights movement'.

The realist objection to the idea of human rights rests on a pessimistic conception of international relations. At its most extreme, this view holds that morality makes no sense in international relations, which are determined only by power. Talk of universal human rights can only be a facade, indulged in for other reasons which have to do with power. Strong states take what they can and weak states accept what they must. Realists point to the essentially anarchic nature of international relations, and by 'anarchy' in this context they mean 'lack of government'. Taken as a whole, the world lacks a single government with a single authority that might impose order. If we were to take the idea of human rights to its logical conclusion, say the realists, we would end up with endless wars of humanitarian intervention as states invaded each other on the grounds of human rights violations. Realists think that when countries talk about human rights, they do so merely as a cover for other interests to do with national power. Interference for political reasons masquerades as a campaign to improve human rights. 'Power works by pretending to be just.'[3]

Advocates of human rights have an answer for each of these objections. Their reply to conservatives and Marxists is to assert a way of thinking about politics that emphasises the value of the individual and presupposes a social contract between the individual and the state. This reminds us that the idea of human rights derives from a particular stream of Western political thought called *liberalism*. In reply to the relativists, supporters of human rights point out that relativism implies tolerance of evil as well as good. To be logically consistent, relativists must not criticise governments which starve, torture and execute their own citizens, and can see no reason to publicise human rights abuses in countries other than their own.

In reply to the realists, human rights proponents say realism is based on outmoded assumptions about international relations. Globalisation, it is argued, is changing the world from an anarchy where all are pitted against each other into a society or even a community where values are increasingly shared by governments and where people are gaining in influence at the expense of states; just as global interdependence is reducing the economic sovereignty of states, so it is diminishing states' moral sovereignty and making them accountable to the whole world for the treatment of citizens. This viewpoint holds that 'cosmopolitan morality', the expression of an emerging international society with shared norms and values, should supersede the morality of states. And cosmopolitan morality naturally gives rise to rights that are held by everybody whatever their culture, religion or way of life.

The terrain of human rights remains deeply contested, especially over the issue of universality versus culture, and some issues exemplify that contestation. Female circumcision, for example, is estimated to have affected more than 130 million women and girls, mostly in Africa. The circumcisers excise tissues around a woman's reproductive organ and in some cases they stitch together the vulva 'in order to narrow the vaginal opening'. The practice, which often produces life-long suffering, has been condemned as a violation of human rights, amounting to a kind of torture and violence against women, yet it is also deeply embedded in cultural practices and beliefs. In some Kenyan societies, female circumcision is a passport to marriage and the uncircumcised woman is shunned by her community.[4] To oppose female circumcision as a violation of human rights, then, is to assert a view that entails a call for cultural practices to be changed, and rests on the assumption that some cultures are better than others. Just as the idea of universal human rights collides with that of state sovereignty, so it also collides with romantic and essentialist notions of culture.

Human rights, after all, are the rights one possesses as a human being, not as the inheritor of a particular cultural tradition.

Universalist and liberal ideas underlie the contemporary movement for human rights and the emergence of international human rights law over the last half-century. The 1948 Universal Declaration of Human Rights was a manifesto, declaring what human rights were, not a treaty which states could sign and observe. The treaty-making process by which declarations become international law has continued for the last 50 years as the UN elaborates on the original pronouncement. The most important of the human rights treaties are the Covenant on Civil and Political Rights and the Covenant on Economic, Social and Cultural Rights. The declaration and the two covenants are together referred to as the International Bill of Rights and are the foundations of international human rights law.

A glance at the International Bill of Rights shows it to be anchored in the Western liberal tradition and influenced by the social liberalism practised in many Western liberal democracies after World War II. It proclaims as civil and political rights the classic liberal freedoms of religion, expression, peaceful assembly, association and movement within a country as well as the freedom from arbitrary arrest and the freedom to vote in periodic elections under universal suffrage. To these it adds the right to be held equal before the law, to be presumed innocent until proved guilty and to own property. The economic, social and cultural rights embodied in the International Bill of Rights include the right to have fair wages and safe working conditions, to form trade unions and to strike as well as to have adequate food, clothing and housing, education and an opportunity to participate in cultural life. Over the last 30 years the UN has elaborated on these basic rights by identifying and codifying human rights in a wide variety of areas. As a nation with strong liberal traditions but weak social democratic ones, the United States has ratified the Covenant on Social and Political Rights but not the Covenant on Social, Economic and Cultural Rights. Australia, more deeply influenced by the labour movement and ideas of social democracy, has ratified both.

People differ in assessing the practice of human rights as much as they do over the idea of human rights. Some think much has been achieved in improving the condition of humankind by constructing an elaborate framework of international human rights law. Others say the proliferation of human rights and of international agreements about them has done nothing to improve the lot of most impoverished people on the planet, and that—if human rights are to mean anything—they should be redefined so as to focus on the core needs that

THE UNIVERSAL DECLARATION OF HUMAN RIGHTS

The United Nations General Assembly adopted the Universal Declaration of Human Rights in December 1948. Western liberal ideas of equality before the law, freedom of expression, and representative democracy inspired many of the 30 articles of the declaration, but as article 23 shows, Western democratic socialism—with its emphasis on the right to work and to form trade unions—also contributed to this enunciation of human rights.

Article 1. All human beings are born free and equal in dignity and rights. They are endowed with reason and conscience and should act towards one another in a spirit of brotherhood.

Article 2. Everyone is entitled to all the rights and freedoms set forth in this Declaration, without distinction of any kind, such as race, colour, sex, language, religion, political or other opinion, national or social origin, property, birth or other status. . . .

Article 3. Everyone has the right to life, liberty and security of person. . . .

Article 5. No one shall be subjected to torture or to cruel, inhuman or degrading treatment or punishment.

Article 6. Everyone has the right to recognition everywhere as a person before the law.

Article 7. All are equal before the law and are entitled without any discrimination to equal protection of the law. All are entitled to equal protection against any discrimination in violation of this Declaration and against any incitement to such discrimination.

Article 8. Everyone has the right to an effective remedy by the competent national tribunals for acts violating the fundamental rights granted him by the constitution or by law.

Article 9. No one shall be subjected to arbitrary arrest, detention or exile. . . .

Article 19. Everyone has the right to freedom of opinion and expression; this right includes freedom to hold opinions without interference and to seek, receive and impart information and ideas through any media and regardless of frontiers. . . .

Article 23.
(1) Everyone has the right to work, to free choice of employment, to just and favourable conditions of work and to protection against unemployment.
(2) Everyone, without discrimination, has the right to equal pay for equal work.

(3) Everyone who works has the right to just and favourable remuneration ensuring for himself and his family an existence worthy of human dignity, and supplemented, if necessary, by other means of social protection.

(4) Everyone has the right to form and to join trade unions for the protection of his interests.

human beings have for food, water, shelter, clothing, security and freedom from arbitrary loss of liberty.[5] By this view, the more human rights there are, the less they mean and they should therefore be confined to what matters most.

HUMAN RIGHTS IN AUSTRALIAN FOREIGN POLICY

People sometimes think Australia should do good in the world by imposing sanctions on countries that violate human rights or attaching conditions to trade with them. Australia should ban sporting contacts, stop development aid, break off diplomatic relations and even go to war. The Australian Greens leader Bob Brown, for example, argues that human rights conditions should be a key part of Australia's free trade agreement with China and should bind both governments and corporations.[6] Others say that to view foreign policy in this way is to run the risk of overextending the usefulness of the concept of human rights. Almost every foreign policy decision, after all, can be construed as having human rights implications. Foreign affairs ministers cannot afford to think this way; instead, they mean something precise when they talk about human rights. They mean either appearing before a UN committee, observing a treaty, changing laws, making representations in foreign capitals, providing technical assistance to judicial systems in regional countries, or engaging in human rights dialogues with other governments.

States may take a number of steps to show they are serious about human rights, or to convey that impression. Those steps can be at different levels: global multilateral, regional multilateral, and bilateral. At the global multilateral level, states may become parties to UN human rights treaties and apply the standards of international human rights law to themselves. This is complicated in Australia by the need for the federal government to negotiate with the states over bringing laws into conformity with treaty obligations, a lengthy and cumbersome process. 'Consenting' to a treaty in Australia usually means a three-step process in which the federal government signs the treaty, then negotiates with state and territory governments, and finally ratifies. A treaty itself does not need the approval of the federal parliament but cannot have any effect until all parliaments legislate in accordance with it. The federal government ratifies or accedes to the treaty by an act of the Governor-General-in-Council only after laws in all parts of Australia have been adjusted.

We should be careful to distinguish here between domestic and international law. When Australia ratifies a UN human rights treaty, it accepts that the provisions of the treaty are legally binding within Australian territory. The treaty is part of international customary law, which cannot be enforced because no supranational body exists to enforce it. National governments possess instruments of coercive authority, such as the police force, to enforce domestic law, but at the international level there are no such instruments, and observance of international law depends upon voluntary agreement by sovereign states to abide by the treaties they ratify. States that ratify treaties agree to report at regular intervals to the UN committees that exist to monitor the observance of the international human rights regime.

The Whitlam government (1972–75) initiated the modern phase of implementing international human rights law in Australia. Whitlam signed the major UN human rights covenants within a few weeks of becoming prime minister, he acceded to treaties on labour standards and refugees, and he passed the *Racial Discrimination Act 1975* to implement a UN treaty on the issue. Hawke and Keating gave Australia a comprehensive and coherent human rights policy for the first time. Australia under Hawke was more willing than ever before to agree to international human rights standards and to apply them to Australian legislation. Hawke ratified the Convention on the Elimination of All Forms of Discrimination Against Women in 1983 and then passed the *Sex Discrimination Act 1984* in accordance with it the following year. He invoked an international environmental treaty to stop the Tasmanian government from flooding national parks. When the case went to the High Court, his government won. He established the Human Rights and Equal Opportunity Commission to monitor Australia's compliance with international human rights agreements. Like Whitlam, Hawke tried to pass a bill of rights and failed, whereas Rudd considered the idea and had a national committee examine it, but then rejected it in favour of what is called Australia's Human Rights Framework. Following the Labor tradition, the Rudd government added a seventh to the list of UN human rights instruments to which Australia is party by ratifying the Convention on the Rights of Persons with Disabilities in 2008.

Under Hawke and Keating as prime ministers in the 1980s and 1990s and to a lesser extent under Rudd and Gillard from 2007, Australia had governments that took treaty obligations seriously and legislated accordingly. Hawke used Australia's international obligations to change the legal landscape on issues such as discrimination on grounds of sex and race and the rights of children and the physically and mentally disabled. Hawke also involved Australia actively in UN efforts to extend human rights law over issues such as the rights of children and migrant workers. The signing of human rights treaties changes no Australian laws automatically. Parliaments must change them. Labor's political will was what made the difference, not the treaties themselves, which many countries sign and then ignore.

Optional protocols to the human rights conventions offer countries the opportunity of voluntarily expanding their acceptance of human rights norms and their enforcement. In 2008 the Rudd government, for example, acceded to a protocol which the Howard government did not like, the Optional Protocol to the Convention on the Elimination of All Forms of Discrimination Against Women, which enables women to take complaints about discrimination directly to the UN and obliges governments to respond. The Rudd government also undertook to set up a parliamentary joint committee on human rights with the power to conduct human rights inquiries, and to introduce 'statements of compatibility', so as to assess whether legislation coming before parliament is compatible with international human rights law. The proposal was referred to the Senate Legal and Constitutional Affairs Committee in 2010 but could not be enacted before the elections of that year.

The second step states may take on human rights, also at a global multi-lateral level, is to approve visits by international observers and permit individuals under their jurisdiction to complain to the UN. They may let the world in and let their people out. Australia regularly appears before the UN Human Rights Council. Australia usually allows human rights delegations from the UN and non-government organisations such as Amnesty International to tour the country and make reports. Labor governments tend to welcome and facilitate such visits, but the Coalition government under John Howard adopted a policy of permitting them only for pressing reasons. The Rudd government even issued a standing invitation to international rapporteurs to come and decide whether Australia is complying with its international human rights obligations. The UN sent a special rapporteur to Australia in 2009, for example, with the task of examining the human rights of Indigenous Australians. He commended the

Rudd government for its national apology to the Aboriginal people but argued that the Northern Territory Emergency Response or 'intervention' raised serious human rights concerns by limiting the capacity of Indigenous Australians to 'control or participate in decisions affecting their lives'.

The third step countries may take, this time at the regional multilateral level, is to be active regionally on human rights issues. Europe, the Americas and Africa all have regional bodies—of varying effectiveness—to monitor the protection of human rights in those parts of the world. No equivalent organisation exists for Asia as a whole or for any region within Asia at the state level, though Australia helps to fund the informal Asia Pacific Forum of National Human Rights Institutions which coordinates and supports the work of human rights commissions in the region.

The fourth step, a bilateral one, is to complain to foreign governments about their treatment of individuals suffering torture, detention for political reasons or other human rights violations. Australia raises hundreds of cases per year with scores of countries, including some that are important to Australia, such as the United States, China and Indonesia. When Australian foreign ministers boast of their human rights record they are usually thinking of Australia's energy in making bilateral 'representations'. We should keep such initiatives in perspective. A representation by an Australian embassy abroad commonly takes the form, at least initially, of a polite inquiry for clarification about a reported violation. Foreign governments are under no compulsion to respond and more often than not they send no reply. In a small minority of cases, perhaps one in every seven, Australia's representation might produce a positive response in the form of an assurance that someone's human rights are being respected or that a detainee will be released. The best results come from concerted action by a number of countries or from representations by Australia to small countries which it influences in other ways, such as those in the South Pacific.

In a few cases Australia has extended bilateral representations to take the form of human rights dialogues, where individual cases can also be raised alongside broader issues. Australia has regular human rights dialogues with China, Vietnam and Laos and conducted one with Iran in 2002. None of these countries can be described as democratic. The human rights dialogue with Iran began with the visit of an Australian delegation to Tehran. The delegation visited a prison and met Iranian leaders, including judges, clerics and women parliamentarians. They exchanged views with the Iranians on constitutional and legal systems, freedom of expression, and the role of national human rights institutions. Then in 2003 Australia hosted a return visit by the Islamic Human Rights Commission of Iran. The regular dialogue with Vietnam typically covers issues such as freedom of expression and religious belief, the treatment of indigenous peoples, and criminal justice. In the case of Laos, an Australian delegation of diplomats and human rights experts visited the Laotian capital Vientiane in 2009 and, among other things, observed a trial at the People's Court for Civil Proceedings. The issues raised in the dialogue included women's rights, minority rights and access to justice.

People disagree about how much human rights dialogues achieve. Supporters say they enable Australia to maintain human rights engagement with authoritarian regimes in a non-confrontational way, whereas critics see them as quarantining issues that ought to be mainstreamed. According to Amnesty International and other groups such as the Australian Greens, human rights should be an integral part of Australia's policies on trade, financial sector reform and foreign aid, not a separate set of issues that is dealt with by diplomats behind closed doors and on a government-to-government basis.[7]

Australia gave strong support to the international human rights regime monitored by the UN during the thirteen Labor years that ended in 1996. Not everyone, however, liked what was happening. Some thought the treaty-making process and accompanying legislation subjected Australians to UN decisions over which they had no control, and by the time the Howard government came to office, many in the Coalition parties harboured suspicions about the whole process of international human rights law monitored by UN committees. They thought it threatened Australian sovereignty, and gave political leverage to domestic critics of their policies on Aboriginal reconciliation, native title and refugees. The Coalition years saw a retreat from Australia's former approach, and a decline in Australia's international reputation as a willing participant in the multilateral human rights regime. As in other areas of foreign policy, the Coalition favoured a practical approach at bilateral and regional level rather than what it saw as Labor grandstanding in multilateral forums.

The Coalition's more sceptical attitude to UN human rights obligations emerged early. When the government detained Cambodian refugees in the Port Hedland detention centre in 1997, the UN Human Rights Committee declared Australia in breach of its international obligations under the International Covenant on Civil and Political Rights. The government rejected the criticism outright. Soon afterwards the government delayed a visit to Australia by the UN rapporteur on racism, and rejected his findings with equal vigour.

The government reduced funding for the Australian Human Rights and Equal Opportunity Commission, cut the numbers of DFAT personnel working on human rights, and did not, at that stage, renew Australia's membership of the UN Commission on Human Rights, the UN body that assessed the global rights situation. The High Court had recognised native title to land in Australia in the Mabo decision of 1992, but the Howard government legislated to restrict the application of that title at the same time as it refused to apologise for Australia's earlier treatment of its Aboriginal citizens, including the forced removal of children from their parents. People seeking refugee status in Australia confronted more and more obstacles, from mandatory detention to visas that granted only temporary protection and prevented reunion with family members.

The Howard government's domestic record on human rights provoked a stream of criticism from abroad. A report on Australia by the UN Committee on the Elimination of Racial Discrimination, released in 2000, was the final straw for a government increasingly resentful of international censure. The report was in some ways complimentary, welcoming the 'numerous legislative measures, institutional arrangements, programmes and policies that focus on racial discrimination' and acknowledging the government's efforts to improve the health, housing, education and employment prospects of Aboriginal Australians. But the report also criticised the government's native title legislation, and the existence in the Northern Territory and Western Australia of mandatory sentencing laws which had a disproportionate impact on young Aboriginal Australians. The Minister for Immigration and Multicultural Affairs, Philip Ruddock, appeared before the UN committee in Geneva, only to face a succession of criticisms. 'Why', he was asked, 'has a country with Australia's resources been unable to ensure that a community representing less than 2 per cent of the population has a decent standard of living?' His reaction on returning to Australia was to blame the UN. The government described the UN's approach as 'blatantly political and partisan' and 'based on an uncritical acceptance of the claims of domestic political lobbies'.[8]

Within a few months the government announced that Australia was partially withdrawing from the UN human rights treaty system. From then on Australia would work with the UN treaty committees, but only selectively; it would accept visits by treaty committees, but only under compelling circumstances; it would reject requests by treaty committees to delay the deportation from Australia of unsuccessful asylum seekers; and it would not sign or ratify the Optional

Protocol to the Convention on the Elimination of All Forms of Discrimination Against Women, which was later ratified under the Rudd government. In line with the new policy, the government then deferred the visit of a UN human rights body to Australia for over two years. The UN Working Group on Arbitrary Detention finally visited Australia's immigration detention centres in 2002, producing a report that met the usual blanket rejection from the government.

While disengaging to some extent from the UN system, Australia also tried to change it. Like many others, the Howard government thought the UN human rights treaty system required radical reform. Not only was it politicised but it was too open to influence by non-government organisations and discriminated against democratically elected governments with good human rights records. Members of treaty committees were meant to act independently of their governments, but many did not; committees did not confine themselves to clearly established and specific breaches of international human rights law, but ranged far and wide in criticising member states; some countries routinely failed to report, ensuring that UN criticism focused on countries that complied, such as Australia. The government therefore announced in 2001 that it was embarking on a program to improve the way the UN human rights committee system worked, by hosting workshops on reform, seeking re-election to the UN Commission on Human Rights and pressing for more resources for the Office of the High Commissioner for Human Rights. Australia returned to the UN Commission on Human Rights for the 2003–05 period and was vice-chair in 2003.

Reform of the UN human rights system was by this time overdue. The crisis in credibility led to the abolition of the old UN Commission on Human Rights and its replacement in 2006 by the UN Human Rights Council, which had 47 member states elected by the General Assembly. The new system was meant to enable the UN to take action to expose human rights abuses around the world, and provided for a Universal Periodic Review under which the human rights situation of all 192 UN member states was to be examined every four years. Now, if people under Australian jurisdiction believe they are suffering from violations of civil and political rights, including racial discrimination, they can take their grievances to the UN Human Rights Council, which can publicise findings worldwide. The Bush administration boycotted the UN Human Rights Council, but the Obama administration reversed that decision and the United States was elected to the Council in 2009.

The debate over the Howard government's human rights record was polarised. On one side were those who liked to see Australia assert its sovereignty and defy international bodies that sought to scrutinise the country's human rights performance. On the other were those who said Australia undermined international human rights law by refusing to accept that the UN has the right to criticise all governments within the system, including democratic ones. They included former Liberal prime minister Malcolm Fraser, who thought the government was diminishing Australia and damaging the UN: 'It is overwhelmingly in our interest to assist the UN and its instrumentalities in establishing a rule of law which internationally can apply to the great and powerful, just as the rule of law can apply to the great and powerful in Australia'.[9] He could see nothing offensive in the 2000 UN report to which the government took such exception. In parliament the Joint Standing Committee on Foreign Affairs, Defence and Trade believed Australia should set an example for the sake of the rule of law internationally. The committee pointed out that countries that abuse human rights are unwilling either to report to UN treaty committees or to cooperate fully with the treaty system: 'it is this unwillingness on the part of states where violations are rife that behoves more open countries like Australia to demonstrate that openness and scrutiny is both tolerated and tolerable'.[10]

THE POLITICS OF HUMAN RIGHTS: CHINA AND AUSTRALIA

At the regional and bilateral level, Australia's approach to human rights cannot be separated from economics. Australian economic connections are increasingly with countries whose governments approach human rights differently from the way most Western governments do. Indonesia, Malaysia and Singapore, for example, have not signed the two main international human rights covenants. Their governments dispute the Western definition of human rights and Western ranking of such rights. Human rights in East Asia pose a problem for Australia, which can proclaim the universality of human rights and criticise regional neighbours, risking economic damage, or else lose credibility by explaining away Asian human rights violations as arising from special circumstances. The problem is becoming more acute as trade with the region grows, and Australia has responded by moderating its criticism of governments in the region, as we can see in the case of China.

China's economy has grown spectacularly ever since the Central Committee of the Chinese Communist Party committed the country to economic reform in 1978. Year by year China has recorded growth rates averaging 9 per cent of gross national product (GNP), rising in some years to over 13 per cent, with the result that Chinese output has more than quadrupled since 1980. The rise of China holds the promise of transforming the lives of a quarter of the world's population and is dramatically enhancing prospects for prosperity in other parts of East Asia and beyond.

Australia was one of the first Western countries to appreciate the significance of China's economic reform. Australia already had good relations with China. Whitlam extended recognition to the People's Republic in 1972 and Fraser inaugurated an Australian aid program. Hawke pursued much closer relations and developed personal rapport in the mid 1980s with key leaders such as the Chinese premier, Zhao Ziyang, and party secretary Hu Yaobang, both of whom visited Australia. Hawke himself went twice to China as prime minister, eager to find new markets for Australian iron ore, wool and wheat. Trade boomed between Australia and China in the mid 1980s and for a few years politicians and policymakers dreamt of a bilateral export trade that would one day dwarf all others. Human rights played little part in these calculations and were seldom raised by either side. Then came the Tiananmen Square incident of June 1989 when the People's Liberation Army did battle with thousands of protesters. Soldiers used machine guns and tanks to regain control of central Beijing and killed at least a thousand people.

Tiananmen thrust human rights to the centre of relations with China, at least in the popular imagination. Australians saw enough of the killings on television to prompt a sudden revulsion towards the Chinese government. Australia's official response appeared to support this sentiment. Hawke cancelled a visit to China. He wept at a memorial service in Parliament House and promised not to send any Chinese in Australia back home at the risk of their lives. He had just read a cable from Beijing describing the deaths there. The effect was to allow at least 20,000 students to stay in Australia and to be granted permanent residency status four years later. The official response was more muted than Hawke's tears suggested. A noisy show of condemnation concealed the real agenda, which was to keep the relationship with Beijing safely on course for Australian trade and investment. Aid commitments to China were honoured and the temporary suspension of new aid lasted only until 1991. Two-way trade was hardly affected. China was too important.

Foreign criticism after Tiananmen spurred the Chinese government to take human rights action of the kind that would be noticed abroad. The authorities discouraged scholarly study of human rights before Tiananmen. Afterwards they fostered it so as to lend intellectual respectability to the official policy which emerged in two white papers, *On Human Rights in China* (1991) and *Progress of Human Rights in China* (1995).

The two foundations of Chinese policy are a belief in the primacy of the right to subsistence, and an insistence that human rights are matters of national sovereignty. China argues that 'for any country or nation, the right to subsistence is the most important of all human rights, without which the other rights are out of the question', and that 'human rights are essentially matters within the domestic jurisdiction of a country'. Accusing other countries of human rights abuses is tantamount to infringing sovereignty. China sees foreign criticism about human rights as threatening domestic stability and with it the enormous advances in development made since 1949 and especially since 1978. China is opposed to 'any country making use of the issue of human rights to sell its own values, ideology, political standards and mode of development', and is especially critical of the United States for focusing on civil and political rights at the expense of all others including rights to subsistence and development in Third World countries. China's interpretation of human rights becomes clear in its response to the American government's annual country reports, which cover China and the rest of the world while omitting the United States itself. China's 2009 report on human rights in the United States, for example, pointed to the prevalence of homelessness, unemployment and violent crimes, the deaths of 30,000 people in gun-related incidents every year, racial discrimination against African-Americans and Hispanics, the torture of prisoners detained in Iraq and elsewhere, the incarceration of more than 7.3 million prisoners whose basic rights were not well protected, the impact of the 50-year blockade on Cuba, and the approval of major arms sales to Taiwan.[11]

When Gareth Evans visited Beijing in 1991 he appeared to have made an extraordinary breakthrough. China customarily refused entry to international human rights teams or UN rapporteurs, but this time the Chinese authorities reversed that position. They invited a foreign human rights delegation—the first ever—to come and see for themselves. The delegation was from Australia, and consisted of members of parliament as well as China experts. It visited China in July 1991, and a second visit followed in 1992. Delegation members focused on the civil and political rights which commonly strike Westerners as the most important human rights. They wanted to know about prisoners of conscience, capital punishment, detention of criminals, the definition of counter-revolutionary acts, the condition of some 200 individual prisoners and the situation in the far western regions of Xinjiang and Tibet. They wrote reports highly critical of Chinese practice on a number of counts, and did not accept China's view that human rights are a purely domestic matter. Nevertheless, China agreed to maintain a human rights dialogue with Australia. The visits seemed to show that China was now willing to give human rights a prominent place in relations with the rest of the world and to accept international human rights norms. In fact China was willing to do the first but not the second. As one delegation member said, the invitation 'was not a change of heart by the Chinese, but a change of tactics'.[12]

Tiananmen gave China reasons to play the game of human rights diplomacy in a new way. In the wake of the massacres the US Congress threatened to abolish China's most-favoured-nation status with the United States. Most-favoured-nation status was a guarantee of access by Chinese goods to the lucrative American market; without it, China would suffer economically. For trade reasons China's leaders wanted to signal Congress that they took Western-style human rights seriously. They did so via a third party, Australia, and later through delegations from France and Switzerland. Not only were the Australian delegations useful for impressing American legislators, Australia later added its voice to the campaign which persuaded the Clinton administration in 1994 to sever the link between human rights and most-favoured-nation status in trade.

China used Australia and Australia used China. The human rights visits served Labor's political purposes. Gareth Evans claimed a notable victory for his human rights advocacy in the form of the first human rights delegation from a foreign country ever to visit the People's Republic. He argued that the mere acceptance of a delegation by China was an advance, indicating a new openness to the discussion of human rights issues by Beijing. From Evans's point of view, the Australian delegations enhanced the human rights credentials of his government, a distinct political asset in the climate of critical opinion created by Labor's response at that time to human rights abuses in Indonesia.

Australia is not silent on human rights problems in China but it is hardly outspoken. Like other Western countries Australia is coming to depend too much on trade with China to risk confrontation on human rights. By 2010 China was Australia's largest trading partner. Australia's approach to human rights in China has therefore become one of quiet diplomacy and caution. For years Australia voted for a resolution criticising China at the UN Human Rights Commission in Geneva. The resolution censured China for persecuting political opponents and called on the Chinese government to free political prisoners. But Australia withdrew support for the resolution after John Howard visited China in 1997.

In return China gave Howard something to show for his visit—the promise of a renewed human rights dialogue, which now occurs annually. In another piece of human rights diplomacy in the late 1990s, the Americans agreed to stop sponsoring an annual resolution at the UN criticising China in return for China signing the UN Covenant on Civil and Political Rights in 1998.

China's official approach to human rights has roots in the humiliation the Chinese suffered historically at the hands of European colonial powers, which took treaty ports and concessions along the Chinese coast and declared their own citizens, as well as many Chinese, to be subject to European rather than Chinese law. China therefore insists that sovereignty has priority over human rights, and does so on the grounds that, if human rights became a principle of international law, enabling countries to judge each other, this would undermine the basic principle of the international system of states, which is the preservation of peace. On the other hand, China wants acceptance as a full player in the international system and must therefore participate in the human rights arrangements that are part of that system. China, like the United States, is a member of the UN Human Rights Council and has been twice elected to it since 2006.

China and Australia both have a vital interest in ensuring that human rights issues do not affect bilateral relations. Speaking at Beijing University in 2008, Kevin Rudd ventured criticism of China's human rights record. He said 'Australia like most other countries recognises China's sovereignty over Tibet. But we also believe it is necessary to recognise there are significant human rights problems in Tibet. The current situation in Tibet is of concern to Australians. We recognise the need for all parties to avoid violence and find a solution through dialogue.'[13] The Chinese government responded by describing Tibet as a purely internal affair, and one in which no foreign country had the right to interfere, but it proceeded to welcome Rudd to official talks.

The Stern Hu and Rabiya Kadeer affairs also threatened to strain Australia–China relations. Stern Hu is an Australian citizen who was responsible for marketing iron ore to Chinese steel mills. He was sentenced by a Shanghai court in 2010 to ten years' imprisonment for taking bribes and stealing trade secrets. Rabiya Kadeer is a US-based activist for the self-determination of the Uighur people, many of whom live in the Chinese province of Xinjiang. When the Melbourne Film Festival planned to screen a documentary about her in 2009, the Chinese government objected, demanding in vain that it not be shown. Here again, neither government stood to gain from allowing these issues to harm a relationship that was of benefit to both countries. The Rudd government invited

China's Vice Premier Li Keqiang on a state visit to Australia later in 2009, when the two sides reaffirmed their commitment to dialogue, engagement and cooperation, recognising that they enjoyed strong economic complementarity.

The annual China–Australia human rights dialogue serves the interests of both governments. For the Chinese government it offers tangible evidence to the world that China takes human rights seriously and is open to foreign criticism; for the Australian government it sends a signal to voters that Australia is prepared to act on human rights even in the case of an important trading partner. Official reports on the process are bland on both sides. The Chinese Ministry of Foreign Affairs, for example, spoke of the positive, candid and constructive atmosphere at the 2009 dialogue, while Australia's ambassador in Beijing, Geoff Raby, talked of engaging frankly with the Chinese in the annual bilateral meetings. Whether the annual dialogue serves the interests of individuals suffering human rights abuses in China or Australia is less clear.

ASSESSMENTS

Almost all basic human rights of the kind found in UN treaties are derived from the constitutional experience of Britain and the United States. They represent profound claims about the nature and purpose of human life and about the proper relationship between people and governments. As Geoffrey Best says, they affirm 'that society and the state can hold together without religious and ideological uniformity, and they are siding with the political philosophies which admit the principle that the state is made for human individuals, not vice versa'.[14]

This Western liberal emphasis in defining human rights was largely taken for granted for as long as the United States and Western Europe were indisputably dominant in global affairs. Some states now question the Western way of defining human rights. African countries revised the Western approach in the 1981 African Charter on Human and Peoples' Rights, which asserts the equality of 'peoples' and their right to freedom from domination, the free use of their resources and so on. Under this charter, human rights belong both to individuals and to vaguely defined groups called *peoples*.

Asian states are mounting a more significant challenge. Human rights in a Western country such as Australia grow out of a familiar tradition. People broadly agree about them. By contrast, human rights in many East Asian countries are highly controversial because they threaten the way things are done, in particular the way governments maintain authority. Governments have a vital interest in meeting this threat by redefining human rights and convincing people that Asian values are superior. During the long economic boom East Asian states grew confident that they were destined for future global influence and should not have to accept lectures from the West about human rights abuses. China, as we have seen, began to define human rights in a Chinese way. The former prime minister of Malaysia, Mahathir Mohamad, argued that 'the norms and precepts for the observance of human rights vary from society to society'. Lee Kuan Yew, the architect of modern Singapore, saw an excess of democracy leading to 'undisciplined and disorderly conditions which are inimical to development'.[15] Mahathir and Lee lamented the extreme individualism of the West, and celebrated the values of community and family. Some observers began to speak of a human rights confrontation between Asia and the West.

Asian states meeting in Thailand in 1993, armed with the influence of an emerging China, produced the Bangkok Declaration. This is the key document redefining human rights in an Asian way and claims culture, development and sovereignty as justifications for Asian governments to interpret human rights as they see fit. The concept of 'Asian values' is so vague as to be meaningless, just as the concept of 'Asia' itself encompasses half the people of the world and all their diverse cultures. Yet academic distinctions of this kind are beside the point in the political arena of human rights. 'Asian values' make sense to governments threatened by the universalisation of human rights.

The Bangkok Declaration confronts Western approaches to human rights in three ways. First, the declaration dilutes the claim that human rights by definition are universal. The Asian countries which signed the declaration affirm the universality of human rights in one paragraph only to undermine it in the next by saying 'they must be considered in the context of a dynamic and evolving process of international norm-setting, bearing in mind the significance of national and regional particularities and various historical, cultural and religious backgrounds'. This is the relativist argument employed not against human rights as such but rather against the claim that they be implemented immediately irrespective of circumstance.

Second, the declaration proclaims a 'right to development', affirms that poverty is a major obstacle in the way of enjoying human rights, and says economic, social and cultural rights are just as important as civil and political ones. Western countries, the United States above all, tend to associate human rights with civil and political rights such as freedom of speech and free voting in democratic elections, rather than with economic rights such as freedom to organise trade unions. Australia gives all human rights equal weight in theory but in practice favours civil and political rights.

Third, the declaration rejects the idea that states can be called to account for human rights abuses. Instead, it emphasises 'the principles of respect for national sovereignty and territorial integrity as well as non-interference in the internal affairs of States, and the non-use of human rights as an instrument of political pressure'. This focus on sovereignty runs counter to the view of many Western countries, including Australia, which says human rights are not solely the internal affair of any country.[16]

The debate about Asian values and the Bangkok Declaration continues, underpinned by the view that liberalism is either a failure in key respects, or inappropriate for Asian cultural conditions, and that Asian societies should assert the value of their own versions of modernity.

Human rights, as these developments show, are not primarily a matter of philosophy or even of international law. They are, above all, a matter of politics. The state in some, though not all, East Asian countries is responsible for violating human rights of all kinds and on a large scale. Some governments detain people without trial, torture them, forcibly move them from their homes, censor expression, prevent free elections and persecute ethnic minorities. East Asian governments want to justify themselves to their own people and the world, and are defining their own version of human rights for pressing political reasons. The establishment of the ASEAN Intergovernmental Commission on Human Rights in 2009 seems unlikely, at least in the opinion of many human rights activists, to change this situation.

Just as human rights are political in East Asia, so they are in the West. Western governments stress certain categories of human rights over others for politically convenient reasons. That is why civil and political rights (freedom of expression, religious belief, fair trial and democratic participation) loom large in the human rights policies of Western countries whereas social and economic rights pale by comparison. The Universal Declaration of Human Rights lists work, equal pay for equal work, protection against unemployment and adequate housing and medical care as human rights, yet none has ever won a prominent place in, say, foreign human rights crusades by the American government.

States find advantage in proclaiming human rights whatever their domestic political record. They want to look good to their own people and other countries. Often a show of commitment internationally is designed merely to impress and brings no improvement. Some countries which have signed human rights treaties appear each year on Amnesty International's list of states that practise torture. And when governments talk about human rights in other countries, they are often engaging in domestic politics.

States are notoriously inconsistent about human rights abuses in foreign countries. In general, they complain if the media makes an issue of abuses, if target states are a long way away or are outcasts in the international community such as North Korea, and if national and moral interest coincide as in the Gulf War, when a larger country invaded a smaller one and jeopardised Western oil supplies. States are less likely to complain about human rights violations in neighbouring countries, those that matter to them economically or strategically, or those that are powerful. Australia conforms to the general pattern on all these counts.

International human rights have a number of dimensions. The domestic dimension—reforming Australian law according to international obligations under the UN treaty system—has changed Australia for the better. Treaties give governments hooks on which to hang laws to stop discrimination on the grounds of gender, age and race, and have made Australia a more civilised place. The regional dimension—bilateral representation and dialogue on human rights—is harder to assess. Human rights activists who want to change the way other states behave tend to think in absolutes whereas governments think in relative terms, balancing human rights against other foreign policy considerations such as trade, investment, aid and security. Activists shape public opinion on key human rights issues and press the government to achieve something. Ministers respond with a flurry of activity but without going as far as people expect. The result is compromise, which critics interpret as betrayal and ministers see as commonsense. The global dimension, expressed through the UN and international human rights law, contributes to international peace and security by fostering a consensus among states on human rights, and deserves the support of Australia for that reason.

FURTHER READING

What are human rights?

Baehr, Peter, *Human Rights: Universality in practice*, Macmillan, London, 1999. (A clear and concise introduction to the law and politics of human rights, including their role in foreign policy.)

Ishay, Micheline, 'What are human rights? Six historical controversies', *Journal of Human Rights*, vol. 3, 2004, pp. 359–71. (Covers the key debates including those over origins of human rights, role of the Enlightenment, cultural relativism.)

Vincent, R.J., *Human Rights and International Relations*, Cambridge University Press, Cambridge, 1986. (A comprehensive and perceptive analysis of all key issues.)

Human rights in Australian foreign policy

Dutton, David, 'Human rights diplomacy', in *Facing North: A century of Australian engagement with Asia. Volume 2: 1970s to 2000*, Peter Edwards and David Goldsworthy, eds, Department of Foreign Affairs and Trade and Melbourne University Press, Melbourne, 2003, pp. 81–129. (Scholarly survey.)

Galligan, Brian, Winsome Roberts and Gabriella Trifiletti, *Australians and Globalisation: The experience of two centuries*, Cambridge University Press, Cambridge, 2001. (Chapter 6 covers the impact of the UN human rights system and international law on Australia.)

Kent, Ann, 'Australia and the international human rights regime', in *The National Interest in a Global Era: Australia in world affairs 1996–2000*, James Cotton and John Ravenhill, eds, Oxford University Press, Melbourne, 2001, pp. 256–78. (Covers a period when Australia's human rights policy internationally was 'fraught with contradiction'.)

Parliament of the Commonwealth of Australia, *Human rights in the Asia-Pacific: Challenges and opportunities*, Joint Standing Committee on Foreign Affairs, Defence and Trade, Canberra, 2010. (Covers the regional human rights situation and the role of Australia including bilateral human rights dialogues.)

Report by the Special Rapporteur on the Situation of Human Rights and Fundamental Freedoms of Indigenous People, James Anaya. Addendum: The Situation of Indigenous Peoples in Australia. UN General Assembly A/HRC/15, 4 March 2010. (Report to the UN Human Rights Council after a visit to Australia in 2009.)

Russell, Ian, Peter van Ness and Beng-Chuat Chua, *Australia's Human Rights Diplomacy*, Australian Foreign Policy Project, ANU, Canberra, 1992. (Human rights in Labor foreign policy.)

Tang, James T.H., ed., *Human Rights and International Relations in the Asia-Pacific Region*, Pinter, London and New York, 1995. (The Bangkok Declaration and the Asian definition of human rights.)

Zifcak, Spencer, *Mr Ruddock Goes to Geneva*, UNSW Press, Sydney, 2003. (How the Australian government reacted to UN criticism of its human rights record.)

——*United Nations Reform: Heading north or south?*, Routledge, London, 2009. (Includes analysis of the UN Human Rights Council, formed in 2006.)

Websites

Amnesty International Australia: <www.amnesty.org.au>
Australian Human Rights and Equal Opportunity Commission: <www.hreoc.gov.au>
Human Rights Watch: <www.hrw.org>
UN Human Rights Council: <www2.ohchr.org/english/bodies/hrcouncil>

Epilogue

The Rudd government, 2007–10, proclaimed that its foreign policy was based upon three pillars: the alliance with the United States; membership of the UN and multilateral institutions; and comprehensive engagement with Asia and the Pacific.

Commitment to the American alliance is common ground between the major political parties in Australia and has been so since the signing of the ANZUS Treaty in 1951. Rudd withdrew Australian troops from Iraq but was as committed to the American alliance as his predecessor. Rudd thought there was 'no more important relationship for Australia than our relationship with the United States of America. We share common interests. More importantly, we share common values. And, for much of the last century, we shared a common history. We are one of the world's oldest continuing democracies. We are one of the United States' oldest continuing allies. We have fought alongside the United States in every major war since US entry into the First World War in 1917.'[1] As a mark of its commitment to fighting a war led by the United States, Australia increased the size of its military force in Afghanistan from 1100 to 1550 a few months after Barack Obama became US president in 2009.

'At the global level', Rudd told parliament in 2008, 'we are committed to multilateral institutions, and in particular the United Nations, to promote a rules-based international order that enhances our security and economy.'[2] In this spirit Rudd announced that Australia would seek a two-year term as a temporary member of the UN Security Council in 2013–14. To be elected, Australia would need to win two-thirds of the votes in the UN General Assembly, 128 out of 192. In order to win the votes of African countries, in 2009 the Rudd government sent the Governor-General Quentin Bryce on a whirlwind tour of Africa, where she visited ten countries in eighteen days. Rudd also increased development aid to

Africa, apparently with a similar purpose in mind. Critics charged the government with spending millions of dollars on a campaign that was likely to fail.

Rudd's response to the global financial crisis, both in foreign and domestic policy, was his greatest achievement as prime minister, and he was at his best when he argued convincingly that the G20, as the more inclusive and representative grouping of economies, should replace the G7 as the leading institution of global governance. The G20, he told the Foreign Policy Association in New York in 2009, had framed and implemented an effective 'global policy response to the gravest global economic crisis we have confronted since the Great Depression.'[3] His management of the climate change issue, on the other hand, was to contribute to his downfall. Rudd's first foreign trip as prime minister was to the 2007 conference of the parties to the UN Framework Convention on Climate Change in Bali, where he was applauded for announcing that Australia would at last ratify the Kyoto Protocol. He believed in creative middle-power diplomacy, and thought Australia could play a valuable role in ensuring that the 2009 Copenhagen climate change conference produced a binding commitment by the nations of the world to reduce emissions of greenhouse gases. But Rudd's foreign policy credibility suffered when no such outcome emerged and Copenhagen proved to be a chaotic and unproductive multilateral conference. Rudd's nuclear initiative lies somewhere between these extremes of activism in the multilateral field and can be seen as a minor diplomatic achievement. The International Commission on Nuclear Non-proliferation and Disarmament sponsored by Australia and Japan produced a comprehensive report which lent momentum to the 2010 NPT conference but it did not influence Australia's nuclear policy.

The key proposal of the Rudd government on its third foreign policy pillar, engagement with Asia and the Pacific, was to reform the regional architecture of East Asia by means of an Asia-Pacific community that would come into being by 2020. Rudd described this as 'a regional institution which spans the entire Asia-Pacific region—including the United States, Japan, China, India, Indonesia and the other states of the region' and one which can 'engage in the full spectrum of dialogue, cooperation and action on economic and political matters and future challenges related to security'.[4] He sent an experienced former Australian Ambassador to Indonesia, Richard Woolcott, to test the idea in Asian capitals, but the response was mixed. Woolcott found that Asian leaders, while being interested in continuing dialogue on the concept, were mostly not in favour of creating yet another regional institution alongside the others, such as ASEAN,

ASEAN Plus Three, the East Asia Summit, APEC and the ASEAN Regional Forum.[5] The future of the proposal was uncertain in 2010.

The Rudd government's management of Australia's most important bilateral relationships differed from country to country. While Australia remained close to the United States, Rudd's ability to speak Mandarin did not guarantee better relations with China. The Chinese government reacted negatively to his criticism of the human rights situation in Tibet and to the depiction of China as a potential military threat in the Defence white paper of 2009. On the other hand, the economic interdependence of Australia and China ensured that pragmatism would predominate and minor difficulties would not be allowed to affect the relationship. Australia benefited from the re-election in 2009 of Susilo Bambang Yudhoyono as president of Indonesia, because he favoured a productive bilateral relationship, though the Rudd government allowed the domestic politics of the refugee issue to intrude too much on it. Rudd recognised the need to improve relations with India, a rising economic power in South Asia, but again domestic developments—in the form of attacks on Indian students in Melbourne—were an irritant in the relationship. Rudd did not concede ground to critics who said Australia should sell uranium to India even though it is not a member state of the NPT.

Continuity with the Howard government characterised Rudd's policy towards small regional neighbours in the Pacific Islands and the Indonesian archipelago. Australia increased aid and helped to build states while being ready to intervene with troops and police when invited to do so. In part because of the cost of state building in Solomon Islands, Howard boosted aid from 0.23 per cent of gross national income in the 2003–04 financial year to 0.28 per cent in 2007–08. Rudd made more aid a key plank of his foreign policy and increased it to 0.33 per cent in 2010–11, promising a massive enlargement to 0.5 per cent by 2015. By the time of the 2010 election, both major parties in Australia had accepted that development assistance should grow.

The process of foreign policy making became even more concentrated in the Department of Prime Minister and Cabinet under Rudd's prime ministership than it had been under Howard. The role of DFAT in foreign policy making was further diminished, especially as the Rudd government reversed most of its promised funding increases to the department.

Julia Gillard became Australia's first female prime minister in June 2010 after the parliamentary party withdrew its support from Kevin Rudd. Within weeks she called a general election, which took place on 21 August. Foreign policy hardly figured in the election campaigns of either the two major parties or the Greens, except in relation to asylum seekers and the military commitment in Afghanistan. Labor and the Coalition both promised to ensure that the claims of asylum seekers were dealt with offshore. Labor said asylum seekers would go to a new regional processing centre in East Timor, the establishment of which would be negotiated with the government of that country; the Coalition promised to reinstate the Howard government's 'Pacific Solution'. Opposition leader Tony Abbott met the president of Nauru in Brisbane during the campaign and announced that Nauru was 'ready, willing and able to reopen that processing centre at short notice'[6], while Opposition immigration spokesman Scott Morrison travelled to Nauru to inspect the mothballed centre and consult with its government. The Greens opposed mandatory detention of asylum seekers and called for their claims to be processed in the metropolitan areas of Australia rather than offshore. The two major parties backed the Australian military presence in Afghanistan, while the Greens favoured withdrawal.

With 50.12 per cent of the two party-preferred vote going to Labor and 49.88 per cent to the Coalition, the election produced a hung parliament in which neither side held a majority. After lengthy consultations, Labor managed to attract promises of support from three independent MPs, enough to govern with a bare majority of one vote after providing the parliament with a speaker.

Soon after being sworn in a second time as prime minister, Julia Gillard travelled to Afghanistan to visit Australian troops and from there to the Asia-Europe Meeting in Brussels. The future of foreign policy under the Gillard minority government depended, above all, on whether her government would survive in the House of Representatives. Assuming that it survived for two or three years, it seemed likely that the moving force in determining the direction of Australia's foreign policy would not be Gillard, who lacked expertise in the field, but Rudd, the new foreign minister. His command of the subject matter of international diplomacy was formidable and, as prime minister, he had played a central role in fashioning policy.

Rudd's experience and personal contacts in foreign capitals were unrivalled among his colleagues in the government. Within hours of becoming foreign minister, Rudd travelled via Pakistan to New York for a UN summit on the Millennium Development Goals and told the UN General Assembly that the Gillard government put the MDGs 'at the heart of our aid program'.[7] In Washington he was welcomed by the American president and the Secretary of State as an old friend. There seemed little doubt that, whatever his deficiencies as a prime minister might have been, Rudd would prove to be an effective Australian foreign minister.

Glossary

Antarctic Treaty regime The internationally agreed set of rules under the Antarctic Treaty and its protocols.

appropriations Authorisations of expenditure by government.

arms control The diplomatic process by which countries agree to limit, regulate and reduce the possession, development and use of weapons, especially weapons of mass destruction.

asymmetry in military affairs Gross disproportion in the military power and technological sophistication of opposing forces in a conflict; exemplified by the phenomenon of the suicide bomber, and the use of primitive weapons by the airline hijackers who attacked the US in 2001.

AUSMIN talks Annual high-level defence and security talks between the US and Australia, military allies under the ANZUS Treaty.

balance of payments A measure of a country's economic transactions with all other countries, in receipts and expenditures, usually calculated monthly and annually.

bilateral, plurilateral and multilateral Australia engages in bilateral diplomacy when it deals with one country on a foreign policy issue, and in multilateral diplomacy when it deals with a number of countries on a foreign policy issue. A further distinction is sometimes made: plurilateral means between more than two countries but not between many. The ASEAN–Australia–New Zealand Free Trade Agreement, with twelve partner states, may be called a plurilateral trade agreement, whereas the Doha Round of the WTO seeks a multilateral trade agreement between 153 member states.

bipartisan Enjoying the support of both major sides of politics. The American alliance enjoys bipartisan support in Australia.

Bretton Woods institutions The International Monetary Fund and the World Bank, which were established following a 1944 conference held in the New Hampshire town of Bretton Woods to determine the shape of international monetary arrangements after World War II. Together with the World Trade Organization, these are sometimes now known as the institutions of global governance.

capital market The institutions, such as stock exchanges, where shares, bonds and other securities or paper assets are bought and sold.

Chapter Seven peacekeeping Peacekeeping as authorised by Chapter VII of the UN Charter; allows UN peacekeepers to enforce peace by military means.

Chapter Six peacekeeping Peacekeeping as authorised by Chapter VI of the UN Charter; restricted to observer missions, securing borders and maintaining truces with light arms.

coalition of the willing In the context of recent events in international affairs, this term refers to groups of countries willing to participate in a military intervention, either with UN authority as in East Timor and Afghanistan or without it, as in Iraq.

Cold War The political and ideological conflict between the Soviet Union and the US, and more broadly between the communist and capitalist worlds, between 1946 and the late 1980s. The Cold War never became a hot war of armed conflict between the two superpowers.

collective security The policy of maintaining international peace by uniting the military forces of all other states against an aggressor state.

commodity A standardised good traded in bulk, such as wool, wheat, sugar or iron ore. Commodities remain Australia's most important exports.

complex peace operations Expanded peacekeeping characteristic of UN interventions since the end of the Cold War, and involving a wide range of UN responsibilities in restoring stability and temporarily governing territories shattered by conflict.

continental defence A defence doctrine that emphasises defending the continent of Australia and its offshore waters against attack.

cooperative intervention Armed or unarmed intervention by one state in another whose government invites or agrees to it.

decolonisation The process by which the former colonies of European states gained their political independence. Most African, South-East Asian and Pacific Island countries were once colonies.

de facto recognition Public acknowledgement by a state that another state, as a matter of observable fact, exercises authority over a particular territory, but without acceptance that this authority is legal or should continue indefinitely.

defence self-reliance A defence doctrine that Australia's military forces should be large and well-equipped enough to defend Australia against a conventional attack without outside help.

de jure recognition Public acknowledgement by a state that another state legally exercises authority over a particular territory.

détente Relaxation of political tensions in international affairs. The Cold War was punctuated by occasional periods of détente between the two superpowers, as in the mid 1970s.

Doha Round The WTO-sponsored multilateral trade negotiations that began at Doha in the Persian Gulf state of Qatar in 2001. Australia, together with many developing countries, hoped the Doha Round would produce liberalisation of global agricultural trade. The Doha Round was continuing in 2010.

environmentalism The view that the natural environment must be protected from degradation by human activity; in Australia, this view is held by many groups and individuals, and is expressed at the party-political level by the Greens.

exchange rate The price of one currency in terms of another.

fissile material Material needed to sustain a nuclear explosion based on fission, that is, splitting the atom. Fissile material is a byproduct of the civilian nuclear energy industry.

floating the currency A policy of allowing a currency such as the Australian dollar to find its own value according to market forces, without government action to determine the rate at which it will exchange with other currencies.

foreign economic policy Foreign policy as it applies to economic issues such as trade, investment or policy coordination in economic matters.

forward defence A defence doctrine, long influential in Australian defence thinking, that emphasises fighting the enemy overseas, usually with Australian troops acting as auxiliaries in support of a much larger Allied force.

framework convention An international agreement, characteristic of diplomacy on global environmental issues, imposing no immediate legal obligations on signatory states but initiating a process of future negotiations that will impose such obligations.

francophone Africa The French-speaking countries of Africa such as Senegal, Chad and Côte d'Ivoire.

free trade A policy of unrestricted trade with other countries in goods and services, with no tariffs, quotas or other obstacles to imports or exports. Free trade in services is increasingly important and contentious.

good governance An approach to the process of governing that emphasises being efficient, accountable, transparent and responsive to the public; that favours globalisation and a market-oriented economic policy; and that is seen by many aid donors, such as Australia, as playing a key role in solving the problems of developing countries.

gross domestic product A measure of national economic activity; includes all economic activities in a country whether owners are resident or not; excludes activities of national companies abroad.

gross national income Previously known as the gross national product, this is a measure of national economic activity that encompasses gross domestic product, and adds to it income received from other countries minus payments made to other countries.

hedge funds Investment funds that, among other things, bet on movements in markets and that commonly employ borrowed money to do so.

humanitarian intervention Intervention, usually armed, by one state in another for the purpose of relieving human suffering and loss of life; there is no presumption in the concept of humanitarian intervention that the government of the target state should agree to it.

industry policy A policy of government intervention in industry, to facilitate restructuring, offer protection from competition, or improve international competitiveness.

intellectual property rights The rights of private property in ideas embodied in books, music, software, videos, films, brand names and inventions of all kinds; these are mostly protected by copyright and patent laws which may apply within a country or, increasingly, across the globe under WTO agreements.

International Court of Justice Established by the UN, sits in The Hague, and rules on issues of international law.

international human rights covenants The agreements that, together with the Universal Declaration of Human Rights, are the foundation of international human rights law. They are the Covenant on Civil and Political Rights and the Covenant on Economic, Social and Cultural Rights.

international norms Standards of international practice that states accept as a consequence of changing circumstances. Some say there is a new international norm in favour of humanitarian intervention, and that it is exemplified by the UN doctrine of the responsibility to protect.

interoperability The ability of two or more nations' defence forces to operate with each other's military equipment, procedures and military doctrines.

Keynesian consensus A view of the way economies work, inspired by the British economist John Maynard Keynes, and shared by the governments of advanced industrialised countries during the long boom from World War II to the 1970s. Keynesians believed that government intervention, in particular to manage the level of demand, was required in order to produce full employment in capitalist economies. When governments spent money to stimulate economies following the global financial crisis in 2008, they were returning to Keynesian economic policy.

liberal internationalism A policy approach to foreign policy emphasising international cooperation, multilateral agreements and respect for the authority of the UN.

mandatory detention Compulsory confinement; in Australia's case, of asylum seekers in detention centres.

mercenaries Soldiers employed not by governments but by private companies that charge for their services. The privatisation of military forces is increasing worldwide.

microstate An unusually small independent country, typically with a population of fewer than 1 million.

Millennium Development Goals A set of development targets to be achieved by developing countries by 2015 and 2020. They were adopted by the UN in 2000, reaffirmed by the UN since, and accepted by Australia as key criteria by which the success of Australian development aid will be measured.

moral hazard Moral hazard is a lack of incentive to guard against risk because of protections enjoyed against that risk. In the context of the aftermath of the global financial crisis, some say that moral hazard applies to large banks and financial institutions, which may cause another crisis in the future through lax lending because they know governments will bail them out with taxpayers' funds.

neo-liberal economics A view of the way economies work, shared by governments of advanced industrialised countries to a greater or lesser extent since the 1970s. Neo-liberals reject the Keynesian consensus, and argue that economies work best when they are most influenced by market forces rather than by government intervention or regulation. Neo-liberal economics was shaken by the global financial crisis, which, many argued, showed that governments had relied too much on markets to create economic stability.

nuclear deterrence The doctrine that nuclear weapons deter nuclear war for as long as they guarantee the destruction of nuclear-armed enemies.

nuclear posture The nuclear powers' declared purpose for possessing nuclear weapons. The US changed its nuclear posture in 2010.

nuclear proliferation The spread of nuclear weapons into the possession of states that have not had them before, or into the possession of non-state organisations or individuals.

nuclear terrorism Terrorism carried out by exploding either nuclear weapons or radiological weapons that spread radioactive materials by means of a conventional explosive.

official aid Aid given by the West to Russia and former Communist countries in eastern Europe during the transition from communism to capitalism; to be distinguished from official development aid, which goes to developing countries in Africa, Asia, the Pacific and Latin America.

prerogative of the Executive Exclusive privilege of the prime minister and Cabinet, as in their authority to commit Australian military forces to war without parliamentary approval.

privatise Transfer publicly owned assets or enterprises to private ownership.

protectionism The policy of preventing foreign competition with domestic industries by imposing tariffs, quotas and other trade barriers. Australia was protectionist for most of the twentieth century.

puppet government A government controlled by the government of another country.

ratify Confirm or make valid a treaty, usually following the incorporation of the treaty's provisions into law.

regional security In Australia's case, the security and peaceful development of nearby regions such as South-East Asia and the Pacific Islands.

reserve currency A currency used as foreign exchange reserves by other countries. The US dollar is the major reserve currency.

right to self-determination Right of a 'nation' or 'people', the exact meanings of which are undefined, to determine who shall govern them; reaffirmed by the UN in 1960; usually involves the formation of a new state.

Secretary of State The American equivalent of Australia's minister for foreign affairs. The US Department of State deals with US foreign policy.

shadow ministers Opposition politicians who 'shadow' government ministers by specialising in areas of policy for which they act as the Opposition's spokespersons.

smart sanctions *Sanctions* are acts by a state to compel another state to follow a particular policy. *Smart sanctions* are such acts designed to cause minimum harm to ordinary people in the offending country, while putting maximum pressure on targeted groups such as government ministers or the elite.

sovereign debt default Failure by a government to pay its debts.

sovereign state A state with no constitutional ties to any other, and in which the government has complete responsibility for domestic and foreign policy.

sovereignty as responsibility The doctrine that sovereignty is not absolute but incurs obligations by states towards their citizens. The doctrine is related to that of the responsibility to protect, which asserts that where states fail in their obligations to protect citizens from the worst human rights abuses the international community has the right to intervene.

stimulus packages The name given to the spending programs undertaken during the global financial crisis by many governments, including Australia's, in order to stimulate economic activity and avert recession or depression.

tariff A tax or duty imposed by a government on imports.

temporary protection visa Official endorsement on a passport or travel document permitting the holder to remain in Australia for a specified period before being required to leave; proposed by Pauline Hanson; initiated by the Howard government; abolished by the Rudd government; applied to asylum seekers.

trade in services Trade which is not in things. Trade in things is 'merchandise trade'. These days much trade is in 'invisibles' such as banking, insurance, telecommunication, tourism and education, and takes the form of companies or individuals in one country buying services from those in another.

trade liberalisation Opening trade to market forces by removing tariffs, quotas and other government restrictions.

transition economy An economy changing from communist central direction to the capitalist free market, either abruptly as in the case of Russia or more gradually as in the case of the People's Republic of China.

UN human development index The United Nations' annual ranking of nations measuring people's standard of living and quality of life, according to criteria such as life expectancy, adult literacy, school enrolments, and income per head adjusted for local prices.

UN human rights mechanisms The means by which the UN seeks to protect human rights worldwide, through the UN Human Rights Council, the committees that oversee adherence to human rights treaties, and the sending of UN observers to participating states.

UN special rapporteur Observer authorised by the UN to report on the state of affairs in a country.

verification regime An agreed process between states to ensure that each is abiding by the terms of an international agreement. Verification regimes are the most important parts of arms control agreements between the US and Russia.

veto power The power to negate a resolution. The single vote of a permanent member of the UN Security Council is enough to outvote all the rest.

White Paper A detailed statement of government policy in a particular area such as foreign affairs or defence.

Notes

Introduction

1 James L. Richardson, 'Liberalism', in *An Introduction to International Relations: Australian perspectives*, Richard Devetak, Anthony Burke and Jim George, eds, Cambridge University Press, Cambridge, 2007, p. 48.
2 Katrina Lee-Koo, 'Feminism', in *Introduction*, Devetak, Burke and George, eds, p. 84.
3 DFAT, *In the National Interest: Australia's foreign and trade policy white paper*, Canberra, 1997, pars 6, 111, 112.
4 Kevin Rudd, 'Undermining our best chance: Australia's dying multilateralism', Evatt Foundation Paper, 2002 at <http://evatt.labor.net.au/publications/papers/37.html>.

Chapter 1

1 Alan Watt, *The Evolution of Australian Foreign Policy 1938–1965*, Cambridge University Press, Cambridge, 1967, p. 51.
2 Quoted in Watt, *Evolution*, p. 55.
3 Churchill to Curtin, 20 February 1942, in *Documents on Australian Foreign Policy 1937–49*, W.J. Hudson and H.J.W. Stokes, eds, vol. v, AGPS, Canberra, 1982, pp. 546–7.
4 Curtin to Churchill, 23 February 1942, in *Documents*, Hudson and Stokes, eds, p. 564.
5 Quoted in *Munich to Vietnam: Australia's relations with Britain and the United States since the 1930s*, Carl Bridge, ed., Melbourne University Press, Melbourne, 1991, p. 103.
6 Quoted in Frank Frost, *Australia's War in Vietnam*, Allen & Unwin, Sydney, 1987, p. 16.
7 Quoted in Gregory Pemberton, *All the Way: Australia's road to Vietnam*, Allen & Unwin, Sydney, 1987, pp. 306, 318.
8 T.B. Millar, 'Vietnam', in *Munich to Vietnam*, ed. Bridge, p. 191.
9 T.B. Millar, *Australia in Peace and War: External relations 1788–1977*, Australian National University Press, Canberra, 1978, pp. 405–6.
10 Neville Meaney, 'The United States' in *Australia in World Affairs 1971–75*, W.J. Hudson, ed., Allen & Unwin, Sydney, 1980, p. 183.
11 Jeffrey T. Richelson and Desmond Ball, *The Ties that Bind: Intelligence cooperation between the UKUSA Countries—the United Kingdom, the United States of America, Canada, Australia and New Zealand*, Allen & Unwin, Sydney & Boston, 1985, p. 259.

Chapter 2

1 Carolyn O'Brien, 'Problems in Australian foreign policy, July–December 1986', *Australian Journal of Politics and History*, vol. 33, no. 2, 1987, p. 11.

2 Department of Foreign Affairs, *Backgrounder*, 19 July 1991, p. 3.

3 *Sydney Morning Herald*, 17 December 1986.

4 Senate, Hansard, 11 December 1991.

5 Department of Foreign Affairs, *Backgrounder*, 27 July 1983.

6 Department of Foreign Affairs, *Australian Foreign Affairs Record*, December 1983, p. 799.

7 *Sydney Morning Herald*, 29 February 1992.

8 DFAT, *In the National Interest: Australia's foreign and trade policy white paper*, Canberra, 1997, par. 3.

Chapter 3

1 Patrick Keefe, 'The leak was me', *New York Review of Books*, vol. 51, no. 10, 10 June 2004, p. 39.

2 Alexander Downer, 'Securing Australia's interests—Australia's foreign policy priorities', *Australian Journal of International Affairs*, vol. 59, no. 1, 2005, p. 9.

3 Murray Goot, 'Neither entirely comfortable nor wholly relaxed: Public opinion, electoral politics, and foreign policy', in *Trading on Alliance Security: Australia in world affairs 2001–2005*, James Cotton and John Ravenhill, eds, Oxford University Press, 2007, pp. 253–304.

4 Julia Gillard (Prime Minister of Australia), press conference, 24 June 2010.

5 Andrea Benvenuti, 'Issues in Australian foreign policy July to December 2005', *Australian Journal of Politics and History*, vol. 52, no. 2, 2006, p. 278.

6 Quoted in Paul Kelly, *The March of Patriots: The struggle for modern Australia*, Melbourne University Press, 2009, p. 434.

7 Robert Manne, ed., *The Howard Years*, Black Inc. Agenda, Melbourne, 2004, p. 50.

8 Ann Capling, 'Australia's trade policy dilemmas', *Australian Journal of International Affairs*, vol. 62, no. 2, 2008, pp. 229–44.

9 Kelly, *The March of Patriots*, 2009, p. 571.

10 Matt McDonald, 'Perspectives on Australian foreign policy 2004', *Australian Journal of International Affairs*, vol. 59, no. 2, 2005, p. 156.

11 Maryanne Kelton, 'Perspectives on Australian foreign policy, 2005,' *Australian Journal of International Affairs*, vol. 60, no. 2, 2006, pp. 229–46.

12 Quoted in Roy Campbell McDowell, *Howard's Long March: The strategic depiction of China in Howard government policy, 1996–2006*, ANU E Press, 2009, p. 34.

13 David Walton, 'Future directions in Australia–Japan relations: An Australian perspective', *Australian Journal of International Affairs*, vol. 60, no. 4, 2006, pp. 598–605.

14 House of Representatives, Hansard, 5 June 2002, p. 2825.

15 Quoted in Michael Clarke, 'Issues in Australian foreign policy, July to December 2007', *Australian Journal of Politics and History*, vol. 52, no. 2, 2008, p. 279.

16 Quoted in John Lee, 'Issues in Australian foreign policy, January to June 2007', *Australian Journal of Politics and History*, vol. 53, no. 4, 2007, p. 602.

Chapter 4

1 Department of the Prime Minister and Cabinet, *Cabinet Handbook*, 6th edn, July 2009, attachment 1.
2 Lowy Institute, *Australia's Diplomatic Deficit: Reinvesting in our instruments of international policy. Blue Ribbon Panel Report*, 2009, pp. viii–xi.
3 Allan Gyngell and Michael Wesley, *Making Australian Foreign Policy*, Cambridge University Press, Cambridge, 2007, 2nd edn, p. 148.
4 Bill Hayden, *Hayden: An autobiography*, Angus & Robertson, Sydney, 1996, p. 398.
5 Gareth Evans and Bruce Grant, *Australia's Foreign Relations in the World of the 1990s*, 2nd edn, Melbourne University Press, Melbourne, 1995, p. 52; Gareth Evans (Minister for Foreign Affairs), ministerial statement 'Government response to Commission of Inquiry into the Australian Secret Intelligence Service', 1 June 1995.
6 Rodney Tiffen, 'Marching to whose drum?—Media battles in the Gulf War', *Australian Journal of International Affairs*, vol. 46, no. 1, May 1992, p. 47.
7 Don Greenlees and Robert Garran, *Deliverance: The inside story of East Timor's fight for freedom*, Allen & Unwin, Sydney, 2002, p. 270.
8 Gyngell and Wesley, *Making Australian Foreign Policy*, 2nd edn, pp. 165–70.
9 Evans and Grant, *Australia's Foreign Relations*, pp. 33–4.
10 DFAT, *Advancing the National Interest: Australia's foreign and trade policy white paper*, Canberra, 2003, p. vii.
11 DFAT, *Annual Report, 08/09*, Canberra, 2009, p. 14.
12 ASIS Resource Statement—Budget estimates for 2009/10 as at Budget May 2009.
13 *Intelligence on Iraq's Weapons of Mass Destruction*, Parliamentary Joint Committee on ASIO, ASIS and DSD, Canberra, 2004, par. 2.29.
14 *Sydney Morning Herald*, 19 June 2004.
15 House of Representatives, Hansard, 21 January 1991.

Chapter 5

1 Alexander Downer (Minister for Foreign Affairs), 'The challenge of conflict, international law responds', speech to the International Law Conference, Adelaide, 27 February 2004.
2 Kevin Rudd (Prime Minister of Australia), press conference, United Nations, New York, 30 March 2008.
3 'Appendix B. United Nations Security Council Resolutions Relating to the Situation Between Iraq and Kuwait', in *Australia's Gulf War*, Murray Goot and Rodney Tiffen, eds, Melbourne University Press, Melbourne, 1992, p. 243.
4 *The National Security Strategy of the United States of America*, Washington, 2002, p. 15.
5 Ivo H. Daalder and James M. Lindsay, *America Unbound: The Bush revolution in foreign policy*, Brookings Institution Press, Washington DC, 2003, p. 145.
6 *Sydney Morning Herald*, 3 March 2004.
7 DFAT, *East Timor in Transition 1998–2000: An Australian policy challenge*, Canberra, 2001, p. 132.
8 Ramesh Thakur, 'From collective to cooperative security? The Gareth Evans vision of the United Nations', in *The New Agenda for Global Security: Cooperating for peace and beyond*, Stephanie Lawson, ed., Allen & Unwin, Sydney, 1995, p. 25.

9   Gareth Evans, 'Future directions for the United Nations', *Melbourne University Law Review*, vol. 20, no. 1, June 1995, p. 178.

10 ICISS, *The Responsibility to Protect: Report of the International Commission on Intervention and State Sovereignty*, Ottawa, 2001, p. vii, xii; UN General Assembly, *Implementing the Responsibility to Protect: Report of the Secretary-General*, A/63/677, 12 January 2009, par. 5.

11 UN General Assembly, 60/1. *World Summit Outcome*, 24 October 2005, par. 138–9.

12 Coalition foreign policy statement, 'A confident Australia', 1996 election; Department of Defence, *Australia's Strategic Policy*, Canberra, 1997, p. 33.

13 Anthony Milner, 'Balancing "Asia" against Australian values', in *The National Interest in a Global Era: Australia in world affairs 1996–2000*, James Cotton and John Ravenhill, eds, Oxford University Press, Melbourne, 2001, p. 44.

Chapter 6

1   Kevin Rudd (Prime Minister of Australia), speech at the launch of the Defence white paper, Garden Island, 2 May 2009.

2   Department of Defence, *Defending Australia in the Asia Pacific Century: Force 2030*, Canberra, 2009, par. 6.13.

3   *Review of Australia's Defence Capabilities: Report to the Minister for Defence by Mr Paul Dibb*, Canberra, 1986, pp. 31, 33, 37.

4   *Defending Australia in the Asia Pacific Century*, par. 6.5.

5   Department of Defence, *The Defence of Australia 1987*, Canberra, 1987, pp. vii, 6, 31.

6   Brendan Nelson (Minister for Defence), 'The ANZUS alliance', address to the Bradfield Forum, 8 September 2006.

7   Stephen Smith (Minister for Foreign Affairs), 'Questions without notice', 24 February 2010.

8   Article 2 of the Australian–Indonesian Security Agreement, signed on 18 December 1995 in Desmond Ball and Pauline Kerr, *Presumptive Engagement: Australia's Asia-Pacific security policy in the 1990s*, Allen & Unwin, Sydney, 1996, p. 144.

9   DFAT, *East Timor in Transition 1998–2000: An Australian policy challenge*, Canberra, 2001, p. 145.

10 Eleanor Hall, 'A failure of leadership in foreign affairs', *The Drum*, 11 March 2010, <www.abc.net.au>.

11 Kevin Rudd (Prime Minister of Australia), speech at the launch of the Defence white paper, Garden Island, 2 May 2009.

Chapter 7

1   *Eliminating Nuclear Threats: A practical agenda for global policymakers. Report of the International Commission on Nuclear Non-proliferation and Disarmament*, Canberra and Tokyo, 2009.

2   Remarks by Barack Obama (President of the United States), Hradcany Square, Prague, Czech Republic, 5 April 2009.

3   Winston Churchill (Prime Minister of Great Britain), speech to the House of Commons, 1 March 1955.

4   Department of Defence, *Defending Australia in the Asia Pacific Century: Force 2030*, Canberra, 2009, pars 4.59, 6.34.

5 George P. Shultz, William J. Perry, Henry A. Kissinger and Sam Nunn, 'A world free of nuclear weapons', *The Wall Street Journal,* 4 January 2007.
6 Steve Coll, 'The Cabinet of Dr Strangelove', *New York Review of Books,* LVII, 3, 25 Feb.–10 March 2010, p. 30.
7 Michael Pugh, *The ANZUS Crisis, Nuclear Visiting and Deterrence,* Cambridge University Press, Cambridge, 1989, p. 36.
8 *Disarmament and Arms Control in the Nuclear Age,* Parliamentary Joint Committee on Foreign Affairs and Defence, Canberra, 1986, pp. 701–2.
9 *Report of the Canberra Commission on the Elimination of Nuclear Weapons,* Canberra, 1996, p. 9.
10 *Defending Australia in the Asia Pacific Century: Force 2030,* par. 9.103.
11 *Eliminating Nuclear Threats: A practical agenda for global policymakers: Report of the International Commission on Nuclear Non-proliferation and Disarmament,* par. 2.30.
12 ' "Al-Qaeda-link" Cern worker held', BBC News Online, 9 October 2009.
13 Seymour M. Hersh, 'Defending the arsenal: In an unstable Pakistan, can nuclear warheads be kept safe?', *The New Yorker,* 16 November 2009, pp. 28–35.
14 John Mueller, *The Atomic Terrorist,* International Commission on Nuclear Non-proliferation and Disarmament, 2009, p. 9.
15 Ken Berry, *Review of Recent Literature on Nuclear Issues,* International Commission on Nuclear Non-proliferation and Disarmament, 2008, pars 3.6–3.8.
16 Andrew O'Neil, 'Shifting policy in a nuclear world: Australia's non-proliferation strategy since 9/11' in *Australian Foreign Policy in the Age of Terror,* Carl Ungerer, ed., University of New South Wales Press, Sydney, 2008, p. 95.
17 Marianne Hanson, 'Issues in Australian foreign policy, January to June 2005', *Australian Journal of Politics and History,* vol. 51, no. 4, 2005, p. 577.
18 Barack Obama (President of the United States), statement on the release of the Nuclear Posture Review, the White House, 6 April 2010.
19 *Communiqué of the Washington Nuclear Security Summit,* 13 April 2010, par. 1.
20 2010 Review Conference of the Parties to the Treaty on the Non-proliferation of Nuclear Weapons, *Final Document,* New York, 2010.
21 DFAT, 'Successful NPT Review Conference', media release, 30 May 2010.
22 *Australian Government's response to the International Commission on Nuclear Non-proliferation and Disarmament (ICNND) Report,* 3 May 2010.
23 'Fraser backs Rudd on nuclear weapons', *Sydney Morning Herald,* 8 April 2009.

Chapter 8

1 *Australia's International Development Cooperation 2004–05,* Canberra, 2004, p. 21.
2 Department of Defence, *Defending Australia in the Asia Pacific Century: Force 2030,* Canberra, 2009, par. 4.35.
3 Interview on ABC Television *7:30 Report,* 25 June 2003.
4 Don Greenlees and Robert Garran, *Deliverance: The inside story of East Timor's fight for freedom,* Allen & Unwin, Sydney, 2002, p. 94.
5 Nick Warner (RAMSI Special Coordinator), 'Operation Helpem Fren: Rebuilding the nation of Solomon Islands', speech to the National Security Conference, 23 March 2004.

6   Howard to Habibie, 19 December 1998, in *East Timor in Transition 1998–2000: An Austra-lian policy challenge*, DFAT, Canberra, 2001, pp. 181–2.

7   'Australian Government historic policy shift on East Timor', media release, Alexander Downer, 12 January 1999.

8   Hugh White, 'The road to INTERFET: Reflections on Australian strategic decisions concern-ing East Timor, December 1998–September 1999', *Security Challenges*, vol. 4, no. 1 (Autumn 2008), pp. 69–87.

9   John Howard (Prime Minister of Australia), 'Australia's strategic future', address to the Australian Strategic Policy Institute (ASPI) conference, Canberra, 5 July 2007.

10 Alexander Downer (Minister for Foreign Affairs), 'Development in the Pacific', address to ANU seminar, 14 October 2003.

11 Jacinta O'Hagan, 'Humanitarianism and armed intervention', in *An Introduction to Interna-tional Relations: Australian perspectives*, Richard Devetak, Anthony Burke and Jim George, eds, Cambridge University Press, Cambridge, 2007, p. 339.

Chapter 9

1   Niall Ferguson et al., 'The crisis and how to deal with it', *New York Review of Books*, vol. 56, no. 10, 11 June 2009.

2   Jeff Madrick, 'How we were ruined and what we can do', *New York Review of Books*, vol. 56, no. 2, 12 February 2009.

3   Kevin Rudd, 'The global financial crisis', *The Monthly*, February 2009, pp. 20–9.

4   Lenore Taylor and David Uren, *Shitstorm: Inside Labor's darkest days*, Melbourne University Press, Melbourne, 2010, p. 125.

5   The G-20 Toronto Summit Declaration, 26–27 June 2010.

6   'Leaders' statement: The Pittsburgh Summit', 24–25 September 2009.

7   Joint doorstop interview with Kevin Rudd (Prime Minister of Australia) and Wayne Swan (Treasurer), Pittsburgh, 25 September 2009.

8   Geoffrey R.D. Underhill, 'Conceptualizing the changing global order', in *Political Economy and the Changing Global Order*, Geoffrey R.D. Underhill and Richard Stubbs, eds, Macmillan, London, 1994, p. 19.

Chapter 10

1   Joan Edelman Spero, *The Politics of International Economic Relations*, 4th edn, Routledge, London, 1992, p. 70.

2   Paul Krugman, 'Regionalism versus multilateralism: Analytical notes' in *Asia Pacific Region-alism: Readings in international economic relations*, Ross Garnaut and Peter Drysdale, eds, Harper Educational, Sydney, 1994, p. 167.

3   DFAT, *In the National Interest: Australia's foreign and trade policy white paper*, Canberra, 1997, p. 43.

4   Anthony Milner, 'Balancing "Asia" against Australian values', in *The National Interest in a Global Era: Australia in world affairs, 1996–2000*, James Cotton and John Ravenhill, eds, Oxford University Press, Melbourne, 2001, p. 48.

5   DFAT, *Advancing the National Interest: Australia's foreign and trade policy white paper*, Canberra, 2003, p. 61.

6   Kevin Rudd, 'Australia and China in the world', 70th Morrison Lecture, Australian National University, 23 April 2010.

Chapter 11

1   Sonja Boehmer-Christiansen, 'The international research enterprise and global environmental change: Climate-change policy as a research process', in *The Environment and International Relations*, John Vogler and Mark F. Imber, eds, Routledge, London and New York, 1996, p. 181.
2   IPCC, *Climate Change 2007: Synthesis Report, summary for policymakers*, pp. 1–5.
3   National Oceanic and Atmospheric Administration, National Aeronautics and Space Administration, United Nations Environment Programme, World Meteorological Organization and the European Commission, *Scientific Assessment of Ozone Depletion: 2006*, p. 6.
4   Gareth Evans, 'Foreign policy and the environment', *World Review*, vol. 30, no. 4, December 1991, pp. 46–55.
5   Lorraine M. Elliott, *International Environmental Politics: Protecting the Antarctic*, St Martin's Press, London, 1994, pp. 209–10; DFAT, *Monthly Record*, October 1991, p. 653.
6   Robyn Eckersley, 'Ambushed: The Kyoto Protocol, the Bush administration's climate policy and the erosion of legitimacy', *International Politics*, vol. 44, 2007, pp. 306–24.
7   Kevin Rudd (Prime Minister of Australia), 'Australia, the region and the world: The challenges ahead', address to the Lowy Institute, 6 November 2009.
8   'UN climate talks too slow: Wong', *The Age*, 10 April 2010.
9   DFAT, *Advancing the National Interest: Australia's foreign and trade policy white paper*, Canberra, 2003, p. 67; Department of Defence, *Defending Australia in the Asia Pacific Century: Force 2030*, Canberra, 2009, par. 4.64.
10 Jon Barnett, 'The worst of friends: OPEC and G-77 in the climate regime', *Global Environmental Politics*, vol. 8, no. 4, November 2008, pp. 1–8.
11 Afelee F. Pita (Ambassador/Permanent Representative of Tuvalu) to the United Nations at the Special Session of the Security Council on Energy, Climate and Security, 17 April 2007, <www.tuvaluislands.com/un/2007/un_2007–04–17.html>.
12 Rio Declaration on Environment and Development, Principle 15.

Chapter 12

1   Development Co-operation Directorate (DCD-DAC), *Table 1: Net Official Development Assistance in 2009*, <www.oecd.org/dataoecd/17/9/44981892.pdf>.
2   'AIG chief says the firm is on "clear path" to repaying bailouts', *Los Angeles Times*, 27 May 2010; David Wessel, *In Fed We Trust: Ben Bernanke's war on the great panic: How the Federal Reserve became the fourth branch of government*, Scribe, Melbourne, 2009, p. 194.
3   Gareth Evans and Bruce Grant, *Australia's Foreign Relations in the World of the 1990s*, 2nd edn, Melbourne University Press, Melbourne, 1995, p. 140; *Australia's Overseas Aid Program 1997–98*, Canberra, 1997, p. vii; *Budget: Australia's International Development Assistance*, 11 May 2010, p. iii.
4   Department of Defence, *Defending Australia in the Asia Pacific Century: Force 2030*, Canberra, 2009, p. 12.
5   Department of Defence, *Australia's National Security: A defence update 2003*, Canberra, p. 23.
6   *The World Today*, ABC Radio, 4 February 2010.

7   Australian Council for International Development, *Analysis: Aid budget 2010/11*, May 2010, p. 16.

8   *Review of the PNG–Australia Development Cooperation Treaty (1999)*, 19 April 2010, p. 26.

9   *Outside-In: A volunteer's reflections on a Solomon Islands community development program*, SSGM Discussion Paper 2008/3, pp. 8–9, <http://rspas.anu.edu.au/papers/melanesia/discussion_papers/08_03.pdf>.

10 Ralph Regenvanu, 'The traditional economy as source of resilience in Vanuatu', in *In Defence of Melanesian Customary Land*, Tim Anderson and Gary Lee, eds, AID/WATCH, Sydney, 2010, p. 32.

Chapter 13

1   Peter H. Bailey, *Human Rights: Australia in an international context*, Butterworths, Sydney, 1990, p. 3.

2   Quoted in R.J. Vincent, *Human Rights and International Relations*, Cambridge University Press, Cambridge, 1986, p. 28.

3   Michael Freeman, 'Human Rights: Asia and the West', in *Human Rights and International Relations in the Asia-Pacific Region*, James T.H. Tang, ed., Pinter, London and New York, 1995, p. 23.

4   Mary Nyangweso Wangila, 'Beyond facts to reality: Confronting the situation of women in "female circumcising" communities', *Journal of Human Rights*, vol. 6, 2007, pp. 393–413.

5   Mirko Bagaric and Penny Dimopoulos, 'International human rights law: All show, no go', *Journal of Human Rights*, vol. 4, no. 1, 2005, pp. 3–21.

6   Bob Brown, 'Turning a blind eye to China', 14 January 2010, <http://greensmps.org.au/blog/turning-blind-eye-china>.

7   *Human Rights in the Asia-Pacific: Challenges and opportunities*, Joint Standing Committee on Foreign Affairs, Defence and Trade, Canberra, 2010, par. 5.113.

8   *Australia's Role in United Nations Reform*, Joint Standing Committee on Foreign Affairs, Defence and Trade, Canberra, 2001, par. 7.39; Spencer Zifcak, *Mr Ruddock Goes to Geneva*, UNSW Press, Sydney, 2003, pp. 13, 23.

9   Zifcak, *Mr Ruddock Goes to Geneva*, p. 43.

10 *Australia's Role in United Nations Reform*, Joint Standing Committee on Foreign Affairs, Defence and Trade, Canberra, 2001.

11 *Full Text of Human Rights Record of the United States in 2009*, <www.chinahumanrights.org/Messages/China/t20100312_555856.htm>.

12 Russell et al., *Australia's Human Rights Diplomacy*, Canberra, 1992, p. 68.

13 'A conversation with China's youth on the future', Peking University, 9 April 2008.

14 Geoffrey Best, 'Justice, international relations and human rights', *International Affairs*, vol. 71, no. 4, 1995, p. 790.

15 *Human Rights and International Relations in the Asia-Pacific Region*, James T.H. Tang, ed., Pinter, London and New York, 1995, pp. 171–2, 232.

16 Bangkok Declaration, pars 5 and 8, in Tang, *Human Rights*, p. 205.

Epilogue

1   Kevin Rudd (Prime Minister), address to the Foreign Policy Association, New York, 24 September 2009, <http://pmrudd.archive.dpmc.gov.au/node/6222>.

2   The First National Security Statement to the Parliament. Address by the Prime Minister of Australia, the Hon. Kevin Rudd MP, 4 December 2008, <http://pmrudd.archive.dpmc.gov.au/node/5424>.

3   Kevin Rudd (Prime Minister), address to the Foreign Policy Association, New York, 24 September 2009, <http://pmrudd.archive.dpmc.gov.au/node/6222>.

4   Kevin Rudd (Prime Minister), 'It's time to build an Asia Pacific Community', address to the Asia Society AustralAsia Centre, 4 June 2008, <www.asiasociety.org.au/speeches/speeches_current/s55_PM_Rudd_AD2008.html>.

5   Frank Frost, *Australia's proposal for an 'Asia Pacific Community': Issues and prospects*, Parliamentary Library Research Paper, 13, 2009–10, 1 December 2009, p. 18.

6   Kirsty Needham and Jessica Wright, 'Abbott on Nauru: How I wish they were there', *Sydney Morning Herald*, 7 August 2010.

7   Kevin Rudd (Foreign Minister), Statement to the High-level Plenary Meeting of the United Nations General Assembly (Millennium Development Goals Summit), New York, 22 September 2010, <www.foreignminister.gov.au/speeches/2010/kr_sp_100922.html>.

Index

For Product Safety Concerns and Information please contact our EU
representative GPSR@taylorandfrancis.com
Taylor & Francis Verlag GmbH, Kaufingerstraße 24, 80331 München, Germany

www.ingramcontent.com/pod-product-compliance
Ingram Content Group UK Ltd.
Pitfield, Milton Keynes, MK11 3LW, UK
UKHW051829180425
457613UK00022B/1172